TEN ENGLISH FARCES

TEN ENGLISH FARCES

Leo Hughes

and

A. H. Scouten

Play Anthology Reprint Series

 BOOKS FOR LIBRARIES PRESS
FREEPORT, NEW YORK

INTERNATIONAL STANDARD BOOK NUMBER:

0-8369-8212-6

LIBRARY OF CONGRESS CATALOG CARD NUMBER:

79-132135

PRINTED IN THE UNITED STATES OF AMERICA

To Our Professors

Harold Newcomb Hillebrand
and
John Earle Uhler

Preface

The object of this collection is to make accessible a representative group of Restoration and eighteenth-century farces once highly popular but now neglected and therefore not easily available. We have no illusions about the intrinsic merit of these little pieces. There is no great literary merit to be found in any one of them. In fact, their significance lies not so much in their merit as in their popularity. As Petit de Julleville puts it, *"Une époque n'est bien connue que si l'on connait bien les choses que cette époque a particulièrement aimées."* Or, to reduce the idea to specific terms, the fact that Isaac Reed, for example, saw nearly twice as many performances of *The Devil to Pay* as he did of *Lear* or *The Way of the World* or *The Careless Husband* tells us nothing about the respective merits of the plays; it does tell us something of Reed and his generation.

We have been governed in our choice of plays by four considerations. We have selected pieces which, for the most part, were highly popular in the eighteenth century. We have tried to give as wide a range, both in time and manner, as the limited number of plays decided upon would allow. We have avoided reproducing works, with the one exception of *The Emperor of the Moon,* to be found in modern editions. We have chosen plays accessible to us in The University of Texas collections.

All of the plays reproduced here were popular in their own day and all but one remained popular for several generations. In the case of some of them—notably *The Bilker Bilk'd, A Duke and No Duke,* and *The Devil to Pay*—the same basic plot can be traced through as much as two centuries of theatrical activity. With farce the criterion of success in the theatre is more important than with any other form. Confinement to the closet may not do a tragedy irreparable damage, but such confinement would be fatal to farce. In fact, *closet farce* is a contradiction in terms. Though farces are often concocted for or even by certain actors and die out when these actors leave the stage, no such piece is reproduced here. Most of the farces given here had the good fortune to fall into congenial hands, so much so that for a time Crispin and Blakes or Nell and Mrs. Clive were almost synonymous, but other Crispins and other Nells arose so that none of these plays was cut short by the demise of an actor. The fate of any given farce, however, is tied up with theatrical taste or fashion, and once the run, however long it may have been, is over, that farce is dead. And once dead to the theatre, it is dead also to the publisher. As a result, a great many plays which have much to reveal concerning the theatrical tastes of bygone days have long since disappeared entirely or been accorded the sometimes dubious prestige of the rare books collection.

The problem of variety and range is a more trying one. We cannot profess to have exhausted all the possibilities here or to have presented anything like the whole range of English farce. We have, however, tried to offer as much variety as possible. There are plays of both foreign and native origin, plays with song and dance or without such embellishments, plays riotous with slapstick or almost decorous in stage behavior. Direct borrowing from foreign sources was somewhat more common in the earlier period; hence the first three plays show Italian and French influence. *The Emperor of the Moon* also reveals the interest in scenic display, being much in the manner of the contemporaneous French *comedie-ballet*. *The Brave Irishman,* coming somewhat later, shows the freedom with which Molière's plays came to be treated in adapting them for the English stage. *Hob* and *The Devil to Pay* are thoroughly English; *The Cobler of Preston,* from Shakespeare, and *The Bilker Bilk'd* represent strands which go all the way back to the sixteenth century in the English theatre and beyond. Again, *The Devil to Pay* and *No Song No Supper* belong to the history of English music drama: the former to the older ballad opera tradition, the latter to comic opera. The *petite comedie* or manners farce, which began to appear about mid-century, is well represented by *Appearance Is Against Them.*

Fielding and the important group writing *petites comedies* around the middle of the eighteenth century, notably Garrick, Foote, and Murphy, we have passed over on two counts: Fielding and Garrick have been edited in recent years. Foote and Murphy, who deserve modern editions, fall somewhat nearer the borderline between farce and comedy; in fact, Foote rejected any other label than *comedy* for his pieces, with no little justification, we may add.

Since for plays of this type there seems to be no particular necessity of providing definitive texts or of choosing the one indisputably best edition, we have used editions from the Wrenn and Aitken Collections of The University of Texas Library. In some cases we have taken the only editions available, even where we may have wished for another; for example, Texas does not have any of the very rare earliest editions of *The Brave Irishman.*' In other cases we have chosen what seemed the most representative version; for example, while the Wrenn Collection contains one of the only three copies of the 18-song 1731 version of *The Devil to Pay* in this country, we have rejected it in favor of the more common 16-song version of 1732 which provided the basis for subsequent stage versions.

In preparing the plays for the printer our object has been to provide authentic yet readable texts. We have made a few additions, either in filling out abbreviations or in marking scene divisions or in supplying a missing or "dropped" letter, but these editorial intrusions have been marked with brackets. Silent changes include modernizing the letter ʃ and transposing *u* and *v*, and *i* and *j* in accordance with modern usage, substituting ordinary capitals for large block initial letters, rectifying obvious errors where a letter was turned or a single piece of italic got mixed in the font, spelling out the speech tags, and occasionally shifting the position of a stage direction to make its intention clearer. Where printing errors obscured the meaning we have used readings from other editions, which we identify.

We wish to acknowledge the help of several persons, more than we can well name here. The staffs of the Library of Congress, Folger, Huntington, New York Public, Yale, and Harvard libraries have all been very gracious. Our greatest debt of gratitude is due to The University of Texas library staff, particularly to Miss Ratchford and Miss Harris. Dr. Avery of Washington State College has kindly allowed us to use his wealth of notes on eighteenth century performances. Dr. Van Lennep has granted us permission to use, in addition to several late eighteenth-century playbills, two manuscripts in the Harvard Theatre Collection, a transcript made by J. P. Kemble of playbills in the Dublin newspapers and an account-book recording the activities of Roger Kemble's provincial troupe around the middle of the eighteenth century. Dr. McManaway has permitted use of the Winston Ms. in the Folger Library. Finally we wish to thank the authorities of The University of Texas for providing the funds for completing the research and publishing this collection.

LEO HUGHES, The University of Texas
A. H. SCOUTEN, The University of Pennsylvania

Contents

Contents

A
Duke and no Duke.

As it is Acted by Their

MajeftiesServants.

To which is now added,

A PREFACE concerning *Farce* :
With an Account of the *Perfonæ*
and *Larvæ*, &c. Of the Ancient
THEATRE.

By *N. TATE*,
SERVANT to Their MAJESTIES.

LONDON:

Printed for *Henry Bonwicke*, at the *Red-Lion* in St. *Paul's*
Church-Yard, 1693.

A Duke and No Duke

Author

It has sometimes been the custom to refer to Nahum Tate in terms of commiseration, as if the world had been slow in recognizing or rewarding his merits,[1] but a more realistic view would seem to be that he got what he deserved and perhaps just a bit more. The son of a preacher, Faithful Tate, or Teate, he was born in Ireland in 1652 and educated there. After being graduated from Trinity University he came to England to seek fame and fortune through literature, his first offering being a volume of poems issued in 1677, five years after his graduation. He then tried his hand at plays, turning out nine of them between 1678 and 1707, most of them tragedies and all but a few of them adaptations. Of these perhaps the most successful was his now notorious emendation of *King Lear*. He was befriended by John Dryden, with whom he collaborated, particularly in *Absalom and Achitophel, Part II*. Not the least successful of his literary undertakings was a version of the Psalms which he and Nicholas Brady produced in 1695 and which "attained ultimately almost universal use" according to the *DNB*. His greatest public triumph came in 1692 when he assumed the laureateship left vacant by the death of Shadwell. Admirers of Dryden may perhaps derive some consolation from the fact that at least a friend succeeded the enemy who had supplanted the laureate of Charles II. Any elation would be tempered, however, by the realization that Tate was an even weaker poet than Shadwell. The legend of some years' standing that Tate was himself supplanted before his death by Rowe seems now to have been disposed of by Mr. H. F. Scott-Thomas.[2] From the latter we learn that Tate died on July 30, 1715, and Rowe was appointed laureate two days later.

---

[1] The writer of the notice in *The Lives and Characters* (1699), perhaps with a view of counterbalancing some of the harsh things in Langbaine's account eight years earlier, says, "He . . . has merit to deserve more than he has met with from others: He is guilty of Modesty, of which few of his Profession know much; and it is the noisy pushing Man in Poetry, as well as other things, that prevails with Fame as well as Fortune."

[2] *Modern Language Notes*, XLIX (1934), 169–71.

Source

A *Duke and No Duke* is based directly upon Sir Aston Cokain's *Trappolin Suppos'd a Prince*, a tragi-comedy composed sometime after 1633 and first published in 1658. Though Tate did not resort to line-by-line borrowing from the earlier play, he did remain fairly close to his source. His greatest changes were in the direction of cutting and simplifying. He reduced Cokain's five acts to three, his characters from twenty-eight to twelve, the number of lines from nearly three thousand to less than half that figure. His only addition was the scene of the Savoyard ambassadors. A more significant change was made, however, in Tate's altering the tone of the play and the characters of some of the principal figures. In keeping with the spirit of the times he made the speech freer and some scenes more lewd than they had been. Trappolin degenerates in character and becomes much more the professional pander than he was in the earlier piece. The admitted gain in realism is offset by the loss of affection for him.

To speak for a moment of the source of Cokain's play, we have here something very interesting indeed. With all the talk one hears of *commedia dell'arte* influences on English drama, there are few unmistakable examples of specific borrowing traceable directly to the Italian improvisators. Here is one of the very few. From Cokain's own account, and a few additional facts, we know that he composed his play after seeing a couple of performances of a similar piece by a *commedia dell'arte* troupe in Venice while he was making his grand tour. And from the researches of Miss Lea we can narrow down the possible sources to a few scenarii and an actual company, the *Affezionati*.[3] Cokain lost some of the flavor in reducing the improvised material to writing, and Tate has allowed still more to escape, but behind the two stand, still clearly visible, the Italians.

Stage History

A *Duke and No Duke* was never a huge success but it lasted well, retaining a moderate popularity until the end of the eighteenth century. Of the period between 1684,[4] when the play was first acted, and

---

[3]See especially her article "Sir Aston Cokayne and the 'Commedia dell'Arte,' " *Modern Language Review*, XXIII (1928), 47–51; also her *Italian Popular Comedy* (Oxford, 1934), *passim*.

[4]Langbaine, writing in 1691 and therefore fairly close to the events he refers to, says that Cokain's own play was performed sometime between the Restoration

1703, when the more or less regular notices in the daily papers begin, we have little definite information. Three records for the first season and a somewhat less specific record for 1693[5] have come down to us. Beginning with 1703 we can trace the course of the play with greater assurance, though our records are far from complete. We find that for some half a century there were few years, especially after the vogue of the farce-afterpiece had been well established by the end of the 1720's, when the play did not see at least a few performances. It occupied the main place in the bills for a longer time than might have been expected. Genest usually lists it alone through the 1730's and 40's, but we learn from the Winston Ms. in the Folger Library that it was followed by an afterpiece as late as May 14, 1744. On January 23, 1746, it was acted after *The Busy Body* at Covent Garden and from then on it remained an afterpiece. Its popularity was particularly great just after the mid-century at Drury Lane, perhaps in part because of Woodward's success in the role of Trappolin.[6] It may have been this increase in popularity which caused Baker to attack the farce as "absurd and impossible" and to wonder "that it should be so frequently represented as it is, or meet with so much Applause even from the very *Canaille*."[7] By the time he was writing, however,

---

and Tate's revision, but it appears that his sole evidence is a prologue which appeared in Duffet's *New Poems* . . . 1676. On the basis of Langbaine's statement, Maidment and Logan, in their edition of Cokain, p. 117, state that the play was acted after the Restoration. Montague Summers, *The Playhouse of Pepys*, p. 245, goes further and gives the date of production as 1675 and the actor of Trappolin as Joe Haines. It is of course impossible to deny that Cokain's play was acted, but the evidence presented by Langbaine is not enough to justify the last claim at least. Maidment and Logan also thought that Cokain's play "appears to have been produced prior to the Restoration," but the evidence seems to us to point in the opposite direction.

[5]See Summers' edition of Downes, p. 234, and Nicoll for the 1684 productions, Sybil Rosenfeld, "The Restoration Stage in Newspapers and Journals," *Modern Language Review*, XXX (1935), 457–58, for the 1693 listing.

[6]MacMillan lists fourteen performances for the 1750–51 season, thirteen for 1751–52, these evidently representing the peak of popularity. Our records show about 160 London performances of Tate's play and about forty performances of the different adaptations for the entire period, 1684–1826.

[7]*Companion to the Play-House* (1764).

the play had begun to fall off, and we get only widely scattered performances up until our last record, for February 17, 1812.[8]

Of the success of the piece outside London there are only meagre accounts. Miss Rosenfeld gives but five entries for the period from 1718 to 1763. We have records of four performances in Edinburgh in the 1750's[9]; in addition there is an Edinburgh cast of 1761 in the 1792 edition. The number is just as small for this country. Odell gives two performances for New York and Pollock three for Philadelphia, all for the period during and shortly after the Revolution. Wright gives one performance for Jamaica.

Other adaptations were much less successful than Tate's. In 1720 John Thurmond turned the play into a pantomime but since his production was unsuccessful it seems not to have been printed, by no means an uncommon fate for pantomimes. Robert Drury's reworking of the play as a ballad opera, *The Devil of a Duke: or, Trapolin's Vagaries* (1732), was also a failure, even though Nicoll's account indicates that Drury was willing to rework the play a second time.[10] In 1733, according to Burns Martin, an adaptation of this ballad opera, entitled *The Devil of a Duke or Trappolin's Vagaries*, with a new scene and thirteen songs by Allan Ramsay, was published in Edinburgh,[11] but no records of its production are given. A much later adaptation of the play was produced on April 13, 1818, at the Surrey Theatre in London and was reviewed by *The European Magazine* as follows:

A new Comic Burletta Spectacle, taken from the Italian, by Sir Aston Cockayne, under the eccentric appellation of 'The Duke, and the Devil!' was this evening completely successful. The whimsical equivoques arising from the constant mis-

---

[8]Nicoll, *History of Early Nineteenth Century Drama*, II, 443. Since Nicoll lists it under "Unknown Authors" and labels it as a burletta, we cannot be sure that this last record is for Tate's piece; it still retained the old title, however.

[9]J. C. Dibdin, *The Annals of the Edinburgh Stage* (1888), lists a performance for January 15, 1755; W. H. Logan, *Fragmenta Scoto-Dramatica* (1835), pp. 22 ff, lists performances for July 9, 1757, and April 6, 20, 1758.

[10]Nicoll lists two editions of Drury's opera for 1732, the second "with additions." His account of the few performances, on the other hand, indicate that the play was withdrawn after the first night so that it "might be shortened."

[11]We have not seen this edition, but Burns Martin in the *Times Literary Supplement*, November 14, 1929, states that he has examined a copy located in Glasgow. For the evidence substantiating Ramsay's authorship of this alteration, see Martin, *Allan Ramsay* (Cambridge, Mass., 1931), pp. 115–6.

takes of the Duke, and his transformed representative Trappolin, kept the audience in continued good humour. . . .[12]

The piece ran four straight weeks, then for a week in July, and tapered off with two performances in August. This last alteration was by T. J. Dibdin, who produced what seems to have been still another alteration, entitled *The Duke and the Devil or, Which is Which?* at Sadlers Wells, February 6, 1826.[13]

Publication

We have examined seven different editions of Tate's farce and noted the probable existence of one more.[14] It is not likely that there were many others. There were some alterations with the passage of time, tending in the usual direction of simplification. Tate's name disappeared from the title page after the first two editions.

A Duke and no Duke. A Farce. As it is Acted by Their Majesties Servants. Written by N. Tate. With the several Songs set to Music. . . . London, Printed for Henry Bonwicke . . . 1685.

A Duke and no Duke. . . . To which is now added, a Preface concerning Farce. . . . By N. Tate, Servant to Their Majesties. London: Printed for Henry Bonwicke . . . 1693.

A Duke and no Duke. . . . London: Printed for J. Turner . . . 1758.

A Duke and no Duke: or Trapolin's Vagaries. . . . In *A Select Collection of Farces.* . . . Edinburgh: Donaldson, 1762.[15]

A Duke and no Duke: or, Trapolin's Vagaries. . . . Glasgow, 1762.

A Duke and no Duke. . . . London: Printed and Sold by W. Oxlade, 1776.

A Duke and no Duke: or Trapolin's Vagaries. . . . In Vol. V, 217–40, *A Collection of the Most Esteemed Farces.* . . . Edinburgh, 1792.

Analysis

This play has some interesting things for us, particularly when it is examined in connection with Cokain's play and the *commedia dell'arte*

---

[12]LXXIII (1818), 343. Summers, *Playhouse of Pepys*, notes this revival but gives the date as July only and mistakes the theatre for Covent Garden.

[13]Nicoll, II, 294.

[14]In an edition of *The Stage Coach* printed by T. Lowndes, London, 1766, there is a list of plays printed and sold by him; among them is *A Duke and no Duke*.

[15]The title of this and other Scottish editions is made up from Tate's original title and the subtitle of Drury's ballad opera adaptation.

behind it. The scenario upon which Cokain drew was a typical one in that the farce element and the leading farce actor dominate the play but do not monopolize it quite. In the Italian comedy, farce was the leading element but it was always accompanied by—perhaps better say it always accompanied—the romantic plot, just as in the *commedia dell'arte* troupe the leaders were invariably the farce actors but no troupe was without a group of young lovers. The romantic plot, always the most stereotyped possible as is this one here, served as the unifying element to which the farce episodes could be tied.

One would expect [writes Alfred Harbage] an Englishman of Cokain's time to convert such material into a mere Bromean comedy of courtship, but such proves not the case. Something of what must have been the spirit of *commedia dell'arte* is preserved—crispness, spontaneity, a certain naivete, and, amidst farcical action and impudent dialogue, an inkling of democratic philosophy.[16]

Also typical of Cokain's source are the horseplay, the use of magic, the bragging soldier, the lecherous and talkative old men, and, most of all, the clever-stupid and often amoral clown. To call attention to some of the examples of the first of these in Cokain's play, note the device of Trappolin's talking to his mistress and his enemy, all in the same breath, in the opening scene, the amusing business of his requiring more and more magic circles to protect him in the conjuring scenes, his riding on Barberino's back in the scene of his return as the counterfeit duke, the ridiculous and drawn-out scenes of his out-curtseying Brunetto in prison, and the *lazzo* with Puchannello.

Of these Tate preserved some but not all and handled those he kept with no particular skill. From his extended comment on Jonson's "humours" characters in the preface which he added to the second edition of this piece,[17] we know that he had a confused notion that much of the secret of farce lay in overdrawn character. He therefore takes Cokain's really sensible and agreeable Duke Lavinio and makes him into a ranting fool, fit for *The Rehearsal*. He likewise increases Trappolin's worst traits until he has become a drunken lecher. Where Cokain's Trappolin is a happy-go-lucky, pleasure-

---

[16]*Cavalier Drama*, p. 133.

[17]Since Tate's long preface to the edition of 1693 is little more than a paraphrase of Agesilai Mariscotti, *De Personis, et Larvis. Syntagmation* (J. G. Graevius, *Thesaurus Antiquitatum Romanorum*, Venice, 1735, IX, 1097–1142), we do not reprint it here. Its chief significance perhaps is that it represents a kind of second-hand defense of a discredited genre.

loving scamp who asks for nothing more than a loaf of bread, a bag of Bologna sausages, a jug of Montefiascone, and his fair Flametta, Tate's Trappolin is a lascivious parasite who would pander his faithful Flametta to Lord Barberino in order to bribe his way out of trouble. As a result Tate has made his characters not more diverting, as befits farce, but less so. The episodes mentioned above in outlining the farce in Cokain's play receive varied treatment in Tate's. Some of the knockabout, such as the scene involving literal horse-play, he deletes entirely, together with the role of Puchannello. Others, such as the conjuring scene, he keeps but shortens and diminishes the fun of. Still others, such as the early scene of double-talk, he retains pretty much in their original state.

PROLOGUE

Written by a Friend of the Author's
Upon the First Drinking of Islington Water.

Gallants,
Who would have thought to have seen so many here,
At such a rambling Season of the Year;
And, what's more strange, All well and Sound, to the Eye!
Pray Gentlemen forgive me if I Lie.
I thought this Season to have turn'd Physician,
But now I see small hopes in that condition:
Yet how if I should hire a Black Flower'd Jump
And plye at Islington, Doctor to Sadler's Pump?
But first let me consult old Erra Pater,
And see what he advises in the matter.
          Let's see——
Venus and Mars, I find in Aries are,
In the Ninth House—a dull dry Bobbing Year.
The Price of Mutton, will run high, 'tis thought,
The Vizard Masks will fall to ten a Groat.
The Moon's in Scorpio's House or Capricorns,
Friends of the City govern well your Horns:
Your Wives will have a mighty Trade this Quarter,
I find they'll never leave their Natural Charter.
For once take my Advice as a true Friend,
When they a Walk to the new Wells pretend.
If you'll avoid your Fate quick hasten after,
They use more ways to Cool, than Drinking Water.

THE PERSONS

LAVINIO, the Great Duke of Tuscany.   Mr. *Wiltshire.*

BRUNETTO, alias HORATIO, Prince of Savoy.   Mr. *Carlile.*
BARBERINO. Lords, Counsellors to LAVINIO.   Mr. *Gillo.*
ALBERTO.   Mr. *Williams.*
TRAPPOLIN. A Parasite, Pimp, Fidler, and Buffoon, transform'd
  by Magick, and Usurper to LAVINIO.   Mr. *Lee.*
MAGO. A Conjurer.   Mr. *Percivall.*
Captain of the Guards.   Mr. *Sanders.*
ISABELLA. The Duchess.   Mrs. *Currer.*
PRUDENTIA. Sister to LAVINIO.   Mrs. *Percivall.*
FLAMETTA. TRAPPOLIN's Sweet-heart.   Mrs. *Twiford.*
Women. Puritan. Embassadours.
Servants and Attendants.
Wiltshire: entire cast supplied from 1685 edition.

The Scene   Florence.

A DUKE AND NO DUKE

ACT I. [SCENE 1.]

TRAPPOLIN *and* FLAMETTA.

TRAPPOLIN. For ever thine Flametta.

FLAMETTA.   Thanks my Dear.
But am not I a fond Fool to believe
  you,
When you have been from me these two
  long days?
I'm sensible I love but too well,
For truly Dear you are a naughty man.

TRAPPOLIN [*aside*]. Pretty Rogue!
how she fires my heart! now could I
cry like any roasted Lobster.—What
would old Lord Barberino give for one
such kind word from her. But young
and poor as she is, she is yet most constant and Virtuous.—Not that I care
much for Virtue neither.—Alas my
Dear, I have been much opprest with
Business since I saw thee. My Honour
was at stake for procuring Convenients
for no less than five Ministers of State.
It 'as been dead trading of late, but
'tis a comfort to see times mend, now
we are upon our Matrimony.

FLAMETTA. Let me Conjure you leave
  these vitious courses,
You must indeed, or we must never
  marry;

SCENE 1: Scene divisions are occasionally noted,
  never numbered; all scene divisions and numbers in brackets have been supplied by the
  editors.

But you will be my Convert and Reform.

TRAPPOLIN. All in good time Love;
it becomes me to see my Betters go
before me, when I do mend I shall certainly do it to purpose, I am so long
about it.——In the mean time I give
thee leave to be honest, and I think
that's fair.——(*Enter* BARBERINO
and Officers.) Whose here my Rival
Lord?

BARBERINO. Here is the Villain with
  his handsome Wench,
And ([what] afflicts me more) an hon-
  est One;
I have these many weeks attempted
  her,
But neither Threats nor Presents can
  prevail.
She must be virtuous, or her Poverty
Could ne'r withstand the Offers I have
  made;
Yet were she virtuous she would ne'r
  allow
This Fidling Parasite, Buffoon and
  Beggar:
But on pretence of his enormities,
I have procur'd this Order from the
  Duke
For his immediate banishment from
  Florence.
Most certainly, he bears some Spell
  about him,
And when he's once remov'd, I shall
  succeed.

TRAPPOLIN. Again my Dear——*My good Lord Barberino, your Honours humble Servant.*——For this free Promise, Love, I ne'er enough can thank Thee——*Your Lordships to command*——No Fortune shall divide or change our Wills.——*Your Honours humble slave*——What's Wealth or Power where Hearts consent like ours?——*Your Lordships Vassal*——When thou dost sigh, thy Trappolin shall weep.——*Your Honour always shall Command Me*——And when thou sings't——

FLAMETTA. We are observ'd.
Learn to be honest, and I am Thine for ever.   *Exit.*

TRAPPOLIN. I beg your Lordships pardon. Your Lordship saw how I was employ'd. The poor wretch has taken a fancy to me, and your Lordship knows I am a Person of liberal Education; That I bear not a Breast of Flint, nor was Nurs't with the Milk of Hircanian Bulls. Now if your Lordship has any thing to Command me, here I stand ready, *I'l fido Trappolino*, your Honours humble Servant in all things possible and impossible.

BARBERINO. You are a sawcy peremptory Villain,
And have too long escap'd the stroak of Justice.

OFFICER. Nor is there such a Coward in all Tuscany,
He's able to corrupt an Army.

TRAPPOLIN. Fear not that Seignior Capitano, for I never mean to come into One.

BARBERINO. So lewd a Pandar ne'er infected City,
What Wife or Daughter of the Noblest Blood
Is safe, where such a Hellish Factor breaths.

TRAPPOLIN. And can your Lordship on your Honour tax me
For want of Diligence in my Vocation?

BARBERINO. Industrious hast thou been in Villany,
But Florence must no longer be the Scene;
This is your Warrant, Captain, from the Duke,

To drive this Miscreant from our City Gates.
And when he's seen again in Tuscany,
That Minute forfeits his abandon'd life.
Thus has our Duke decreed.

TRAPPOLIN. At whose request?

BARBERINO. On mine.

TRAPPOLIN. I am glad to find your Honour has so much Interest in His Highness, and therefore make choice of your Honour as the most proper person to sollicit my Repeal.

BARBERINO. Audacious Slave.

TRAPPOLIN. His Highness knows travelling is chargeable, and besides my Stomach is of no ordinary Dimensions.

BARBERINO. Away with him, if he dispute your Orders
Call for the Parish Whips to your Assistance.

TRAPPOLIN. Seignior Officer you may take his Lordships word when he says a thing. You hear his Lordship hath private business with me, and desires your absence—For certain then his Highness is upon Treaty of Marriage with the Millanese; your Lordship and I, were always of opinion it would come to that.

BARBERINO. Such harden'd Impudence was never seen, Take him away.

TRAPPOLIN. My Lord, my Lord—Such a Primrose in a Corner for your Lordship, never blown upon my Lord;—

BARBERINO. Force him along.

TRAPPOLIN. Flametta my Lord, what says your Lordship to Flametta? There's Eyes and Bubbies! Shall I bring her to your Lordship—Nay my Lord, my Lord. *(they bear him off)*   *Exeunt.*

Enter Duke LAVINIO, ALBERTO,
Guards, and Attendants.

LAVINIO. I'm stung with Adders and shall go distracted;
Let me have breathing room.

ALBERTO. Your Highness knows
I ever have been watchful for your Honour,
And next to that I would preserve your quiet.

LAVINIO. Choice Method, first blow poyson in my Ears,
And after that preach patience to me.

ALBERTO. I fear my Duty has been too officious;
Dread Sir, reflect where was the mighty harm
In holding talk with him by open day?
I hope this fanning will incense the flame. *(Aside.)*

LAVINIO. What harm? the very Bawd to their desires
Could never have Forehead to dispute the harm:
A Virgin and a Princess seen to walk
And hold discourse apart with one of Race
Obscure, at least unknown, and no harm in't?
'Twere lewd, though they had only pray'd together:
Bring the Audacious Traytor to Our Presence. (BRUNETTO *brought in here.)*

BRUNETTO. *(Kneeling.)* Dread Sir, and twice my Noble Conquerour,
First in the Field, in which your Self alone
Could stop my Conquest with resistless Might,
And since in Gen'rous Princely Favours.

LAVINIO. Rise.
I am not us'd to hearken after Praise,
Or Thanks for Benefits by me conferr'd,
For hitherto they always fell on Merit,
Which can at best be call'd but paying Debts.
Only in this Acknowledgment, I hear
Ingratitude from it's own mouth condemn'd:
This Lord, the watchful Argus of my Honour,
Has charg'd you with a Crime will stain the Worth
You shew'd in Battel, and make Valour blush.

ALBERTO. I but inform'd your Highness what I saw.

BRUNETTO. He's prejudic'd, I kill'd his Son in fight
In Service of my Prince, as he of you.

LAVINIO. I have a Sister, dear to me as Fame,

Our Royal Father's only Care and Comfort.
'My Dukedom (said he dying) I bequeath thee,
'A slender Present and thy Due by Birth;
'But with it all the Glory of our Race,
'The spotless Honour of the Medices;
'Preserve the Princely Blood from baseborn taint,
'But most secure it in the weaker part,
'And match Prudentia with her Peer in Birth;
'So shall I with my Ancestors have rest.
Now Sir, how far you have infring'd these Orders,
And brought a guilt unknown upon my head,
I leave yourself to judge: Confess your Crime,
And Torture shall revenge it; smother it,
And Torture shall extort it.

BRUNETTO. My charmed Soul
Came panting to my Lips to meet your Charge,
And beg forgiveness for its high presumption.
But since you talk of Tortures, I disdain
The servile Threats, and dare your utmost Rage;
I love the Princess, and have urg'd my passion,
Tho' I confess all hopeless of return.
This with a Soldiers freedom I avouch,
Who scorns to lodge that Thought he dares not own:
Now Sir, Inflict what punishment you please.
But let me warn you, that your vengeance reach
My head, or neither of us can have rest.

LAVINIO. Chains, Straw and Darkness! this is meer distraction!
To Prison with him; you that waited on him *(They lead off* BRUNETTO.)
Be now his Guard: Thin Diet and no Light;
Such usage may restore him—Vengeance thus
Converts to Charity. *(Enter* PRUDENTIA.) Prudentia,
Your Entrance has prevented me a Visit
To your Apartment, and half sav'd a Chiding;
Yet I must tell you, you have been to blame,

But Sister learn reserv'dness for the future,
Such as becomes your Quality, and hold
That place which Nature and unspotted Virtue
Has hitherto secur'd you in my Heart.

PRUDENTIA. Most gracious Sir, If e're my secret Soul
Admits one thought that is not first submitted
For Approbation to your Royal Will,
The Curse of Disobedience fall upon me;
As I in you have found a Fathers Love,
I shall repay't with more than Filial Duty.

LAVINIO. Vertue and Honour ever guide thy way.
Thou'rt solitary, but shalt quickly enjoy
A sweet Companion in our Royal Bride.
Sforza the Duke of Millain, our old Friend,
Who always in our Wars hath sent us aid,
Here offers me the beauteous Isabella
His Daughter for my Wife, and instantly
We will to Millain on the Expedition,
That Treatment once determin'd, wee'l return
To Florence, where wee'l celebrate our Nuptials
With that Magnificence becomes our State.

PRUDENTIA. Go and be happy Sir in your fair Choice.

BARBERINO. That Blessing's only wanting to our State.

LAVINIO. Lord Barberino and Alberto, you
Whom I have always found most faithful to me,
To you I do commit the Government
Of Tuscany 'till my return; your Power
I leave unlimited, keep open Ear
To just Complaints: Allow and Act no wrong;
Look closely to our Prisoner Brunetto.

ALBERTO. So may your wish't Return be safe and speedy.

LAVINIO. Sister, your tears afflict us; a few Weeks
Shall grace our Court with the fair Millanese.
Lead on, 'tis time we were upon our way. *Exeunt.*

SCENE [2.] *A Desart.*

Enter TRAPPOLIN.

TRAPPOLIN. This banisht life is very doleful——What an inhumane Duke was this to banish me, that never banisht him? At every step I take, my poor Flametta comes into my mind: She met me at the Towns end, and would fain have come along with me, but that I told her she was not banisht, and might not.—Methinks this is a very melancholy place, I have not met a living Body yet, but they had wings or four legs. Let me bethink me where to betake my self, I would to Rome and turn Friar, but that I have too much Learning. A Man of my Occupation might once have finger'd the Polux Ryals in Venice, but now the Gentry go a more compendious way to work, and Pimp for one another; 'tquite spoils all trading. *(Soft Music in the Air.)* What sound is this? Sure this place must needs be haunted: This with a good Dinner were something, but as it is, it feels as if they were playing upon my small Guts. *(Storm and Thunder.)* So now, my airy Fidlers are fallen out amongst themselves; I lik'd their first strein somewhat better. I would his Highness would come and banish me from this place too. *(Storm again,* MAGO *the Conjurer rises.)* What's here? a decrepit old man? Now and I were sure he was of mortal Race, I would set upon him in the name of Famine——But if he should blow Brimstone in my Face there were a hopeful beginner baulk't.

MAGO. Son, Thou art Banish'd—I know all the matter.

TRAPPOLIN. 'Tis true old Friend, I am banish'd—But how the Devil came you to know it?

MAGO. Why, the Devil told me.

TRAPPOLIN. The Devil he did?— Why 'twas e'en his own doing, and so he could give you the best account of it.

MAGO. Be not dismay'd, Preferment waits upon thee, I am so far from hurting thee, That from poor Trappolin, I'le make thee a Prince.

TRAPPOLIN. Look you there again, he knows my name too.—For certain, this must be the Devil's kinsman—A Prince! poor Trappolin thanks you Father Conjurer, but has no mind to domineer in Hell: I know where your Territories lye.

MAGO. Besotted Wretch, Thou does not understand me; I tell thee Son, thou shalt return to Florence—

TRAPPOLIN. And be hang'd there for my labour.

MAGO. Be honour'd there, exalted o're thy Fellows.

TRAPPOLIN. On a Gibbet.

MAGO. There shalt thou shine in wealth, and roul in plenty,
The Treasures of the East shall Court thy wearing;
The haughty Nobles shall seem Pigmies to thee;
All Nature shall be ransack'd for thy Board,
And Art be tir'd to find thee choice of Banquets;
Each day and hour shall yield new Scenes of pleasure,
And crowding Beauties sue for thy Embraces.

TRAPPOLIN. Sure I have pimp'd for this old Fellow formerly, he's so kind— Well, as you say, Father Conjurer (on some private Considerations that I have) this may not do amiss: But how shall it be done?

MAGO. By Eo, Meo, and Areo.

TRAPPOLIN. What they mean, I know not, but I am satisfi'd 'tis by going to the Devil for it, and so much for that matter.

MAGO. Here, seat thee in this Chair.

TRAPPOLIN. To be shav'd Father Conjurer by one of your black Valets? I shall lather under their hands without a Ball.

MAGO. Sit still, and see the wonders of my Art; Eo, Meo, and Areo, rise.

TRAPPOLIN. What will become of this temporal Body of mine?—I am glu'd to my Seat here.——But hear you good Father, must this Retinue of your needs appear?

MAGO. Of indispensible necessity.

TRAPPOLIN. Then good Father let them appear invisibly, I have no great inclination to their Company: For to tell you the truth, I like yours none of the best, you are like the Devil enough to serve my turn.

MAGO. Now by the most prevailing Spell
That e're amaz'd the Powers of Hell;
That mid-night Witches ever try'd,
While Cynthia did her Cresent hide;
While watchful Dogs do bark forbore,
The Wolf to howl, the Sea to roar;
While Robbin do's his midnight Chare,
And Plowmen sweat beneath the Mare;
By all the terrours of my Skill,
Ascend, ascend, and execute my will.
(Lightning and Thunder, Spirits rise, and sink down with TRAPPOLIN.)
Now proud Lavinio, little dost thou know
This secret practise of my just Revenge.
(After a Dance the Spirits rise again, with TRAPPOLIN dressed exactly like the Duke LAVINIO.)

TRAPPOLIN. Oh Father what metal do you take me to be made of? I am not us'd to travel under ground: Oh for a Dram of the Bottle of a Quart or two! Call you this preferment? Marry he deserves it that goes to the Devil for't, but I see no preferment neither.

MAGO. Thou dost not know thy self, look in that Mirrour. (Shews him a Looking glass.)

TRAPPOLIN. Whose there, the Duke? —Your Highness is well return'd: Your faithful Servant Trappolin begs of your Grace to call him home, and hang up this old Wizard; he'l Conjure your Grace out of your wits else, and your Subjects out of your Dominions.—— What's he gone again? He's for his frisque under ground too. I have made way for him, I have work'd like any Mole, and made holes you may thrust Churches through.

MAGO. 'Tis thou thy self that represents the Duke;
What in that Glass thou saw'st is but thy Picture.

TRAPPOLIN. If that be my Picture I am the Picture of the Duke.

MAGO. And shalt be taken for the Duke himself.

TRAPPOLIN. The Dress is just like him, and for ought I knòw, it is Dress that makes a Duke.—Let me see, what must I say now? my Highness is your Highness's humble Servant.—This Conjurer is a rare Fellow.

MAGO. As thou didst here seem to thy self, So shalt thou to the world appear the perfect Duke: To Florence then and take thy State upon thee.

TRAPPOLIN. Trust me for Duking of it: I long to be at it. I know not why every man should not be Duke in his turn.—Father Conjurer, time is precious with us great Persons: However, I should be glad to see you at Court. It may be the better for you, for as I take it, we shall have some change of Ministers, and so farewel.

MAGO. Stay Son, Take this inchanted powder with thee, Preserve it carefully, for at thy greatest need 'Twill give thee aid: When any Foe assaults, Cast but this Magick Powder in his face, and thou shalt see most wonderful effects.

TRAPPOLIN. Good, Now I'm satisfi'd I am the Duke [,] Which some shall rue: Good Father, Fare you well. *(Conju[rer] vanishes.)*
Eo, Meo, and Areo—Pass.   *Exit.*

SCENE [3.] *The Palace.*

BARBERINO *and* FLAMETTA.

FLAMETTA. I do beseech your Honour to repeal
My only joy, my banisht Trappolin;
Take pity on a helpless Virgins tears,
Abandon'd to Distress——You must——
You will——
For as our Sov'raign left his Power with you
He left his Mercies too.·

BARBERINO. Her tears inflame me:
And were this Dukedom which I hold in trust
My due by Birth, I'd give it in exchange
For this sweet Innocence, this Artless Beauty.
Indeed (my pretty One) you wrong your Charms;

Nay I must say, you wrong your Virtue too
By this concern, for an abandon'd Slave,
Devoted to all Crimes; forget and scorn him.

FLAMETTA. I gave my heart before I knew his Vices,
But it will be my triumph to reclaim him,
I do beseech your Honour to call him home.

BARBERINO. And what Return may I expect for this?

FLAMETTA. Goodness has always been it's own reward;
But to convince you that your Courtesie
Shall not be wholly thrown away upon me,
By Day or Night you shall command—

BARBERINO. What?

FLAMETTA. My Prayers.

BARBERINO. A very hopeful Recompence;
What Statesman ever yet took Prayers for pay?
Deluded Maid, thou dost not know thy worth,
This Beauty must not be a Beggars Prize,
Design'd by Nature for a Nobler Sphere.
What can this Minion whose repeal you seek
Perform for thee? What can a Peasant do
To deck thy Youth, or to inrich thy Age?
Come be advis'd, here's Gold and Jewels for thee,
The Pride, the Pomp of Nature shall be thine:
Make all your study how to please your self,
Fortune shall wait to see your wish perform'd.

FLAMETTA. Are you our Prince, my Lord?

BARBERINO. What means that Question?

FLAMETTA. If you were, The Prince should be deny'd.
for thee? What can: from 1685 edition; 1693
edition reads "for thee what can"

BARBERINO. Then much more I.
Why do I trifle thus? I am no Prince,
Yet will not be deny'd;—Who waits
without?

FLAMETTA. Heaven shield me! You
intend no Violence.

BARBERINO. What I intend is Love;
if you refuse,
You make the Rape, that's all: Who
waits I say?

Enter Servant.

FLAMETTA. Help Heaven!

SERVANT. My Lord, my Lord most
unexpected News!

BARBERINO. Come near
And bear this peevish Girl to my Apartment,
Shee'l thank me for the Force.

SERVANT. The Duke, my Lord, his
Highness.

BARBERINO. Take her Slave.

SERVANT. His Highness is return'd
from Millain.

BARBERINO. Ha! The Duke return'd
from Millain? Thou art mad.

SERVANT. Just now arriv'd my Lord,
and coming hither.

BARBERINO. Here! Dispose of her as
I commanded thee,
'Till I find out the meaning of this
Dream.
Ha! that's his voice—And here he comes
in Person:
Let her go Slave.—Away dear Maid,
away. *(Puts her out.)*

Enter TRAPPOLIN *with his Spirits
invisible.*

ALBERTO *from the other side.*

BARBERINO. Great Sir, Upon our
knees we welcome your Return.

TRAPPOLIN. And upon our Legs we
take it:——Hem! hem! *(He struts
about.)*

ALBERTO. Your Highness comes unlook't for, we did not expect
This happy time so soon by fourteen
days.

BARBERINO. So please your Grace,
where is our Dutchess?

TRAPPOLIN. Your Dutchess will not
come 'till the Gods know when; for
my part I know nothing of the matter.
I left my Train behind me and came
unlookt for, to see how you Governed
in my absence, which I fear you have
done scurvily enough.

ALBERTO. How wild he talks!

TRAPPOLIN. Eo, Meo, and Areo, well
stuck to me I'faith—Well Lords, you
never pity my Misfortunes; I have been
robb'd in my journey, had my Horse
taken from me, and if it had not been
for Father Conjurer.

BARBERINO. How Sir?

TRAPPOLIN. I say, if I had not been
a Conjurer, I had ne're got home in
my Royal skin;—Well stuck there again,
Boys, well stuck.

ALBERTO. What means your Highness?

TROPPOLIN. Our Highness means to
take exact account of Affairs; I left an
honest Fellow here, call'd Trappolin.
What become of him?

BARBERINO. Your Highness gave me
charge to banish him.

TRAPPOLIN. Why there's the Pillar
of our State gone. You took him for
Buffoon, but I found him one of the
best Politicians in Christendom; other
Countries will value him, and for ought
I know, he's a Prince by this time—Eo,
Meo, and Areo, true Lads still.

ALBERTO. I am amaz'd!

TRAPPOLIN. Hear me, you Lord Barb
[erino] I love dispatch in Affairs, tell
me therefore what you take to be the
duty of a Statesman?

BARBERINO. To study first his Royal
Masters profit,
And next to that his pleasure; to
pursue
No sinister design of private gain;
Nor pillage from the Crown to raise
his Heirs,
His base-born Brood in Pomp above the
Race
Of old descended Worth; to know
Desert,
And turn the Princes favour on his
Friends;

And keep an open Ear to just Complaints.

TRAPPOLIN. Why there 'tis. I have travel'd, and can tell you what a Statesman should be. I will have him ten times prouder than his Master; I, and ten times richer too. To know none of his old Friends, when he is once in Office; to inform himself who has Merit, that he may know whom to do nothing for; to make Sollicitors wait seven years to no purpose, and to bounce thr'o a whole Regiment of 'em, like a Souldier through the Gantlet.

ALBERTO. This is meer Frenzy.

TRAPPOLIN. And there is another good Friend of mine, Brunetto, where is he?

ALBERTO. Dread Sir, You[r] Highness knows that for his presumption in Courting of your Sister, you confin'd him.

TRAPPOLIN. Nothing but lying in this world! I confine him: 'Tis well known I never had a Sister in my life.

BARBERINO. No Sister, Sir?

TRAPPOLIN. No, Jack Sawce, none that's worth imprisoning a Friend for; honest Brunetto I'le be with thee in the twinkling of a—Eo, Meo, and Areo, sit fast; pass.   *Exit.*

ALBERTO. He cannot counterfeit so much.

BARBERINO. I know 'not; But if he do not, he is surely mad.

ALBERTO. The Heav'ns be merciful! What wild fantastick things he do's? And talks of Eo, Meo, and Areo; Names [u]nheard of in the Court before.

BARBERINO. Some Millain Counts I warrant you. This kindness to Brunetto is most strange.

ALBERTO. Let's after him, and wait his better leisure.   *Exeunt.*

SCENE [4.] *A Prison.*

Re-enter TRAPPOLIN.

TRAPPOLIN. What a dismal Place is here? I'le have it carry'd bodily out of my Dukedom. Alass poor Brunetto,

what has he done to be shut up here?— Oh here he comes! *Enter* BRUNETTO.

BRUNETTO. What can the Duke design by coming hither?
For certain, it must be to see me strangled:
Well let him execute his Tyrant will,
For Death itself were Mercy to this Dungeon.

Great Prince.

TRAPPOLIN. He makes a very low leg, but I scorn to be out done in Courtesie.

BRUNETTO. What can this cruel Mockery intend? Your Highness does forget your self extreamly: I am your Prisoner.

TRAPPOLIN. My best Friend Brunetto.

BRUNETTO. I am astonish't! Sir, upon my knees I do congratulate your safe Return.

TRAPPOLIN. And upon my Knees I do embrace thee, honest Brunetto.

BRUNETTO. I know not what to think or speak. I do beseech your Highness Rise.

TRAPPOLIN. Not without thee: Therefore up I say; away with Complements, I cannot abide them.

BRUNETTO. You honour me above expression.

TRAPOLIN. A Fig for honour, I love thee[,] man; Sirrah Jayler, bring Chairs hither presently.

BRUNETTO. Your Highness.—

TRAPPOLIN. Away with Highness, I say, away with it; call me Lavin, plain Medices.

BRUNETTO. Sure I am awake, this is no Dream?

TRAPPOLIN. We will live merrily together, i'faith we will! Come Sirrah what a while have you been bringing these Chairs? I have known a Pimp made a Prince in less time. Brunetto sit thee down, sit down I say.

Dungeon: period in 1685 edition substituted for comma of 1693 edition.

extreamly: colon supplied from 1685 edition.

BRUNETTO. I will attend your Highness on my Knees.

TRAPPOLIN. Why, I am not thy Father, am I? Sit thee here.

BRUNETTO. On the right hand—That must not be.

TRAPPOLIN. Why an' thou wilt have it there, there let it be.—But hold, I am mistaken, that is on the left hand; that must not be: Dost thou think I have no manners in me. (*They remove their Chairs several times.*)

BRUNETTO. There is no remedy, I must obey.

TRAPPOLIN. Very well,—What now art thou afraid of me? Marry an' thou draws't back, I'le draw back too: Therefore sit still I say, and let us talk.

BRUNETTO. Great Sir, I am unworthy of these honours.
Your Noblest Florentines would be most proud
To be thus grac't.

TRAPPOLIN. I love not these set speeches. Let us talk as if we were in a Tavern together.—Now, I prithee Man, how cams't thou into this damn'd Dungeon?

BRUNETTO. I, now the Storm comes,—Pardon me Dread Soveraign.

TRAPPOLIN. What, on thy Knees again? Dost take me for Mahomet? As well as I can pardon thee, I do pardon thee whatever it be, tho' thou hast kill'd every body.

BRUNETTO. Wherefore this Torture Sir, before my Death,
'Tis Tyranny; your Highness knows my Crime
Was in aspiring to your Royal Sister.

TRAPPOLIN. Wast thou laid up for that: Alas for thee! Hast marry'd her?

BRUNETTO. Beseech your Grace.

TRAPPOLIN. Well, An'thou has not, I would thou hads't; get her consent, and here I give thee mine. So come along with me to Dinner.

BRUNETTO. Your Highness shall command me to my Death.

TRAPPOLIN. I say, Thou shalt have her, and if I had two Sisters thou shoulds't have them both—Who waits there? (BARBERINO, ALBERTO, *Attendants Enter.*) Now my good Lords, you see this Apartment, and you thought fit to have Brunetto shut up here for making Love to my Sister.

ALBERTO. It was your Highness Judgment and Command.

TRAPPOLIN. Jayler, take me these two Coxcombly Lords, and keep them under Lock: They are never well but when they are doing mischief. In my Conscience and Soul, here is such incumbrance of perplexity, that I protest—Come along Friend. *Exit with* BRUNETTO.

BARBERINO. Why, this is meer Distraction.

ALBERTO. We must endure it. (*They go in.*)

ACT II. SCENE [1.] *The Palace.*

Enter TRAPPOLIN.

TRAPPOLIN. This Dukes Life is very pleasant! Did ever any man come to preferment upon lighter terms, I am made a Prince, and Father Conjurer goes to the Devil for't. (*Enter* FLAMETTA.)
Whose here my pretty little Rogue? I mar'l what makes her at Court, tho' I fear this Affair will cost Lord Barberino a Castration.

FLAMETTA. Here is the Duke alone, whom I so long
Have sought for, to petition for repeal
Of my Dear Trappolin:——
I do beseech your Grace
Take pity on a Miserable Maid
Bereav'd of all her Joys.

TRAPPOLIN. All her Joys, that's Me!

FLAMETTA. I humbly beg Poor banish't Trappolin may be recall'd.

TRAPPOLIN [*aside*]. Dear Honeysuckle, she even makes me weep.

FLAMETTA. Great Sir, That you have Noble thoughts.

TRAPPOLIN. I have so.

FLAMETTA. The World is Witness, and by Consequence A heart full of Commiseration.

TRAPPOLIN. 'Tis so; [aside] What a torment is this now, that I must counterfeit with her?—Fair Maiden rise; What is your Name?

FLAMETTA. Flametta.

TRAPPOLIN. Thou shal't fare the better for that:—Trouble not your self, your Trappolin shall be recall'd; and I would I were sacrific'd, if I do not love him as well as I do my self.—Who comes yonder? the Princess.

Enter PRUDENTIA.

FLAMETTA. This is most Gracious.—

TRIPPOLIN. Some of my roguy Lords talk't of hanging him, if er'e he come home again but upon my Honour I swear it, that if they hang him, they shall hang me; and so set thy heart at rest.

FLAMETTA. Heav'n bless your Highness. *Exit.*

TRAPPOLIN. If this be the Princess, I'le be sworn Brunetto was in the Right of it.

PRUDENTIA. Ten thousand Welcomes, Sir: I never found
Such tedious hours since you left the Court.

TRAPPOLIN. Fair Lady, come hither—
You are our Sister you'l say.

PRUDENTIA. I hope my Conduct Sir, has ne'er giv'n Cause
For you to doubt of my Relation to you:
I am your Sister Sir, and Servant.

TRAPPOLIN. I am sorry for't.

PRUDENTIA. I do beseech your Highness, on what ground?

TRAPPOLIN. For a Carnal Reason, that shall be Nameless. But since we are Brother and Sister, we must content our selves as well as we can.

PRUDENTIA [aside]. I am surpriz'd at this: I heard indeed
His Language and Deportment was much alter'd;—
Sir, I am glad to see you safe return'd, But should have been more joyful, had you brought
Your Dutchess with you.

TRAPPOLIN. She'l come soon enough, never fear it: But Sister, To our Affair in hand (for I am Vengeance hungry.)

At my Return here I found Brunetto in Goal, and it appear'd to be for Love of you: Tell me Sister, can you fancy him?

PRUDENTIA. Your Will, Sir, is the square of all my Actions;
I have no Aversion for Brunetto's Passion:
Besides, his Quality, tho' yet conceal'd, Is worthy of your Blood, he is a Prince; His Name Horatio, and the second Son To Savoy's Duke.

TRAPPOLIN. My Friend a Prince; besworn I no more thought of seeing him a Prince than my self: Sister, you shall have my Consent to marry him, and so there's an end. *(A confused noise without.)* What's there to do?

Enter Officer

OFFICER. Dread Sir, This is the Day and Hour, in which your Highness is wont to determine Causes in your Chair of State here. And accordingly here are several Persons come to appeal to your Highness for Justice.

TRAPPOLIN. What! Justice before I have Dined? I tell you, it is a dangerous thing: I had like to have been hang'd once my Self, because the Judge was Fasting;—Well, let them enter. *(He takes the Chair of State.)* Well, here sits the Government: In the first place I would have the Court take notice, that in Affairs of State, I think that words are not be multiply'd, and I think so I shall not do so; and if I do not, no body else must: So that in this Assembly, he that speaks little, will speak better than he that talks much; and he that says nothing, better than they both. *(The People being brought in, A Woman with her Daughter stand forth.)*

WOMAN. I do beseech your Highness to do me Justice;
I have liv'd long with Fame amongst my Neighbours;
My Husband too bore Office in the Parish
'Till he was kill'd in fighting for your Highness,
And left me but this dear and only Daughter,
Whom this old Sinner has debauch'd, And spoil'd her Fortune.

TRAPPOLIN. Debauch'd? That is to say, lay with her? and got her Maidenhead.

WOMAN. Your Highness has a most discerning Judgment.

TRAPPOLIN. And how did he do this? Lawfully by the help of a Pimp, or without it?

WOMAN. O most unlawfully! For Sir, he has a Wife and Son too of his own Inches.

TRAPPOLIN. A Son of his own Inches; good, Then the Decision of this Cause is easie: Do you hear Woman, we will have that Son debauch'd, you shall get that Son's Maidenhead, and spoil his Fortune.

WOMAN. I do beseech your Grace, what?—

TRAPPOLIN. No replying after Sentence.—Whose Cause is next.

Another Woman stands forth.

WOMAN. Great Duke of Tuscany, vouchsafe to hear me:
I am a poor and helpless Widow, one
That had no Comfort left me but my Child,
Whom this vile Minion Whipp the Coach-man here
Being Drunk, drove over him and left him dead.
I do beseech your Highness, make my Case
Your own, and think what sad Distress—

TRAPPOLIN. Hold, hold, I will have no flourishing—This Cause requires some half a Minutes Consideration more than the former: Whipp you say, being drunk drove over your Child and kill'd him; why look you Woman, Drink will make a Coachman a Prince, and *Vice versâ* by the Rule of Proportion, a Prince a Coachman, so that this may be my own Case another time; however, that shall make no obstruction of Justice:—Therefore Whipp shall lye with you, and be suspended from driving, till he has got you another Child.—

WOMAN. So please your Grace, this is still worse.

TRAPPOLIN. No replying after Sentence.—Whose next?

A Puritan stands forth.

PURITAN. So please your temporal Authority.

TRAPPOLIN. How now! my mortifi'd Brother of Geneva, what carnal Controversie are you ingaged in?

PURITAN. Verily, there is nothing carnal in my Cause: I have sustained violence, much violence, and must have Compensation from the ungodly.

TRAPPOLIN. What is your Grievance?

PURITAN. I will pour it forth in the words of Sincerity.

TRAPPOLIN. I care not a Farthing for Sincerity, let me have it in Brevity.

PURITAN. This Person here is by Occupation a Mason or Tiler, as the language of the world termeth it; whilest therefore I stood contemplating a new Mansion that I had prepared unto my self the same time that this Person occupied his Vocation aloft thereon, or rather should have occupied; such was his wicked negligence, that he fell from the top of the building most unconscionably upon my outward man, even with all his carnal weight, and almost bruised me unto the Death, I being clad in thin Array (through the immoderate heat of the Season) namely, five Cassocks or Coats, seven Cloaks, and one dozen of quilted Caps.

TRAPPOLIN. Believe me, Sirs a most important matter! If such enormities go unpunish'd, what Subject can be safe? Why if any perverse Fellow take a Pique against his Neighbour, it is but getting up 8 or 10 or 14 stories high, and so fall down upon him as he stands thinking no harm in the Street: I do therefore Decree, That this Tiler shall stand below, while you get upon the Battlements of the House, and fall down upon him.

PURITAN. This is still most monstrous.

TRAPPOLIN. As for petty Causes, let them wait till we have Dined—Eo, Meo, and Areo!—Come along Sister. *Exeunt.*

[SCENE 2.]

Enter Duke LAVINIO, ISABELLA the Dutchess, Ladies, and Attendants.

LAVINIO. My hearts best Treasure,
charming Isabella;
You are most welcome to the Court of
Florence,
And when I lose the sense of such a
Blessing;
And cease to make your happiness my
study,
Let me become a Tributary Lord,
And hold my Birth-right at anothers
will.

ISABELLA. Dread Sir, I know and
prize my happiness:
Blest doubly in your Fortunes and your
Love.

LAVINIO. My absence from Affairs so
long, requires
My close Attendance now for some few
hours;
Then I'le return to settle Loves Account,
With flaming heart at Beauties 'Altar
bow,
And pay my Vows with double Adora-
tion.
Meanwhile, our Princess and her Train
once more
Shall welcome you to Florence:
Attend the Dutchess in.
Ex. all but LAVINIO *and Guards.*
The Face of things seems alter'd since
I went;
Some strange fantastick humour has
possest
In general the Citizens of Florence.
As yet I have met with none, but who
amaze me;
And speak of Matters done by me, as if
I had been here before my Dutchess
came.
Call Barberino and Alberto to me;
They'l soon resolve—(BARBERINO *and*
ALBERTO *appear through the*
Grates.)

BARBERINO. Most Gracious Sir,
Pitty your Subjects, and most faithful
Servants.

LAVINIO. Confusion! Are my Eyes
and Ears both charm'd?
Our Deputies whom we did leave in trust
Of our whole Power, chain'd, shackl'd,
and in Jayl!
Set them at large, and in my Presence
now
Before this Minute can expire, or I
Shall go distracted 'ere I know the
Cause.

Sure some ill Spirit has possest
My Subjects minds when I was gone;
D'ye know me?

BARBERINO. The Duke of Florence
our most gracious Master.

LAVINIO. Are not you call'd Barberino, you Alberto,
My prudent faithful Counsellours to
whom
I left the Government of Tuscany?

ALBERTO. We are your Loyal Subjects, tho' your Prisoners.

LAVINIO. How came you so?

BARBERINO. Great Sir, Your self
knows well: 'Twas only for obeying your
Commands.

LAVINIO. A Plot, a general Plot upon
my Wits;
Tell me the meaning, jest not with my
Rage,
I charge you do not, therefore speak
sense to me;
Or on your naked hearts I'le read the
Riddle.

ALBERTO. Alass! what shall we say?
Great Sir, you know
That none except your Royal self could
do it,
And to your Sacred Justice we appeal
How far we have deserv'd.

LAVINIO. Perdition! Furies
Where will this end? Gods! I shall
burst with Choler.
Be merciful good Heav'n, and give me
Temper.

ALBERTO. Amen good Heaven: I fear
the fatal want.

LAVINIO. Some Frenzie has on the
poor Wretches seiz'd,
Or else they durst not thus to tempt my
Fury.
Indeed I was to blame in threatning
you,
Who so much need my pity: My good
Lords,
I do beseech you to collect your Wits,
well: colon supplied from 1885 edition.
A Plot: 1685 edition reads "By Heav'n a general
    Plot"
Sacred: from 1685 edition; "Sacreed" in 1693
    edition.

And tell me gently how you came in Prison.

BARBERINO. By the Prosperity of Tuscany, Your Highness left us there.

LAVINIO. When did I so?

ALBERTO. The self same time you went in Person thither to free Brunetto.

LAVINIO. The self same time that I went thither to free Brunetto: Death, whom? What Brunetto?

BARBERINO. Your Prisoner taken in the Mantuan Wars.

LAVINIO. The more I search, the more I am confounded,
Quite lost within a Labyrinth of wonders.

ALBERTO. Gods! how he speaks, as if all we were mad,
And he had done nothing.

LAVINIO. I will yet have patience:
Tell me my Lords, if you are very sure
That you are well and Masters of your Sense.

BARBERINO. If e're your Highness knew us so we are.

LAVINIO. Yet give me leave to think what I do know;
I can sustain no more.—Come hither Captain.
These Lords affirm, that I put them in Prison,
How say you to't?

CAPTAIN. Great Sir, your Highness did,
You saw them left in Custody that Minute
You freed Brunetto.

LAVINIO. He's in the same Tale:
Tho' they are alike depriv'd of sense,
Yet do they all agree in what they say;
But why, good Captain, I will reason't with you,
Should I desire Brunetto's liberty?
Would it not be a foul dishonour think you
To the Great Family of Medices,
To cast away our Sister upon one
We neither yet know whom, nor what he is:
I pray you therefore Captain, if you have

Any small fragment of your Wits remaining
Reply accordingly.

CAPTAIN.   Sir, it is certain,
That if your Highness should bestow your Sister,
On such a one as you are pleas'd to mention,
The Conduct would surprize the world; but Sir,
I heard your self, distinctly I did hear you,
To call Brunetto, Prince Horatio,
The second Son to the Duke of Savoy.

LAVINIO.   Vengeance!
My wonder is so great, that I want words
Wherewith to give it vent: I see that all
My Subjects being distracted, think me mad.

CAPTAIN. Nay more, Your Highness gave the Princess charge
That she prepar'd herself, for in two days
You'd see her marry'd to the Prince Horatio.

LAVINIO. Enough! Yet Gods I'le hold my Reason yet.
Florence I left a most ingenious City,
But find it wofully at my Return
Possest with strange unheard of Lunacy.
Captain, I swear to you by my Dukedom,
I'd rather send for that Brunetto's head,
Than such a message as you say I did.

CAPTAIN. Beseech Your Highness look, let your own eyes
Convince you of the Truth of what I said.

Enter BRUNETTO *and* PRUDENTIA.

BRUNETTO. Divine Prudentia, All thy Sexes Charms
In thee are centred, and from that fair Union
Receive a fresh unspeakable Addition;
Your Brother's good ev'n to a Miracle,
And gave me thraldom, but to raise my Joy.

PRUDENTIA. Indeed it speaks a Noble Nature in him
To call: from 1685 edition; 1693 edition has "to call"

To Crown Desert, though in an Enemy.
And now I must confess without a blush,
You long have been my hearts dear
secret choice,
But never durst give Ear to your Addresses
'Till by my Brothers free consent allow'd.

BRUNETTO. Said you Consent? Alass!
That Name falls short
Of his Transcendent Grace: He's earnest
for us,
Urges and drives us to the Bow'r of Joy.

LAVINIO. Furies and Scorpions drive
you, Whirlwinds part you.

PRUDENTIA. My Royal Brother.

LAVINIO. Damn'd Infernal Creature!
More false than Helen, and the greater
Plague.

BRUNETTO. I did suspect at first 'twas
his Distraction
That favour'd my aspiring hopes, and
now
I fear't has chang'd his mind to my
undoing.

PRUDENTIA. Wherein Dear Sir, have
I deserv'd this Usage?
Was't not your Order?

LAVINIO. Sulphur choak thy voice:
I'le spend no Breath upon a thing so
vile.
You Sir, My new made Favourite, come
near
And tell me, are you Son to Savoy's
Duke?

BRUNETTO. Your Highness knows I
am his Second.

LAVINIO. I know you are his Second?
Blood and Fire.
This Frenzy has seiz'd him too.
Then know Sir, were you Savoy's Eldest
Son,
My Sister once deserv'd a better Match;
And she shall rather in a Monastery
Sigh out a weary Life without Devotion,
Than be your Wife.—To Prison with
the Boaster
'Till Savoy fetch him thence. *(The
Guards hurry him off.)*

BARBERINO. This relishes of Reason.

ALBERTO. Heav'n preserve This temper, and restore the State of Florence.

LAVINIO. Come Lords, and lend your
best Assistance to me,
Sleep shall not close my Eyes, nor food
refresh me,
'Till we have search't this Mischief to
the Core;
Wee'l stop at no extreams of Blood or
Torture,
Baulk no rough Means that may our
Peace secure;
Such desp'rate Ill's must have as desp'rate Cure.

Exeunt. manet PRUDENTIA.

PRUDENTIA. Unhappy Florence! more
unhappy I
To see a Prince and Brother thus decay'd,
Bereav'd of Reason, and made less than
Man!
My dear Horatio, grieve not at this
Usage,
But rather pity thy Oppressors Fate.

Enter TRAPPOLIN.

TRAPPOLIN. Whose here? the Princess in Tears? Dear Sister, how dost
thou do? Come, I know your Grievance,
and out of my Natural affection have
taken care for you; you marry the
Prince Horatio this Night.

PRUDENTIA [*aside*]. One Minute then
has chang'd his sullen humour! Why
then Sir, have you made him a close
Prisoner?

TRAPPOLIN. A Prisoner say you?—
Run Guards and fetch him to our Presence.—Do not so much abuse your self
dear Sister, to think I would confine
my Friend to Prison.

PRUDENTIA. You did it Sir this Minute, he's scarce there yet.

TRAPPOLIN. Madam Sister, If I did,
it was in my Drink, and certainly I had
some politick Reason for it, which I
have now forgot,—Some more Wine
Slave to clear my Understanding.

(BRUNETTO *brought in here.*)
BRUNETTO. How soon his mind is
chang'd? The Heaven's be prais'd.

TRAPPOLIN. Dear Prince Horatio an'
you do not forgive my Locking you in
Prison, I shall never be merry again,
and so here is to you dear Prince
Horatio.

BRUNETTO. Upon my knees I pay my humblest Thanks.

TRAPPOLIN. Come, come, Take her along Man, take her along, I know Lovers would be private, and so agree the rest among your selves.

(BRUNETTO *leads off* PRUDENTIA.)

BARBERINO *and* ALBERTO *passing over the Stage.*

TRAPPOLIN. Who's yonder? my Lords Banishers at large agen? will the Government never be able to drink in quiet for 'em? Seize those Traytors there, and carry them to Prison. And do you hear Sirrah, it shall be Treason for any body to let them out.

OFFICER. Unless by order from your Highness.

TRAPPOLIN. Orders from my Highness? I tell you Rascal, it shall be Treason to let them out, tho' I command it my self. Away with them, go.

(*Enter* ISABELLA.) What Bona Roba have we here now?

ISABELLA. My Dearest Lord.

TRAPPOLIN. For her Dress and Beauty, she may be a Dutchess, who are you Madam?

ISABELLA. Do you not know me Sir?

TRAPPOLIN. It seems she is none of the wisest, tho'.

ISABELLA. How am I alter'd since I came from Millain?

TRAPPOLIN. Oh! 'tis the Dutchess: You are our Wife, you'l say?

ISABELLA. Sir:

TRAPPOLIN. I am glad of it I promise you; come kiss then incontinently.

ISABELLA. What mean you Sir? You are merrily dispos'd.

TRAPPOLIN. Madam Dutchess, I am somewhat jovial indeed, I have been drinking freely, and so kiss me again.

ISABELLA. My Lord.

we here: from 1685 edition; "hear" in 1693 edition.
mean you Sir?: question mark supplied from 1685 edition.

TRAPPOLIN. You are a handsome Woman I promise you, and tell me Madam Dutchess, am not I a proper handsome Fellow?

ISABELLA. Sir, Do not jest with me, you know you are The Man whom I esteem above the World.

TRAPPOLIN. What a winning look was there too?—To Bed my Dear, to Bed.—I'le but take 'tother Flask, to put State Affairs out of my head, and then— Ah! ha! ha! *Exeunt.*

ACT III. [SCENE 1.]

Enter LAVINIO.

LAVINIO. You Glorious Planets that do nightly guide
The giddy Ships upon the Ocean Waves,
If some of your malignant Influences
Have rais'd this madness in my Subjects minds,
Let some of your more gentle Aspects now
Restore them to their Sense.
(BARBERINO *and* ALBERTO *appear in Prison.*)
I am astonish'd, Heaven's! What do I see?
My Lords imprison'd? Free them instantly
Without reply, for should you answer me,
I know you'l say I did it, and distract me.

CAPTAIN. His ill Fit's off again.

LAVINIO. I do not think that since the Infancy
And first Creation of the World, a madness
Pestiferous and equal unto this
Was ever known, all-Gracious Heav'n reveal
The fatal Cause, or lay our Cities waste.

BARBERINO. Most Gracious Soveraign, How have we deserv'd
Thus to be made the scorn of Vulgar Eyes?

LAVINIO. Yet send me Patience Heav'n!
I wonder Lords, that you of all my Subjects,
Whom I have known to bear the Noblest Judgments,

Should thus distract your selves in your
wild Fits:
You run to Prison of your own accord,
And say, I sent you.

ALBERTO. Most Royal Sir, we grieve
to see these days;

You did command us thither.

LAVINIO. I?

BARBERINO. Your Highness self.

LAVINIO. You are both deceived, to
act such idle Errors,
And lay the blame on me.

CAPTAIN. So please your Grace, You
did again commit 'em,
That very hour in which you set them
free.

LAVINIO. I commit them?
I tell you all with sorrow, witness
Heav'n
How deep that sorrow is! you are all
mad:
Therefore in this small interval of Sense,
Betake you with one voice to your
Devotion,
And pray the incens'd Gods to be ap-
peas'd
And keep you from Relapse.

BOTH. Heav'n bless your Highness.
Ex. All but LAVINIO.

LAVINIO. Plague, Famine, War, the
ruinous Instruments
Wherewith incensed Deities do punish
Poor Mankind for mis-deeds, had they
all fall'n
Upon this City, it had been a thing
To be lamented, but not wonder'd at.

Enter ISABELLA.

ISABELLA. My Lord, I have this hour
expected you.

LAVINIO. O, my dear Isabella, I have
brought thee
From Millain flourishing with all De-
lights,
Into a City full of men distracted.

ISABELLA. He is not sober yet: Go
in and sleep Sir.
You do not well my Lord, thus to betray
Your weakness to the publick view.

Royal Sir: comma after "Royal" deleted to follow 1685 reading.

LAVINIO. Oh, Heavens! My Wife and
all.

ISABELLA. What say you Sir?

LAVINIO. My Isabella, Thou hast
cause to curse me
For bringing thee into a place infected;
The Air is poyson'd, and I wonder now
How I have scap'd so long.

ISABELLA. I pray go sleep.

LAVINIO. Why Isabella?

ISABELLA. You have drunk too much.

LAVINIO. Madness unmatch'd!
She's farther gohe than any of the rest.
Dear Isabella, retire into thy Chamber;
Compose thy thoughts a while, and I'le
come to thee,
There we'l beseech the angry Gods to-
gether,
That they would yet remove this heavy
Ill.   *Ex.* ISABELLA.

Enter BRUNETTO *and* PRUDENTIA.
What do I see? Brunetto unconfin'd;
I am astonish'd how he came at large;
Whom I would have to lie in Prison,
walk
In freedom, and whom I would have in
freedom,
Run of themselves to Prison.—Hell!
They kiss,
Embrace before my Eyes! My Guards
there.

BRUNETTO. Ha! He's chang'd again.

PRUDENTIA. My Noble Brother.

LAVINIO.   Off.
Hadst thou thy Reason, and shouldst
offer this,
I'd study Tortures for thee; as thou art,
I pity thy misfortunes.—Seize your
Prisoner:
Next time I see him free, your head is
forfeit.

PRUDENTIA. Wonder on Wonders, I
beseech you Sir
By all the bonds of Nature, for what
cause?

LAVINIO. It is in vain to answer
frantick People.   *Exeunt.*

[SCENE 2.]

Scene Draws, and Shews TRAPPOLIN
asleep, Flasks of Wine by him.

Dear Isabella,: comma supplied from 1685 edition.

TRAPPOLIN. What a Princely Nap have I taken!—But as I remember I was to have gone to my Dutchess, or dreamt so.—Give me a Bumper. (BARBERINO and ALBERTO enter.) My Lords at large again?

BARBERINO. Long live your Highness.

TRAPPOLIN. Amen.

ALBERTO. And happily.

TRAPPOLIN. Amen for that too— But my small Friends how came you hither? I thought you had been under Lock and Key.

BARBERINO. Alass! he is relaps'd as bad as ever.

TRAPPOLIN. Sirrah Captain, Why kept you not these Vermine up till I bid you let them out?

CAPTAIN. So please your Grace, I did.

TRAPPOLIN. Will you lie Rascal to my Princely Face? (He throws Wine in his Face.)

CAPTAIN. Gods! will this Humor never leave him?

BARBERINO. We must in again.

TRAPPOLIN. To Kennel with them, walk my good Lords Banishers, your Honours know the way. Along with them. Trugh! Trugh!

ALBERTO. There is no remedy.
(They are carried off.)

TRAPPOLIN. Thus far I take it, we have kept the Government in good Order; now for my Dutchess, lead to her Graces Apartment.
Officer enters.

OFFICER. Ambassadours from Savoy desire admittance.

TRAPPOLIN. What are their Names?

OFFICER. Sir, I presum'd not to enquire.

TRAPPOLIN. Then what's their Business?

OFFICER. That Sir were presumption.

TRAPPOLIN. Thou insolent Varlet, What a Vulgar Fellow dost thou take me for, to speak with Strangers before *Grace,*: comma supplied from 1685 edition.

I know their Business?—Well Sirrah, set a Bumper by our Chair of State, and bring them to our Presence.

OFFICER. What can this mean?
[Exit.]

TRAPPOLIN. Suppose now, that those should be Spies upon our Government, in the shape of Ambassadours: Loving Subjects, if that be their business, I shall be frank and tell them, they have the wrong Sow by the Ear. For as the Ancients were wont to say, (those Ancients were a wise Nation) it was with them a principle Maxime, *Some wiser than some:* Trust me for Politicks, I'faith.
Enter Ambassadours.

1 EMBASSADOUR. Dread Sir, By us the Duke of Savoy sends
To greet your Nuptials with the Millanese,
Wishing all happiness to great Lavinio.

TRAPPOLIN. 'Tis civilly done, by my Troth, and there is no Love lost, I can assure him.

2 EMBASSADOUR [aside]. Is this the so much fam'd Lavinio,
Renown'd for Wisdom and Severity.

TRAPPOLIN. I say, it shews his good Nature as well as his Breeding, and so here's his good health.

1 EMBASSADOUR. This is most strange.

TRAPPOLIN. So much for Ceremony, now to our Business: For what can more befit a Prince than Business, Which always is best done *Propriâ Personâ:* I therefore Spice my Mornings Draught my self.

2 EMBASSADOUR. I am astonish'd.

TRAPPOLIN. The next prime Quality is for a Prince
Well to inform him of neighbouring Courts,
What Customs and Diversions are in use;
But chiefly by what Politicks they steer,
What Method in Affairs of State they take,
Whereby to square his own Concerns at home:
I therefore ask, What Wine you have in Savoy?

1 EMBASSADOUR [*aside*]. This is gross Mockery.

2 EMBASSADOUR [*aside*]. Or utter Frenzy.
We come not Sir to trifle, and 'tis time We now declare the Order of our Message:
Our Royal Master is at last informed, His only Brother, and his Dukedoms Heir,
Lyes here confin'd in close Imprisonment;
Release him instantly, and we are Friends:
Refuse us: and our sole Reply is War.

TRAPPOLIN. If you bring nothing but War, e'en carry it back with you again: We can drink and quarrel fast enough amongst our selves;—But heark you, For the sake of some Dukes that shall be nameless, before I treat with your Master, I must know by what Title he holds.

1 EMBASSADOUR. By Native and Legitimate Claim.

TRAPPOLIN. That is as much as to say, I am an Usurper.

2 EMBASSADOUR. By most unquestioned and immediate Right From Heav'n.

TRAPPOLIN. As who should say, my Preferment came from the Devil.

1 EMBASSADOUR. We ask your final Answer, Peace or War.

TRAPPOLIN. My final Answer is, to tell no man my Pleasure, till I know it my self.

2 EMBASSADOUR [*aside*]. Let us declare for Arms then, and away.

1 EMBASSADOUR [*aside*]. It cannot be with this Fantastick Tale;
To bring this strange account, will speak us mad,
And with our Prince ne'er gain the least Belief.

TRAPPOLIN. Look you Sirs, Your Master and I, can agree to fall out at our leisure; but if he pretend to love the Prince Horatio better than I do, he is a very uncivil Person, and so I shall tell him when I next light into his Company.

1 EMBASSADOUR. Heaven's! this is still more strange.

TRAPPOLIN. Will he fight for him?

2 EMBASSADOUR. He'l Conquer for him, Florence shall confess it.

TRAPPOLIN. Then I have one familiar Question more, Will he Pimp for him?

1 EMBASSADOUR. Prodigious!

TRAPPOLIN. Not Pimp for him? Let him pretend no further; If he ne'er Pimp'd for him, his claim is done. Will he give him his Sister?

2 EMBASSADOUR. That were foul Incest; and besides, he has none.

TRAPPOLIN. Why no more have I, nor ever had in my life, and yet I have given him mine.—But as for your Princess, let her set her heart at rest; for if my Friend must not have her, I will marry her my self.

1 EMBASSADOUR. What, while your Millanese is living?

TRAPPOLIN. That I confess I had forgot, Care for the State has turn'd my Brain:—But here is to our better Understanding. (*Drinks.*)

2 EMBASSADOUR. This is beyond all sufferance, gross affront;
And Florence shall in Blood lament the Folly.

TRAPPOLIN. In the name of Mars, then let your Master know, I care not, when we meet at the head of our Army—to crack a Bottle.

Exeunt severally.

[SCENE 3.]

Enter LAVINIO *hastily.*

LAVINIO. I've found, I've found at last the fatal Riddle:
It must be so, the Gods inspire the Thought,
Call Barberino and Alberto to me.
[*Enter Servant.*]

SERVANT. From Prison Sir?

LAVINIO. From Prison Slave, what mean'st thou?

SERVANT. Your Highness but this Minute sent them thither;
Nor will your Officer at my Request

Release them, 'twas so strict a Charge
you gave.

LAVINIO. Here take my Signet for a
Token: Bid them   [*Exit Servant.*]
Attend me instantly in my Apartment.
It must, it must be so, some spiteful
Fiend
Permitted by the Heav'ns assumes my
shape:
And what I do, undoes; no other Cause
Remains in Nature for these strange
Effects;
Pity me Gods, your lab'ring Minister;
Remove this Plague, and save the State
of Florence.   *Exit.*

Enter TRAPPOLIN, *as going to the
Dutchesse's Bed-Chamber.*

TRAPPOLIN. The next is the Dutchesse's Bed-Chamber.—and yonder she is
fast asleep.—What a Neck and Breast
is there?—Now do I reckon that my
Friend Brunetto and I shall encounter
much about a time. I ought to have
seen him a Bed first, but my Natural
Affection to my Dutchess prevail'd above
my Manners.

Re-Enter Servant.

SERVANT. Here is your Ring again
Sir.

TRAPPOLIN. What Ring?

SERVANT. Your Signet Sir, which
you sent me with, I have according to
your Order releas'd the Lords.

TRAPPOLIN. Give it me: Now, go
Slave commend me to Brunetto, and
bid him start fair.

SERVANT. From Prison Sir?

TRAPPOLIN. From Prison say you?
—Here take my Signet with you again,

and release him: and say, I charge him
on his Allegiance to go to Bed to the
Princess immediately; make all fast
without there; I can find the way to
her Grace by my self: Away. *Ex. Servants, &c. (As he is going in, he meets*
LAVINIO *entring.)*

LAVINIO. 'Tis strange they come not
yet—What do I see?

From Prison Sir? : "from" in 1693 edition; reading of 1685 edition restored.
From Prison say you? : "Prom" in 1693 edition;
reading of 1685 edition restored.

This is the Hellish Phantasm that has
bred
All this Confusion in our Court; good
Gods
How he resembles me! That I my self
Would almost take him for my self:
What art thou?

TRAPPOLIN. I am Lavinio Duke of
Tuscany.

LAVINIO. He speaks too, and usurps
my Name.
If thou art a Fiend, the gracious
Heav'ns be kind,
And put a Period to thy wild proceed-
ings;
But if thou art a Witch, I'le have thee
burnt.

TRAPPOLIN. Burnt? Traytor, burn
your lawful Duke!

LAVINIO. I'le try if thou hast sub-
stance, struggle not,
For thou mayst sooner break from
Hercules:
I'le have thee flead from thy enchanted
skin,
In which thou represents my person.

TRAPPOLIN. I say, beware of Treason; flea off my skin?

LAVINIO. Guards, Guards, Guards.

TRAPPOLIN. Guards, Guards.

LAVINIO. A Traytor, a Traytor.

TRAPPOLIN. A Traytor, a Traytor.
(As they strive and call together, TRAP-
POLIN *flings the enchanted Powder in
his Face,* LAV[INIO] *quits his hold.)*
There's some of Father Conjurer's Powder for you; what it will do for me I
know not, but there 'tis.

LAVINIO. The Sorcerer has blinded
me.

TRAPPOLIN. Ay, so would Powder of
Post for the present; but if this be all
the wonderful Effects, I'le save my
skin while I may.   *(He runs off.)*

LAVINIO. Stop, stop the Traytor, help!
Guards, Guards!   *(Runs after him.)*

Enter ISABELLA *in her Night-
Gown.*

ISABELLA. Sure I did hear the Duke
by Husbands Voice

help! : from 1685 edition; question mark in 1693
edition.

As in distress, and calling out for help;
Or did I dream? It must be more than
so:
Nay, as I thought, I saw two Figures of
him
One coursing of the other:—The noise
continues still—
Who waits? All Deaf? *(Rings a bell.)*
What, no Attendance here? What can
this mean?
This is the private passage to the
Princesse's Chamber.
I'le see if all be as silent there. *Exit.*

Re-Enter TRAPPOLIN.

TRAPPOLIN. What will become of
me? I shall never have the heart to
swagger it out with him: The Guards
are coming too:—Oh rare Powder!
'thas done the work I'faith.

*Re-Enter LAVINIO, transform'd into
the Likeness of TRAPPOLIN.*

LAVINIO. I have thee, and will hold
thee, wert thou Proteus.

Enter Captain and Guards.

TRAPPOLIN. Help Subjects, help your
Duke's assaulted.

CAPTAIN. Audacious Slave.

LAVINIO. Death and Furies.

CAPTAIN. What? Trappolin return'd?

OFFICER. He is distracted sure.

TRAPPOLIN. No, no, Trappolin was
too honest to assault his natural Prince,
this is some Villain transform'd by
Magick to his likeness, And I will have
him flea'd out of his enchanted skin.

LAVINIO. Blood and Vengeance.

TRAPPOLIN. Look to him carefull, till
you have our further Orders: Now
once more for my Dutchess. *Exit.*

LAVINIO. Unhand me Slaves, I am
the Duke your Sovereign.

ALL. Ha! ha! ha!

LAVINIO. That Villain that went out,
a damn'd Imposter.

OFFICER. Foul Treason, stop his
mouth.

CAPTAIN. Alass, he is Lunatik.

What?: punctuation supplied from 1685 edition.

LAVINIO. Why did you let th'Impostor
Devil scape?

CAPTAIN. Compose thy self poor
Trappolin.

LAVINIO. What mean the Slaves by
Trappolin?   *Enter Servant.*
Sir, Are you come? Where is my Ring?

SERVANT. Trappolin come home? And
as great a Knave, it seems as ever:
He has heard the Duke sent me with
his Ring, and this impudent Rogue
thinks to get it.

LAVINIO. The Slaves are now gone
mad another way.
They take the Counterfeit for their true
Prince,
And me it seems for one I do not know.

Sure some amongst my Subjects yet
will know me,
Then Slaves, your Heads shall answer
for this Crime.

Enter FLAMETTA.

FLAMETTA. I am or'ejoy'd, you are
welcome home my Dear;
I fear'd alass, I ne're should see you
more:
Indeed my Dear, you are beholden to
me;
'Twas I that won the Duke for your
Repeal.

LAVINIO. Blood and Fire!

FLAMETTA. This unkind to treat me
with such coldness,
After so long an Absence; have you
then
Forgot my Truth and Constancy?

LAVINIO. Off Strumpet.

FLAMETTA. Dost thou reward me thus
for all the Pains I took for thy Return
to Florence?

LAVINIO. Leave me, Or I will spurn
thee from me.

FLAMETTA. O faithless Men! Women
by me take heed
How you give credit to the perjur'd Sex.
Have I all thy long Banishment been
true,
Refus'd Lord Barberino with his Gifts;
And am I slighted thus?

it seems: from 1685 edition; 1693 edition has
"seem"

LAVINIO. What means the Harlot?
Heav'n, Earth, and Hell, have all conspir'd together,
To load me with a Crime unknown before. (*Enter* BARBERINO *and* ALBERTO.)
My Lords, You never came in better Season.
For never was your Prince so much distres't;
My very Guards deny me for their Master,
And take a Wizard for the Duke of Florence.

BARBERINO. What means the Vagabond, how came he home?
I hope the Duke will take care to reward him.
Say Captain, which way is our Royal Master?

LAVINIO. Nay then, Destruction is turned loose upon me.

FLAMETTA. Alas, he is mad! Distracted with his Banishment.

Enter ISABELLA *and* PRUDENTIA.

PRUDENTIA. The Vision you relate is wonderful,
And all these strange disorders in the Court
Must needs proceed from some prodigious Cause.

LAVINIO. That is the Princesse's voice; Prudentia, Sister,
Pity your Brother, speak to these mad Subjects
That do not know their Prince.

PRUDENTIA. What Fellow's this?

CAPTAIN. Off Sirrah.

LAVINIO. Is she bewitched too?—My Dear Isabella
Thou sure wilt own the Duke thy Husband:—Ha:
She turns away in wonder: By the Bonds
Of Duty, and of Nature, I conjure you
To do me Right, and own the Duke your Lord.
Alberto, Barberino, Prudentia, Isabella.

ALL. Ha! ha! ha!

ISABELLA. What do you with this frantick wretch? look to him and lodge him in the Hospital.

LAVINIO. Confusion! Nay then 'tis time to lay me thus on Earth,
And grow one Piece with it.
(*Throws himself down.*)

Enter BRUNETTO.

BRUNETTO. Your Highness humble Servant,—Dear Prudentia,
The Duke once more consents to make us happy,
Here is his Royal Signet for our Marriage.

Enter TRAPPOLIN.

TRAPPOLIN. Eo, Meo, and Areo, rare Boys still.—I am out of breath with looking for her; the Bed I found, but no Dutchess, and not one of her Women can tell me where she is:—Why here they are now all on a Bundle. Dear Pigs-ney, what a naughty Trick was this, to Spirit your self away, when you know how frighted I am with lying alone?—My Princely Friend, Hast thou consummated? That sneaking look of thine confesses thee Guilty: Well, marry'd or not marry'd, I am resolv'd to see you a Bed together incontinently.

LAVINIO. The Devil you shall.
(*Rising up hastily.*)

FLAMETTA. Dear Trappolin be quiet. You will destroy your self and me——I do beseech your Grace, Forgive him; alass, he is Lunatik.

LAVINIO. Oh Heav'ns! endure this Impostor thus
With his Enchantments to bewitch your Eyes.

TRAPPOLIN. Alass, poor Trappolin! That ever such good Parts as thine should come to this.

ALBERTO. Will he e're suffer this abuse?

BARBERINO. I know not, perhaps one Madman will pity another.

LAVINIO. Ye Florentines, I am Lavinio;
I am the Tuscan Duke; this an Impostor
That by damn'd Magick, and Infernal Arts
Has rais'd these strange Chimaera's in the Court.

ALBERTO. Your Highness is too patient.

FLAMETTA. Sweet Trappolin be rul'd.

TRAPPOLIN. Shew him a Glass.

LAVINIO. What do I see? even thus
I seem to them:
Plagues, Death, and Furies, this is
Witchcraft all:
Still I assert my Right, I am Lavinio.
(Breaks the Glass.)

TRAPPOLIN. Nay then, I see hee'l
ne're come to good; to Prison with him,
take him away. (As they seize him,
Thunder and Lightning breaks forth,
MAGO rises.)

MAGO. Turn thee Lavinio Duke of
Tuscany.

LAVINIO. Ha: who art thou that
own'st my Power and Title,
Disclaim'd by all my Subjects?

ALL. This is strange.

TRAPPOLIN. Father Conjurer here?—
I warrant he's going to the Devil now,
and calls at Court for Company.

LAVINIO. What e're thou art, dissolve
this Magick Mist;
Restore my State, and right an injur'd
Prince.

MAGO. My Spells alone can do it.

LAVINIO. I know that voice.

MAGO. Remember Guiscardi the Tus-
can Count,
Whom twelve years since, thou didst
unjustly banish;
Which tedious hours I chiefly have
apply'd
To Magick Studies, and in just Revenge
Have rais'd these strange disorders in
thy Court;
Now, Pardon what is past, I'le set all
Right.

LAVINIO. I swear by all the Honours
of my State,
By both my Dukedoms, Florence and
Sienna,
I pardon what is past.

TRAPPOLIN [aside]. So here is his
Grace and the Devil upon Articles of
Agreement, and excluding me from the
Treaty:—Well, I'le e'en banish my
self whilest I have the Authority in my
own hands: I have got a handsome Face
by the Bargain, and it would grieve

me to be flea'd out of it, and therefore
I will steal off as silently as I can.
[Exit.]

MAGO. Then take that Chair. (He
places LAVINIO in the Chair. Thunder
and Lightning again.)

BRUNETTO. What mean those Prodi-
gies?

MAGO. Ye Noble Florentines suspend
your fears,
And you shall see the wonders of my
Skill.
Thus with my Powerful Wand I Crown
thy Brow
With grateful slumbers till my Charms
are wrought.
You Spirits fram'd of milder Elements,
You that Controul the black malicious
Fiends,
Ascend, ascend, and execute my Will.
(Soft Musick. Spirits rise and dance
about LAVINIO, who by a device is
transform'd before the Audience into
his own Appearance, and Habit.)

ALL. The Duke: Good Heav'n: How
have our Eyes been Charm'd? Long
live your Highness.

LAVINIO. Where have I Been? Sure
all has been a Dream.

MAGO. Your Royal Word is past, you
pardon all;

LAVINIO. I do, and weep for joy
To see my Subjects to their Sense restor'd.

MAGO (To Brunetto). Brave Prince
Horatio, your elder Brother, The Duke
of Savoy's dead.

LAVINIO. Then he is Savoy. Sir, I
entreat forgiveness of what's past, And
wish you Joy,
(Gives him PRUDENTIA.)

BRUNETTO [and] PRUDENTIA. You
Crown our Happiness.

LAVINIO. Methinks, we have all been
scatter'd in a Storm,
And thus by Miracle met here together
Upon the happy shore.—Horatio,
Lords,
Prudentia, Wife, let me embrace you
all.

(TRAPPOLIN brought in by Spirits,
in his own likeness.)

Here is th' Impostor, Gods! what abject Things,
When in your Hands, prove Scourges of a State.

TRAPPOLIN. Good Father Conjurer, for old Acquaintance sake! Beseech your Grace, use Moderation. (To LAVINIO.) You see by me what a Prince may come to.

LAVINIO. Thy Pardon's granted, but depart the Realm.

FLAMETTA. Dear Trappolin embrace the happy Fate, and take me with thee.

TRAPPOLIN (To BRUNETTO). My Lord,—I have stood your Lordship's Friend.

BRUNETTO. In Savoy I'le requite thee Trappolin.

TRAPPOLIN. Savoy, Girl, Savoy—. a Count, a Count I warrant thee.

MAGO. Son Trappolin, I am thy natural Father;
And Since my Banishment from Florence, have
Sustain'd much Hardship, serv'd the Turk in's Galleys.

TRAPPOLIN. By your leave Father Conjurer, you have serv'd the Devil too.

MAGO. But from this Hour renounce my wicked Arts.

LAVINIO. So, lasting Happiness on Florence fall;
Our Plague's remov'd, and now we'll pass the Time
In Courtly Joys; our Tuscan Poets shall
From these Disorders, frame Fantastick Scenes

sake!: exclamation point supplied from 1685 edition.

To entertain our beauteous Millanese:
Each Accident at leisure well recite,
Misfortunes past, prove Stories of Delight.

SONGS.

A Song written by Sir George Etherege

Tell me no more I am deceiv'd,
While Silvia seems so kind;
And takes such care to be believ'd,
The Cheat I fear to find
To flatter me should Falshood lye
Conceal'd in her soft Youth;
A thousand times I'd rather die,
Than see the unhappy Truth;

II

My Love all Malice shall outbrave,
Let Fops in Libels rail;
If she the Appearances will save,
No Scandal can prevail:
She makes me think I have her Heart,
How much for that is due?
Tho she but act the tender part,
The Joy she gives is true.

A Song written by a Lady.

I.

Ah poor Olinda! never boast
Of Charms that have thy Freedom cost,
They threw at Hearts, and thine is lost.
Yet none thy Ruine ought to blame,
His Wit first blew me to a Flame,
And fans it with the Wings of Fame.

II.

In vain I do his Person shun,
I cannot from his Glory run,
That's Universal as the Sun.
In Crowds his Praises fill my Ear,
Alone his Genius does appear,
He, like a God, is ev'ry where.

A Song written by a Person of Quality.

Who can resist my Celia's Charms?
Her Beauty wounds and Wit disarms;
When these their mighty Forces joyn,
What Heart's so strong but must resign?
Love seems to promise in her Eyes,
A kind and lasting Age of Joys;
But have a care, their Treason shun,
I look'd, believ'd, and was undone,
In vain a thousand ways I strive,
To keep my fainting Hopes alive;
My Love can never find Reward,
Since Pride and Honour is her Guard.

NOTES

Page 13: *Lee:* Among the famous low comedians who followed Anthony Leigh in the role of Trappolin were Ned Shuter, Woodward, Palmer, Tom Edwin, and, according to Montague Summers, Edward Fitzwilliam.

Mrs. Percivall: later to be the wife of the ill-starred William Mountfort and still later of Jack Verbruggen.

Puritan: prominent eighteenth-century actors of this part were Hippisley at Covent Garden and Suett at Drury Lane.

Page 13. *and Reform:* here, some twelve years before the production of Cibber's *Love's Last Shift,* can be found Nahum Tate presenting the new point of view— that a feminine mind was capable of reforming the most debased and degenerate of men.

Page 17. *sink down:* Trappolin is dropped through the large trap on the outer stage where he can change into the robes of the Duke.

Page 18. *Artless Beauty:* the entire passage is illustrative of the contemporary trend of placing emphasis on "virtue in distress," a tendency that was manifesting itself in the plays of Banks and later of Rowe and many others. The neoclassicist Tate is using the phrase "Artless Beauty" as an encomium, though in a few lines afterwards he will return to the conventional attitude of "Pomp of Nature."

Page 20. *Enter Brunetto:* Trappolin has entered from one of the side doors to the outer stage, and a "flat" has been drawn in the inner stage revealing a painted set of a prison. See Summers, *Restoration Theatre,* pp. 223–4. The bringing of chairs by the jailer also shows that Trappolin and Brunetto were on the same level.

Page 22. *Carnal Reason:* although Tate omits the scene in Cokain's play where Trappolin required Flametta to disrobe, garment by garment, he here introduces a licentious and prurient passage which has no foundation in the source.

Second Son: here Tate gets into trouble by not changing all of Cokain's references to Horatio's relation to the Duke of Savoy. Throughout the play Horatio will be called alternately the second son and then the brother of the Duke of Savoy.

for Justice: Summers, in his *Playhouse of Pepys,* pp. 244, 275, and Maidment and Logan, in their edition of Cokain's plays, p. 108, list the Sieur D'Ouville's *Contes aux heures perdues* (1644) as the source for the petitioners' scene. Although Cokain probably composed his play before 1644, there is also evidence to indicate that in this scene he was still following his Italian source. Beside Trappolin's sentence upon Whipp, the coachman, Miss Lea cites the following passage from *Il Finto Principe, II,* a production of which Cokain may have seen:

> *Qui si fa il lazzo che Cola da audienza, vien gente con memoriali,*
> *del'asino, della Donna pregna, del creditore e della Piazza morta.*

THE
EMPEROR
OF THE
MOON:
A
FARCE.

As it is Acted by Their

𝕸𝖆𝖏𝖊𝖘𝖙𝖎𝖊𝖘 𝕾𝖊𝖗𝖛𝖆𝖓𝖙𝖘,

AT THE
QUEENS THEATRE.

Written by Mrs. *A. Behn.*

The second Edition.

LONDON,

Printed by *R. Holt,* for *Joseph Knight,* and *Francis
Saunders,* at the *Blew-Anchor* in the lower Walk of the
New Exchange, 1688.

THE
EMPEROR
OF THE
MOON:
A
FARCE.

As it is Acted by Their

Majesties Servants

AT THE

QUEEN'S THEATRE.

Written by Mrs. A. Behn.

The Second Edition.

LONDON,

Printed by R. E. &c. for Joseph Knight, and Francis
Saunders, at the Blue Anchor in the Lower Walk of the
New Exchange, 1688.

The Emperor of the Moon

Author

Even the briefest sketch of the life of Aphra Behn involves one in controversial details. No one has yet appeared with a biography of our first professional woman writer which solves the vexed question of her early life. She has had her defenders in recent years,[1] defenders willing to accept even some of the most romantic details of the early memoirs, but she has also sustained a vigorous attack which has dismissed practically all of the accounts related of her early life as sheer fiction.[2] Professor Bernbaum would have us disregard not only the implausibly romantic Oroonoko episode, but the whole Surinam adventure as well. More recently Mr. Platt[3] has brought forward another elaborate version of these early years, a version which in spite of its elaborateness and striking novelty will no doubt win supporters if for no other reason because it provides a reasonable middle ground. This is not to assert, however, that Mr. Platt lacks convincing evidence to bolster his argument.

But without any longer mystifying the reader who may not be familiar with the controversial details let us give briefly such facts and reasonable inferences as we have. Mrs. Behn was born Aphra Amis in Wye, July, 1640. She apparently did spend some time in South America, though her story of the high station she occupied there was probably a facile invention of her later years. She may have been married for a few brief years to a merchant of Dutch ancestry named Behn. She certainly did spend some time in Holland in 1666–67 in the secret service of the English government, though the records indicate that she provided very little information and a

---

[1]Perhaps the leaders among her champions have been Mr. Summers and Miss Sackville-West. More recently Edward Wagenknecht has offered his tribute, "In Praise of Mrs. Behn," *The Colophon*, Pt. XVIII (1934), [n. p.]. This article is just what its title says; it adds scarcely anything new.

[2]Her most vigorous assilant has been Professor Bernbaum, whose articles in the *Kittredge Anniversary Papers* and in *PMLA*, both 1913, have left very little of the old seventeenth-century memoirs undamaged.

[3]H. G. Platt, Jr., "Astrea and Celadon: an Untouched Portrait of Aphra Behn," *PMLA*, XLIX (1934), 544–59.

great many requests for funds, which she was denied.[4] Eventually she came home on borrowed money and, after a brief period spent in getting free of the burden of the loan and the shadow of prison, she settled down to the literary career which was to earn her fame. She died in 1689. It is hardly necessary to give a detailed list of her productions, of which there were many, for Mrs. Behn was a prolific writer of plays, novels, and verse. In twenty years she turned out around twenty plays and half as many novels. The plays were remarkable, even in an age far from puritanical, for the frankness of both language and incident. Most of them were comedies of intrigue with a generous mixture of farce; of the whole group only *The Rover* and the *Emperor of the Moon* enjoyed a very enduring success. The novels ran a great deal more to sentiment and for that reason proved more popular to the eighteenth century. Of these, *Oroonoko,* which was turned into a highly popular tragedy by Thomas Southerne, was easily the most popular.

Source

In dedicating her play to the Marquis of Worcester Mrs. Behn divulged the source of her plot: "A very barren and thin hint of the plot I had from the Italian, and which, even as it was, was acted in France eighty odd times without intermission. 'Tis now much alter'd, and adapted to our English Theatre and genius. . . ." "The Italian" from which she got her "thin hint" was the *commedia dell'arte* piece called *Arlequin empereur dans la lune,* 1684, for which Fatouville provided the French scenes. Actually there is more than a hint of the Italian-French play here, though Mrs. Behn has provided almost as much of her own material as she borrowed. It is not possible to be certain how she came by the imported material, but the most reasonable conjecture would seem to be that she, or some friend, saw the piece performed often enough to retain the substance of the six or eight scenes from which she borrowed. It is difficult to believe, as Summers does, that she had access to a printed copy of the play. He speaks of an edition "published in its entirety" in 1684 and adds, "Mrs. Behn of course used the edition of 1684."[5] In comparing her play with its admitted source Summers implies that he has compared

---

[4]Fortunately the Calendar of State Papers has provided some trustworthy material for the students of Mrs. Behn's life to work on, if not to agree over.

[5]*The Works of Aphra Behn,* III, 387.

the English *Emperor* of 1687 with the French *Empereur* of 1684. Unfortunately there are some suspicious details here. First of all, to speak of these Italian-French productions of the early 1680's as "published in their entirety" is to show an unawareness of what actually was happening. There could be no "entire" play, for only the French scenes were written down; the Italian ones were still played *al improviso*. Secondly, if there is a 1684 edition still extant it has eluded such diligent searchers as Professor Lancaster.[6] Thirdly, a detailed examination of Summers' observations and comparisons reveals pretty clearly that he had a copy of the scenes from Gheradi before him and not the earlier edition of which he speaks with such confidence.[7] To sum up, it seems safest at present to accept the view that the material taken from the *commedia dell'arte* scenes came from observing the play, not from reading a printed text.

In comparing Mrs. Behn's play with the French scenes from *Arlequin empereur dans la lune*, as printed later in Gherardi's *Theatre italien*, we note the following borrowings. She borrowed the "*Scene du desespoir*" in which Harlequin attempts suicide by tickling himself to death. The few details of the scene are reasonably close to the French but there is no direct taking over of speeches. From the "*Scene de la fille de chambre*" she borrowed a few of Harlequin's satirical jibes, but there is no close paralleling here. The highly farcical scene in which Harlequin slips from his hiding place to tag Bellemante's verses is an elaboration of Isabella's narration of how the same thing happened to her. The business of the jealous young lovers hidden in the closet parallels the remainder of the French "*Scene d'Isabelle et Colombine*." Similar rough parallels and piece-meal borrowings occur for the "*Scene du Fermier*," the "*Scene de l'apoticaire*," the "*Scene de l'ambassade, et du voyage dans l'empire de la lune*," and the "*Scene derniere*," in which one of the most

---

[6]For the most thorough and reliable account of activities of the *Theatre Italien* in English—or for that matter in any language—see H. C. Lancaster, *History of French Dramatic Literature*, Pt. IV, Vol. II, Chaps. xi ff. Professor Lancaster informs us that he has never seen an edition of Fatouville's play antedating Gherardi but that Soleinne lists an undated edition for Troyes.

[7]Even his description of the Gherardi collection indicates that Summers has not informed himself of the nature of the work or its interesting history.

striking parallels in the whole play occurs, the repeated comment of the old man on Arlequin's answer, *"C'est tout comme ici!"*[8]

Much of Mrs. Behn's play is altogether independent of Fatouville's, for example, the elaborate tapestry scene[9] and most of the telescope scene.

Stage History

Gosse tells us, in his article on Mrs. Behn in the *DNB*, that the *Emperor of the Moon* was a failure, but it would appear that either he had failed to inform himself of the play's fortunes or else he had a remarkably high standard for theatrical success. No play which retains even a small place in the repertory for seventy years and more can be dismissed in such high-handed fashion, and that is precisely what the play did. In Gosse's defense it might be said that there is very little in Genest and other works on stage history to guard him against such an error. But the newspapers have a great many entries scattered over a period running to the end of 1748[10] and accounting for four or five London theatres; our own accounts gathered from newspapers and other sources show slightly over one hundred and thirty performances of the play between its first production in December, 1687, and the last for which we have a record, in December, 1748. The British Museum has a copy of a 1777 edition of the play, "with alterations," produced at the Patagonian theatre, but we have no information on its reception at this date, nearly a century after the initial production.

Cibber tells, with characteristic verve, the story of Will Pinketh-man's unsuccessful attempt in September, 1702, to play Harlequin without the traditional mask, perhaps in deference to the members of his audience who disliked this obvious label on imported goods.[11]

---

[8]There is every reason to believe that Cibber had this passage in mind when he comments, apropos of something or other, "Why may I not then say, as some Fool in a French Play does upon a like Occasion—*Justement, comme chez nous!*" *Apology*, II, 220.

[9]Mrs. Behn may have taken this idea from another *commedia dell'arte* piece, Fatouville's *Arlequin Jason ou la toison d'or.*

[10]From Genest's accounts of the 1748–49 season we learn of the elaborate plans for reviving Mrs. Behn's farce and the dismal results. Drury Lane had a much better cast than Covent Garden, particularly with Woodward as Harlequin, but evidently even the best acting could no longer keep the piece running.

[11]*Apology*, I, 150 ff.

Pinkethman, no doubt with mask restored, played Mrs. Behn's farce at his summer theatre at Richmond in 1710, according to Miss Rosenfeld, but aside from this notice and another for Dublin, 1758, given by Genest, we know nothing of performances outside London.

Publication

The history of publication of *The Emperor of the Moon* may be summarized briefly by stating that there are four editions of the play alone, two at the time it first appeared and two nearly a century later, and four editions in collections of Mrs. Behn's works, from early in the eighteenth century to early in the twentieth.

The Emperor of the Moon: a Farce . . . Written by Mrs. Behn. London: Printed by R. Holt, for Joseph Knight, and Francis Saunders . . . 1687.

The Emperor of the Moon. . . . The Second Edition. . . . 1688.

The Emperor of the Moon. . . . In Vol. II, *Plays Written by the late Ingenious Mrs. Behn.* . . . The Second Edition. London, Printed for M. W. and sold by W. Meadows . . . 1716.

The Emperor of the Moon. . . . In Vol. IV, *Plays.* . . . The Third Edition. London: Printed for Mary Poulson . . . 1724.

The Emperor of the Moon. . . . 1757.[12]

The Emperor of the Moon. A dialogue—pantomime, written by Mrs. Behn; with alterations. . . . T. Sherlock: London, 1777.

The Emperor of the Moon. . . . In Vol. IV, *Plays, Histories, and Novels.* . . . London: John Pearson, 1871.[13]

The Emperor of the Moon. . . . In Vol. III, *Works of Aphra Behn,* ed. Montague Summers. London: William Heinemann; Stratford-on-Avon: A. H. Bullen, 1915.

Analysis

This farce is another of the Italian school, like Tate's *Duke and No Duke* or Ravenscroft's *Scaramouch.* This time the romantic plot has almost disappeared under the farcical scenes heaped upon it with no higher motive than to provide laughs. Not only has the romantic plot been reduced to the merest thread; what is left is treated with no

---

[12]This and the next listed here we have not seen but have taken the information from the *British Museum Catalogue.*

[13]This is merely a reprint of the 1724 edition of the plays and the 1725 edition of the novels.

sign of seriousness. The play begins with a commonplace situation: a father refuses to marry his daughter and niece to suitable young lovers; he has higher ambitions for them. Yet we soon discover that he is literally lunatic and will take no less than the man in the moon. With so hopelessly silly a guardian, the young ladies have virtually no problem in eluding him. So the dramatist needs to devote no attention to the intrigue and can concentrate on the farce episodes.

A second feature of the play appealing to contemporary audiences is its extravaganza; its opportunities for lavish scenes, for song and dance. Like the little *comedies-ballets* Molière wrote for Louis or like *Mamamouchi*, which Ravenscraft concocted from a couple of Molière's plays, this play provides ample scope for the costume maker and the scene painter.

Most interesting to us, however, are the *burle*, the farce turns, with which the play is strewn. Most of these had doubtless resulted from generations of experience on the stage by the Italian comedians, who had elaborated them and tested them before hundreds of audiences until they knew just how often to repeat a turn or prolong a scene to get the greatest number of laughs.[14] To take a few examples, let us look at the suicide episode in the first act. Gherardi labels it *"Scene du desespoir"* and adds an editorial note in which he describes Harlequin's acting, changing his voice as he carries on a dialogue with himself and so on. No one, he concludes, has ever seen it acted without agreeing that it is *"une des plus plaisantes qu'on ait jamais joué sur le theâtre italien."* Then there are the various shorter tricks[15] in I, iii, in which Harlequin and Scaramouch grope about in the dark, assume grotesque postures, which the playwright tries to give in detailed stage directions, thrust fingers into each other's mouth, and so on. These represent the most elementary kind of buffoonery but in capable hands they can be extremely comic on the stage. A scene

---

[14] It may not be inappropriate to note here that the Marx Brothers, among the leading farceurs of their generation, found themselves badly handicapped in the novel circumstances of movie production where there was no audience to register its response to their buffoonery.

[15] In defining *burla* Miss Lea says, "A 'burla,' to use the technical term, is something between a 'lazzo,' or comic turn, and a regular sub-plot. . . ." *Italian Popular Comedy*, I, 186. From her description we suppose that *burla* would be the appropriate term to apply to the tickling scene described above, *lazzi* to the brief tricks considered here, and *sub-plot* to the whole business of Harlequin and Scaramouch's rivalry for the hand of Mopsophil.

not borrowed from Fatouville but quite possibly suggested by other performances of the Italians is the one in which the actors assume poses as figures in a tapestry—the device of pretending to be a post or tree or other inanimate object being as old as farce itself. Perhaps, to take just one more, the most elaborate *burla* is the one involving Harlequin's lightning-like changes of character when he is attempting to drive past the official without paying the fee, a scene borrowed from Fatouville's "*Scene du Fermier de Donfront*," as it is called in Gherardi. The stage direction in the French reproduction gives a more striking description of what is intended here. While the officer is running out to call the clerk, we are told, "*Arlequin pendant ce temps change de juste-au-corps & de chapeau, & paroit en boulanger, avec une chemisette rogue et un bonnet blanc de laine; & son souflet se trouve changé en charlette.*" Here is the very essence of farce, rapid, clever, ludicrous in the extreme.

To the Lord Marquess of Worcester, &c.

My Lord,

It is a common Notion, that gathers as it goes, and is almost become a vulgar Error, That Dedications in our Age, are only the effects of Flattery, a form of Complement, and no more; so that the Great, to whom they are only due, decline those Noble Patronages that were so generally allow'd the Ancient Poets; since the Awful Custom has been so scandaliz'd by mistaken Addresses, and many a worthy Piece is lost for want of some Honourable Protection, and sometimes many indifferent ones traverse the World with that advantageous Passport only.

This humble Offering, which I presume to lay at your Lordships Feet, is of that Critical Nature, that it does not only require the Patronage of a great Title, but of a great Man too, and there is often times a vast difference between those two great Things; and amongst all the most Elevated, there are but very few in whom an Illustrious Birth and equal Parts compleat the Hero; but among those, your Lordship bears the first Rank, from a just Claim, both of the Glories of your Race and Vertues. Nor need we look back into long past Ages, to bring down to ours the Magnanimous deeds of your Ancestors: We need no more than to behold (what we have so often done with wonder) those of the Great Duke of Beauford, your Illustrious Father, whose every single Action is a glorious and lasting President to all the future Great ones; whose unshaken Loyalty, and all other eminent Vertues, have rendred him to us, something more than Man, and which alone, deserving a whole Volume, wou'd be here but to lessen his Fame, to mix his Grandeurs with those of any other; and while I am addressing to the Son, who is only worthy of that Noble Blood he boasts, and who gives the World a Prospect of those coming Gallantries that will Equal those of his Glorious Father; already, My Lord, all you say and do is admir'd, and every touch of your Pen reverenc'd; the Excellency and Quickness of your Wit, is the Subject that fills the World most agreeably. For my own part, I never presume to contemplate your Lordship, but my Soul bows with a perfect Veneration to your mighty Mind; and while I have ador'd the delicate effects of your uncommon Wit, I have wish'd for nothing more than an Opportunity of expressing my infinite Sense of it; and this Ambition, my Lord, was one Motive of my present Presumption, in the Dedicating this Farce to your Lordship.

I am sensible, my Lord, how far the Word Farce might have offended some, whose Titles of Honour, a Knack in dressing, or his Art in writing a Billet Deux, had been his chiefest Talent, and who, without considering the Intent, Character, or Nature of the thing, wou'd have cry'd out upon the Language, and have damn'd it (because the Persons in it did not all talk like Hero's) as too debas'd and vulgar to entertain a Man of Quality; but I am secure from this Censure, when your Lordship shall be its Judge, whose refin'd Sence, and Delicacy of Judgment, will, thro' all the humble Actions and trivialness of Business, find Nature there, and that Diversion which was not meant for the Numbers, who comprehend nothing beyond the Show and Buffoonry.

A very barren and thin hint of the Plot I had from the Italian, and which, even as it was, was acted in France eighty odd times without intermission. 'Tis now much alter'd, and adapted to our English Theatre and Genius, who cannot find an Entertainment at so cheap a Rate as the French will, who are content with almost any Incoherences, howsoever shuffled together under the Name of a Farce; which I have endeavour'd as much as the thing wou'd bear, to bring within the compass of Possibility and Nature, that I might as little impose upon the Audience as I cou'd; all the Words are wholly new, without one from the Original. 'Twas calculated for His late Majesty of Sacred Memory, that Great Patron of Noble Poetry, and the Stage, for whom the Muses must for ever mourn, and whose Loss, only the Blessing of so Illustrious a Successor can ever repair; and 'tis a great Pity to see that best and most useful diversion of Mankind, whose Magnificence of old was the most certain sign of a flourishing State, now quite undone by the Misapprehension of the Ignorant, and Misrepresentings of the Envious, which evidently shows the World is improv'd in nothing but Pride, Ill Nature, and affected Nicety; and the only diversion of the Town now, is high Dispute, and publick Controversies in Taverns, Coffee-houses, &. and those things which ought to be the greatest Mysteries in Religion, and so rarely the Business of Discourse, are turn'd into Ridicule, and look but like so many fanatical Stratagems to ruine the Pulpit as well as the Stage. The Defence of the first is left to the Reverend Gown, but the departing Stage can be no otherwise restor'd, but by some leading Spirits so Generous, so Publick, and so Indefatigable as that of your Lordship, whose Patronages are sufficient to support it, whose Wit and Judgment to defend it, and whose Goodness and Quality to justifie it; such Encouragement wou'd inspire the Poets with new Arts to please, and the Actors with Industry. 'Twas this that occasion'd so many Admirable Plays heretofore, as *Shakespear's*, *Fletcher's*, and *Johnson's*, and 'twas this alone that made the Town able to keep so many Play-houses alive, who now cannot supply one. However, my Lord, I, for my part, will no longer complain, if this Piece find favour in your Lordship's Eyes, and that it be so happy to give your Lordship one [h]ours Diversion, which is the only Honour and Fame is wish'd to crown all the Endeavours of,

My Lord,
  Your Lordship's
    Most humble, and
      Most Obedient
        Servant
          A. Behn.

PROLOGUE

Spoken by Mr. JEVERN.

Long, and at vast Expense the industrious Stage
Has strove to please a dull ungrateful Age:
With Hero's and with Gods we first began,
And thunder'd to you in Heroick Strain.
Some dying Love-sick Queen each Night you injoy'd,
And with Magnificence, at last were cloy'd:
Our Drums and Trumpets frighted all the Women;
Our fighting scar'd the *Beaux* and *Billet Deux* Men.
"So Spark in an Intrigue of Quality,
"Grows weary of his splendid Drudgery;
Hates the Fatigue, and cries a Pox upon her,
What a damn'd bustle's here with Love and Honour?
    In humbler Comedy, we next appear
No Fop or Cuckold, but slap-dash we had him here;
We show'd you all, but you malicious grown,
Friends Vices to expose, and hide your own;
Cry, Damn it——This is such or such a one.
Yet nettled, Plague, What do's the Scribler mean,
With his damn'd Characters, and Plot obscene?
No Woman without Vizard in the Nation,
Can see it twice, and keep her Reputation——that's certain
Forgetting—
That he himself, in every gross Lampoon,
Her lewder Secrets spreads about the Town;
Whilst their feign'd Niceness is but cautious Fear,
Their own Intrigues shou'd be unravel'd here.
    Our next Recourse was dwindling down to Farce,
Then—'Zounds, what Stuff's here? 'tis all o'er my——
Well, Gentlemen, since none of these has sped,
'Gad, we have bought a share i'th speaking Head.
So there you'l save a Sice,
You love Good Husbandry in all but Vice:
Whoring and Drinking, only bears a Price.

*The Head rises upon a twisted Post, on a Bench, from under
the Stage. After JEVERN speaks to its Mouth.*

         Oh!————Oh!————Oh!
STENTOR. Oh!————Oh!————Oh!

*After this it sings Sawny, Laughs, crys, God bless the King
in order.*

STENTOR *Answers.* Speak lowder Jevern, if you'd have me
           repeat;
         Plague of this Rogue, he will betray
         the Cheat.

He speaks lowder, it answers indirectly.

————Hum————There 'tis again,
Pox of your Echo with a Northern Strain.
Well, ————This will be but a nine days wonder too;
There's nothing lasting but the Puppets Show.
What Ladies heart so hard, but it wou'd move,
To hear *Philander* and *Irene's* Love?
Those Sisters too, the scandalous Wits do say,
Two nameless, keeping *Beaux,* have made so gay;
But those Amours are perfect Sympathy,
Their Gallants being as meer Machines as they.
Oh! how the City Wife, with her noon Ninny,
Is charm'd with, Come into my Coach—Mis *Jinny,* Mis *Jinny.*
But overturning—*Frible* crys—Adznigs,
The jogling Rogue has murther'd all his Kids.
The Men of War cry Pox on't, this is dull,
We are for rough Sports,—Dog Hector, and the Bull.
Thus each in his degree, Diversion finds,
Your sports are suited to your Mighty Minds;
Whilst so much Judgment in your Choice you show,
The Puppets have more Sence than some of you.

PERSONS NAMES

DOCTOR BALIARDO.   Mr. *Underhil.*
SCARAMOUCH, his Man.   Mr. *Lee.*
PEDRO, his Boy.
DON CINTHIO, DON CHARMANTE, both Nephews to the Vice-Young Mr. *Powel.*
    Roy, and Lovers of ELARIA and BELLEMANTE.   Mr. *Mumford.*
HARLEQUIN, CINTHIO's Man.   Mr. *Jevern.*
Officer and Clark
ELARIA, Daughter to the DOCTOR.   Mrs. *Cooke.*
BELLEMANTE, Niece to the DOCTOR.   Mrs. *Mumford.*
[FLORINDA]
MOPSOPHIL, Governante to the young ladies.   Mrs. *Cory.*
The Persons in the Moon, are DON CINTHIO, Emperor;
    DON CHARMANTE, Prince of Thunderland. Their At-
    tendants, Persons that represent the Court Cards.
KEPLER and GALILEUS, two Philosophers.
Twelve Persons representing the Figures of the twelve
    Signs of the Zodiack.
Negroes, and Persons that Dance.
Musick, Kettle-Drums, and Trumpets.

The Scenes, Naples.

ACT I. SCENE 1.

A Chamber.

Enter ELARIA and MOPSOPHIL.

I.

A Curse upon that faithless Maid,
Who first her Sexes Liberty betray'd;
Born free as Man to Love and Range,
Till Nobler Nature did to Custom change:
Custom, that dull excuse for fools,
Who think all Vertue to consist in Rules,

II.

From Love our Fetters never sprung,
That smiling God, all-Wanton, Gay and young,
Shows by his Wings he cannot be
Confined to a restless Slavery;
But here and there at random roves,
Not fixt to glittering Courts or shady Groves.

III.

Then he that Constancy Profest,
Was but a well dissembler at the best;
And that imaginary sway
She feigned to give, in seeming to obey,
Was but the height of Prudent Art,
To deal with greater Liberty her Heart.

(After the Song ELARIA gives her Lute to MOPSOPHIL.)

ELARIA. This does not divert me: Nor nothing will, till Scaramouch return, And bring me News of Cinthio.

MOPSOPHIL. Truly I was so sleepy last Night, I know nothing of the adventure, for which you are kept so close a Prisoner to Day, and more strictly guarded than usual.

ELARIA. Cinthio came with Musick last Night under my Window, which my Father hearing sallied out with his Mirmidons upon him, and clashing of Swords I heard, but what hurt was done, or whether Cinthio were discovered to him, I know not; but the Billet I sent him now by Scaramouch, will occasion me soon intelligence.

MOPSOPHIL. And see Madam where your trusty Roger comes.

Enter SCARAMOUCH peeping on all sides before he enters.
You may advance, and fear none but your Friends.

SCARAMOUCH. Away and keep the door.

ELARIA. Oh dear Scaramouch! hast thou been at the Vice-Roy's?

SCARAMOUCH. Yes, yes.—*(In heat.)*

ELARIA. And hast thou deliver'd my Letter to his Nephew Don Cinthio?

SCARAMOUCH. Yes, Yes, what should I deliver else?

ELARIA. Well—and how does he?

SCARAMOUCH. Lord, how shou'd he do? Why, what a Laborious thing it is to be a Pimp? *(Fanning himself with his Cap.)*

ELARIA. Why, well he shou'd do.

SCARAMOUCH. So he is, as well as a Night adventuring Lover can be—he has got but one wound, Madam.

ELARIA. How! wounded say you? Oh Heavens! 'Tis not Mortal?

SCARAMOUCH. Why I have no great skill,—but they say it may be Dangerous.

ELARIA. I Die with fear; where is he wounded?

SCARAMOUCH. Why, Madam, he is run—quite thorough the—heart,—but the Man may Live, if I please.

ELARIA. Thou please! Torment me not with Riddles.

SCARAMOUCH. Why Madam, there is a certain cordial Balsam, called a fair Lady; which outwardly applyed to his Bosom, will prove a better cure than all your Weapon-Salve, or Sympathetick Powder, meaning your Ladyship.

ELARIA. Is Cinthio then not wounded?

SCARAMOUCH. No otherwise than by your fair Eyes, Madam; he got away unseen and unknown.

ELARIA. Dost know how precious time is, and dost thou Fool it away thus? what said he to my Letter?

SCARAMOUCH. What should he say?
ELARIA. Why a hundred dear, soft things of Love, kiss it as often, and bless me for my goodness.

SCARAMOUCH. Why so he did.

ELARIA. Ask thee a thousand questions of my health after my last nights fright.

SCARAMOUCH. So he did.

ELARIA. Expressing all the kind concern Love cou'd inspire, for the punishment my Father has inflicted on me, for entertaining him at my Window last Night.

SCARAMOUCH. All this he did.

ELARIA. And for my being confin'd a Prisoner to my Apartment, without the hope or almost possibility of seeing him any more.

SCARAMOUCH. There I think you are a little mistaken, for besides the Plot that I have laid to bring you together all this Night,—there are such Stratagems a brewing, not only to bring you together, but with your Fathers consent too; Such a Plot, Madam.

ELARIA. Ay that wou'd be worthy of thy Brain; prethee what—

SCARAMOUCH. Such a device!

ELARIA. I'm impatient.

SCARAMOUCH. Such a Conundrum,— well if there be wise Men and Conjurers in the World, they are intriguing Lovers.

ELARIA. Out with it.

SCARAMOUCH. You must know, Madam, your Father, (my Master the Doctor,) is a little Whimsical, Romantick, or Don Quick-sottish, or so.—

ELARIA. Or rather Mad.

SCARAMOUCH. That were uncivil to be supposed by me; but Lunatick we may call him without breaking the Decorum of good Manners; for he is always travelling to the Moon.

ELARIA. And so Religiously believes there is a World there, that he discourses as gravely of the People, their Government, Institutions, Laws, Manners, Religion and Constitution, as if he had been bred a Machiavel there.

SCARAMOUCH. How came he thus infected first?

ELARIA. With reading foolish Books, Lucian's *Dialogue of Icaromenippus,* who flew up to the Moon, and thence to Heaven; an Heroick business called, *The Man in the Moon,* if you'll believe a Spaniard, who was carried thither, upon an Engine drawn by wild Geese; with another Philosophical Piece, *A Discourse of the World in the Moon;*

with a thousand other ridiculous Volumes too hard to name.

SCARAMOUCH. Ay, this reading of Books is a pernicious thing. I was like to have run Mad once, reading *Sir John Mandivel;*—but to the business,—I went, as you know, to Don Cinthio's Lodgings, where I found him with his dear Friend Charmante, laying their heads together for a Farce.

ELARIA. A Farce.—

SCARAMOUCH. Ay a Farce, which shall be called,—*the World in the Moon.* Wherein your Father shall be so impos'd on, as shall bring matters most magnificently about.—

ELARIA. I cannot conceive thee, but the design must be good since Cinthio and Charmante own it.

SCARAMOUCH. In order to this, Charmante is dressing himself like one of the Cabalists of the *Rosicrucian* Order, and is coming to prepare my credulous Master for the greater imposition. I have his trinkets here to play upon him, which shall be ready.

ELARIA. But the Farce, where is it to be Acted?

SCARAMOUCH. Here, here, in this very House; I am to order the Decoration, adorn a Stage, and place Scenes proper.

ELARIA. How can this be done without my Father's knowledge?

SCARAMOUCH. You know the old Apartment next the great Orchard, and the Worm-eaten Gallery, that opens to the River; which place for several years no body has frequented, there all things shall be Acted proper for our purpose.

Enter MOPSOPHIL *running.*

MOPSOPHIL. Run, run, Scaramouch, my Masters Conjuring for you like Mad below, he calls up all his little Devils with horrid Names, his *Microscope,* his *Horoscope,* his *Telescope,* and all his *Scopes.*

SCARAMOUCH. Here, here,—I had almost forgot the Letters; here's one for you, and one for Mrs. Bellemante. *(runs out.)*

Enter BELLEMANTE *with a Book.*

BELLEMANTE. Here, take my Prayer Book, Oh *Marrois charé.* *(Embraces her.)*

Marrois: 1687 edition has *ma tres chear.*

ELARIA. Thy Eyes are always laughing, Bellemante.

BELLEMANTE. And so would yours had they been so well imployed as mine, this Morning. I have been at the Chapel, and seen so many Beaus, such a Number of Plumees, I cou'd not tell which I shou'd look on most; sometimes my heart was charm'd with the gay Blonding, then with the Melancholy Noire, annon the amiable brunet, sometimes the bashful, then again the bold; the little now, anon the lovely tall! In fine, my Dear, I was embarass'd on all sides, I did nothing but deal my heart *tout au tour.*

ELARIA. Oh there was then no danger, Cousin.

BELLEMANTE. No, but abundance of Pleasure.

ELARIA. Why, this is better than fighting for Charmante.

BELLEMANTE. That's when he's present only, and makes his Court to me; I can sigh to a Lover, but will never sigh after him,—but Oh the Beaus, the Beaus, Cousin that I saw at Church.

ELARIA. Oh you had great Devotion to Heaven then!

BELLEMANTE. And so I had; for I did nothing but admire its handywork, but I cou'd not have pray'd heartily if I had been dying; but a deuce on't, who wou'd come in and spoil all but my Lover Charmante, so drest, so Gallant, that he drew together all the scatter'd fragments of my heart, confin'd my wandering thoughts, and fixt 'em all on him; Oh how he look'd, how he was dress'd! *(Sings)*

Chivalier, a Chevave Blond,
Plus de Mouche, Plus de Powdre
Pleus de Ribbons et Cannons.

—Oh what a dear ravishing thing is the beginning of an Amour?

ELARIA. Thou'rt still in Tune, when wilt thou be tame, Bellemante?

BELLEMANTE. When I am weary of Loving, Elaria.

ELARIA. To keep up your Humor, here's a Letter from your Charmante.

BELLEMANTE *(reads).* "Malicious Creature, when wilt thou cease to torment me, and either appear less charming or more kind. I languish when from you, and am wounded when I see you, and yet I am eternally Courting my Pain. Cinthio and I are contriving how we shall see you to Night. Let us not toil in vain; we ask but your consent; the pleasure will be all ours; 'tis therefore fit we suffer all the fatigue. Grant this, and Love me, if you will save the Life of

Your Charmante."

—Live then Charmante! Live as long as Love can last!

ELARIA. Well, Cousin, Scaramouch tells me of rare designs a hatching, to relieve us from this Captivity; here are we mew'd up to be espous'd to two Moon-calfs for ought I know; for the Devil of any Humane thing is suffer'd to come near us, without our Governante and Keeper, Mr. Scaramouch.

BELLEMANTE. Who, if he had no more Honesty, and Conscience, than my Unkle, wou'd let us pine for want of Lovers; but Heaven be prais'd, the Generosity of our Cavaliers has open'd their obdurate Hearts with a Golden key, that let's 'em in at all opportunities. Come, come, let's in, and answer their Billet Deux. *Exeunt.*

SCENE 2. *A Garden.*

Enter DOCTOR, *with all manner of Mathematical Instruments, hanging at his Girdle;* SCARAMOUCH *bearing a Telescope twenty (or more) Foot long.*

DOCTOR. Set down the Telescope— Let me see, what Hour is it?

SCARAMOUCH. About six a Clock, Sir.

DOCTOR. Then 'tis about the Hour, that the great Monarch of the upper World enters into his Closet; Mount, mount the Telescope.

SCARAMOUCH. What to do, Sir?

DOCTOR. I understand, of certain moments Critical, one may be snatch'd of such a mighty consequence to let the sight into the secret Closet.

SCARAMOUCH. How, Sir, Peep into the Kings Closet; under favour, Sir, that will be something uncivil.

DOCTOR. Uncivil, it were flat Treason if it shou'd be known, but thus unseen, and as wise Politicians shou'd, I take Survey of all: This is the States man's peeping hole, thorow which he Steals the secrets of his King, and seems to wink at distance.

SCARAMOUCH. The very key-hole,Sir, thorow with which half an Eye, he sees him even at his Devotion, Sir. *(A knocking at the Garden Gate.)*

DOCTOR. Take care none enter—

(SCARAMOUCH *goes to the Door.)*

SCARAMOUCH. Oh, Sir, Sir, here's some strange great Man come to wait on you.

DOCTOR. Great Man! from whence?

SCARAMOUCH. Nay, from the Moon World, for ought I know, for he looks not like the People of the lower Orb.

DOCTOR. Ha! and that may be; wait on him in. *Exit* SCARAMOUCH.

Enter SCARAMOUCH *bare, bowing before* CHARMANTE, *drest in a strange Fantastical Habit, with* HARLEQUIN: *Salutes the Doctor.*

CHARMANTE. Doctor Baliardo, most learned Sir, all Hail; Hail from the great Caballa—of Eutopia.

DOCTOR. Most Reverend Bard, thrice welcome. *(Salutes him low.)*

CHARMANTE. The Fame of your great Learning, Sir, and Vertue, is known with Joy to the renown'd Society.

DOCTOR. Fame, Sir, has done me too much Honour, to bear my Name to the renown'd Caballa.

CHARMANTE. You must not attribute it all to Fame, Sir, they are too learned and wise to take up things from Fame, Sir; our intelligence is by ways more secret and sublime, the Stars, and little Daemons of the Air inform us all things, past, present, and to come.

DOCTOR. I must confess the Count of Gabalist, renders it plain, from Writ Divine and Humane, there are such friendly and intelligent Daemons.

CHARMANTE. I hope you do not doubt that Doctrine, Sir, which holds that the Four Elements are Peopl'd with Persons of a Form and Species more Divine than Vulgar Mortals—those of the fiery Regions we call the *Salamanders*, they beget Kings and Heroes, with Spirits like their Deietical Sires; the lovely Inhabitants of the Water, we call Nymphs. Those of the Earth are Gnomes or Fayries. Those of the Air are Silfs. These, Sir, when in Conjunction with Mortals, beget Immortal Races. Such as the first born Man, which had continu'd so, had the first Man ne'er doated on a Woman.

DOCTOR. I am of that opinion, Sir, Man was not made for Woman.

CHARMANTE. Most certain, Sir, Man was to have been Immortaliz'd by the Love and Conversation of these Charming Silfs and Nymphs, and Woman by the Gnomes and Salamanders, and to have stock'd the World with Demy-Gods, such as at this Day inhabit the Empire of the Moon.

DOCTOR. Most admirable Philosophy and Reason.—But do these Silfs and Nymphs appear in shapes?

CHARMANTE. Of the most Beautiful of all the Sons and Daughters of the Universe: Imagination it self, Imagination is not half so Charming: and then so soft, so kind! but none but the Caballa and their Families are blest with their Divine Addresses. Were you but once admitted into that Society.—

DOCTOR. Ay, Sir, what Vertues or what Merits can accomplish me for that great Honour?

CHARMANTE. An absolute abstinence from carnal thought, devout and pure of Spirit; free from Sin.

DOCTOR. I dare not boast my Vertues, Sir; Is there no way to try my Purity?

CHARMANTE. Are you very secret.

DOCTOR. 'Tis my first Principle, Sir—

CHARMANTE. And one, the most material in our Rosicrucian order. Please you to make a Trial.

DOCTOR. As how, Sir, I beseech you?—

CHARMANTE. If you be thoroughly purg'd from Vice, the opticks of your sight will be so illuminated, that glancing through this Telescope, you may behold one of those lovely Creatures, that people the vast Region of the Air.

DOCTOR. Sir, you oblige profoundly.

CHARMANTE. Kneel then, and try your strength of Vertue, Sir.—Keep your Eye fixt and open. *(He looks in the Telescope.)*

(While he is looking, CHARMANTE *goes to the Door to* SCARAMOUCH, *who waited on purpose without, and takes a Glass with a Picture of a Nymph on it, and a light behind it, that as he brings it, shows to the Audience. Goes to the end of the Telescope.)*

—Can you discern, Sir?

DOCTOR. Methinks I see a kind of Glorious Cloud drawn up—and now—'tis gone again.

CHARMANTE. Saw you no figure?

DOCTOR. None.

CHARMANTE. Then make a short Prayer to Alikin, the Spirit of the East; shake off all Earthly thoughts, and look again. *(He prays.* CHARMANTE *puts the Glass into the Mouth of the Telescope.)*

DOCTOR.—Astonisht, Ravisht with delight, I see a Beauty young and Angel like, leaning upon a Cloud.—

CHARMANTE. Seems she on a Bed, then she's reposing, and you must not gaze—

DOCTOR. Now a Cloud Veils her from me.

CHARMANTE. She saw you peeping then, and drew the Curtain of the Air between.

DOCTOR. I am all Rapture, Sir, at this rare Vision—Is't possible Sir, that I may ever hope the Conversation of so Divine a Beauty?

CHARMANTE. Most possible, Sir; they will Court you, their whole delight is to Immortalize—Alexander was begot by a *Salamander*, that visited his Mother in the form of a Serpent, because he wou'd not make King Philip Jealous, and that famous Philosopher Merlin, was begotten on a Vestal *Nun*, a certain Kings Daughter, by a most beautiful young *Salamander* as indeed all the Heroes, and men of mighty minds are.

DOCTOR. Most excellent!

CHARMANTE. The Nymph Egeria inamour'd on Numa Pompilius, came to him invisible to all Eyes else, and gave him all his Wisdom and Philosophy. Zoroaster, Trismegistus, Apuleius, Aquinas, Albertus Magnus, Socrates, and Virgil had their Zilphid, which foolish people call'd their Daemon or Devil. But you are wise, Sir.—

DOCTOR. But do you imagine, Sir, they will fall in Love with an old Mortal?

CHARMANTE. They love not like the Vulgar, 'tis the Immortal Part they doat upon.

DOCTOR. But, Sir, I have a Neece and Daughter which I love equally, were it not possible they might be Immortaliz'd?

CHARMANTE. No doubt on't, Sir, if they be Pure and Chast.

DOCTOR. I think they are, and I'll take care to keep 'em so; for I confess, Sir, I wou'd fain have a Hero to my Grandson.

CHARMANTE. You never saw the Emperor of the Moon, Sir, the mighty Iredonozar.

DOCTOR. Never, Sir; his Court I have, but 'twas confusedly too.

CHARMANTE. Refine your Thoughts Sir, by a moments Prayer, and try again. *(He prays.* CHARMANTE *claps the Glass with the Emperor on it, he looks in, and sees it.)*

DOCTOR. It is too much, too much for mortal Eyes! I see a Monarch seated on a Throne—But seems most sad and pensive.

CHARMANTE. Forbear then, Sir, for now his Love-Fit's on, and then he wou'd be private.

DOCTOR. His Love-Fit, Sir!

CHARMANTE. Ay, Sir, the Emperor's in Love with some fair Mortal.

DOCTOR. And can he not Command her?

CHARMANTE. Yes, but her Quality being too mean, he struggles tho' a King, 'twixt Love and Honour.

DOCTOR. It were too much to know the Mortal, Sir?

CHARMANTE. 'Tis yet unknown, Sir, to the Cabbalists, who now are using all their Arts to find her, and serve his Majesty; but now my great Affair deprives me of you: To morrow Sir, I'll wait on you again; and now I've try'd your Vertue, tell you Wonders.

DOCTOR. I humbly kiss your Hands, most Learned Sir. (CHARMANTE *goes out.* DOCTOR *waits on him to the Door, and returns; to him* SCARAMOUCH. *All this while* HARLEQUIN *was hid in the Hedges, peeping now and then, and when his Master went out he was left behind.)*

SCARAMOUCH. So, so Don Charmante has plaid his part most exquisitely; I'll in and see how it works in his Pernicranium.—Did you call, Sir?

DOCTOR. Scaramouch, I have for thy singular Wit and Honesty, always had a Tenderness for thee above that of a Master to a Servant.

SCARAMOUCH. I must confess it, Sir.

DOCTOR. Thou hast Vertue and Merit that deserves much.

SCARAMOUCH. Oh Lord, Sir!

DOCTOR. And I may make thee great, —all I require, is, that thou wilt double thy diligent Care of my Daughter and my Neece, for there are mighty things design'd for them, if we can keep 'em from the sight of Man.

SCARAMOUCH. The sight of Man, Sir!

DOCTOR. Ay, and the very Thoughts of Man.

SCARAMOUCH. What Antidote is there to be given to a young Wench, against the Disease of Love and Longing?

DOCTOR. Do you your Part, and because I know thee Discreet and very Secret, I will hereafter discover Wonders to thee—On pain of Life, look to the Girls; that's your Charge.

SCARAMOUCH. Doubt me not, Sir, and I hope your Reverence will reward my faithful Service with Mopsophil, your Daughters Governante, who is Rich, and has long had my Affection, Sir.

(HARLEQUIN, *Peeping, cries—*
"Oh Traitor!")

DOCTOR. Set not thy Heart on Transitories, mortal, there are better things in store—besides, I have promis'd her to a Farmer for his Son.—Come in with me, and bring the Telescope.

Exit. DOCTOR *and* SCARAMOUCH.

(HARLEQUIN *comes out on the Stage.*)

HARLEQUIN. My Mistress Mopsophil to marry a Farmers Son! What am I then forsaken, abandon'd by the false fair One!
—If I have Honour, I must die with Rage;
Reproaching gently, and complaining madly.
—It is resolv'd, I'll hang my self— No, —When did I ever hear of a Hero that hang'd himself? no—'tis the Death of Rogues. What if I drown my self?— No,—Useless Dogs and Puppies are drown'd; a Pistol or a Caper on my own Sword wou'd look more nobly, but that I have a natural aversion to Pain. Besides, it is as Vulgar as Ratsbane, or the sliceing of the Weasand. No, I'll die a Death uncommon, and leave behind me an eternal Fame. I have somewhere read in an Author, either Ancient or Modern, of a Man that laugh'd to death. —I am very Ticklish, and am resolv'd—to die that Death.—Oh Mopsophil, my cruel Mopsophil! (*Pulls off his Hat, Sword and Shooes.*)—And now, farewell the World,

fond Love, and mortal Cares. *(He falls to tickle himself, his Head, his Ears, his Arm-pits, Hands, Sides, and Soals of His Feet; making ridiculous Cries and Noises of Laughing several ways, with Antick Leaps and Skips, at last falls down as dead.)*·

Enter SCARAMOUCH.

SCARAMOUCH. Harlequin was left in the Garden, I'll tell him the News of Mopsophil. *(Going forward, tumbles over him.)* Ha, what's here? Harlequin Dead! *(Heaving him up, he flies into a Rage.)*

HARLEQUIN. Who is't that thus wou'd rob me of my Honour?

SCARAMOUCH. Honour, why I thought thou'dst been dead.

HARLEQUIN. Why so I was, and the most agreeably dead.—

SCARAMOUCH. I came to bemoan with thee, the common loss of our Mistriss.

HARLEQUIN. I know it Sir, I know it, and that thou'rt as false as she: Was't not a Covenant between us, that neither shou'd take advantage of the other, but both shou'd have fair Play, and yet you basely went to undermine me, and ask her of the Doctor; but since she's gone, I scorn to quarrel for her— But let's like loving Brothers, hand in hand, leap from some Precipice into the Sea.

SCARAMOUCH. What, and spoil all my Cloths? I thank you for that; no I have a newer way: you know I lodge four pair of Stairs high, let's ascend thither, and after saying our Prayers.—

HARLEQUIN.—Prayers! I never heard of a dying Hero that ever pray'd.

SCARAMOUCH. Well, I'll not stand with you for a Trifle—Being come up, I'll open the Casement, take you by the Heels, and fling you out into the Street,—after which, you have no more to do, but to come up and throw me down in my turn.

HARLEQUIN. The Achievement's great and new; but now I think on't, I'm resolv'd to hear my Sentence from the mouth of the perfidious Trollop, for yet I cannot credit it.

I'll to the Gypsie, tho' I venture banging, To be undeceiv'd, 'tis hardly worth the hanging. *Exeunt.*

SCENE [3]. *The Chamber of*

BELLEMANTE.

Enter SCARAMOUCH *groping.*

SCARAMOUCH. So, I have got rid of my Rival, and shall here get an Opportunity to speak with Mopsophil, for hither she must come anon, to lay the young Ladies Night-things in order; I'll hide my self in some Corner till she come. *(Goes on to the further side of the Stage.)*

Enter HARLEQUIN *groping.*

HARLEQUIN. So, I made my Rival believe I was gone, and hid my self, till I got this Opportunity to Mopsophil's Apartment, which must be hereabouts, for from these Windows she us'd to entertain my Love. *(Advances.)*

SCARAMOUCH. Ha, I hear a soft Tread,—if it were Mopsophil's, she wou'd not come by Dark. (HARLEQUIN *advancing runs against a Table and almost strikes himself backwards.)*

HARLEQUIN. What was that?—a Table,—There I may obscure my self.— *(Groping for the Table.)* What a Devil, is it vanish'd?

SCARAMOUCH. Devil, — Vanish'd, — What can this mean? 'Tis a Mans Voice.—If it shou'd be my Master the Doctor, now I were a dead Man;—he can't see me,—and I'll put my self into such a Posture, that if he feel me, he shall as soon take me for a Church Spout as a' Man. *(He puts himself into a Posture ridiculous, his Arms akimbo, his Knees wide open, his Back-side almost touching the Ground, his Mouth stretched wide, and his Eyes staring. HARLEQUIN groping, thrusts his Hand into his Mouth, he bites him, the other dares not cry out.)*

HARLEQIN. Ha, what's this? all Mouth, with twenty Rows of Teeth.— Now dare not I cry out, least the Doctor should come, find me here, and kill me. —I'll try if it be mortal. *(Making damnable Faces and Signs of Pain, he*
Scene 3: the text has "Scene 2."

draws a Dagger. SCARAMOUCH *feels the Point of it, and shrinks back, letting go his Hand.)*

SCARAMOUCH. Who the Devil can this be? I felt a Poniard, and am glad I sav'd my Skin from pinking. *(Steals out.* HARLEQUIN *groping about, finds the Table, on which there is a Carpet, and creeps under it, listening.)*

Enter BELLEMANTE, *with a Candle in one Hand, and a Book in the other.*

BELLEMANTE. I am in a *Belle* Humor for Poetry to Night,—I'll make some *Boremes* on Love. *(She writes and Studies.) Out of a great Curiosity, —A Shepherd did demand of me.—* No, no,—*A Shepherd this implor'd of me.—(Scratches out, and Writes a new,)* Ay, ay, so it shall go.—*Tell me, said he,—Can you Resign?—Resign,* ay,— what shall Rhime to *Resign? —Tell me, said he,—(She lays down the Tables, and walks about.)* HARLEQUIN *peeps from under the Table, takes the Book, writes in it, and lays it up before she can turn. (Reads.)* Ay, ay,—So it shall be, —*Tell me, said he, my Bellemante; —Will you be kind to your Charmante? (Reads those two Lines, and is amaz'd.)* —Ha, —Heav'ns! what's this? I am amaz'd! —And yet I'll venture once more.—*(Writes and studies. Writes.)—I blush'd, and veil'd my wishing Eyes. (Lays down the Book and walks as before. —Wishing Eyes—*(HARLE-QUIN *writes as before.) —And answer'd only with my Sighs. (She turns and takes the Tablet.)* —Ha, —what is this? Witchcraft or some Divinity of Love? some Cupid sure invisible.— Once more I'll try the Charm.— (BELLEMANTE *writes.) Cou'd I a better way my Love impart? (Studies and walks.) Impart—(He writes as before.) And without speaking, tell him all my Heart.—*'Tis here again, but where's the Hand that writ it? *(Looks about.)* —The little Diety that will be seen But only in his Miracles. It cannot be a Devil, For here's no Sin or Mischief in all this.

Enter CHARMANTE. *She hides the Tablet, he steps to her and snatches it from her and Reads.*

Out of a great Curiosity,
A Shepherd this implor'd of me;
Tell me, said he, my Bellemante,
Will you be kind to your Charmante?
I blush'd, and veil'd my wishing Eyes,
And answer'd only with my Sighs:
Cou'd I a better way my Love impart;
And without speaking, tell him all my Heart?

CHARMANTE. Whose is this different Character? *(Looks angry.)*

BELLEMANTE. 'Tis yours for ought I know.

CHARMANTE. Away, my Name was put here for a blind. What Rhiming Fop have you been clubbing Wit withal?

BELLEMANTE. Ah, *mon Dieu!* — Charmante Jealous!

CHARMANTE. Have I not cause?— Who writ these Boremes?

BELLEMANTE. Some kind assisting Diety, for ought I know.

CHARMANTE. Some kind assisting Coxcomb, that I know. The Ink's yet wet, the Spark is near I find.—

BELLEMANTE. Ah, *Mal heureus!* How was I mistaken in this Man?

CHARMANTE. Mistaken! What, did you take me for, an easie Fool to be impos'd upon?—One that wou'd be cuckolded by every feather'd Fool; that you shou'd call a—*Beau un Gallant Huome.* 'sdeath! Who wou'd doat upon a fond She-Fop?—A vain conceited Amorous Cocquet.

(Goes out, she pulls him back.)

Enter SCARAMOUCH, *running.*

SCARAMOUCH. Oh Madam! hide your Lover, or we are all undone.

CHARMANTE. I will not hide till I know the thing that made the Verses.

DOCTOR *(calling as on the Stairs).* Bellemante, Neece,—Bellemante.

SCARAMOUCH. She's coming, Sir.— Where, where shall I hide him?—Oh, the Closet's open? *(Thrusts him into the Closet by force.)*

[*Enter* DOCTOR.]

DOCTOR. Oh Neece! Ill Luck, Ill Luck, I must leave you to night; my Brother the Advocate is sick, and has sent for me; 'tis three long Leagues,

and dark as 'tis, I must go.—They say he's dying. Here, take my Keys, *(Pulls out his Keys, one falls down.)* and go into my Study, and look over all my Papers, and bring me all those Mark'd with a Cross and Figure of Three, they concern my Brother and me. *(She looks on SCARAMOUCH, and makes pitiful Signs, and goes out.)* —Come Scaramouch and get me ready for my Journey, and on your Life let not a Door be open'd till my Return.
Exit.

Enter MOPSOPHIL. HARLEQUIN *peeps from under the Table.*

HARLEQUIN. Ha! Mopsophil, and alone!

MOPSOPHIL. Well, 'tis a delicious thing to be Rich; what a World of Lovers it invites: I have one for every Hand, and the Favourite for my Lips.

HARLEQUIN. Ay, him wou'd I be glad to know. *(And peeping.)*

MOPSOPHIL. But of all my lovers, I am for the Farmer's Son, because he keeps a Calash—and I'll swear a Coach is the most agreeable thing about a man.

HARLEQUIN. Ho, ho!

MOPSOPHIL. Ah me,—What's that? *(He answers in a shrill Voice.)*

HARLEQUIN. The Ghost of a poor Lover, dwindl'd into a Hey-ho. *(He rises from under the Table and falls at her Feet. SCARAMOUCH enters. She runs off squeaking.)*

SCARAMOUCH. Ha, my Rival and my Mistress!— Is this done like a Man of Honour, Monsieur Harlequin, to take Advantages to injure me? *(Draws.)*

HARLEQUIN. All advantages are lawful in Love and War.

SCARAMOUCH. 'Twas contrary to our League and Covenant; therefore I defy thee as a Traitor.

HARLEQUIN. I scorn to fight with thee, because I once call'd thee Brother.

SCARAMOUCH. Then thou art a Poltron, that's to say a Coward.

HARLEQUIN. Coward, nay, then I am provok'd, come on—

SCARAMOUCH. Pardon me, Sir, I gave the Coward, and you ought to strike. *(They go to fight ridiculously, and ever as* SCARAMOUCH *passes,* HARLEQUIN *leaps aside, and skips so nimbly about, he cannot touch him for his Life; which after a while endeavouring in vain, he lays down his Sword.)* —If you be for dancing, Sir, I have my Weapons for all occasions. (SCARA-MOUCH *pulls out a Fleut Deux, and falls to Playing.* HARLEQUIN *throwns down his, and falls a Dancing; after the Dance, they shake Hands.)*

HARLEQUIN. He my Bone Ame— Is not this better than Duelling?

SCARAMOUCH. But not altogether so Heroick, Sir. Well for the future, let us have fair Play; no Tricks to undermine each other, but which of us is chosen to be the happy Man, the other shall be content.

ELARIA *(within).* Cousin Bellemante, Cousin.

SCARAMOUCH. 'Slife, let's be gone, lest we be seen in the Ladies Apartment. (SCARAMOUCH *slips* HARLEQUIN *behind the Door.)*

Enter ELARIA.

ELARIA. How now, how came you here?

SCARAMOUCH *(signs to* HARLEQUIN *to go out).* I came to tell you Madam, my Master's just taking Mule to go his Journey to Night, and that Don Cinthio is in the Street, for a lucky moment to enter in.

ELARIA. But what if any one by my Fathers Order, or he himself, shou'd by some chance surprise us?

SCARAMOUCH. If we be I have taken order against a Discovery. I'll go see if the old Gentleman be gone, and return with your Lover. *(Goes out.)*

ELARIA. I tremble, but know not whether 'tis with Fear or Joy.

Enter CINTHIO.

CINTHIO. My Dear Elaria— *(Runs to imbrace her, she starts from him.)*—Ha, —Ha, —shun my Arms, Elaria!

ELARIA. Heavens! Why did you come so soon?

CINTHIO. Is it too soon, when are 'tis safe, Elaria?

ELARIA. I die with fear—Met you not Scaramouch? He went to bid you wait a while; What shall I do?

CINTHIO. Why this Concern? none of the House has seen me. I saw your Father taking Mule.

ELARIA. Sure you mistake, methinks I hear his Voice.

DOCTOR (below). —My Key— The Key of my Laboratory.—Why, Knave, Scaramouch, where are you?—

ELARIA. Do you hear that, Sir?—Oh, I'm undone!—Where shall I hide you? —He approaches—(She searches where to hide him.)—Ha, my Cousins Closet's open,—step in a little.— (He goes in, she puts out the Candle. Enter the Doctor. She gets round the Chamber to the Door, and as he advances in, she steals out.)

DOCTOR. Here I must have dropt it; a Light, a Light—there—

Enter CINTHIO from the Closet, pulls CHARMANTE out, they not knowing each other.

CINTHIO. Oh this perfidious Woman! no marvel she was so surpriz'd and angry at my Approach to Night.—

CHARMANTE. Who can this be?— but I'll be prepar'd—(Lays his hand on his Sword.)

DOCTOR. Why, Scaramouch, Knave, a Light! (Turns to the Door to call.)

Enter SCARAMOUCH with a Light, and seeing the two Lovers there, runs against his Master, puts out the Candle, and flings him down, and falls over him. At the entrance of the Candle, CHARMANTE slips from CINTHIO into the Closet. CINTHIO gropes to find him; when MOPSO-PHIL and ELARIA, hearing a great Noise, enter with a Light. CINTHIO finding he was discover'd, falls to acting a Mad Man, SCARAMOUCH helps up the doctor, and bows.

DOCTOR. Ha,—a Man,—and in my House,—Oh dire Misfortune!—Who are you, Sir?

CINTHIO. Men call me Gog Magog, the Spirit of Power;.
My Right-hand Riches holds, my Left-hand Honour.
Is there a City Wife Wou'd be a Lady?
—Bring her to me,
Her easie Cuckold shall be dubb'd a Knight.

ELARIA. Oh Heavens! a mad Man, Sir.

CINTHIO. Is there a Tawdry Fop wou'd have a Title?
A rich Mechanick that wou'd be an Alderman?
Bring 'em to me,
And I'll convert that Coxcomb, and that Block-head, into Your Honour, and Right Worshipful.

DOCTOR. Mad, stark mad! Why, Sirrah, Rogue—Scaramouch—How got this mad Man in? (While the Doctor turns to SCARAMOUCH, CINTHIO speaks softly to ELARIA.)

CINTHIO. Oh, thou perfidious Maid! who hast thou hid in yonder conscious Closet? (Aside to her.)

SCARAMOUCH. Why Sir, he was brought in a Chair for your Advice, but how he rambl'd from the Parlour to this Chamber, I know not.

CINTHIO. Upon a winged Horse, Iclyped Pegasus,
Swift as the fiery Racers of the Sun,
—I fly—I fly—
See how I mount, and cut the liquid Sky. (Runs out.)

DOCTOR. Alas poor Gentleman, he's past all Cure—But, Sirrah, for the future, take you care that no young mad Patients be brought into my House.

SCARAMOUCH. I shall, Sir,—and see —here's your key you look'd for.

DOCTOR. That's well; I must be gone—Barr up the Doors, and upon Life or Death let no man enter. (Exit Doctor, and all with him, with the light. CHARMANTE peeps out—and by degrees comes all out list'ning every step.)

CHARMANTE. Who the Devil cou'd that be that pull'd me from the Closet? but at last I'm free and the Doctors gone; I'll to Cinthio, and bring him to pass this Night with our Mistresses.
(Exit.)

As he is gone off, enter CINTHIO
groping.

CINTHIO. Now for this lucky Rival, if
his Stars will make this last part of his
Adventure such. I hid my self in the
next Chamber, till I heard the Doctor
go, only to return to be ʃeveng'd. *(He
gropes his way into the Closet, with
his Sword drawn.)*

Enter ELARIA *with a Light.*

ELARIA. Scaramouch tells me Charmante is conceal'd in the Closet, whom
Cinthio surely has mistaken for some
Lover of mine, and is jealous but I'll
send Charmante after him, to make my
peace and undeceive him. *(Goes to the
door.)*—Sir, Sir, where are you? they
are all gone, you may adventure out.

(CINTHIO *comes out.)* —Ha,—Cinthio
here!—

CINTHIO. Yes Madam, to your shame
—Now your Perfidiousness is plain—
False Woman, 'Tis well your Lover had
the Dexterity of escaping, I'd spoil'd
him making Love else. *(Gets from her,
she holds him.)*

ELARIA. Prethee hear me.

CINTHIO. —But since my Ignorance
of his Person saves his Life, live and
possess him, till I can discover him.
(Goes out.)

ELARIA. Go peevish Fool—
Whose Jealousie believes me given to
Change,
Let thy own Torments be my just
Revenge.

The End of the first Act.

ACT II. SCENE 1.

An Antick Dance.

After the Musick has plaid, enter
ELARIA [;] *to her* BELLE-
MANTE.

ELARIA. Heavens, Bellemante! Where
have you been?

BELLEMANTE. Fatigu'd with the most
disagreeable Affair, for a Person of my
Humour, in the World. Oh how I hate
Business, which I do no more mind,
than a Spark does the Sermon, who is
ogling his Mistress, at Church all the

while: I have been ruffling over twenty
Reams of Paper for my Uncles Writings.

Enter SCARAMOUCH.

SCARAMOUCH. So, so, the Old Gentleman is departed this wicked World,
and the House is our own for this
Night.—Where are the Sparks? Where
are the Sparks?

ELARIA. Nay, Heaven knows.

BELLEMANTE. How! I hope not so,
I left Charmante confin'd to my Closet,
when my Unkle had like to have surpriz'd us together: Is he not here?—

ELARIA. No he's escap'd, but he. has
made sweet doings.

BELLEMANTE. Heavens Cousin!
What?

ELARIA. My Father was coming ʼinto
the Chamber, and had like to have
taken Cinthio with me, when, to conceal him, I put him into your Closet,
not knowing of Charmante's being there,
and which, in the Dark, he took for a
Gallant of mine; had ʼnot my Fathers
Presence hinder'd, I believe there had
been Murder commited; however, they
both escap'd unknown.

SCARAMOUCH. Pshaw, is this all?
Lovers Quarrels are soon adjusted; I'll
to 'em, unfold the Riddle, and bring
'em back—take no care, but go in and
dress you for the Ball; Mopsophil has
Habits which your Lovers sent to put
on: the Fiddles Treat, and are all prepar'd.—*Exit.*

Enter MOPSOPHIL.

MOPSOPHIL. Madam, your Cousin
Florinda, with a Lady, is come to visit
you.

BELLEMANTE. I'm glad on't, 'tis a
good wench, and we'll trust her with
our Mirth and Secret. *(They go out.)*

Scene 2. *Changeʂ to the Street.*

*Enter Page with a Flambeaux, follow'd
by* CINTHIO; *passes over the Stage.*
SCARAMOUCH *follows* CINTHIO *in
a Campain Coat.*

SCARAMOUCH. 'Tis Cinthio—Don
Cinthio — *(Calls: he turns.)* — Well,
what's the Quarrel?—How fell ye out.

CINTHIO. You may inform yourself I believe, for these close Intrigues cannot be carried on without your knowledge.

SCARAMOUCH. What Intrigues, Sir? be quick, for I'm in hast.

CINTHIO. Who was the Lover I surpriz'd i'the'Closet?

SCARAMOUCH. *Deceptio visus*, Sir; the Error of the Eyes.

CINTHIO. Thou Dog—I felt him too; but since the Rascal escaped me—I'll be Reveng'd on thee—*(Goes to beat him, he running away, runs against* HARLEQUIN, *who is entring with* CHARMANTE, *and is like to throw 'em both down.)*

CHARMANTE. Ha,—What's the matter here?—

SCARAMOUCH. Seignior Don Charmante—*(Then he struts courageously in with 'em.)*

CHARMANTE. What, Cinthio in a Rage! Who's the unlucky Object?

CINTHIO. All Man and Woman Kind: Elaria's false.

CHARMANTE. Elaria false! take heed, sure her nice Vertue is Proof against the Vices of her Sex.—Say rather Beelemante.
She Who by Nature's light and wavering.
The Town contains not such a False Impertinent.
This Evening I surpriz'd her in her Chamber
Writing of Verses, and between her Lines,
Some Spark had newly pen'd his proper Stuff.
Curse of the Jilt, I'll be her Fool no more.

HARLEQUIN. I doubt you are mistaken in that, Sir, for 'twas I was the Spark that writ the proper Stuff. To do you Service—

CHARMANTE. Thou!

SCARAMOUCH. Ay we that spend our Lives and Fortunes here to serve you,—to be us'd like Pimps and Scowndrels.— Come, Sir,—satisfie him who

'twas hid i'th Closet when he came in and found you.

CINTHIO. Ha,—is't possible? Was it Charmante?

CHARMANTE. Was it you, Cinthio? Pox on't, what Fools are we, we cou'd not know one another by Instinct?

SCARAMOUCH. Well, well, dispute no more this clear Case, but lets hasten to your Mistresses.

CINTHIO. I'm ashm'd to appear before Elaria.

CHARMANTE. And I to Bellemante.

SCARAMOUCH. Come, come, take Heart of Grace; pull your Hats down over your Eyes; put your Arms across; sigh and look scurvily; your simple Looks are ever a Token of Repentance; come—come along. *Exeunt Omnes.*

Scene [3.] *Changes to the inside of the House.*

The Front of the Scene is only a Curtain or Hangings to be drawn up at Pleasure.

Enter ELARIA, BELLEMANTE, MOPSOPHIL, [FLORINDA,] *and Ladies dress'd in Masking Habits.*

ELARIA. I am extremely pleas'd with these Habits, Cousin.

BELLEMANTE. They are *Ala Gothic* and *Uncommune*.

FLORINDA. Your Lovers have a very good Fancy, Cousin, I long to see 'em.

ELARIA. And so do I. I wonder why Scaramouch stays so, and what Success he has.

BELLEMANTE. You have cause to doubt, you can so easily acquit your self; but I, what shall I do? who can no more imagine who shou'd write those Boremes, than who I shall love next, if I break off with Charmante.

FLORINDA. If he be a Man of Honour, Cousin, when a Maid protests her Innocence—

BELLEMANTE. Ay, but he's a Man of Wit too, Cousin, and knows when Women protest most, they likely lye most.

ELARIA. Most commonly, for Truth needs no asseveration.

BELLEMANTE. That's according to the Disposition of your Lover, for some believe you most, when you most abuse and cheat'em; some are so obstinate, they wou'd damn a Woman with protesting, before she can convince 'em.

ELARIA. Such a one is not worth convincing, I wou'd not make the World wise at the expence of a Vertue.

BELLEMANTE. Nay, he shall e'en remain as Heaven made him for me, since there are Men enough for all uses.

Enter CHARMANTE and CINTHIO, dress'd in their Gothic Habits. SCARAMOUCH, HARLEQUIN and Musick. CHARMANTE and CINTHIO kneel.

CINTHIO. Can you forgive us?
    (*ELARIA takes him up.*)

BELLEMANTE. That, Cinthio, you're convinc'd, I do not wonder; but how Charmante's Goodness is inspir'd, I know not. *(Takes him up.)*

CHARMANTE. Let it suffice, I'm satisfy'd, my Bellemante.

ELARIA. Pray know my Cousin Florinda. *(They Salute the Lady.)*

BELLEMANTE. Come let's not lose time, since we are all Friends.

CHARMANTE. The best use we can make of it, is to talk of Love.

BELLEMANTE. Oh! we shall have time enough for that hereafter; besides you make Love in Dancing as well as in Sitting; you may gaze, sigh,— and press the Hand, and now and then receive a Kiss, what wou'd you more?

CHARMANTE. Yes, with a little more.

BELLEMANTE. We were unreasonable to forbid you that cold Joy, nor shall you wish long in vain, if you bring Matters so about, to get us with my Uncle's Consent.

ELARIA. Our fortunes depending solely on his Pleasure, which is too considerable to lose.

CINTHIO. All things are order'd as I have written you at large; our Scenes and all our Properties are ready; we have no more to do but to banter the old Gentleman into a little more Faith, which the next Visit of our new Cabalist Charmante will compleat. *(The Musick Plays. Enter some Anticks and dance. They all sit still the while.)*

ELARIA. Your dancers have perform'd well, but 'twere fit we knew whom we trusted with this Evenings Intrigue.

CINTHIO. Those, Madam, who are to assist us in carrying on a greater Intrigue, the gaining of you. They are our Kinsmen.

ELARIA. Then they are doubly welcome. *(Here is a Song in Dialogue, with Fleut Deux and Harpsicals. Shepherd and Shepherdess; which ended, they all dance a Figure Dance.)*

CINTHIO. Hark, what Noise is that? sure 'tis in the next Room.

DOCTOR *(within)* Scaramouch, Scaramouch! (*SCARAMOUCH runs to the Door, and holds it fast.*)

SCARAMOUCH. Ha,—the Devil in the likeness of my old Masters Voice, for 'tis impossible it shou'd be he himself.

CHARMANTE. If it be he, how got he in? did you not secure the Doors?

ELARIA. He always has a Key to open 'em; Oh! what shall we do? there's no escaping him; he's in the next Room, through which you are to pass.

DOCTOR *[without]*. Scaramouch, Knave, where are you?

SCARAMOUCH. 'Tis he, 'tis he, follow me all—(*He goes with all the Company behind the Front Curtain.*)

DOCTOR *(without).* I tell you, Sirrah, I heard the Noise of Fiddles.

PETER *(without).* No surely, Sir, 'twas a Mistake. *(Knocking at the Door.)*

(*SCARAMOUCH having plac'd them all in the Hanging, in which they stand without Motion in Postures. He comes out. He opens the Door with a Candle in his hand.)*

Enter the Doctor and PETER with a Light.

SCARAMOUCH. Bless me, Sir! Is it you or your Ghost.

DOCTOR. 'Twere good for you, Sir, if I were a thing of Air; but as I am a substantial Mortal, I will lay it on as substantially—*(Canes him. He cries.)*

SCARAMOUCH. What d'ye mean, Sir? what d'ye mean?

DOCTOR. Sirrah, must I stand waiting your Leisure, while you are Rogueing here? I will Reward ye. *(Beats him.)*

SCARAMOUCH. Ay, and I shall deserve it richly, Sir, when you know all.

DOCTOR. I guess all, Sirrah, and I heard all, and you shall be rewarded for all. Where have you hid the Fiddles you Rogue?

SCARAMOUCH. Fiddles, Sir!—

DOCTOR. Ay, Fiddles, Knave.

SCARAMOUCH. Fiddles, Sir! — Where?

DOCTOR. Here,—here I heard 'em, thou false Steward of thy Masters Treasure.

SCARAMOUCH. Fiddles, Sir! Sure 'twas Wind got into your Head, and whistled in your Ears, riding so late, Sir.

DOCTOR. Ay, thou false Varlet there's another Debt I owe thee, for bringing me so damnable a Lye: my Brother's well—I met his Valet but a League from Town, and found thy Roguery out. *(Beats him. He cries.)*

SCARAMOUCH. Is this the Reward I have for being so diligent since you went?

DOCTOR. In What, thou Villain? in what? *(The Curtain is drawn up, and discovers the Hangings where all of them stand.)*

SCARAMOUCH. Why look you, Sir, I have, to surprise you with Pleasure, against you came home, been putting up this Piece of Tapestry, the best in Italy, for the Rareness of the Figures, Sir.

DOCTOR. Ha—Hum—It is indeed a stately Piece of Work; how came I by 'em?

SCARAMOUCH. 'Twas sent your Reverence from the Vertuoso, or some of the Cabbalists.

DOCTOR. I must confess, the Workmanship is excellent,—but still I do insist I heard the Musick.

SCARAMOUCH. 'Twas then the tuning of the Spheres, some Serenade, Sir, from the Inhabitants of the Moon.

DOCTOR. Hum,—from the Moon,— and that may be—

SCARAMOUCH. Lord, d'ye think I wou'd deceive your Reverence?

DOCTOR. From the Moon, a Serenade, —I see no signs on't here, indeed it must be so — I'll think on't more at Leisure.—*(Aside.)*—Prithee what Story's this? *(Looks on the Hangings.)*

SCARAMOUCH. Why, Sir,—'Tis.—

DOCTOR. Hold up the Candles higher, and nearer. (PETER *and* SCARAMOUCH *hold Candles near. He takes a Perspective and looks through it; and coming nearer,* HARLEQUIN, *who is plac'd on a Tree in the Hangings, hits him on the Head with his Trunchion. He starts, and looks about. He sits still.*

SCARAMOUCH. Sir.—

DOCTOR. What was that struck me?

SCARAMOUCH. Struck you, Sir! Imagination.

DOCTOR. Can my Imagination feel, Sirrah?

SCARAMOUCH. Oh, the most tenderly of any part about one, Sir!

DOCTOR. Hum—That may be—

SCARAMOUCH. Are you a great Philosopher, and know not that, Sir?

DOCTOR *(aside).* This Fellow has a glimpse of Profundity—*(Looks again.)* —I like the Figures well.

SCARAMOUCH. You will, when you See 'em by Day-light, Sir.

(HARLEQUIN *hits him again. The Doctor sees him.*

DOCTOR. Ha, —Is that Imagination too?—Betray'd, Betray'd, undone; run for my Pistols, call up my Servants,

Peter, a Plot upon my Daughter and My Neece, *(Runs out with* PETER.*)*

(SCARAMOUCH puts out the Candle, they come out of the Hanging, which is drawn away. He places 'em in a Row just at the Entrance.)

SCARAMOUCH. Here, here, fear nothing, hold by each other, that when I go out, all may go; that is, slip out, when you hear the Doctor is come in again, which he will certainly do, and all depart to your respective Lodgings.

CINTHIO. And leave thee to bear the Brunt?

SCARAMOUCH. Take you no care for that, I'll put it into my Bill of Charges, and be paid all together.

Enter the Doctor with Pistols, and PETER.

DOCTOR. What, by dark? that shall not save you Villains, Traytors to my Glory and Repose.—Peter, hold fast the Door, let none escape. *(They all slip out.)*

PETER. I'll warrant you, Sir. *(Doctor gropes about, then stamps and calls.)*

DOCTOR. Lights there—Lights—I'm sure they could not scape.

PETER. Impossible, Sir.

Enter SCARAMOUCH undress'd in his Shirt, with a Light. Starts.

SCARAMOUCH. Bless me!—What's here?

DOCTOR. Ha,—Who art thou?

(Amaz'd to see him enter so.)

SCARAMOUCH. I, who the Devil are you, and you go to that? *(Rubs his Eyes, and brings the Candle nearer. Looks on him.)* Mercy upon us!—Why, what is't you, Sir, return'd so soon?

DOCTOR. Return'd! *(Looking sometimes on him, sometimes about.)*

SCARAMOUCH. Ay, Sir, Did you not go out of Town last night, to your Brother the Advocate?

DOCTOR. Thou Villain, thou question'st me, as if thou knew'st not that I was return'd.

SCARAMOUCH. I know, Sir! how shou'd I know? I'm sure I am but just wak'd from the sweetest Dream—

DOCTOR. You dream still, Sirrah, but I shall wake your Rogueship.— Were you not here but now, shewing me a piece of Tapestry, you Villain?—

SCARAMOUCH. Tapestry?—(MOP-SOPHIL *list'ning all the while.*)

DOCTOR. Yes, Rogue, yes, for which I'll have thy Life.—*(Offering a Pistol.)*

SCARAMOUCH. Are you stark mad, Sir; or do I dream still?

DOCTOR. Tell me, and tell me quickly, Rogue, who were those Traytors that were hid but now in the Disguise of a piece of Hangings. *(Holds the Pistol to his Breast.)*

SCARAMOUCH. Bless me! you amaze me, Sir. What conformity has every Word you say, to my rare Dream: Pray let me feell you, Sir,—Are you Humane?

DOCTOR. You shall feel I am, Sirrah, if thou confess not.

SCARAMOUCH. Confess, Sir! What should I confess!—I understand not your Cabbalistical Language; but in mine, I confess that you have wak'd me from the rarest Dream—Where methought the Emperor of the Moon World was in our House, Dancing and Revelling; and methoughts his Grace had fallen desperately in Love with Mistress Elaria, and that his Brother, the Prince, Sir, of Thunderland, was also in Love with Mistress Bellemante; and methoughts they descended to court 'em in your Absence.—And that at last you surpriz'd 'em, and that they transform'd themselves into a Suit of Hangings to deceive you. But at last, methought you grew angry at something, and they all fled to Heaven again; and after a deal of Thunder and Lightning, I wak'd, Sir, and hearing Humane Voices here, came to see what the Matter was. *(This while the Doctor lessens his signs of Rage by degrees, and at last stands in deep contemplation.)*

DOCTOR. May I credit this?

SCARAMOUCH. Credit it! By all the Honour of your House, by my unseperable Veneration for the Mathematicks, 'tis true, Sir.

DOCTOR (aside).—That famous Rosicrucian, who yesterday visited me, told me—the Emperor of the Moon was in Love with a fair Mortal—This Dream is Inspiration in this Fellow—He must have wonderous Vertue in him, to be worthy of these Divine Intelligences.— But if that Mortal shou'd be ELARIA! but no more, I dare not yet suppose it— perhaps the thing was real and no Dream, for oftentimes the grosser part is hurried away in Sleep, by the force of Imagination, and is wonderfully agitated—This Fellow might be present in his Sleep,—of this we've frequent Instances—I'll to my Daughter and my Neece, and hear what knowledge they may have of this.

MOPSOPHIL [aside]. Will you so? I'll secure you, the Frolick shall go round.   [Exit.]

DOCTOR. Scaramouch, If you have not deceiv'd me in this Matter, time will convince me farther; if it rest here, I shall believe you false—

SCARAMOUCH. Good Sir, suspend your Judgment and your Anger then.

DOCTOR. I'll do't, go Back to Bed—

Ex. DOCTOR and PETER.

SCARAMOUCH. No, Sir, 'tis Morning now—and I'm up for all day.—This Madness is a pretty sort of a pleasant Disease, when it tickles but in one Vein—Why here's my Master now, as great a Scholar, as grave and wise a Man, in all Argument and Discourse, as can be met with, yet name but the Moon, and he runs into Ridicule, and grows as mad as the Wind.

Well Doctor, if you can'st be madder yet,
We'll find a Medicine that shall cure your Fit.
—Better than all Galenists.

[SCENE 4.]

*Scene Draws off. Discovers ELARIA,
BELLEMANTE, and MOPSOPHIL
in Night-Gowns.*

MOPSOPHIL. You have your Lessons, stand to it bravely, and the Town's our own, Madam. *(They put themselves in Postures of Sleeping, leaning on the Table,* MOPSOPHIL *lying at their Feet.)*

Enter DOCTOR, *softly.*

DOCTOR. Ha, not in Bed! this gives me mortal Fears.

BELLEMANTE. Ah, Prince— *(She speaks as in her Sleep.)*

DOCTOR. Ha, Prince! *(Goes nearer and listens.)*

BELLEMANTE. How little Faith I give to all your Courtship, who leaves our Orb so soon. *(In a feign'd Voice.)*

DOCTOR. Ha, said she Orb?

(Goes nearer.)

BELLEMANTE. But since you are of a Celestial Race,
And easily can penetrate
Into the utmost limits of the Thought,
Why shou'd I fear to tell you of your Conquest?—
And thus implore your aid. *(Rises and runs to the Doctor. Kneels and holds him fast. He shews signs of Joy.)*

DOCTOR. I am Ravish'd!

BELLEMANTE. Ah, Prince Divine, take Pity on a Mortal—

DOCTOR. I am rapt!

BELLEMANTE. And take me with you to the World above.

DOCTOR. The Moon, the Moon she means, I am Transported, Overjoy'd, and Ecstasy'd. *(Leaping and jumping from her Hands, she seems to wake.)*

BELLEMANTE. Ha, my Uncle come again to interrupt us!

DOCTOR. Hide nothing from me, my dear Bellemante, since all already is discover'd to me—and more—

ELARIA. Oh, why have you wak'd me from the softest Dream that ever Maid was blest with?

DOCTOR. What—what, my best Elaria? *(With over-joy.)*

ELARIA. Methought I entertain'd a Demi-God, one of the gay Inhabitants of the Moon.

BELLEMANTE. I'm sure mine was no Dream—I wak'd, I heard, I saw, I spoke—and danc'd to the Musick of the Spheres, and methought my glorious Lover ty'd a Diamond Chain about my Arm—and see 'tis all substantial.

(Shows her Arm.)

ELARIA. And mine a Ring, of more than mortal Lustre.

DOCTOR. Heaven keep me moderate! least excess of Joy shou'd make my Vertue less. *(Stifling his Joy.)* —There is a wonderous Mystery in this. A mighty Blessing does attend your Fates. Go in, and pray to the chast Powers above To give you Vertue fit for such rewards. *(They go in.)*—How this agrees with what the learned Cabbalist inform'd me of last Night! He said, that great Iredonozar, the Emperor of the Moon, was inamour'd on a fair Mortal. It must be so—and either he descended to Court my Daughter Personally, which, for the Rareness of the Novelty, she takes to be a Dream; or else, what they and I beheld, was Visionary, by way of a sublime Intelligence—and possibly—'tis only thus—the People of that World converse with Mortals.—I must be satisfy'd in this main Point of deep Philosophy. I'll to my Study, for I cannot rest, Till I this weighty Mystery have discuss'd. *Exit. very gravely.*

SCENE [5.] *The Garden.*

Enter SCARAMOUCH *with a Ladder.*

SCARAMOUCH. Tho' I am come off *en Cavalier* with my Master, I am not with my Mistress, whom I promised to console this Night, and is but just I shou'd make good this Morning; 'twill be rude to surprize her Sleeping, and more Gallant to wake her with a Serinade at her Window. *(Sets the Ladder, to her Window, fetches his Lute and goes up the Ladder.)* *He Plays and Sings this Song.*

When Maidens are young and in their Spring
Of Pleasure, of Pleasure, let 'em take their full
  Swing,
    Full Swing,—full Swing,—
  And Love, and Dance, and Play, and Sing.
For Silvia, believe it, when Youth is done,
There's nought but hum drum, hum drum, hum
    drum;
There's nought but hum drum, hum drum, hum
    drum.

Then Silvia be wise—be wise—be wise,
Tho' Painting and Dressing, for a while, are
    Supplies,
    And may—surprise—
  But when the Fire's going out in your Eyes,
  It twinkles, it twinkles, it twinkles, and dies.
And then to hear Love, to hear Love from you,
I'd as lief hear an Owl cry—Wit to woo,
    Wit to woo, Wit to woo.

Enter MOPSOPHIL *above.*

MOPSOPHIL. What woful Ditty-making mortal's this? That ere the Lark her early Note has sung, Does doleful Love beneath my Casement thrum.— —Ah, Senior Scaramouch, is it you?

SCARAMOUCH. Who shou'd it be, that takes such pains to sue?

MOPSOPHIL. Ah, Lover most true Blew!

Enter HARLEQUIN *in Womens Cloths.*

HARLEQUIN. If I can now but get admittance, I shall not only deliver the young Ladies their Letters from their Lovers, but get some opportunity, in this Disguise, to slip this Billet Deux into Mopsophil's Hand, and bob my Comrade Scaramouch.—Ha,—What do I see?—My Mistress at the Window, courting my Rival! Ah Gypsie!—

SCARAMOUCH.—But we lose precious time, since you design me a kind Hour in your Chamber.

HARLEQUIN. Ah Traytor!

MOPSOPHIL. You'll be sure to keep it from Harlequin.

HARLEQUIN. Ah yes, he, hang him Fool, he takes you for a Saint.

SCARAMOUCH. Harlequin! —Hang him, shotten Herring.

HARLEQUIN. Ay, a Cully, a Noddy.

MOPSOPHIL. A meer Zany.

HARLEQUIN. Ah, hard hearted Turk.

MOPSOPHIL. Fit for nothing but a Cuckold.

HARLEQUIN. Monster of Ingratitude! How shall I be reveng'd; (SCARAMOUCH *going over the Balcony.*) — Hold, hold, thou perjur'd Traytor. *(Cryes out in a Womans Voice.)*

MOPSOPHIL. Ha, — Discover'd! — A Woman in the Garden!

HARLEQUIN. Come down, come down, thou false perfidious Wretch.

SCARAMOUCH. Who, in the Devils Name, art thou? And to whom dost thou speak?

HARLEQUIN. To thee, thou false Deceiver, that hast broke thy Vows, thy Lawful Vows of Wedlock—*(Bawling out.)* Oh, oh, that I shou'd live to see the Day! *(Crying.)*

SCARAMOUCH. Who mean you, Woman?

HARLEQUIN. Whom shou'd I mean, but thou—my lawful Spouse?

MOPSOPHIL. Oh Villain! —Lawful Spouse!—Let me come to her. (SCARAMOUCH *comes down, as* MOPSOPHIL *flings out of the Balcony.)*

SCARAMOUCH. The Woman's mad—hark ye Jade—how long have you been thus distracted?

HARLEQUIN. E're since I lov'd and trusted thee, false Varlot.—See here,—the Witness of my Love and Shame.

(Bawls, and points to her Belly.)

Just then MOPSOPHIL *enters.*

MOPSOPHIL. How! with Child!—Out Villain, was I made a Property?

SCARAMOUCH. Hear me.

HARLEQUIN. Oh, thou Heathen Christian!—Was not one Woman enough?

MOPSOPHIL. Ay, Sirrah, answer to that.

SCARAMOUCH. I shall be sacrific'd.

MOPSOPHIL. I am resolv'd to marry to morrow—either to the Apothecary or the Farmer, men I never saw, to be reveng'd on thee, thou tarmagant Infidel.

Enter the DOCTOR.

DOCTOR. What. Noise, what Out-cry, what Tumult's this?

HARLEQUIN. Ha,—the Doctor!—What shall I do?—*(Gets to the Door,* SCARAMOUCH *pulls her in.)*

DOCTOR. A Woman!—some Bawd I am sure—Woman, what's your. Business here?—ha—

HARLEQUIN. I came, an't like your Seigniorship, to Madam the Governante here, to serve her in the Quality of a *Fille de Chambre*, to the young Ladies.

DOCTOR. A *Fille de Chambre!* 'tis so, a she-Pimp,—

HARLEQUIN. Ah Seignior—*(Makes his little dapper Leg instead of a Courtsie.)*

DOCTOR. How now, what do you mock me?

HARLEQUIN. Oh, Seignior!— *(Gets nearer the door.)*

MOPSOPHIL. Stay, stay, Mistriss, and what Service are you able to do the Seigniors Daughters?

HARLEQUIN. Is this Seignior Doctor Baliardo, Madam?

MOPSOPHIL. Yes.

HARLEQUIN. Oh! He's a very handsome Gentleman—indeed—

DOCTOR. Ay, ay, what Service can you do, Mistriss?

HARLEQUIN. Why, Seignior, I can tye a Crevat the best of any Person in Naples, and I can comb a Periwig—and I can—

DOCTOR. Very proper Service for young Ladies; you I believe, have been *Fille de Chambre* to some young Cavaliers.

HARLEQUIN. Most true, Seignior, why shou'd not the Cavaliers keep *Filles de Chambre*, as well as great Ladies *Vallets de Chambre?*

DOCTOR *(aside).* Indeed 'tis equally reasonable.—'Tis a Bawd—But have you never serv'd Ladies?

HARLEQUIN. Oh yes! I serv'd a Parsons Wife.

DOCTOR. Is that a great Lady?

HARLEQUIN. Ay surely, Sir, what is she else? for she wore her Mantoes of *Brokad de or*, Petticoats lac'd up to the Gathers, her Points, her Patches, Paints and Perfumes, and sate in the uppermost Place in the Church too.

MOPSOPHIL. But have you never serv'd Countesses. and Dutchesses?

HARLEQUIN. Oh, yes, Madam! the last I serv'd, was an Aldermans Wife in the City.

MOPSOPHIL. Was that a Countess or a Dutchess?

HARLEQUIN. Ay, certainly—for they have all the Money; and then for Cloaths, Jewels, and rich Furniture, and eating, they outdo the very *Vice-Reigne* her self.

DOCTOR. This is a very ignorant running Bawd,—therefore first search her for Billets Deux, and then have her Pump'd.

MARLEQUIN. Ah, Seignior,—Seignior. —(SCARAMOUCH *searches him, finds Letters.)*

SCARAMOUCH. —Ha, —to Elaria— and Bellemante?—*(Reads the Outside, pops 'em into his Bosom.)*—These are from their Lovers— Ha, a Note to Mopsophil,—Oh, Rogue! have I found you?

HARLEQUIN. If you have, 'tis but Trick for your Trick, Seignior Scaramouch, and you may spare the Pumping.

SCARAMOUCH. For once, Sirrah, I'll bring you off, and deliver your Letters. —Sir, do you not know who this is?— Why 'tis a Rival of mine, who put on this Disguise to cheat me of Mistriss Mopsophil.—See here's a Billet to her.—

DOCTOR. What is he?

SCARAMOUCH. A Mungrel Dancing-Master; therefore, Sir, since all the Injury's mine, I'll pardon him for a Dance, and let the Agility of his Heels save his Bones, with your Permission, Sir.

DOCTOR. With all my Heart, and am glad he comes off so comically.

HARLEQUIN *Dances. A knocking at the Gate.* SCARAMOUCH *goes and returns.*

SCARAMOUCH. Sir, Sir, here's the rare Philosopher who was here yesterday.

DOCTOR. Give him Entrance, and all depart.

Enter CHARMANTE.

CHARMANTE. Blest be those Stars, that first Conducted me to so much Worth and Vertue, you are their Darling, Sir, from whom they wear their brightest Lustre. Your Fortune is establish'd, you are made, Sir.

DOCTOR. Let me contain my Joy— *(Keeping in an impatient Joy.)* May I be worthy, Sir, to apprehend you?

CHARMANTE. After long Searching, Watching, Fasting, Praying, and using all the vertuous means in Nature, whereby we solely do attain the highest knowledge in Philosophy; it was resolv'd, by strong Intelligence—you were the happy Sire of that Bright Nymph, that had effascinated, charm'd and conquer'd the mighty Emperor Iredonozar— the Monarch of the Moon.

DOCTOR *(aside).* I am—undone with Joy! ruin'd with Transport— Can it— can it, Sir,—be possible—*(Stifling his Joy, which breaks out.)*

CHARMANTE. Receive the Blessing, Sir, with moderation.

DOCTOR. I do, Sir, I do.

CHARMANTE. This very Night, by their great Art, they find He will descend, and show himself in Glory. An Honour, Sir, no Mortal has receiv'd This sixty hundred years.

DOCTOR. Hum—Say you so, Sir? no Emperor ever descend this sixty hundred years? *(Looks sad.) (Aside.)*— Was I deceiv'd last night?

CHARMANTE. Oh! Yes, Sir, often in disguise, in several Shapes and Forms, which did of old occasion so many Fabulous Tales of all the Shapes of Jupiter—but never in their proper Glory, Sir, as Emperors. This is an Honour only design'd to you.

DOCTOR. And will his Grace—be here in Person, Sir? *(Joyful.)*

CHARMANTE. In Person—and with him, a Man of mighty Quality, Sir,—'tis thought—the Prince of Thunderland—but that's but whisper'd, Sir, in the Cabbal, and that he loves your Neece.

DOCTOR. Miraculous? how this agrees with all I've seen and heard—To Night, say you, Sir?

CHARMANTE. So 'tis conjectur'd, Sir,—some of the Cabbalist—are of opinion—that last night there was some Sally from the Moon.

DOCTOR. About what hour, Sir?

CHARMANTE. The Meridian of the Night, Sir, about the hours of twelve or one, but who descended, or in what Shape, is yet uncertain.

DOCTOR. This I believe, Sir.

CHARMANTE. Why, Sir?

DOCTOR. May I communicate a Secret of that Nature?

CHARMANTE. To any of the Cabbalist, but none else.

DOCTOR. Then know—last night, my Daughter and my Neece were entertain'd by those illustrious Heroes.

CHARMANTE. Who Sir? the Emperor and Prince his Cousin?

DOCTOR. Most certain, Sir. But whether they appear'd in solid Bodies, or Fantomical, is yet a Question, for at my unlucky approach, they all transform'd themselves into a Piece of Hangings.

CHARMANTE. 'Tis frequent, Sir, their Shapes are numerous, and 'tis also in their Power to transform all they touch, by virtue of a certain Stone—they call the *Ebula.*

DOCTOR. That wondrous *Ebula,* which Gonzales had?

CHARMANTE. The same—by Virtue of which, all weight was taken from him, and then with ease the lofty Traveller flew from Parnassus Hill, and from Hymettus Mount, and high Gerania, and Acrocorinthus, thence to Taygetus, so to Olympus Top, from whence he had but one step to the Moon. Dizzy he grants he was.

DOCTOR. No wonder, Sir, Oh happy great Gonzales!

CHARMANTE. Your Vertue, Sir, will render you as happy—but I must hast—this Night prepare your Daughter and your Neece, and let your House be Dress'd, Perfum'd, and Clean.

DOCTOR. It shall be all perform'd, Sir.

CHARMANTE. Be modest, Sir, and humble in your Elevation, for nothing shews the Wit so poor, as Wonder, nor Birth so mean as Pride.

DOCTOR. I humbly thank your Admonition, Sir, and shall, in all I can, struggle with Humane Frailty. *(Brings* CHARMANTE *to the Door bare.) Ex.*

Enter SCARAMOUCH *peeping at the other Door.*

SCARAMOUCH. So, so, all things go gloriously forward, but my own Amour, and there is no convincing this obstinate Woman, that 'twas that Rogue Harlequin in Disguise, that claim'd me; so that I cannot so much as come to deliver the young Ladies their Letters from their Lovers. I must get in with this damn'd Mistress of mine, or all our Plot will be spoil'd, for want of Intelligence.—Hum,—The Devil does not use to fail me at a dead Lift. I must deliver these Letters, and I must have this Wench—tho' but to be reveng'd on her for abusing me.—Let me see—she is resolv'd for the Apothecary or the Farmer. Well, say no more honest Scaramouch, thou shalt find a Friend at need of me—and if I do not fit you with a Spouse, say that a Woman has out-witted me.

The End of the Second Act.

ACT III. SCENE 1.

The Street, with the Town Gate, where an Officer stands with a Staff like a London Constable.

Enter HARLEQUIN *riding in a Calash, comes through the Gate towards the Stage, dress'd like a Gentleman sitting in it. The Officer lays hold on his Horse.*

OFFICER. Hold, hold, Sir, you, I suppose, know the Customs that are due to this City of Naples, from all Persons that pass the Gates in Coach, Chariot, Calash, or *Siege Voglant*.

HARLEQUIN. I am not ignorant of the Custom, Sir, but what's that to me?

OFFICER. Not to you, Sir! what Privilege have you above the rest.

HARLEQUIN. Privilege, for what, Sir?

OFFICER. Why, for passing, Sir, with any of the before named Carriages.

HARLEQUIN. Ar't mad?—Dost not see I am a plain Baker, and this my Cart, that comes to carry Bread for the Vice-Roy's, and the Cities Use?—ha—

OFFICER. Are you mad, Sir, to think I cannot see a Gentleman Farmer and a Calash, from a Baker and a Cart?

HARLEQUIN. Drunk by this Day—and so early too? Oh you're a special Officer; unhand my Horse, Sirrah, or you shall pay for all the Damage you do me.

OFFICER. Hey day! here's a fine Cheat upon the Vice-Roy; Sir, pay me, or I'll seize your Horse.—(HARLEQUIN *strikes him. They scuffle a little.*) —Nay, and you be so brisk, I'll call the Clerk from his Office. *(Calls.)* Mr. Clerk, Mr. Clerk. *(Goes to the Entrance to call the Clerk, the mean time* HARLEQUIN *whips a Frock over himself, and puts down the hind part of the Chariot, and then 'tis a Cart.)*

Enter CLERK.

CLERK. What's the matter here?—

OFFICER. Here's Fellow, Sir, will perswade me, his Calash is a Cart, and refuses the Customs for passing the Gate.

CLERK. A Calash—Where?—I see only a Carter and his Cart. *(The Officer looks on him.)*

OFFICER. Ha,—What Devil, was I blind?

HARLEQUIN. Mr. Clerk, I am a Baker, that come with Bread to sell, and this Fellow here has stopt me this hour, and made me lose the Sale of my Ware—and being Drunk, will out-face me I am a Farmer, and this Cart a Calash—

CLERK. He's in an Error Friend, pass on—

HARLEQUIN. No, Sir, I'll have satisfaction first, or the Vice-Roy, shall know how he's serv'd by Drunken Officers, that Nuisance to a Civil Government.

CLERK. What do you demand, Friend?

HARLEQUIN. Demand,—I demand a Crown, Sir.

OFFICER. This is very hard—Mr. Clerk—If ever I saw in my Life, I thought I saw a Gentleman and a Calash.

CLERK. Come, come, gratifie him, and see better hereafter.

OFFICER. Here, Sir,—If I must, I must—*(Gives him a Crown.)*

CLERK. Pass on, Friend — *(Exit Clerk.* HARLEQUIN *unseen, puts up the Back of his Calash, and whips off his Frock, and goes to drive on. The Officer looks on him, and stops him again.)*

OFFICER. Hum, I'll swear it is a Calash—Mr. Clerk, Mr. Clerk, come back, come back—(Runs out to call him. [HARLEQUIN] *changes as before.)*

Enter OFFICER *and* CLERK.

OFFICER. Some Sir, let your own Eyes convince you, Sir,—

CLERK. Convince me, of what, you Sott?

OFFICER. That this is a Gentleman, and that a—ha,— *(Looks about on* HARLEQUIN.)

CLERK. Stark Drunk, Sirrah! if you trouble me at every Mistake of yours thus, you shall quit your Office.—

OFFICER. I beg your Pardon, Sir, I am a little in Drink I confess, a little Blind and Mad—Sir,—This must be the Devil, that's certain. *(The Clerk goes out,* HARLEQUIN *puts up his Calash again, and pulls off his Frock and drives out.)*—Well, now to my thinking, 'tis as plain a Calash again, as ever I saw in my Life, and yet I'm satisfy'd 'tis nothing but a Cart. *Exit.*

SCENE [2] *changes to the Doctors House.*

The Hall.

Enter SCARAMOUCH *in a Chair, which set down and open'd, on all sides, and on the top represents an Apothecaries Shop, the Inside being painted with Shelves and Rows of Pots and Bottles;* SCARAMOUCH *sitting in it dress'd in Black, with a short black Cloak, a Ruff, and little Hat.*

SCARAMOUCH. The Devil's in't, if either the Doctor, my Master, or Mopsophil, know me in this Disguise—And thus I may not only gain my Mistress, and out-wit Harlequin, but deliver the Ladies those Letters from their Lovers, which I took out of his Pocket this Morning, and who wou'd suspect an Apothecary for a Pimp? Nor can the Jade Mopsophil, in Honour refuse a Person of my Gravity, and so well set up.—*(Pointing to his Shop)*—Hum, the Doctor here first, this is not so well, but I'm prepar'd with Impudence for all Encounters. *(Enter the* DOCTOR. SCARAMOUCH *Salutes him gravely.)* —Most Reverend Doctor Baliardo— *(Bows.)*

DOCTOR. Seignior—*(Bows.)*

SCARAMOUCH. I might, through great ‹Pusillanimity, blush—to give you this Anxiety, did I not opine you were as Gracious as Communitive and Eminent; and tho' you have no Cognizance of me, your Humble Servant,—yet I have of you—you being so greatly fam'd for your Admirable Skill, both in Galenical and Paracelsian *Phoenomena's*, and other approv'd Felicities in Vulnerary, Emeticks and purgative Experiences.

DOCTOR. Seignior,—your Opinion honors me—a rare Man this.

SCARAMOUCH. And though I am at present busied in writing—those few Observations I have accmulated in my Peregrinations, Sir, yet the Ambition I aspir'd to, of being an Ocular and Aurial Witness of your Singularity, made me trespass on your sublimer Affairs.

DOCTOR. Seignior.—

SCARAMOUCH.—Besides a violent Inclination, Sir, of being initiated into the Denomination of your Learned Family,

by the Conjugal Circumference of a Matrimonial Tye, with that singularly accomplish'd Person—Madam, the Governante of your Hostel.

DOCTOR *(aside).* Hum—A sweet-heart for Mopsophil!

SCARAMOUCH. And if I may obtain your Condescension to my Hymeneal Propositions, I doubt not my Operation with the Fair One.

DOCTOR. Seignior, she is much honour'd in the Overture, and my Abilities shall not be wanting to fix the Concord. —But have you been a Traveller, Sir?

SCARAMOUCH. Without Circumlocution, Sir, I have seen all the Regions beneath the Sun and Moon.

DOCTOR. Moon, Sir! You have never travell'd thither, Sir?

SCARAMOUCH. Not in *Propria Persona*, Seignior, but by speculation, I have, and made most considerable Remarques on that incomparable *Terra Firma*, of which I have the compleatest Map in Christendom—and which Gonzales himself omitted in his *Cosmographia* of the *Lunar Mundus.*

DOCTOR. A Map of the *Lunar Mundus*, Sir! may I crave the Honour of seeing it?

SCARAMOUCH. You shall, Sir, together with the Map of *Terra Incognita*, a great Rarity, indeed, Sir.

Enter BELLEMANTE.

DOCTOR. Jewels, Sir, worth a Kings Ransome.

BELLEMANTE. Ha, —What Figure of a Thing have we here—Bantering my Credulous Uncle? —This must be some Scout sent from our *Forlorn Hope*, to discover the Enemy, and bring in fresh Intelligence. —Hum, —That Wink tipt me some Tidings, and she deserves not a good Look, who understands not the Language of the Eyes. —Sir, Dinner's on the Table.

DOCTOR. Let it wait, I am imploy'd— *(She creeps to the other side of* SCARAMOUCH, *who makes Signs with his Hand to her.)*

BELLEMANTE. Ha,— 'tis so, —This fellow has some Novel for us, some Let-

ters or Instructions, but how to get it—
(As SCARAMOUCH *talks to the* DOC-
TOR, *he takes the Letters by degrees
out of his Pocket, and unseen gives 'em
to* BELLEMANTE *behind him.)*

DOCTOR. But this Map, Seignior; I
protest you have fill'd me with Curiosity.
Has it signify'd things so exactly, say
you?

SCARAMOUCH. Omitted nothing,
Seignior, no City, Town, Village or
Villa, no Castle, River, Bridge, Lake,
Spring or Mineral.

DOCTOR. Are any, Sir, of those admirable Mineral Waters there, so frequent in our World?

SCARAMOUCH. In abundance, Sir,
the Famous Garamanteen, a young
Italian, Sir, lately come from thence,
gives us an account of an excellent
Scaturigo, that has lately made an Ebu-
lation there, in great Reputation with
the Lunary Ladies.

DOCTOR. Indeed, Sir! be pleas'd
Seignior, to 'solve me some Queries
that may enode some apparences of the
Virtue of the Water you speak of.

SCARAMOUCH [*aside*]. Pox upon him,
what Questions he asks—but I must on
—Why, Sir, you must know,—the Tinc-
ture of this Water upon Stagnation,
Ceruberates, and the Crocus upon the
Stones Flaveces; this he observes—to
be, Sir, the Indication of a Generous
Water.

DOCTOR. Hum— *(Gravely Nodding.)*

SCARAMOUCH. Now, Sir, be pleas'd
to observe the three Regions, if they
be bright, without doubt Mars is powerful; if the middle Region or Camera
be pallid, *Filia Solis* is breeding.

DOCTOR. Hum.

SCARAMOUCH. And then the third
Region, if the Faeces be volatil, the
Birth will soon come in Balneo. This
I observed also in the Laboratory of
that Ingenious Chymist Lysidono, and
with much Pleasure animadverted that
Mineral of the same Zenith and Nader,
of that now so famous Water in Eng-
land, near that famous Metropolis, call'd
Islington.

DOCTOR. Seignior—

SCARAMOUCH. For, Sir, upon the
Infusion, the Crows Head immediately
procures the Seal of Hermes, and had
not *Lac Virginis* been too soon suck'd
up, I believe we might have seen the
Consummation of *Amalgena.* (BELLE-
MANTE *having got her Letters, goes
off. She makes Signs to him to stay a
little. He Nods.)*

DOCTOR. Most likely, Sir.

SCARAMOUCH. But, Sir, this Garamanteen relates the strangest Operation
of a Mineral in the Lunar World, that
ever I heard of.

DOCTOR. As how, I pray, Sir?

SCARAMOUCH. Why, Sir, a Water
impregnated to a Circulation with *Fema*
Materia; upon my Honour, Sir, the
strongest I ever drank of.

DOCTOR. How, Sir! did you drink of
it?

SCARAMOUCH. I only speak the
words of Garamanteen, Sir.—Pox on
him, I shall be trapt. *(Aside.)*

DOCTOR. Cry Mercy, Sir,—*(Bows.)*

SCARAMOUCH. The Lunary Physicians, Sir, call it *Urinam Vulcani,* it
Calibrates every ones Excrements more
or less according to the Gradus of the
Natural Calor.—To my Knowledge, Sir,
a Smith of a very fiery Constitution, is
grown very Opulent by drinking these
Waters.

DOCTOR. How Sir, grown Rich by
drinking the Waters, and to your
Knowledge?

SCARAMOUCH. The Devil's in my
Tongue, to my Knowledge, Sir, for
what a man of Honour relates, I may
safely affirm.

DOCTOR. Excuse me, Seignior,—*(Puts
off his Hat again gravely.)*

SCARAMOUCH. For, Sir, conceive me
how he grew Rich, since he drank those
Waters he never buys any Iron, but
hammers it out of *Stercus Proprius.*

Enter BELLEMANTE *with a Billet.*
Fema: Summers emends to Prima.

BELLEMANTE. Sir, 'tis three a Clock and Dinner will be cold.—(*Goes behind* SCARAMOUCH, *and gives him the Note, and goes out.*)

DOCTOR. I come Sweet-heart; but this is wonderful.

SCARAMOUCH. Ay, Sir, and if at any time Nature be too infirm, and he prove Costive, he has no more to do, but to apply a Loadstone *ad Anum.*

DOCTOR. Is't possible?

SCARAMOUCH. Most true, Sir, and that facilitates the Journey *per Viscera* —But I detain you, Sir, another time— Sir,—I will now only beg the Honor of a Word or two with the Governante, before I go.—

DOCTOR. Sir, she shall wait on you, and I shall be proud of the Honour of your Conversation.—(*They bow. Exit* DOCTOR.*)*

Enter to him HARLEQUIN, *dress'd like a Farmer, as before.*

HARLEQUIN. Hum—What have we here, a Taylor, or a Tumbler?

SCARAMOUCH. Ha—Who's this?— Hum—What if it shou'd be the Farmer that the Doctor has promis'd Mopsophil to? My heart misgives me. (*They look at each other a while.*) Who wou'd you speak with, Friend?

HARLEQUIN [*aside*] This is, perhaps, my Rival, the Apothecary.— Speak with, Sir, why, what's that to you?

SCARAMOUCH. Have you Affairs with Seignior Doctor, Sir?

HARLEQUIN. It may be I have, it may be I have not. What then, Sir?—

While they seem in angry Dispute, Enter MOPSOPHIL.

MOPSOPHIL. Siegnior Doctor tells me I have a Lover waits me, sure it must be the Farmer or the Apothecary. No matter which, so a Lover, that welcomest man alive. I am resolv'd to take the first good Offer, tho' but in Revenge of Harlequin and Scaramouch, for putting Tricks upon me.—Ha, —Two of 'em!

SCARAMOUCH. My Mistress here! (*They both Bow and Advance, both putting each other by.*)

MOPSOPHIL. Hold Gentlemen,—do not worry me. Which of you wou'd speak with me?

BOTH. I, I, I, Madam—

MOPSOPHIL. Both of you?

BOTH. No, Madam, I, I.

MOPSOPHIL. If both Lovers, you are both welcome, but let's have fair Play, and take your turns to speak.

HARLEQUIN. Ay, Seignior, 'tis most uncivil to interrupt me.

SCARAMOUCH. And disingenious, Sir, to intrude on me. (*Putting one another by.*)

MOPSOPHIL. Let me then speak first.

HARLEQUIN. I'm Dumb.

SCARAMOUCH. I Acquiesce.

MOPSOPHIL. I was inform'd there was a Person here had Propositions of Marriage to make me.

HARLEQUIN. That's I, that's I— (*Shoves* SCARAMOUCH *away.*)

SCARAMOUCH. And I attend to that consequential *Finis.* (*Shoves* HARLEQUIN *away.*)

HARLEQUIN. I know not what you mean by your *Finis*, Seignior, but I am come to offer my self this Gentlewomans Servant, her Lover, her Husband, her Dog in a Halter, or any thing.

SCARAMOUCH. Him I pronounce a Poltroon, and an Ignominious Utensil, that dares lay claim to the Renowned Lady of my *Primum Mobile;* that is, my best Affections.—(*In Rage.*)

HARLEQUIN. I fear not your hard Words, Sir, but dare aloud pronounce, if Donna Mopsophil like me, the Farmer, as well as I like her, 'tis a Match, and my Chariot is ready at the Gate to bear her off, d'ye see.—

MOPSOPHIL (*Aside*). Ah, how that Chariot pleads.—

SCARAMOUCH. And I pronounce, that being intoxicated with the sweet Eyes of this refulgent Lády, I come to tender her my noblest Particulars, Being already most advantageously set up with the circumstantial Implements of my Occupation. (*Points to the Shop.*)

MOPSOPHIL. A City Apothecary, a most Gentile Calling—Which shall I chuse?—Seignior Apothecary, I'll not expostulate the Circumstantial Reasons that have occasion'd me this Honour.—.

SCARAMOUCH. Incomparable Lady, the Elegancy of your Repertees most excellently denote the Profundity of your Capacity.

HARLEQUIN. What the Devil's all this? Good Mr. Conjurer stand by— and don't fright the Gentlewoman with your Elegant Profondities. (Puts him by.)

SCARAMOUCH. How a Conjurer! I will chastise thy vulgar Ignorance, that yclips a Philosopher, a Conjurer. (In Rage.)

HARLEQUIN. Losophers!—Prethee, if thou bee'st a Man, speak like a Man— then.

SCARAMOUCH. Why, what do I speak like? What do I speak like?

HARLEQUIN. What do you speak like—why you speak like a Wheel-Barrow.

SCARAMOUCH. How!—

HARLEQUIN. And how! (They come up close together at half Sword. Parry; stare on each other for a while, then put up and how to each other civilly.)

MOPSOPHIL. Thats well Gentlemen, let's have all Peace, while I survey you both, and see which likes me best. (She goes between 'em, and surveys 'em both, they making ridiculous Bows on both sides and Grimaces the while.)

MOPSOPHIL. —ha, —now on my Conscience, my two foolish Lovers— Harlequin and Scaramouch; how are my Hopes defeated?—but Faith I'll fit you both. (She views 'em both.)

SCARAMOUCH (Aside). So she's considering still, I shall be the happy Dog.

HARLEQUIN (Aside). She's taking aim, she cannot chuse but like me best.

SCARAMOUCH. Well, Madam, how does my Person propagate. (Bowing and Smiling.)

MOPSOPHIL. Faith, Seignior, now I look better on you, I do not like your Phisnomy so well as your Intellects; you discovering some Circumstantial Symptoms that ever denote a Villainous Inconstancy.

SCARAMOUCH. Ah, you are pleas'd, Madam.—

MOPSOPHIL. You are mistaken, Seignior, I am displeas'd at your Grey Eyes, and Black Eye-brows and Beard, I never knew a Man with those Signs, true to his Mistriss or his Friend. And I wou'd sooner wed that Scoundrel Scaramouch, that very civil Pimp, that meer pair of Chymical Bellows that blow the Doctors projecting Fires, that Deputy-Urinal Shaker, that very Guzman of Salamanca, than a Fellow of your infallible Signum Mallis.

HARLEQUIN. Ha, ha, ha,—you have your Answer, Seignior Friskin—and may shut up your Shop and be gone.— Ha, ha, ha.—

SCARAMOUCH (Aside.) Hum, sure the Jade knows me—

MOPSOPHIL. And as for you, Seignior.

HARLEQUIN. Ha, Madam—(Bowing and Smiling.)

MOPSOPHIL. Those Lanthorn Jaws of yours, with that most villainous Sneer and Grin, and a certain fierce Air of your Eyes looks altogether most Fanatically—which with your notorious Whey Beard, are certain Signs of Knavery and Cowardice; therefore I'd rather wed that Spider Harlequin, that Sceleton Buffoon, that Ape of Man, that Jack of Lent, that very Top, that's of no use, but when 'tis whipt and lasht, that pitious Property I'd rather wed than thee.

HARLEQUIN. A very fair Declaration.

MOPSOPHIL. You understand me— and so adieu sweet Glister-pipe, and Seignior dirty Boots, Ha, ha, ha.— (Runs out. They stand looking simply on each other, without speaking a while.)

SCARAMOUCH (Aside). That I shou'd not know that Rogue Harlequin.

HARLEQUIN (Aside). That I shou'd take this Fool for a Physician.—How long have you commenc'd Apothecary, Seignior?

SCARAMOUCH. Ever since you turn'd Farmer.—Are not you a damn'd Rogue to put these Tricks upon me, and most dishonourably break all Articles between us?

HARLEQUIN. Are not you a damn'd Son of a————something—to break Articles with me?

SCARAMOUCH. No more Words, Sir, no more words, I find it must come to Action,—Draw.—*(Draws.)*

HARLEQUIN. Draw, so I can draw, Sir.—*(Draws. They make a ridiculous cowardly Fight. Enter the Doctor, which they seeing, come on with more Courage. He runs between 'em and with his Cane beats the Swords down.)*

DOCTOR. Hold—hold—What mean you, Gentlemen?

SCARAMOUCH. Let me go, Sir, I am provok'd beyond measure, Sir.

DOCTOR. You must excuse me, Siegnior—*(Parlies with* HARLEQUIN.*)*

SCARAMOUCH *(Aside).* I dare not discover the fool for his Masters Sake, and it may spoil our intrigue anon; besides, he'll then discover me, and I shall then be discarded for bantering the Doctor. —A Man of Honour to be so basely affronted here.—*(The Doctor comes to appease* SCARAMOUCH.*)*

HARLEQUIN. Shou'd I discover this Rascal, he wou'd tell the Old Gentleman I was the same that attempted his House to day in Womens Cloths, and I shou'd be kick'd and beaten most unsatiably.

SCARAMOUCH. What, Seignior, for a man of Parts to be impos'd upon, —and whipt through the Lungs here—like a Mountebanks Zany for sham Cures—Mr. Doctor, I must tell you 'tis not Civil.

DOCTOR. I am extreamely sorry for it, Sir,—and you shall see how I will have this fellow handled for the Affront to a Person of your Gravity, and in my House—Here Pedro,—*(Enter* PEDRO.*)*—Take this intruder, or bring some of your Fellows hither, and toss him in a Blanket—*(Exit* PEDRO. HARLEQUIN *going to creep away,*

SCARAMOUCH *holds him.)*

HARLEQUIN. Hark ye, bring me off, or I'll discover all your Intrigue. *)Aside to him.)*

SCARAMOUCH. Let me alone—

DOCTOR. I'll warrant you some Rogue that has some Plot on my Neece and Daughter—

SCARAMOUCH. No, no, Sir, he comes to impose the grossest Lye upon you that ever was heard of.

Enter PEDRO *with others, with a Blanket. They put* HARLEQUIN *into it, and toss him.*

HARLEQUIN. Hold, hold,—I'll confess all, rather than indure it.

DOCTOR. Hold,—What will you confess, Sir? *(He comes out. Makes sick Faces.)*

SCARAMOUCH.—That he's the greatest Impostor in Nature. Wou'd you think it, Sir? he pretends to be no less than an Ambassador from the Emperor of the Moon, Sir—

DOCTOR. Ha,—Ambassador from the Emperor of the Moon—*(Pulls off his hat.)*

SCARAMOUCH. Ay, Sir, thereupon I laugh'd, thereupon he grew angry,—I laugh'd at his Resentment, and thereupon we drew—and this was the high Quarrel, Sir.

DOCTOR. Hum,—Ambassador from the Moon. *(Pauses.)*

SCARAMOUCH. I have brought you off, manage him as well as you can.

HARLEQUIN. *(Aside.)* Brought me off, yes, out of the Frying-Pan into the Fire. —Why, how the Devil shall I act an Ambassador?

DOCTOR. It must be so, for how shou'd either of these know I expected that Honour? *(He addresses him with profound Civility to* HARLEQUIN.*)* Sir, if the Figure you make, approaching so near ours of this World, have made us commit any indecent Indignity to your high Character, you ought to pardon the Frailty of our Mortal Education and Ignorance, having never before been blest with the Descention of any from your World.—

HARLEQUIN. *(Aside.)* What the Devil shall I say now?—I confess I am as you see by my Garb, Sir, a little Incognito, because the Publick Message I bring, is very private—which is, that the mighty Iredonozar, Emperor of the Moon—with his most worthy Brother, the Prince of Thunderland, intend to Sup with you to Night—Therefore be sure you get good Wine—Tho' by the way let me tell you, 'tis for the Sake of your Fair Daughter.

SCARAMOUCH. I'll leave the Rogue to his own Management.—I presume by your whispering, Sir, you wou'd be private and humbly begging Pardon, take my Leave. *Exit.*

HARLEQUIN. You have it Friend. Does your Neece and Daughter Drink, Sir?

DOCTOR. Drink, Sir?

HARLEQUIN. Ay, Sir, Drink hard.

DOCTOR. Do the Women of your World drink hard, Sir?

HARLEQUIN. According to their Quality, Sir, more or less; the greater the Quality, the more Profuse the Quantity.

DOCTOR. Why that's just as 'tis here; but your Men of Quality, your Statesmen, Sir, I presume they are Sober, Learned and Wise.

HARLEQUIN. Faith, no, Sir, but they are, for the most part, what's as good, very Proud, and promising, Sir, most liberal of their Word to every fauning Suiter, to purchase the state of long Attendance, and cringing as they pass; but the Devil of a Performance, without you get the Knack of bribing in the right Place and Time; but yet they all defy it, Sir.—

DOCTOR. Just, just as 'tis here.—But pray sir, How do these Great Men live with their Wives?

HARLEQUIN. Most Nobly, Sir, My Lord keeps his Coach, my Lady, hers; my Lord his Bed, my Lady hers; and very rarely see one another, unless they chance to meet in a Visit, in the Park, the Mall, the Tour, or at the Bassett-Table, where they civilly Salute and part, he to his Mistriss she to play.

DOCTOR. Good lack! just as 'tis here.

HARLEQUIN. —Where, if she chance to lose her Money, rather than give out, she borrows of the next Amorous Coxcomb, who, from that Minute, hopes, and is sure to be paid again one way or other, the next kind Opportunity.

DOCTOR.—Just as 'tis here.

HARLEQUIN. As for the young Fellows that have Money, they have no Mercy upon their own Persons, but wearing Nature off as fast as they can, Swear, and Whore, and Drink, and Borrow as long as any Rooking Citizen will lend, till having dearly purchased the Heroick Title of a Bully or a Sharper, they live pity'd of their Friends, and despis'd by their Whores, and depart this Transitory World, diverse and sundry ways.

DOCTOR. Just, just, as 'tis here.

HARLEQUIN. As for the Citizen, Sir, the Courtier lies with his Wife, he, in revenge, Cheats him of his Estate, till Rich enough to marry his Daughter to a Courtier, again give him all—unless his Wives Over-Gallantry break him; and thus the World runs round.—

DOCTOR. The very same 'tis here.— Is there no preferment, Sir, for Men of Parts and Merit?

HARLEQUIN. Parts and Merit! What's that? a Livery, or the handsome tying a Crevat, for the great Men prefer none but their Footmen and Vallets.

DOCTOR. By my Troth, just as 'tis here. —Sir, I find you are a Person of most profound Intelligence—under Favour, Sir,—Are you a Native of the Moon or this World?—

HARLEQUIN. The Devils in him for hard Questions.—I am a Neapolitan, Sir.

DOCTOR. Sir, I Honour you; good luck, my Countryman, How got you to the Region of the Moon, Sir?

HARLEQUIN. —A plaguy inquisitive old Fool—Why, Sir,—Pox on't, what shall I say?—I being—one day in a musing Melancholy, walking by the

Seaside—there arose, Sir, a great Mist, by the Suns exhaling of the Vapours of the Earth, Sir.

DOCTOR. Right, Sir.

HARLEQUIN. In this Fog or Mist, Sir, I was exhaled.

DOCTOR. The Exhalations of the Sun, draw you to the Moon, Sir?

HARLEQUIN. I am condemn'd to the Blanket again.—I say, Sir, I was ex-hal'd up, but in my way—being too heavy, was dropt into the Sea.

DOCTOR. How, Sir, into the Sea?

HARLEQUIN. The Sea, Sir, where the Emperors Fisher-man casting his Nets, drew me up, and took me for a strange and monstrous Fish, Sir,—and as such, presented me to his Mightiness,—who going to have me Spitchcock'd for his own eating.—

DOCTOR. How, Sir, eating.—

HARLEQUIN. What did me I, Sir, (Life being sweet) but fell on my Knees, and besought his Gloriousness not to eat me, for I was no Fish but a Man; he ask'd me of what Country, I told him of Naples; whereupon the Emperor overjoy'd, ask'd me if I knew that most Reverend and most Learned Doctor Baliardo, and his fair Daughter. I told him I did: where-upon he made me his Bed-fellow, and the Confident to his Amour to Seigniora Elaria.

DOCTOR. Bless me, Sir! how came the Emperor to know my Daughter?

HARLEQUIN. —There he is again with his damn'd hard Questions.—Know her, Sir,—Why—you were walk-ing abroad one day.—

DOCTOR. My Daughter never goes abroad, Sir, farther than our Garden.—

HARLEQUIN. Ay, there it was indeed, Sir,—and as his Highness was taking a Survey of this lower World—through a long Perspective, Sir,—he saw you and your Daughter and Neece, and from that very moment, fell most des-perately in Love.—But hark—the sound of Timbrils, Kettle-Drums and Trum-pets.—The Emperor, Sir, is on his Way,—prepare for his Reception. (A

strange Noise is heard of Brass Ket-tles, and Pans, and Bells, and many tinkling things.)

DOCTOR. I'm in a Rapture—How shall I pay my Gratitude for this great Negotiation? —but as I may, I humbly offer, Sir,—(Presents him with a Rich Ring and a Purse of Gold.)

HARLEQUIN. Sir, as an Honour done the Emperor, I take your Ring and Gold. I must go meet his Highness.—(Takes Leave.)

Enter to him SCARAMOUCH, as himself.

SCARAMOUCH. Oh, Sir! we are astonish'd with the dreadful sound of the sweetest Musick that ever Mortal heard, but know not whence it comes. Have you not heard it, Sir?

DOCTOR. Heard it, yes, Fool,—'Tis the Musick of the Spheres, the Em-peror of the Moon World is descending.

SCARAMOUCH. How, Sir, no marvel then, that looking towards the South, I saw such splendid Glories in the Air.

DOCTOR. Ha,—saw'st thou ought de-scending in the Air?

SCARAMOUCH. Oh, yes, Sir, Won-ders! hast to the old Gallery, whence, with the help of your Telescope, you may discover all.—

DOCTOR. I wou'd not lose a moment for the lower Universe.

Enter ELARIA, BELLEMANTE, MOP-SOPHIL, dress'd in rich Antick Habits.

ELARIA. Sir, we are dress'd as you commanded us, What is your farther Pleasure?

DOCTOR. —It well becomes the Hon-our you're design'd for, this Night to wed two Princes—Come with me and know your happy Fates.

Ex. DOCTOR and SCARAMOUCH.

ELARIA. Bless me! My Father, in all the rest of his Discourse, shows so much Sense and Reason, I cannot think him mad, but feigns all this to try us.

BELLEMANTE. Not Mad! Marry Heaven forbid, thou art always creat-ing Fears to startle one; why if he be not mad his want of Sleep this eight and forty hours, the Noise of strange unheard of Instruments, with the Fantastick Splendor of the unusual Sight, will so turn his Brain and dazle him, that in Grace of Goodness, he may be Mad: If he be not;—come let's after him to the Gallery, for I long to see in what showing Equipage our Princely Lovers will address to us.

Exeunt.

SCENE [3.] *The Last.*

The Gallery richly adorn'd with Scenes and Lights.

Enter DOCTOR, ELARIA, BELLE-MANTE, *and* MOPSOPHIL. *Soft Musick is heard.*

BELLEMANTE. Ha.—Heavens! what's here?—what Palace is this?—No part of our House, I'm sure—

ELARIA. 'Tis rather the Apartment of some Monarch.

DOCTOR. I'm all amazement too, but must not show my Ignorance.—Yes, Elaria, this is prepar'd to entertain two Princes.

ELARIA. 'Tis all amazement too, but must not show my Ignorance.—Yes, Elaria, this is prepar'd to entertain two Princes.

BELLEMANTE. Are you sure on't, Sir? are we not, think you, in that World above, I often heard you speak of? in the Moon, Sir?

DOCTOR *(Aside).* How shall I resolve her?—For ought I know, we are.

ELARIA. Sure, Sir, 'tis some Inchantment.

DOCTOR. Let not thy Female Ignorance prophane the highest Mysteries of Natural Philosophy: To fools it seems Inchantment—but I've a Sense can reach it,—sit and expect the Event. —Hark—I am amaz'd, but must conceal my Wonder—that Joy of Fools— and appear wise in Gravity.

BELLEMANTE. Whence comes this charming Sound, Sir?

DOCTOR. From the Spheres—it is familiar to me.

The Scene in the Front draws off, and shews the Hill of Parnassus; a noble large Walk of Trees leading to it, with eight or ten Negroes upon Pedestals, rang'd on each side of the Walks. Next Kepler and Galileus descend on each side, opposite to each other, in Chariots, with Perspectives in their Hands, as viewing the Machine of the Zodiack. Soft Musick plays still.

DOCTOR. Methought I saw the Figure of two Men descend from yonder Cloud, on yonder Hill.

ELARIA. I thought so too, but they are disappear'd, and the wing'd Chariot's fled.

Enter KEPLER *and* GALILEUS.

BELLEMANTE. See, Sir, they approach.—*(The Doctor rises, and Bows.)*

KEPLER. Most Reverend Sir, we from the upper World thus low salute you.— Kepler and Galileus we are call'd, sent as Interpreters to Great Iredonozar, the Emperor of the Moon, who is descending.

DOCTOR. Most Reverand Bards—profound Philosophers—thus low I bow to pay my humble Gratitude.

KEPLER. The Emperor, Sir, Salutes you, and your fair Daughter.

GALILEUS. And, Sir, the Prince of Thunderland salutes you and your fair Neece.

DOCTOR. Thus low I fall to thank their Royal Goodness. *(Kneels. They take him up.)*

BELLEMANTE. Came you, most Reverend Bards, from the Moon World?

KEPLER. Most Lovely Maid, we did.

DOCTOR. May I presume to ask the manner how?

KEPLER. By Cloud, Sir, through the Regions of the Air, down to the fam'd Parnassus; thence by Water, along the River Helicon, the rest by Post, upon two wing'd Eagles.

DOCTOR. Sir, are there store of our World inhabiting the Moon?

KEPLER. Oh, of all Nations, Sir, that lie beneath it in the Emperors Train!

Sir, you will behold abundance; look up and see the Orbal World descending; observe the Zodiack, Sir, with her twelve Signs.

(Next the Zodiack descends, a Symphony playing all the while; when it is landed, it delivers the twelve Signs: Then the Song, the Persons of the Zodiack being the Singers. After which, the Negroes Dance and mingle in the Chorus.)

A Song for the Zodiack.

Let murmuring Lovers no longer Repine,
  But their Hearts and their Voices advance;
Let the Nymphs and the Swains in the kind
  Chorus joyn,
  And the Satyrs and Fauns in a Dance.
Let nature put on her Beauty of May,
  And the Fields and the Meadows adorn;
Let the Woods and the Mountains resound with
  the Joy,
  And the Echoes their Triumph return.

Chorus

  For since Love wore his Darts,
    And Virgins grew Coy;
  Since these wounded Hearts,
    And those cou'd destroy,
There ne'er was more Cause for your Triumphs and Joy.
Hark, hark, the Musick of the Spheres,
  Some Wonder approaching declares;
Such, such, as has not blest your Eyes and Ears
  This, thousand, thousand, thousand years.
See, see what the Force of Love can make,
  Who rules in Heaven, in Earth and Sea;
Behold how he commands the Zodiack,
  While the fixt Signs unhinging all obey.
    Not one of which, but represents
      The Attributes of Love,
    Who governs all the Elements
      In Harmony above.

Chorus

  For since Love wore his Darts,
    And Virgins grew Coy;
  Since these wounded Hearts,
    And those cou'd destroy,
There ne'er was more Cause for your Triumphs and Joy.
The wanton Aries first descends,
  To show the Vigor and the Play,
  Beginning Love, beginning Love attends,
When the young Passion is all over Joy,
He bleats his soft Pain to the fair curled Throng,
And he leaps, and he bounds, and Loves all the
  day long.
At once Loves Courage and his Slavery
  In Taurus is express'd,
Tho' oe'r the Plains the Conqueror be,
  The Generous Beast
Does to the Yoke submit his Noble Breast,
While Gemini smiling and twining of Arms,
  Shows Loves soft Indearments and Charms.
And Cancer's slow Motion the degrees do
  express;
  Respectfully Love arrives to happiness.
  Leo his strength and Majesty,
  Virgo his blushing Modesty,
  And Libra all his Equity.
  His Subtility does Scorpio show,
And Sagittarus all his loose desire,

By Capricorn his forward Humour know,
And Aqua Lovers Tears that raise his Fire,
While Pisces, which intwin'd do move,
Show the soft Play, and wanton Arts of
  Love.

Chorus

For since Love wore his Darts,
  And Virgins grew Coy;
Since these wounded Hearts,
  And those cou'd destroy,
There ne'er was more Cause for your Triumphs and Joy.

KEPLER. See how she turns, and sends her Signs to Earth.—Behold the Ram—Aries—see Taurus next descends; then Gemini—see how the Boys embrace.—Next Cancer, then Leo, then the Virgin; next to her Libra—Scorpio, Sagittary, Capicorn, Aquarius,—Pisces. This eight thousand years no Emperor has descended, but Incognito, but when he does to make his Journey more Magnificent, the Zodiack, Sir, attends him.

DOCTOR. 'Tis all amazing, Sir.

KEPLER. Now, Sir, behold, the Globick World descends two thousand Leagues below its wonted Station, to show Obedience to its proper Monarch. *(After which, the Globe of the Moon appears, first, like a new Moon; as it moves forward it increases, till it comes to the Full. When it is descended, it opens, and shews the Emperor and the Prince. They come forth with all their Train, the Flutes playing a Symphony before him, which prepares the Song. Which ended, the Dancers mingle as before.)*

A Song.

All Joy to Mortals, Joy and Mirth
  Eternal Io's sing;
The Gods of Love descend to Earth,
  Their Darts have lost the Sting.
The Youth shall now complain no more
  On Silvia's needless Scorn,
But she shall love, if he adore,
  And melt when he shall burn.

The Nymph no longer shall be shy,
  But leave the jilting Road;
And Daphne now no more shall fly
  The wounded panting God;
But all shall be serene and fair,
  No sad Complaints of Love
Shall fill the Gentle whispering Air,
  No echoing Sighs the Grove.

Beneath the Shades young Strephon lies,
  Of all his Wish possess'd;
Gazing on Silvia's charming Eyes,
  Whose Soul is there confess'd.
All soft and sweet the Maid appears,
  With Looks that know no Art,
And though she yields with trembling Fears,
  She yields with all her Heart.

KEPLER. —See, Sir, the Cloud of Foreigners appears, French, English, Spaniards, Danes, Turks, Russians, Indians, and the nearer Climes of Christendom; and lastly, Sir, behold the mighty Emperor.—*(A Chariot appears, made like a Half Moon, in which is CINTHIO for the Emperor, richly dress'd and, CHARMANTE for the Prince, rich, with a good many Heroes attending. CINTHIO'S Train born by four Cupids. The Song continues while they descend and land. They address themselves to ELARIA and BELLEMANTE.—DOCTOR falls on his Face, the rest bow very low as they pass. They make signs to KEPLER.)* The Emperor wou'd have you rise, Sir, he will expect no Ceremony from the Father of his Mistriss. *(Takes him up.)*

DOCTOR. I cannot, Sir, behold his Mightiness—the Splendor of his Majesty confounds me—

KEPLER. You must be moderate, Sir, it is expected. *(The two Lovers make all the Signs of Love in dumb show to the Ladies, while the soft Musick plays again from the End of the Song.)*

DOCTOR. Shall I not have the Joy to hear their Heavenly Voices, Sir?

KEPLER. They never speak to any Subject, Sir, when they appear in Royalty, but by Interpreters, and that by way of Stentraphon, in manner of the Delphick Oracles.

DOCTOR. Any way, so I may hear the Sence of what they wou'd say.

KEPLER. No doubt you will—But see the Emperor commands by signs his Foreigners to dance—*(Soft Musick changes.)*

(A very Antick Dance. The Dance ended, the Front Scene draws off, and shows a Temple, with an Altar, one speaking through a Stentraphon from behind it. Soft Musick plays the while.)

KEPLER. Most Learned Sir, the Emperor now is going to declare himself, according to his Custom, to his Subjects. Listen—

STENTRAPHON. Most Reverend Sir, whose Vertue did incite us,

Whose Daughters Charms did more invite us;

We come to grace her with that Honour, That never Mortal yet had done her, Only once Jove was known in Story, To visit Semele in Glory. But fatal 'twas, he so enjoy'd her, Her own ambitious Flame destroy'd her. His Charms too fierce for Flesh and Blood, She dy'd embracing of her God. We gentler marks of Passion give, The Maid we love, shall love and live; Whom visibly we thus will grace, Above the rest of humane Race. Say, is't your Will that we shou'd Wed her, And nightly in Disguise Bed her.

DOCTOR. The Glory is too great for Mortal Wife. *(Kneels with Transport.)*

STENTRAPHON. What then remains, but that we consummate This happy Marriage in our splendid State?

DOCTOR. Thus low I kneel, in thanks for this great Blessing.

(CINTHIO takes ELARIA by the Hand; CHARMANTE BELLEMANTE; two of the Singers in white being Priests, they lead 'em to the Altar, the whole Company dividing on either side. Where, while a Hymeneal Song is sung, the Priest joins their Hands. The Song ended, and they Marry'd, they come forth; but before they come forward,—two Chariots descend, one of one side above, and the other on the other side; in which is HARLEQUIN dress'd like a Mock Hero, with others, and SCARAMOUCH in the other, dress'd so in Helmets.)

SCARAMOUCH. Stay mighty Emperor, and vouchsafe to be the Umpire of our Difference. *(CINTHIO makes signs to KEPLER.)*

KEPLER. What are you?

SCARAMOUCH. Two neighbouring Princes to your vast Dominion.

HARLEQUIN. Kinghts of the Sun, our Honourable Titles. And fight for that fair Mortal, Mopsophil.

MOPSOPHIL. Bless us!—my two precious Lovers, I'll warrant; well, I had better take up with one of them, than lie alone to Night.

SCARAMOUCH. Long as two Rivals have we Lov'd and Hop'd,
Both equally endeavour'd, and both fail'd;
At last by joint Consent we both agreed
To try our Titles by the Dint of Lance,
And chose your Mightiness for Arbitrator.

KEPLER. The Emperor gives Consent.—*(They both, all arm'd with gilded Lancers and Shields of Black, with Golden Suns painted. The Musick plays a fighting Tune. They fight at Barriers, to the Tune.—HARLEQUIN is often Foil'd, but advances still; at last SCARAMOUCH throws him, and is Conqueror; all give Judgment for him.)*

KEPLER. The Emperor pronounces you are Victor.—*(To SCARAMOUCH.)*

DOCTOR. Receive your Mistress, Sir, as the Reward of your undoubted Valour—*(Presents MOPSOPHIL.)*

SCARAMOUCH. Your humble Servant, Sir, and Scaramouch, returns you humble thanks.—*(Puts off his Helmet.)*

DOCTOR. Ha,—Scaramouch—*(Bawls out, and falls in a Chair. They all go to him.)* My heart misgives me—Oh, I am undone and cheated every way.—*(Bawling out.)*

KEPLER. Be patient, Sir, and call up all your Vertue,
You're only cur'd, Sir, of a Disease
That long has raign'd over your Nobler Faculties.
Sir, I am your Physician, Friend and Counsellor;
It was not in the Power of Herbs or Minerals,
Of Reason, common Sense, and right Religion,
To draw you from an Error that unmann'd you.

DOCTOR. I will be Patient, Gentlemen, and hear you.—Are you not Ferdinand?

KEPLER. I am,—and these are Gentlemen of Quality,

That long have lov'd your Daughter and your Neece.
Don Cinthio this, and this, Don Charmante,
The Vice-Roys Nephews, both.—
Who found, as men—'twas impossible to enjoy 'em,
And therefore try'd this Stratagem.—

CINTHIO. Sir, I beseech you, mitigate your Grief,
Altho' indeed we are but mortal men,
Yet we shall Love you,—Serve you, and obey you—

DOCTOR. Are not you then the Emperor of the Moon? And you the Prince of Thunderland?

CINTHIO. There's no such Person, Sir.
These Stories are the Fantoms of mad Brains,
To puzzle Fools withal—the Wise laugh at 'em,
—Come Sir, you shall no longer be imposed upon.

DOCTOR. No Emperor of the Moon,—and no Moon World!

CHARMANTE. Ridiculous Inventions. If we'd not lov'd you, you'd been still impos'd on; We had brought a Scandal on your Learned Name, And all succeeding Ages had despis'd it.

DOCTOR. *(He leaps up.)* Burn all my Books, and let my Study Blaze,
Burn all to Ashes, and be sure the Wind Scatter the vile Contagious Monstrous Lyes.—Most Noble Youth—you've honour'd me with your Alliance, and you, and all your Friends, Assistances in this Glorious Miracle, I invite to Night to revel with me.—Come all and see my happy Recantation of all the Follies Fables have inspir'd till now. Be pleasant to repeat your Story, to tell me by what kind degrees you Cozen'd me—I see there's nothing in Philosophy—*(Gravely to himself.)* Of all that writ, he was the wisest Bard, who spoke this mighty Truth.—
"He that knew all that ever Learning writ,
"Knew only this—that he knew nothing yet."

EPILOGUE.

To be spoken by Mrs. COOK.

With our old Plays, as with dull Wife it fares,
To whom you have been marry'd tedious years.
You Cry—She's wonderous good, it is confess'd,
But still 'tis *Chapon Boüillé* at the best;
That constant Dish can never make a Feast:
Yet the pall'd Pleasure you must still pursue,
You give so small encouragement for new;
And who wou'd drudge for such a wretched Age,
Who want the Bravery to support one Stage?
The wiser Wits have now new Measures set,
And taken up new Trades, that they may Eat,
No more your nice fantastick pleasures serve,
Your Pimps you pay, but let your Poets starve.
They long in vain for better Usage hop'd,
Till quite undone and tir'd, they dropt and dropt;
Not one is left will write for thin third day,
Like desperate Pickeroons, no Prize no Pay;
And when they've done their best, the Recompence,
Is, Dam the Sot, his Play wants common Sense.
Ill natur'd Wits, who can so ill requite
The Drudging Slaves, who for your Pleasure write.
    Look back on flourishing Rome, ye proud Ingrates,
And see how she her thriving Poets treats:
Wisely she priz'd 'em at the noblest Rate,
As necessary Ministers of State,
And contributions rais'd to make 'em great.
They from the publick Bank she did maintain,
And freed from want, they only writ for Fame;
And were as useful in a City held,
As formidable Armies in the Field.
They but a Conquest over men pursu'd,
While these by gentler force the Soul subdu'd.
Not *Rome* in all her happiest Pomp cou'd show
A greater Caesar than we boast of now;
Augustus Reigns, but Poets still are low.
    May Caesar live, and while his Mighty Hand
Is Scattering Plenty over all the Land;
With God-like Bounty recompencing all,
Some fruitful drops may on the Muses fall;
Since honest Pens do his just cause afford
Equal Advantage with the useful Sword.

FINIS.

NOTES

Though *The Emperor of the Moon* was printed in 1915 by Montague Summers, there is some justification for the present edition in that the editors have attempted to preserve a more faithful rendering of the Restoration text. Except for spelling out the speech tags in full and changing names from *italic* to roman type, few changes have been made. Summers' practice of numbering the scenes has been followed, and a few asides have been placed before a speech instead of after it.

Otherwise the reader will find the text printed directly from its source, in contrast to the 1915 edition where all sorts of changes in spelling, punctuation, and capitalization have been made. An excellent illustration may be found if one compares vol. III, p. 397, line 31 of Summers' edition with the passage on page 51 of the present text. Summers has "I die with Fear,"; our reading is "I Die with fear;". Summers' reading appears quite natural, for the printers regularly capitalized the initial letter of nouns; the only drawback is that the line was not so printed in the source: the verb was capitalized and not the noun.

The Anatomist:

OR,

The Sham Doctor.

Written by Mr. *Ravenscroft*.

WITH

The LOVES

OF

Mars and Venus.

A Play Set to MUSIC.

Written by Mr. *Motteux*.

As they are Acted together at the New
Theatre, in *Little Lincolns-Inn-Fields*.

LONDON,
Printed, and are to be Sold by R. *Baldwin*, near the
Oxford Arms in *Warwick lane*. 1697.

The Anatomist

Author

No very full account of Edward Ravenscroft can be given. From the dedication of *The Anatomist* to his kinsman we learn that he professed to be able to trace his family back to William the Conqueror, but of even such essential details as the date and place of his own birth we have no information. Ravenscroft first came into public notice in 1672 when, as a member of the Middle Temple, he wrote his first play, *The Citizen Turn'd Gentleman*, and had it produced at Dorset Garden in July. Perhaps to gain additional notice the playwright assaulted Dryden in the prologues to this and his next play, *The Careless Lovers* (1673), and had the satisfaction of nettling the Laureate into a sharp retort.

Ravenscroft continued his neglect of the law in favor of the theatre, turning out some ten plays in the next twenty-five years. Few of these pieces require any extended comment. They are almost all concocted of borrowed materials, thrown together carelessly, aimed at the least critical members of the contemporary audience. Aside from *The Anatomist* the only one to keep the stage for more than a generation was the clever and salacious *London Cuckolds* (1681), which remained popular with at least some part of the theatre-going public until past the middle of the eighteenth century, only to be banned by Garrick at one theatre and shortly afterwards dropped at the other.[1]

For his second last offering Ravenscroft joined with French exile P. A. Motteux, perhaps best known for his translation of *Don Quixote*, and between them they turned out the right combination of slapstick, sound, and show to please the taste of the day. *The Anatomist; or, the Sham Doctor . . . with the Loves of Mars and*

---

[1]Mr. Summers, *Restoration Comedies* (1922), pp. xxxiii ff., is particularly incensed at the stage historians who have suggested that the play was banned at Covent Garden by royal command shortly after Garrick dropped it in 1751. He seems to be right in denying the royal command but he fails to make much of a case for the continued popularity of the piece from what he could find in Genest. The latter records the full-length play for the last time for November 9, 1758. We do not know what changes were made in the two-act version played at Covent Garden, April 10 and 12, 1782.

Venus. After this popular success Ravenscroft wrote one more play, *The Italian Husband,* and then faded from sight. We know nothing more of his later years or of the time and place of his death.

Source

The Anatomist was taken from Hauteroche's *Crispin medecin,* first performed about 1670.[2] In general Ravenscroft was content to borrow line after line from the French playwright, making only two kinds of alterations. Where it was necessary to fit Motteux's *Mars and Venus* scenes into the production he made some attempt to provide realistic transitions. More significant for our purposes, however, are the changes made in Act III, where the English piece becomes much more boisterously farcical than its source. It is possible but scarcely probable that the idea of putting old Gerald on the dissecting table and then having him flee in terror was borrowed from the *commedia dell' arte.*[3] It is far more likely that Ravenscroft, trained in the ways of farce, saw a chance to repeat a scene with variations since such repetitiousness is the very essence of farce.

Stage History

Ravenscroft's farce was first produced at Lincoln's Inn Fields in November, 1696[4] and enjoyed unusual success in that troubled period of theatrical history. Coupled with a musical rendering of the Mars and Venus story by P. A. Motteux, it seems to have caught the fancy of audiences eager for song and show. In fact, it was one of three plays which, according to a contemporary, "kept up" the theatre for "two or three years."[5] Actual records of performances during the period are rare, as they are for all plays produced then. We discover, however, that *The Anatomist* was still being performed with its original companion piece in 1704 at Lincoln's Inn Fields. Some time later it became the cus-

[2]E. T. Norris, "The Original of Ravenscroft's *Anatomist,*" *Modern Language Notes,* XLVI (1931), 522–26.

[3]Miss Lea describes a similar mock dissection occurring in a play by Lachi based on a traditional scenario. *Italian Popular Comedy* (Oxford, 1934), I, 190.

[4]Letter of Robert Jennens (HMC, Cowper Mss., II, 367).

[5]*Comparison between the Two Stages* (1702), p. 33. For additional testimony on the early popularity of *The Anatomist* see Ravenscroft's dedication of the piece, Downes, and the letter by Jennens cited above.

tom to give it, or the combination, along with an afterpiece, as at Drury Lane in 1710 or at Lincoln's Inn Fields between 1714 and 1720, when it was produced with a variety of farces as after-pieces. Scattered records of performances,[6] virtually all at Lincoln's Inn Fields and Covent Garden, occur until 1736, at which time Rich's company dropped the play from the repertory.

Eventually Ravenscroft's farce was bound to become an after-piece and it did so at Goodman's Fields,[7] where it was played with several different tragedies about the time the theatre in the East End was emerging from obscurity because of the presence in the company of David Garrick. Few changes in the play were necessary, most of them involving the excision of Motteux' scenes and the reduction of the farce to a single act.

Additional changes occurred, probably around 1743 at Drury Lane, in the part of the Doctor. The actor Charles Blakes being a consummate mimic of the French, the part of the Doctor was changed to *Monsieur le medicin*, the chief alteration being the addition of a great many French words to the medical jargon spoken by that character.[8]

---

[6]From the incomplete records provided by the *Daily Courant* and the *Daily Advertiser;* Genest is not able to give us much help in this period. For a very sensible correction of the errors growing out of Riccoboni's interesting account of his experiences at a performance of the play at Lincoln's Inn Fields see the article by Norris cited above.

[7]The *Daily Advertiser* lists ten performances between February, 1741, and May, 1742, all of them afterpieces. The first use of *The Anatomist* as an afterpiece may have occurred somewhat earlier. In the *Craftsman* for February 28 and March 6 and 13 and in the *Grub-Street Journal* for March 18, 1736, John Hippisley ran some elaborate announcements of his benefit per-formance to be given Monday, March 22. The bill was to consist of *The Recruiting Officer* to be followed by *Flora*. However, in the *Craftsman for Saturday*, March 20, he changed the afterpiece to *The Anatomist*, "the part of old Gerall [sic] by Mr. Hippisley." Since both the *Daily Advertiser* and the *Gentleman's Magazine* give the afterpiece for March 22 as *Flora* we cannot be certain that Hippisley's change was carried out. Just what took place at Punch's Theatre on Friday, March 14, 1740, for which Nicoll records a per-formance of *The Sham Doctor* must also remain uncertain.

[8]Genest, IV, 59. Genest's comment on Blakes' excellence in the part is no doubt based on the account in the list of plays appended to *Scanderbeg* (1747), where *The Anatomist* is described as a "mean Performance" and its admitted popularity credited to "one Actor [Mr. *Blakes*] who is inimitable in his mimicking a *Frenchman*."

The Anatomist remained a stock afterpiece throughout the second half of the century, as may be seen from the list of over 150 performances given by MacMillan for Drury Lane during Garrick's career of thirty years there. According to Genest's account, Covent Garden did not touch the piece again until 1786 and then only for one performance,[9] but there were widely scattered performances at Drury Lane toward the end of the century and up until Genest's last entry, for May, 1805.

Records for the provinces are meager but there are indications of some popularity. Miss Rosenfeld cites performances for but a single theatre, Bath, and for one season only, 1751–52. However, from a manuscript record of the performances of Roger Kemble's troupe for the 1766–68 seasons we discover that Ravenscroft's farce, invariably called *The Sham Doctor,* was one of the more popular afterpieces in the company's repertory.[10] The accounts for Dublin and Edinburgh are even sparser.[11]

In this country *The Anatomist* was popular for some time. It was first presented to American audiences at the midpoint of the eighteenth century and retained at least some popularity for a century, the last record we have being for New York in 1849.[12]

---

[9]A preliminary announcement at the foot of a playbill for Friday, December 22, in the Harvard Theatre Collection promises *The Beggar's Opera* and *The Anatomist,* "Second Time at this Theatre" for tomorrow, but the bill for December 23 is lacking. Genest has one of his infrequent confusions in dating just at this point, giving December 23 for 20, but it is reasonably clear that he had no bill for the days between December 20 and 27.

[10]In the Harvard Theatre Collection. The company was performing at Coventry, Worcester, Bromsgrove, and Bath.

[11]From a transcript by J. P. Kemble of records in the Dublin *Journal,* also in the Harvard Theatre Collection, we learn of a performance in Dublin in February, 1751. Three records, for the 1757–58 season in Edinburgh, are reproduced by W. H. Logan, *Fragmenta Scoto-Dramatica,* pp. 21, 24. Additional evidence for Scotland may be had from the two Edinburgh editions, both of which give a cast for Edinburgh, 1781.

[12]From the accounts of Seilhamer, Miss Willis, Odell, Pollock, James, Hoole, and Wright we learn of thirty-nine performances in various cities in the United States and one in Jamaica. The first performances were in 1752, in Annapolis and Williamsburg (Seilhamer, I, 34; Odell, I, 52–53), and the last in 1849, in New York (Odell, X, 562). Seilhamer, I, 61, calls attention to Dunlap's statement that *The Anatomist* "stood first on the Hallam list for popularity and profit" but cautions us about accepting Dunlap's word and suggests that the honor should go to *The Devil to Pay.*

Publication

During the century and a half *The Anatomist* remained in the
repertory in Great Britain and America it went through at least
ten editions. These may be divided into two groups or stages. In
the first forty years or so, while the farce was still joined with the
Mars and Venus story, it retained its three-act form. After that
it was published without Motteux' scenes, at least once in two
acts, usually in one. In this latter form there were few changes
beyond deleting the transitions Ravenscroft had put in to join his
scenes with those of his collaborator. Quite understandably, no
toning down of the author's farcical additions occurred.

The Anatomist: or, the Sham Doctor. Written by Mr. Ravenscroft.
   With the Loves of Mars and Venus . . . London, Printed, and
   are to be Sold by R. Baldwin . . . , 1697.[13]

The Anatomist; or, the Sham-Doctor: Written by Mr. Ravenscroft.
   With the Loves of Mars and Venus... . . London: Printed for
   J. Darby, for A. Bettesworth and F. Clay, M.DCC.XXII.

The Anatomist; or, the Sham-Doctor: Written by Mr. Ravenscroft.
   With the Loves of Mars and Venus... . . London: Printed for
   W. Feales . . . , R. Wellington . . . , and C. Corbett . . . , J. Brind-
   ley . . . , A. Bettesworth, and F. Clay, in Trust for B. Wellington. MDCCXXXV.

The Anatomist; or, the Sham-Doctor . . . London: Printed for Hawes,
   Clarke and Collins, S. Crowder, T. Longman, T. Lownds, and
   C. Corbett. MDCCLXIII.

The Anatomist: or, the Sham Doctor . . . London: Printed for the
   Proprietors, and sold by T. Davies. . . . [n.d.)[14]

The Anatomist; or, the Sham Doctor. By Mr. Ravenscroft. In Vol. I
   of the *Supplement to Bell's British Theatre,* London, 1784.

The Anatomist: or the Sham Doctor. By Mr. Ravenscroft. In Vol. I
   of *A Collection of the Most Esteemed Farces and Entertainments.*
   . . . Edinburgh, 1792.

The Anatomist; or, the Sham Doctor. A Farce. By Mr. Ravenscroft.
   London: Printed for C. Whittingham . . . for John Sharpe . . . ,
   1805. In Vol. XIII of *Sharpe's British Theatre.*

---

[13]A copy in the Folger Library with a slight variation in the first signature
and a corrected spelling of the name of one of the actors may be described
as a second issue of this first edition.

[14]Most libraries apparently follow the *British Museum Catalogue* in giving
the date as 1762, but the printed cast is of the period around 1771, which may
be taken as a more satisfactory approximate date.

The Anatomist; or, the Sham Doctor, a Farce, by Edward Ravenscroft . . . London: Printed for John Cawthorne . . . 1807. In
Vol. VI of *Cawthorne's Minor British Theatre.*

The Anatomist; or, the Sham Doctor. A farce. In two acts. By Mr.
Ravenscroft. Philadelphia: Published by Thomas H. Palmer.
1822.

Analysis

Although Professor Lancaster speaks of the French source of *The
Anatomist* as a comedy,[15] it is scarcely more than a farce. Ravenscroft's adaptation is clearly farcical. The satirical value of the piece
is almost nil, for the satire both of physicians and of May-December
marriages had long since become threadbare. Nor is the plot of any
significance. As Lancaster points out concerning *Crispin medecin,*
there is no real conflict; the girl's mother, who "rules the roost," is
wholly opposed to old Gerald's marrying her daughter. The outcome
can never be in doubt. The only item of interest left, then, is the
clever tricks and hair-breadth escapes of Crispin.

Ignoring the exposition and the stereotyped satire of absent-minded
physicians and henpecked husbands, we come to three or four major
pieces of farce business in Acts II and III. First Crispin is trapped
in the doctor's office and at Beatrice's suggestion plays the role of
cadaver, thus combining two familiar devices of farce, disguise and
the pretence of inanimation. In this situation he must endure both
the humiliation of being described as a rogue—always amusing to
an audience when the one insulted hears but is powerless to retort—
and of being threatened with dismemberment, the highly technical
terms used by the doctor not making the prospect any more cheerful.
The dramatist prevents the scene from reaching its obvious climax
by having Beatrice save Crispin, and we are ready for the next episode, Crispin's playing physician.

In this traditional scene, perhaps the only thing requiring comment
is the skilfull manner in which the dramatist carries the clever-stupid
servant over some very thin ice. His ignorance gets him into ridiculous difficulties, even with his thick-witted patients or with the dodder-
ing physician, but his cleverness, plus Beatrice's, always rescues him
in time.

---

[15]*A History of French Dramatic Literature in the Seventeenth Century,* III,
769, 774.

In the third episode, the one in which Old Gerald and Martin break through Crispin's flimsy story of his master's doings at the university, Ravenscroft makes somewhat pointless use of Crispin's *"medicus sum"* and "systol and diastole," one of his weakest alterations of the French play. The scene ends in true slapstick as Old Gerald aims a blow at Crispin and tumbles when the latter dodges. Crispin thereupon dumps Martin on top of his master and scurries off.

The big farce episode, which provides the main interest in Act III, is the English dramatist's own concoction. By a clever use of repetition he provides much the same situation as that in which Crispin was stretched on the table, except that now Crispin is the surgeon, rendered even more ludicrous by his "German" accent, and the superannuated lover the frightened victim, stripped to his drawers. What a pair of clever *farceurs* could do with such an opportunity may readily be imagined. Beatrice adds to the scene by her suggestions.

PROLOGUE

Spoken by Mr. BETTERTON.
Written by Mr. MOTTEUX.

To day no Pageant Decoration,
This Lord May'rs Show began the Reformation:
Yet is our Entertainment odd and new;
We've in our Show the First of Cuckolds too:
And what we call a Masque some will allow
To be an Op'ra, as the World goes now.
So is your poysoning Quack miscall'd a Doctor,
And your worst Mimick calls himself an Actor.
So your dull Scribler (to our Cost we knew it)
Writes a damn'd Play, and is misnam'd a Poet.
Once Song and Dance cou'd buoy up want of Thinking,
But now these Bladders can't prevent its Sinking:
Plays grow so heavy, that those helps are vain;
Three times they sink, and never rise again.
Well, if our Neighbors the Precedence claim,
For good dull Stuff we'll not dispute with them.
Our Medley is perhaps as much too light,
But let it pass—We don't take Money yet by weight.
By Sympathy, 't should please the Beaux, I know,
For in all things an Op'ra's like a Beau.
Both Beau and Op'ra on the Stage are seen;
Both odd in Dress, and shifting still the Scene;
Each dances, sings, and moves like a Machine.
To be admir'd, 'tis at a vast Expence;
It loves soft words, but cares not much for Sense;
For by its Nature 'twas design'd for show;
Why, 'tis an Op'ra but to dress a Beau.
But one unlucky diff'rence stands between;
Op'ra's are paid, but Beaux pay to be seen,
(Those who don't come to sharp an Act I mean.)
For your own sakes, we beg Applause of you;
Since 'twill revenge you on the Scribbling Crew.
For, if this takes, strait crys each senseless Elf,
Dem-me, I'd write as well as this my self.
With that, he writes a thing, which we refuse,
Then, wondring how we durst affront his Muse,
Strait in a huff he gives it t'other House;
Who either slight it, or 'twill be its Lot
To get as much as their last Op'ra got.

Prologue: another prologue and the epilogue have been omitted.

DRAMATIS PERSONAE.

OLD MR. GERALD.
YOUNG MR. GERALD.
THE DOCTOR.
WIFE to the DOCTOR.
MRS. ANGELICA, their Daughter.
BEATRICE, the Maid.
MARTIN, Servant to OLD GERALD.
CRISPIN, the SHAM DOCTOR, Servant to YOUNG GERALD.
SIMON, a Country-fellow.
WAITING-WOMAN.

Mr. *Bright.*
Mr. *Hodson.*
Mr. *Underhill.*
Mrs. *Leigh.*
Mrs. *Bowman.*
Mrs. *Lawson.*
Mr. *T. Harris.*
Mr. *Bowen.*
Mr. *Trout.*
Mrs. *Robinson.*

ACT I. SCENE 1.

Enter before the Curtain, ANGELICA, BEATRICE.

ANGELICA. Is my Mother ready, is she coming to hear the Musick?

BEATRICE. Yes Madam, and is extreamly pleas'd; she loves Musick wonderfully.

ANGELICA. So do I Beatrice; we are much beholden to my singing Master.

BEATRICE. Yes Madam! But you are more beholden to your Lover, young Mr. Gerald.

ANGELICA. How so!

BEATRICE. You know he has left the University for your sake, and has been this month in Town, waiting opportunities to see you: He brought with him some words of his own composing to entertain you, they are set by your own Master: By this means he hopes to get admittance to discourse you, and breath his Love Ejaculations in your Ear.

ANGELICA. How can that be? He is known both by my Father and Mother.

BEATRICE. No matter for that; he is in disguise, and sits amongst the Instrumental Musick as one of them.

ANGELICA. How shall I know him?

BEATRICE. By his Eye, as you do a Pheasant, he'll be looking on you all the while.

ANGELICA. But how will he come to speak to me?

BEATRICE. Trust that to chance, at least it will be a pleasure to see one another: It is a delight to Lovers to steal looks, tho it be at Church.

ANGELICA. Sure Love and Devotion are near a kin, they are each bred in the Soul, and Musick is the food of both.

BEATRICE. Here comes your Father and Mother.

Enter DOCTOR and WIFE.

WIFE. Come Husband, stay and hear the Musick, my Daughter's Master will take it ill else, it was provided for the Playhouse, and he has brought 'em all here to practice it over in form: You'll have time enough to visit your Patients.

DOCTOR. Let 'em begin presently then, for time is precious to men of business.

WIFE. The Musick strikes up already. Sit down, Husband, Daughter, and Beatrice, take you your places over against us.

They all sit down, and the first Musical entertainment begins. After that they rise and speak.

DOCTOR. Well, now my time is out, I must be gone.

WIFE. This is not all: This is but the Prologue to what follows; you must hear the rest.

DOCTOR. I must go visit a Nobleman that is my Patient just now, but I'le return anon: In the mean time take all the performers in to Breakfast, and treat 'em with some bottles of Wine.

WIFE. By that time you'll come again.

DOCTOR. Ay, my dear Wife, farewell.
Exit.

WIFE. Gentlemen, pray all walk into the next Room, and take part of a small Entertainment. Come Daughter. *Exeunt* WIFE, ANGELICA, *and Performers.*

Enter CRISPIN.

CRISPIN. Beatrice, tell Mrs. Angelica my Master wou'd fain come too, but dares not, for fear he should be knówn to be in Town. Besides, he and I have some business, but we'll be here again anon.

BEATRICE. Well, well, get you gone Crispin. I am call'd. *Exeunt severally.*

SCENE 2.

Enter OLD GERALD, *and* MARTIN.

MARTIN. You are resolv'd Sir, to Marry you say?

OLD GERALD. I am; and to that end, I have sent my Son to the University, to mind his Study, and be out of the way.

MARTIN. May I, Sir, be so bold, to ask the Ladies name, you intend to make your Wife?

OLD GERALD. Madam Angelica the Doctor's Daughter.

MARTIN. Sure, Sir, you're not in earnest, she's not above fifteen; that Match Sir, would be fitter for your Son.

OLD GERALD. My Son? I don't intend that he shall Marry yet, these seven years.

MARTIN. But Sir, consider well before you Marry.

OLD GERALD. I have thought enough, she's handsome, young, and sprightly.

MARTIN. But these are qualities will not agree with an old mans constitution.

OLD GERALD. Old! Coxcomb: I an't so old

MARTIN. No Sir, if you had been contemporary with the Patriarchs, you had been counted now a very youth, but in this short-liv'd age we live in, Sir, you are, as one may say, worn to the stumps.

OLD GERALD. Hold your prating; Threescore is mans ripe Age.

MARTIN. Yes, and his rotten Age too; but you, if I mistake not, are threescore and ten.

OLD GERALD. No more of Age: 'Tis a thing never to be inquired into, but when you are buying Horses.

MARTIN. How? Not in Marriage Sir.

OLD GERALD. Not if a man be very rich.

MARTIN. Can you believe Sir, the old Doctor her Father, and the Gentlewoman her Mother, who is a notable wise governing Woman, will bestow their Daughter, and their only Heir, upon a man so old, where there's no hopes of Grand Children to inherit what they have, without an Act of Parliament to enable him.

OLD GERALD. Hold your tongue I say; you are my Servant, not my Councellor I take it Sir; this is my own concern; when I am Married, I doubt not but I shall behave my self, as a married man ought.

MARTIN. But if the Doctor won't consent to it.

OLD GERALD. That I am sure of, he has promis'd me, and he's a man of his word.

MARTIN. That indeed is something: but Sir, you know the Wife there wears the Breeches; and if the grey Mare be the better Horse, you'll find it difficult to bestride the Filly.

OLD GERALD. I know she is a little domineering; and I know too that Mr. Doctor is a Wise Man; his gravity and prudence, will manage her well enough; he who can cure mad folks, scorns to be Wife-ridden.

MARTIN. Many have try'd in vain; a man sometimes may sooner break his own heart, than his Wife's will. But see Sir, here's the Doctor.

Enter DOCTOR.

DOCTOR. Mr. Gerald, good morrow to you Sir.

OLD GERALD. Mr. Doctor, I was coming to speak to you.

DOCTOR. Come; let me feel your pulse.

OLD GERALD. It needs not Sir.

DOCTOR. T'other hand.

OLD GERALD. That's not my business.

DOCTOR. No, but 'tis mine, your Pulse Sir is disordered.

OLD GERALD. You mistake me, my—

DOCTOR. Put out your tongue, your tongue.

OLD GERALD. No matter for my tongue.

DOCTOR. Do you sleep well?

OLD GERALD. Yes, very well. But Sir—

DOCTOR. How is your Stomach? have you a good Appetite.

OLD GERALD. Yes Mr. Doctor, but I come—

DOCTOR. And do you digest well what you eat?

OLD GERALD. Yes very well, but will you hear me Sir?

DOCTOR. And all those other benefits of nature.

OLD GERALD. I have 'em regularly. But Mr. Doctor—

DOCTOR. Nay if you eat well, drink well, sleep well, digest well, and after all this should not be well, it would be wonderful. But I lose time, I must visit my other Patients. Your Servant Sir.

OLD GERALD. Stay, good Sir, stay, I have had patience to hear you talk, and to no purpose neither; now 'tis my turn to speak, and to some purpose.

DOCTOR. Dispatch then; I'm in haste.

OLD GERALD. 'Tis not about my health I came to you, no 'tis another affair.

DOCTOR. What affair?

OLD GERALD. That, that you know of.

DOCTOR. What I say?

OLD GERALD. The business that I spoke of.

DOCTOR. When?

OLD GERALD. When? more than once.

DOCTOR. Where?

OLD GERALD. At several places; at your house and mine.

DOCTOR. What was it then?

OLD GERALD. About your Daughter.

DOCTOR. What about your Daughter?

OLD GERALD. About my marrying her.

DOCTOR. O, was it nothing else? I thought 't had been something of consequence. As to that matter I have given my promise; chuse your own time, Marry her when you please.

OLD GERALD. And have you broke it to your Wife?

DOCTOR. No, but my will is hers, she submits to what I think fit. I am and will be master. I thank Heaven, I have discretion, and can rule a Wife, as a wise Husband ought.

OLD GERALD. I doubt it not.

DOCTOR. If once my Wife should contradict my will, she should soon find what metal I am made of. I thank my Stars we have no domestick broyls, my Wife submits to me in all things.

OLD GERALD. If you think fit then, let's acquaint her with it, 'tis a formality all Mothers may expect.

DOCTOR. You say well; stay here, I'le call her! *Exit.*

OLD GERALD. Well Martin, what say you now?

MARTIN. I see the Doctor is your friend; so far all's well; but mark the end I say still.

Re-enter DOCTOR *and* WIFE.

DOCTOR. My dearest, here's our good friend Mr. Gerald come purposely to see you.

WIFE. Sir, your Servant. Tho my Husband's a Physitian, I am glad to see you're in good health.

Servant: from 1722 edition; text reads "you Servant."

OLD GERALD. Speak to her Mr. Doctor, tell her the business.

DOCTOR. Do you speak first.

OLD GERALD. 'Tis properer for you.

DOCTOR. No, no, you'll explain your self much better. Lovers are eloquent.

OLD GERALD. But you have the Authority of a Husband, and may without ceremony open the matter to her.

DOCTOR. No, you must break the Ice, you shall see my power if she resists.

WIFE. Pray Gentlemen, what's this contest about, and why was I call'd hither?

OLD GERALD. A foolish punctilio of honor; and something Mr. Doctor has to acquaint you with.

DOCTOR. Our kind friend, Mr. Gerald here, has a mind to marry our Daughter, Love.

OLD GERALD. Yes Madam; and upon such terms as few Parents are displeas'd with. You may scruple my age, but when you know, I will take her without a Portion, and mean to settle a good joynture on her, allow her handsomely for Pin-Money, keep her a Coach, a Chariot, and two Footmen; and give her every New-years-day, a hundred Guineas in an Embroidered Purse, to fool away; I hope, that scruple will be remov'd. Besides, Mr. Doctor has given his consent already, and I doubt not, but yours will come as easily.

WIFE. Hold there, good Mr. Gerald; these things require consideration; your Ages are most unsutable. Many young Women have been ruin'd by such unequal Matches. Youth and Age cannot agree: An old Man may be fond of a young Woman, but a young Woman of an old Man never. But to avoid all inconveniencies, and fatal accidents, that may happen to our Family, by such a disproportion'd Marriage, I must tell you plainly, you shan't have my consent; and I hope you will not take it ill of me.

OLD GERALD. But your Husband, Madam, has given me his word.

WIFE. What if he has? He gave it then without consideration. When he comes to weigh all circumstances as he ought, he must, and will be of my mind too.

OLD GERALD. Speak Mr. Doctor, did not you absolutely promise me?

WIFE. He who indiscreetly promises, may with good reason call it back. He did it without my knowledge or consent, therefore't was but a half promise, Sir.

OLD GERALD. But, Mr. Doctor, a Man of Honour ought to keep his word, and stand to what he says. Speak then, have you not promised me your Daughter?

DOCTOR. 'Tis true, I cannot deny it.

WIFE. How! can you not? we'll talk of that hereafter. Well Mr. Gerald, promise, or not promise, all's one for that, I deny my consent, and that's enough.

DOCTOR. But Wife, dear Wife—

WIFE. Wife me no Wife's, but hold your foolish prating; sure I know better than you what's befitting for our Daughter.

DOCTOR. But my dear, we ought—

WIFE. I know we ought to be wiser than to make foolish promises; or if you were so childish not to keep 'em. Come Mr. Gerald, set your Heart at rest, you shall never marry my Daughter; there's my resolution. I will not be the jest of the whole Town. Who would not split their sides to hear a couple of old fools call one another, Father and Son? away, away for shame. *Exit.*

MARTIN. Sir, Sir, Mr. Doctor.

DOCTOR. Well, what say you?

MARTIN. If once my Wife should contradict my will! She should soon find what metal I am made of. I thank my Stars we have no domestick broyls, my Wife submits to me in all things.

OLD GERALD. Martin says true; this lesson you read to us, before you call'd your Wife, good Mr. Doctor.

But, Mr. Doctor: from 1722 edition; text reads "But, Mr Dr"

DOCTOR. 'Tis very true; and 'tis as true, this was no proper place to shew my authority; our Passion must be govern'd by our Reason; my Moderation must cool her Intemperance: Had I presently flown to the top o'th' house, we had made fine work on't. I'll take a more convenient opportunity to discourse this matter with her; in the mean time, leave it to me: I have given my word, and I will—I will—come trust to me: I warrant you.

MARTIN. Yes Sir, leave it to Mr. Doctor, he'l do wonders; he is a Lyon in private, but you saw he was a Lamb in publick: But I fear you had better take the Wife's word, than the Husband's, 'tis plain she rules the Roast.

DOCTOR. You are a fool, and know not what you say.

MARTIN. But I know, Sir, you had a furious repulse at the Half Moon, you were beaten out of your Trenches too; you'll have no better luck at the Conterscarp: If you dare venture to storm, I fear you will be beaten off, with such a shameful loss, you will be forc'd to raise the Siege, and glad you scape unwounded.

DOCTOR. Hold your tongue, you are a sawcy Knave.

MARTIN. I have done; I won't dispute Titles with Mr. Doctor.

DOCTOR. Well Mr. Gerald, once more leave all to me: I tell you I will do it; that's sufficient. *Exit.*

MARTIN. Now, Sir, have you the same hopes you had of Marrying Mrs. Angelica? You see her Mother's an imperious Woman, and will never give her consent to it: The Doctor I confess is an able Physician, and an excellent man in his way, but yet he has the fortune to be Hen-peck'd, and must submit, as many wise and learned men have done; therefore you must not build upon his promises: Besides, I do not find you have got the Daughter's consent yet; and that's the main point of all.

OLD GERALD. You say true, Martin; I must think of that. Stay, is not that Crispin yonder?

Enter CRISPIN.

CRISPIN. O Sir, your Servant: I am glad I have found you. Good morrow Martin.

MARTIN. Good morrow Crispin.

OLD GERALD. What cause brings you to Town?

CRISPIN. Your Son, my Master, sent me in all haste.

OLD GERALD. For what?

CRISPIN. That Letter will inform you.

OLD GERALD (*reads*). Honoured Father, Hoping you are in good health, as I am, thanks be to God, at the present writing hereof: This is to let you understand that all my Money's gone, and my Cloaths worn so bare, that you may, as the saying is, see my Breech thro my Pocket-holes.

MARTIN. A fine Epistle.

OLD GERALD. This is not my Sons stile, nor is't his hand: This is some Roguery of yours Sirrah.

CRISPIN. To tell you the plain truth, Sir, I lost I know not how, my Masters Letter on the Road; and baiting at a little Village, it hapned to be the Sextons house, who sold a Cup of notable good Ale: There I got him to write this Letter for me. I know my Master sent for Money, and Cloaths, pray read the rest.

OLD GERALD. No, I have read enough.

MARTIN. You dictated this Letter to the Sexton, Crispin.

CRISPIN. I did so? what of that?

MARTIN. Nothing, but that the stile is very eloquent.

CRISPIN. I think so: I have not been at the University with my Master 4 months, for nothing.

OLD GERALD. Has my Son spent all his Money in so short a time? he has been prodigal.

CRISPIN. He could not help it, he was forc'd to treat at his first coming,

Sir: I shall be his Steward for the future, and manage matters better.

OLD GERALD. Look you do. I have some business now, about an hour hence come home to me. Follow me Martin. *Ex [eunt]* OLD GERALD *and* MARTIN.

CRISPIN. So far all's well: If I can screw a good summ out' of him, I do my Masters business; the old Gentleman must not know he is in Town, nor must my Master know I lost his Letter. O, here he comes.

Enter YOUNG GERALD.

YOUNG GERALD. I sent you with my Letter to my Father; why are you loytering here?

CRISPIN. 'Tis done, Sir.

YOUNG GERALD. What is done, Sir?

CRISPIN. Your business, Sir, is done effectually: I met your Father here, just in this place; gave him your Letter; he read it o're and o're, and said the stile was admirable; was overjoy'd to see how the University had improv'd you; then I made him an eloquent Oration, to let him see how I had profited: This melted his hard heart, made his old Eyes twinkle like flames in the bottom of two Sockets. At last he bid me come home to him some half an hour hence; by that time, Sir, the Money will be ready.

YOUNG GERALD. Did he ask no questions? how I had spent my Money? what company I kept? or how I behav'd my self in the University?

CRISPIN. He had no time for that; when I come home to him, perhaps he may.

YOUNG GERALD. Be careful Crispin; should he suspect—

CRISPIN. He shall pump nothing out of me, I warrant you.

YOUNG GERALD. But Martin is a notable sly youth.

CRISPIN. You think, because I cannot write and read as he can, that I have less wit than Martin; I warrant you I'll be upon my Guard, I'll deal well enough with him. But now, Sir,

let me question you a little; how durst you venture abroad by day light? Should your Father—

YOUNG GERALD. I know it Crispin, but as soon as you were gone, Angelica sent her Maid to me, bid me meet her here; something of consequence has hapned to her, and I'm in pain to know the meaning of it. See, she is here.

Enter ANGELICA.

YOUNG GERALD. My dear Angelica.

ANGELICA. Mr. Gerald! I am glad my Maid found you, you have made haste.

YOUNG GERALD. Can you blame me for that? My love was too impatient to wait; I have a thousand doubts and fears: why did you send for me? what has happen'd, Madam? tell me my Angelica, and ease my loaded heart.

ANGELICA. I could not prevail upon my self to stay till you came. O Gerald! 'twill surprize you when I tell you, your Father is in love.

YOUNG GERALD. You mock me Madam.

ANGELICA. No, 'tis too true; he has askt me of my Father and my Mother, offers to settle a large Joynture on me, and Marry me without a Portion too. These are proposals few Parents will refuse.

YOUNG GERALD. The Laws of Nature, tho not of Nations, forbid such unequal Matches.

ANGELICA. But Money, Gerald! what will not Money do?

YOUNG GERALD. 'Tis true; for Money Mothers sell their Daughters.

ANGELICA. Yes, and for Money, most Daughters sell themselves.

YOUNG GERALD. A Beau for money, will Marry an old wither'd Witch, with rotten Lungs, no Teeth, one Eye, and half a Nose.

ANGELICA. For Money, Soldiers sell their lives.

YOUNG GERALD. And Priests their consciences.—But my Angelica; your

Father is a wise and learned Man, he is not mercenary, he won't sell you.

ANGELICA. You are mistaken, Sir, he has given his promise to your Father.

YOUNG GERALD. Then all my hope is vanish'd.

ANGELICA. Not so; you have no reason to despair. You say my Father's wise, and learned too; now I say, my Mother has no learning, but more wisdom, for she has positively refused to give him her consent.

YOUNG GERALD. O you revive me! my drooping Soul drinks up your words, as the parch'd Earth does a refreshing shower! what's to be done, Crispin?

ANGELICA. I told you my Mother lov'd Musick most immoderately: She is much pleased with it. I will let her know that it was your contrivance, and acquaint her with our love, and try to make her of our party. Stay hereabouts, if I succeed, Beatrice shall give you notice.

YOUNG GERALD. Do my dear Lov'd, Angelica: Good luck attend you.

CRISPIN. Has the Devil Lechery got possession of my old Master's head? I am sure he left his Breeches long ago. Let me see; he has to my knowledge, been bewitch'd about some 15 years.

YOUNG GERALD. This was the cause I was remov'd, and sent to the University.

CRISPIN. He shall quickly find we lost no time there; we have studied hard, studied Fortification, we can Entrench; if he can Mine, Sir, we can Countermine.

YOUNG GERALD. Now go, fetch the money from my Father instantly, you shall find me hereabouts at your return. *Exit.*

CRISPIN. Well, of all your Father's follies, this is the worst.
When old men fall in Love, they're surely curst.

SCENE [3.] *A Hall in the Doctors House.*

Scene 3: text has "Scene 2."

Enter the Doctor's WIFE, ANGELICA, *and* BEATRICE.

WIFE. Is the Room in order, Beatrice, for the Musick to go on with the entertainment?

BEATRICE. Yes, Madam.

WIFE. 'Tis very well. Go see how long it will be to dinner.
Come, my Angelica, be free and merry,
Trust to thy Mother's conduct, and her kindness;
Thy Father shall not sell thee while I live.
While you remain obedient and discreet,
It shall be all the study of my life,
To make you happy, Child.

ANGELICA.   Oh my dear Mother!
Let me receive this blessing on my Knees.
If ever I am disobedient to you?
Or e're abuse this mighty goodness to you,
May I become the out-cast of your Family;
Disown'd by you, dispis'd by all good Women,
and hated by young Gerald.

Enter YOUNG GERALD.

WIFE. Here he comes.
You're welcome, Sir; if mine is not sufficient,
You shall have her welcome too,
And that, I hope will please you.

YOUNG GERALD. Please me! Ay, more
Than wealth to Misers, freedom to a Slave,
Or a Reprieve to one condemn'd to die.

ANGELICA. Oh, Mr. Gerald!
I have the most indulgent Mother living.
Your Father's liberal offers to the Doctor
Cannot prevail on her.

YOUNG GERALD. How shall I thank You, Madam, as I ought?
How pay the mighty debt due you both?
Due to your wisdom, and her matchless love?
If all the duty, the profound respect
That ever pious Son paid his own Mother

Ay, more: emended from "I" after 1722 text.

Can merit so much Happiness, if deserve it,
The business of my life shall be to
please her.
My truth, my constancy, and perfect
love,
No time shall alter, nor no chance
remove.

WIFE. Do this, my Son, and Heaven
will bless you both.

Enter BEATRICE.

BEATRICE. My Master, Madam, has
sent word, he can't be at home till
dinner-time, but wou'd have you go on
with the Musick.

WIFE. Then we'll loose no more time;
come let us seat our selves; I long to
hear more.

Here comes the second Musical Enter-
tainment: After which they rise and
speak.

WIFE. We'll hear the rest after Dinner.

BEATRICE. Desire the Gentlemen all
to walk in.

YOUNG GERALD. I must not be seen
by your Husband; therefore I'll take
my leave.

WIFE. I know it, Mr Gerald. Your
Servant Sir.

ANGELICA. Sir your Servant.

YOUNG GERALD. Adieu my Life, my
Dear, Angelica. *Exit.*

WIFE. Two things, and only two, Angelica; I always lov'd, and lov'd em
passionately.

ANGELICA. What were those, Madam?

WIFE. My Husband, and good Musick.

ANGELICA. And in that Madam, I
follow your example.

WIFE. Yes Child, but take this rule
with you;
Discretion is a Womans safest guard.
She shuns Vain Glory, Malice, Strife,
and Pride,
When Reason and good Nature is her
Guide.

ACT II. SCENE 1.

Enter DOCTOR.

DOCTOR. Beatrice, I say; where are
you?

Enter BEATRICE.

BEATRICE. Here, Sir, here.

DOCTOR. See all things are in order
here in my Laboratory. Many Virtuosi
will be here, to see my curious Dissection, and hear the leacture I intend to
read on a dead Body, which every
moment I expect to be sent in from the
place of Execution.

BEATRICE. Why do you choose this
back Apartment at the end of the Garden? You us'd to do it in the Great
Hall formerly.

DOCTOR. My Wife will have it so, and
that's enough; the body may be brought
in privately, at that back door, for so
I order'd it: Besides, the wrangling
disputations of self-conceited, obstinate
Physicians, who come to see my operation, will at this distance less disturb
the Neighborhood: they will maintain
their notions with more noise, than
Betters in a Cock-pit.

BEATRICE. 'Tis observ'd you Doctors
rarely agree in your opinions, Sir, which
makes some affirm, Physick itself is a
very uncertain Science.

DOCTOR. That's true; but yet the
fault's not in the Art.

BEATRICE. It must be in the Professors then.

DOCTOR. And so it is; but this is not
your business.

BEATRICE. I only speak my simple
judgment Sir.

DOCTOR. The Body will be here immediately: let 'em carry it into the
Vault, 'tis cooler there: in the mean
time I'll make some visits to my Patients who are near. Ha! Beatrice, let
me see, what have you there?

BEATRICE. Where, Sir, What do you
mean?

DOCTOR. There, Sirrah, there. Let's
see those pretty Bubbies.

BEATRICE. Fye Sir, you make me
blush.

DOCTOR. Faith I will see 'em; I
and feel 'em too.

BEATRICE. You old men have such odd fancies in you.

DOCTOR. I am a Cock o'th' Game, you little Rogue.

BEATRICE. You strut, and crow, and clap your Wings indeed, but all to little purpose.

DOCTOR. Ah you unlucky Chitt! I cou'd, I cou'd—

BEATRICE. But you forget your Patients Sir.

DOCTOR. That's true indeed: well when I am come again. *Exit.*

BEATRICE. I find all Husbands, old, and young, are still for variety; which is a certain sign of an ill stomach: well if ever it be my fortune to Marry one who serves me so, I'll say no more, but that which is sauce for a Goose, shall be sauce for a Gander too. *(Enter CRISPIN.)* Crispin! What brings you hither now?

CRISPIN. I have been almost half an hour hankering about the back door: I saw the Doctor come forth just now, and then I ventur'd to slip in.

BEATRICE. Secure that door then, while I fasten this; we will not be surpriz'd: now what's the business?

CRISPIN. My Master, poor man's at his wits end, he walks and starts, then stops and muses, then he walks again: What Madam Angelica told him about his Father has distracted him. I have a Letter for her.

BEATRICE. Give it me.

CRISPIN. Stay Beatrice, let me look on you a little: what hast thou been doing to thy self? I never saw thee so handsome in my life.

BEATRICE. Indeed?

CRISPIN. No indeed: thou hast stolen some of thy Lady's Wash; it can't be natural; come, let me try.

BEATRICE. Stand off, you fool.

CRISPIN. Now I think on't, I have not had one kiss since I came from the University.

BEATRICE. Keep your distance, you had best: I will not make you so familiar with me.

CRISPIN. Say you so: Harkee, Gentlewoman, what made you here alone with Mr Doctor? This place is very private, at a convenient distance from the house too.

BEATRICE. One who was hang'd this morning is to be Dissected here: I must set everything in order for it; the Body will be sent in presently.

CRISPIN. We have prepar'd another Entertainment for you Lady. *(Knocking.)* Here, let me out quickly.

DOCTOR *(within).* Open the door.

BEATRICE. What shall I do? it is my Master.

CRISPIN. Let me out I say.

BEATRICE. Here, come to the other door. *(Knocking at the other door.)*

WIFE *(within).* Where are you, Beatrice?

BEATRICE. O Heaven! 'tis my Mistress, she's at the other door.

CRISPIN. The Devil she is.

BEATRICE. If she were not there, I would let you down into the Vault.

DOCTOR *(within).* Ho Beatrice! open the door I say.

CRISPIN. What will become of me?

BEATRICE. Here, here, lay your self at length upon this Table: I'll say you are the dead Body sent from the Gallows.

CRISPIN. Oh Beatrice—

BEATRICE. No more; do as I bid you. *(CRISPIN lies at his full length on the Table. BEATRICE opens the door.)*

Enter DOCTOR.

DOCTOR. You made me wait sufficiently. I had forgot some Medicines I prepar'd; I must go up and fetch 'em. *Exit.*

BEATRICE. Now I'll let in my Mistress.

Enter WIFE.

WIFE. How were you employ'd, you could open the door no sooner?

BEATRICE. I was busie in taking in this Executed Body, I made all the haste I could.

Re-enter DOCTOR.

DOCTOR. 'Tis very well. Adieu, I am in haste. *Exit.*

WIFE. Beatrice, set all his Instruments in order: my Daughter and I will make a visit: I do not love such sights, they make me melancholy.

BEATRICE. I'll be careful in your absence. *(Exit* WIFE.*)* Now, Crispin, is my invention good? *(*CRISPIN *rises.)*

CRISPIN. You've brought me bravely off; but I'll be gone for fear of an after-clap.

DOCTOR *(within)*. Beatrice, Beatrice, open the door again. *(Knocks.)*

BEATRICE. 'Tis my Master, to the same posture quickly.

CRISPIN. The Devil take him.

Enter DOCTOR.

DOCTOR. I think I am bewitcht to day; I have taken the wrong Medicines. What's that there?

BEATRICE. The Body from the Gallows, Sir; the fellows that brought it would not carry it into the Vault.

DOCTOR. How came they to send him with his Cloaths on?

BEATRICE. They'll call for 'em to morrow.

DOCTOR. 'Tis very well. Ha! the Body's warm: I have a mind to make an experiment immediately. Go, Beatrice, fetch me my Incision Knives, Amputation Knife, Dismembring Saw, with the Threads, Pins, and all the other Instruments I laid ready in my Closet.

BEATRICE. But Sir, your Patients expect you now.

DOCTOR. An hour or two hence will serve.

BEATRICE. Should any of 'em dye in the mean time?

DOCTOR. That's not my fault; if any of 'em are in so much danger, my visit will do 'em no good now.

BEATRICE. I have heard you say, Sir, a proper dose given at a lucky time—

DOCTOR. Go, bring me only my Incision Knife; for while the natural heat remains, I shall more easily come at the Lacteal Veins, which convey the Chyle to the Heart, for Sanguification, or encrease of Blood.

BEATRICE. But, Sir, you won't begin the Anatomy before the Doctors come.

DOCTOR. Fetch it, I say.

BEATRICE. Well, Sir, since I must. *Exit.*

DOCTOR. He's not ill shap'd, nor is he very ill featur'd; and yet his visage retains much discontent and trouble. Well, still all the Rules of Metoposcopy and Physiognomy are false, if this was not a Rogue that very well deserv'd hanging. This Incision pleases me extremely; I'll open his Belly from the *Xiphoid Cartilage,* quite along to the *Os Pubis.* I feel his Heart pant yet: If any of my fellow Physicians were here now, especially those who doubt the Harveyan Doctrine, I'd let 'em plainly see the Circulation of the Blood thro the *Systole* and *Diastole.*

Enter SURGEON.

SURGEON. O Doctor! I am glad I have found you: My Lord is much worse since yesterday; you must visit him immediately.

DOCTOR. I'll come anon; I am very busie now.

SURGEON. My Lord's so very ill, you must go with all speed to him.

DOCTOR. Go you before I say, and let him blood, I'll be with him in an hour.

SURGEON. Sure Bleeding can't be proper in his circumstances.

DOCTOR. I say let him blood: Sure I know what I do.

SURGEON. His case is alter'd much, Sir, since you saw him.

DOCTOR. Once more, I say, go bleed him.

SURGEON. But Sir—

DOCTOR. Bleed him, I say: 'Tis fine indeed when Surgeons shall teach Physicians.

SURGEON. I will not Bleed him, I am sure it will be his death: Let who will do it for me; and so farewel. *Exit.*

DOCTOR. Farewel, Sir, if you won't, another shall.

Enter BEATRICE, who was listning.

BEATRICE. I have been looking all about Sir, and cannot find your Incision Knife: Besides, Sir, a fine Lady call'd at the door just now, in a great Gilt Coach, and charg'd me to send you to my Lord's immediately.

DOCTOR. Ha!

BEATRICE. In haste Sir, in all haste.

DOCTOR. Sayst thou—

BEATRICE. He's dying Sir, he's dying.

DOCTOR. What shou'd I go for then?

BEATRICE. You must go Sir, you shall go—you are sent for.

DOCTOR. The Devil's in the Wench— *(She turns him round.)*

BEATRICE. They are in haste, in haste Sir.

DOCTOR. Well I go then: Let the Body be carry'd into the Vault.

BEATRICE. It shall, Sir; but lose no more time: be gone. So, joy go with you. *(She turns him out.)*

CRISPIN. And I, without more words, will be gone presently.

BEATRICE. Whither in such haste?

CRISPIN. Whither, with a vengeance! Let me out I say: you must fetch the Incision Knife, with a pox t'ye, and all the other damnable Instruments, to rip me up alive, and make minc'd meat of me! A curse on his *Systol* and *Dyastole.*

BEATRICE. You are mistaken, Crispin: when I went out I did not go to fetch the Instruments, I went to hide 'em, where I was sure he cou'd never find 'em.

CRISPIN. I thought indeed, you could not have the heart to see a man who loves you as I do, so barbarously dismembred; and therefore I lay still.

BEATRICE. Well, stay here a while; I'll run and give Angelica the Letter, and return instantly.

CRISPIN. I beg your pardon, I'll stay no longer in this room.

BEATRICE. Why so?

CRISPIN. The very thought of that damn'd Incision Knife puts me into a cold sweat? I'll stay for you in the street.

BEATRICE. Away, you sot.

CRISPIN. I had rather be a Sot than an Anatomy, I will not have my Flesh scrap'd from my Bones. I will not be hung up for a Skeleton in Barber-Surgeons-Hall.

BEATRICE. Stay but a little.

CRISPIN. Yes in the street. There I shall not be in danger of your damn'd Amputation Knife, and your Dismembring Saw, with a pox to him.

BEATRICE. Alas! poor Crispin.

CRISPIN. Fear makes me think every thing I see an Instrument to rip me up, from the Systole to the Dyastole.

BEATRICE. He had a mind to be acquainted with your inside, Crispin.

CRISPIN. The Devil pick his Bones for't. I shall never recover my self till I get out of this cursed place. *(Knocking again.)* Ah! The Spirit's come again! Open the door, I'll rush out like a Lyon.

BEATRICE. Have a care, or you'll spoil all.

CRISPIN. If the Doctor catches me here, he will spoil all. Amputation and Incision will spoil all.

BEATRICE. Come, lay your self upon the Table quickly; he has no Instruments.

CRISPIN. Not I; for ought I know, he may have some about him, his Pockets may be fill'd with Knifes, Pins, Threads, Saws, and the Devil and all.

BEATRICE. Well thought on: Here hangs my Master's Gown and Cap, you shall strait put 'em on, and tell him you are a Physician, just come from the University, and understanding a dead Body was to be dissected by him, came to hear his Lecture.

CRISPIN. Where is the dead Body, fool?

BEATRICE. I'll tell him, 'tis carried into the Vault, as he commanded.

CRISPIN. Give me the Robes then: I'de rather act the Doctor than the dead Body. So, now I hope I need not fear his peeping into my *Os Pubis*, with a pox to him. *(Puts on the Gown.)*

BEATRICE. But if he should find out your ignorance!

CRISPIN. I'll venture that; the World bely's 'em, or there are many great Physicians, as great Fools as my self. I have good natural Parts, Beatrice, if they scape but Incision and Amputation.

BEATRICE. So; now I'le let him in.

Enter a Waiting Woman.

WOMAN. Is Mr Doctor within?

BEATRICE. No.

WOMAN. Why do you deny him to me? There he is.

CRISPIN. Well, what's your business with me, Mistress! Speak.

WOMAN. My Lady has lost her little Lap-dog, which she lov'd better than any Relation in the World. She lays the fault on me, and grieves and takes on as if 'twere her only Child. I fear she'll grow Distracted if we find it not. Now, Sir, knowing that you are not only a learned Physitian, but that you understand Astrology and the like—

CRISPIN. Ay, ay, I understand one, as well as the other.

WOMAN. Therefore, Sir, I bring you a Fee, and desire you to tell me some tidings of him.

CRISPIN. Have you brought the Dogs Water with you?

WOMAN. His Water? the Dog's lost, Sir.

CRISPIN. Lost—why—ay, what then?

BEATRICE. The Rascal stumbles confoundedly—You do not mind, Sir, the Dog is not sick, he is lost.

CRISPIN. Oho—lost how long since he was lost?

WOMAN. Two days ago.

CRISPIN. At what hour?

WOMAN. At eleven in the morning.

CRISPIN. What colour?

WOMAN. Black and White.

CRISPIN. Enough, enough.

WOMAN. Well, he's a rare Man, if he can tell me where to find the Dog.

BEATRICE. Never doubt him; he will do it certainly.

CRISPIN. You say 'tis two days since?

WOMAN. Yes, Sir.

CRISPIN. About eleven a clock?

WOMAN. Yes.

CRISPIN. Black and White?

WOMAN. Very right, Sir.

CRISPIN. Beatrice, what's in that Box there in your hand?

BEATRICE. Some Pills my Master gave me to lay up.

CRISPIN. O ho! Some Pills? Give me the Box.

BEATRICE. To what purpose?

CRISPIN. Hold your peace; here, take these Pills.

WOMAN. For what, an't please your Worship?

CRISPIN. Your Lady's Dog is lost.

WOMAN. Yes, Sir.

CRISPIN. And you would find him again?

WOMAN. With all my heart.

CRISPIN. Take these Pills then.

WOMAN. Will these Pills make me find the Dog again?

CRISPIN. Yes, they will make you find him; for they're of a very searching nature. There I was witty, Beatrice.

WOMAN. But, Sir—

CRISPIN. Go, do as I bid you.

WOMAN. Here are just five, Sir, must I take 'em all?

CRISPIN. Yes, all five, and all at once.

WOMAN. There is your Fee, Sir, if these Pills help us to the Dog again, you'll have my Lady, and the whole Family for your Patients: and so your Servant, Sir. *Exit.*

BEATRICE. Ha Crispin! Is not this better than being a dead Body. You no sooner Commenc'd Doctor, but you got a Doctor's Fee. *(She shuts the Door.)*

CRISPIN. Two new Crown-pieces; 'tis a brave Trade indeed: Here a man gets his Money easily.

BEATRICE. I could not chuse but smile to hear your ignorance O silly! The Dog's Water? And what would you have done, but for my Box of Pills? Give Pills to find a Dog? Ha, Ha!

CRISPIN. What would you have a man do, who can neither write nor read? Come let me disrobe my self; I'll wait for you in the street. *(Knocking.)*

BEATRICE. Hark, some body knocks again.

CRISPIN. O Lord! If this should be the Doctor?

BEATRICE. There's no remedy? You must brazen it out.

Enter SIMON.

SIMON. Is Mr Doctor within?

BEATRICE. What's your business?

SIMON. I'de speak with him.

BEATRICE. From whom?

SIMON. Why from my zelf.

BEATRICE. Why do you know him, friend?

SIMON. I come to ask him one Question, and you ask me a score.

BEATRICE. He's not at home to every Body; therefore I must know.

SIMON. Then I neither know him, nor he me. I pray is he at home to receive Money? I bring a Fee.

CRISPIN. Who are you Friend?

SIMON. Why they call me at our Town, Simon the infant; but my name is Simon Burly.

CRISPIN. Well, what's your business? quick.

SIMON. I am told you're an Astrologer, as well as Doctor.

CRISPIN. What then?

SIMON. Why then, I question you, an't please ye, whether Alice Draper, a young Maid in our Town, that I love, has that love for me again as she pretends to have. Because there is an arch Attorney's Clark, that is often in her Company, and I don't know—

CRISPIN. Hold, what kind of Woman is she?

SIMON. Why, she is a sprightly, cleaver, well built Wench, with a fine featly Face, brown Hair, ruddy com-Complection; a good crummy Lass, and treads well on her Pastons.

CRISPIN. Sprightly, proper, well built, featly Face, brown Hair, ruddy complection'd; a crummy Lass, and treads well on her Pastons.

SIMON. Ay marry does she.

CRISPIN. Here, take these Pills.

SIMON. Pills?

CRISPIN. Yes, take 'em.

SIMON. How, Pills?

CRISPIN. Yes of Pills. You must take the number Ten, because of your great Bulk.

SIMON. I have taken Pills to purge with-all; but Wounds can they—

CRISPIN. Go to I say; they'll purge the Head, and clear the understanding wonderfully. Ours is a Science you know nothing of.

BEATRICE. Tell him they are Cephalick Pills. *(BEATRICE whispers him.)*

CRISPIN. Ay, ay; These are Cephalick Pills. But that is Heathen *Greek* to you: If you understood *Latin*, I could talk to the purpose to ye.

SIMON. I am a piece of a Scollard I must tell you: *Intelligo, Domine, Linguam Latinam.*

CRISPIN. Poh, poh, I know that; but that's Out-Landish *Latin*. There's several sorts of *Latin*: There's Law-*Latin*, Priests *Latin*, and Doctor's-*Latin;* as for example: *Olo Purgatum, Physicum, Vomit—um—guts—out—um*—and so forth: Our *Latin* is quite another thing from School *Latin*.

SIMON. I think it may be so?

CRISPIN. Go, do as I bid ye.

SIMON. I had best give you your Fee first.

CRISPIN. I, I, that's well consider'd.

SIMON. Pills—

CRISPIN. Ay, Pills.

SIMON. Ten Pills.

CRISPIN. Just ten: Dispatch—away,

SIMON. If these should do the business—

CRISPIN. I understand you; I shall have more of your custom then; go, go, farewel—

SIMON. These knowing Men, your Lawyers, and Physitians, when they have once finger'd the Money, are so hasty to be rid of a man, they'll not give one word into the bargain: Good day to ye, Sir.

CRISPIN. The like to you, Friend. *(Exit SIMON.)* Two Crowns and a half a Guinea got already; this is a gainful and no painful Trade.

BEATRICE. Learned Mr Doctor, I must have snacks.

CRISPIN. And so thou shalt; there's my last Fee for thee, you cannot say but I dealt nobly by you.

BEATRICE. Thank you; this will buy Pins.

CRISPIN. Hark! *(Knocking.)*

BEATRICE. There's more Fees coming.

CRISPIN. My heart misgives me. Ah, what will become of me! it is the Devil himself.

Enter DOCTOR.

DOCTOR. Have you done every thing as I order'd, Beatrice?

BEATRICE. Yes, Sir, the Body's carried into the Vault. Just before you came in this Gentleman, some Doctor, I suppose of your acquaintance; I presume he intends to be present at your Anatomy Lecture.

DOCTOR. Sir, tho I have not the honour yet to know you, you are very welcome, Sir. I shall not begin my dissection till to morrow morning; then if you please to honour me with your presence, you may, perhaps, hear something that is curious, and out of the common Road.

CRISPIN. I have heard much, Sir, of your great Abilities, and shall not fail you; for your reputation, Mr Doctor, is a reputation—that—as I may say—or as—in fine, Sir, I will not fail to wait on you—

BEATRICE. Sir, if you please to retire out of this Room—

DOCTOR. By and by—I have not done with the Doctor yet. Pray, Sir, let me consult with you a little, about the case of a sick person, who is my Patient now.

CRISPIN. Do me the honour to excuse me now; I have business of mighty consequence, that requires my departure instantly,—but to morrow, Mr Doctor—

DOCTOR. Stay a little, I'le give you his Case in two words. You must know, my Patient, Sir, has labour'd many months first under a Tertian, then under a Quartan, and now 'tis turn'd to a Quotidian: The Fever we have pretty well abated, yet after all,—besides a great disposition he has to sleep, which very much fatigues him,—that which he spits from him, is very white—now, Sir, in my judgment that's an ill symptom, for a *Pituita alba aqua inter cutem supervenit*, says Hipocrates, and this you know well enough, the Greeks call *Leucophelgmateia*—so then according to Hipocrates, this white spitting, or *Pituita alba* is an evident sign, that the Hydropsie, or Dropsie will succeed. Now, Sir, what say you is the most soveraign Remedy to be given in this Case to hinder this evil consequence?

CRISPIN. Why, Sir, I must tell you—but to what purpose? you have no need of my opinion, you are a man famous for understanding—so that—and as it were—in fine, I will not speak one word more to this purpose.

DOCTOR. Pray, Sir, speak freely; I shall be proud to have your opinion of this case.

CRISPIN. No matter, Sir, for my opinion; for tho I know enough—and all that—yet I had rather—

DOCTOR. I act openly, Sir, I am not like some Physitians that I know, so fond of my own opinion, Sir, that rather than consult with other Doctors, they'll let a Patient dye under their hands; wherefore speak freely, I am prepar'd to give you my attention.

CRISPIN. Why then, Sir, in this sort of Malady, I do not know but that—or when—or as it may be very near this Case—or so, Sir—

DOCTOR. Humh—

CRISPIN. What think you of—a—dose of Pills?

DOCTOR. How! Pills, Sir? that would ruin all we have done.

CRISPIN. O you mistake me, Sir, I don't advise you, Sir, to give him Pills. I only mention'd, Sir, a dose of Pills which I had took my self this morning, Sir, which have not yet done working, and force me to leave you something abruptly, Sir.

DOCTOR. Pray let me know your Lodging e're you go. I shall be glad of the honour of your acquaintance—and—

CRISPIN. I am grip'd most damnably—

Enter WIFE, ANGELICA, *and* BEATRICE.

BEATRICE. Quickly, Madam, or he'll be discover'd.

WIFE. Enough—O Husband—Husband, come away, have a care—have a care—

DOCTOR. Of what Wife?—

WIFE. Turn that ill look'd fellow out of Doors—away with him—let him not speak a word.

CRISPIN. Madam—

WIFE. Away with him—

CRISPIN. Madam—Madam—

WIFE. Away with him, away with him, away with him—

CRISPIN. Madam—Madam—Madam—Madam—Madam

BEATRICE *and* ANGELICA *thrust out* CRISPIN. *He turning round is forced quite to the Door. Exit.*

WIFE. Ah, dear Husband, you must excuse me for intruding so hastily—

DOCTOR. What was the matter, Wife?

WIFE. Did you know this Gentleman.

DOCTOR. I suppose him to be some young Callow Doctor just wander'd from his Nest, the University.

WIFE. No, no, he's a High German Doctor—a Great Negromancer, a Conjurer, one that deals in the black Art, and raises Spirits—

DOCTOR. How do you know?—

WIFE. Some of our Neighbors that saw him come in at the back Door—came privately and told me so—and bid me have a care of him.—I was frighted almost out of my Wits—and shan't come to my self a good while—

DOCTOR. Oh Wife, fear nothing, 'tis but silly peoples talk.

WIFE. Indeed I am much frighted—

DOCTOR. Come, come, divert your self, and think no more on't.

WIFE. Ay, well thought on—Beatrice are the performers ready to go on with their Musical Entertainment?

BEATRICE. Yes, Madam, they stay but for your coming.

WIFE. Come then we'll go in; Husband you shall stay and sit with me—

Musick has a strange influence o're me, that will bring me to my self agen.

DOCTOR. I will Wife—   DOCTOR, WIFE, ANGELICA *exeunt.*

WIFE. Daughter, come you along with us.

Enter CRISPIN *peeping in.*

CRISPIN. Beatrice are they gone—

BEATRICE. What makes you here—I thought I had thrust you out of doors.

CRISPIN. You did so—but wondering what you all meant, I slipt in agen—to listen—

BEATRICE. It was my contrivance to bring you off, you Blockhead, you had been discovered else—

CRISPIN. This was better however, than Incision, Dissection, and Amputation. Therefore now I'le be gone in earnest, I fairly have escap'd all these disasters, And wou'd not run the Risque again. for twenty Masters.

BEATRICE. Faint hearted, Crispin! In spight of all ill luck in Love's His- 'tries, I'de venture Limb and Life to serve my Mistress.

Here comes in the third Musical Entertainment.

ACT III. SCENE 1.

Enter OLD GERALD.

I am resolv'd to bribe Beatrice, and make her of my party; she is a notable young witty Wench, and governs her young Mistress as she pleases; the Devil's in her if she's Money proof: I see her coming forth. *(Enter* BEATRICE.*)* Beatrice, Beatrice, a word with you.

BEATRICE. To me, Sir, do you speak?

OLD GERALD. Yes, yes, to you, my pretty, little, witty, smiling Rogue; hold up your head, here's Money for you; ha!

BEATRICE. Two pieces of Broad Gold? What is this for, Sir?

Wife: question mark after "Wife" removed to follow reading of 1722 edition.

OLD GERALD. One for thy good Will, and one for thy good Word.

BEATRICE. As how, Sir, I beseech you?

OLD GERALD. Promise me one thing, I will make 'em ten, make 'em ten presently; and if you succeed after- ward, a hundred.

BEATRICE. I marry, Sir, you speak now to the purpose?

OLD GERALD. You know I have ob- tain'd the Doctor's promise, to marry his Daughter, fair Angelica.

BEATRICE. You have, Sir.

OLD GERALD. Her Mother refuses her consent to it.

BEATRICE. She does so.

OLD GERALD. Now Child, if you could get for me the young Lady's consent—

BEATRICE. To marry, Sir?

OLD GERALD. Ay, ay, to marry her.

BEATRICE. Is that all? Come, Sir, she may look further, and fare worse—

OLD GERALD. That's well said; there's another piece for that.

BEATRICE. I thank you, Sir.

OLD GERALD. I know you rule her as you please.

BEATRICE. Some times she hearkens to me.

OLD GERALD. Now if you will com- mend me to her often—

BEATRICE. As how, Sir?

OLD GERALD. As thus. By telling her how rich I am, and that I love her so, I can deny her nothing. 'Tis true, I have a Son, an only Son, but him I have remov'd, on purpose to make way for her.

BEATRICE. That was wisely done, Sir.

OLD GERALD. Ay, was it not? Tell her all Happiness consists in wealth, that she may make me settle almost all I have on her, and the Children I shall have by her.

BEATRICE. And do you think you shall have Children by her?

OLD GERALD. Why not? I am hale, and very lusty, Beatrice. Well, if thou dost this for me, besides a hundred pounds I'le give thee on the day I Marry her, I'le get thee with Child too, give thee a good Portion, and Marry thee to an honest Shop-keeper.

BEATRICE. Fye, fye; you offer me too much in conscience, Sir; but for my young Mistress, Sir—

OLD GERALD. Ay; am I sure of thy assistance there?

BEATRICE. Yes, Sir, I'le do my weak endeavour for you; I'le begin presently; I'le set you forth with commendations, Sir.

OLD GERALD. How, how my pretty Rogue?

BEATRICE. Why thus, Sir—if I may be so bold as to advise you, Madam, take Mr Gerald, let him be your Husband—says she presently, which Mr Gerald meanest thou? O Madam, say I, the Father certainly; the Son's a young extravagant, idle fellow; his Father means to disinherit him, unless he mends his manners.

OLD GERALD. And so I do; that of my Son was well put in. Go on.

BEATRICE. O but he's old, she cries— true Madam, say I, but then he's rich too, very rich; when e're he dies, he'll leave you wealth enough to make you a Lady.

OLD GERALD. That she may be before, if she pleases me.

BEATRICE. I'le tell her so. But she may say, old men are cross and peevish—no, say I, he's mild, and humble, a fine, sweet temper'd Gentleman, he'll doat upon you, he'll never make you jealous, he will not run after other Women, as all young fellows do.

OLD GERALD. That was well thought on.

BEATRICE. O Madam, you know not what a fine thing it is to be an old Man's darling.

OLD GERALD. Good agen.

BEATRICE. Says she, his Teeth are naught—O but his Breath is sweet— his Eyes, says she, are sunk—O but,

say I, he sees without Spectacles— says she—he's an old musty fusty stinking—

OLD GERALD. Enough, enough. When shall I see her, Beatrice.

BEATRICE. This very afternoon, you cannot have a fitter opportunity, you know the Doctor, is much abroad, my old Mistress will be absent too. If you'll be walking about four a clock, near our back Door, I'le let you in privately into the Anatomy Room, there shall she meet you, Sir.

OLD GERALD. Hold up thy hand, I'le make the three broad pieces ten. There, will these incourage thee?

BEATRICE. You are a wise Client, Sir, you will not starve a good Cause, I see.

OLD GERALD. I scorn it, Beatrice.

BEATRICE. One thing I must advise you, Sir; be vigorous, press your suit home to her: for I must tell you, there's a young, debauch'd lew'd fellow, just such another as your own Son is, who haunts her every where, makes violent love to her, watches all opportunities to speak to her, is always making Presents, sending Letters to her: I'le watch him narrowly, I'le spoil his sport; I'le manage Mr Gerald's Cause so well, if I get not my young Mistress for him, I'le forfeit my Maidenhead.

OLD GERALD. Come hither; I must kiss thee; I will kiss thee, thau art a pretty, witty, merry Rogue, and I'le— provide for thee.

BEATRICE. Farewel, Sir, remember four a clock, if you brought some Jewels, with you, Necklaces, Rings, and Bracelets, only to shew her, Sir, young Girls, you know are mightily taken with such fine things.

OLD GERALD. I'le do't, my Girl; I'le do't. I'le home and pick out of my Cabinet the best of all my Pawns, and bring 'em to her. But first I'le be spruc'd up; I will be shav'd and wash'd, and perfum'd too; put on a clean Band, and my best Bob-wig, my new Hat, and put a clean Handerchief in my Pocket, and then—at four a clock—ay that's the hour. *Exit* OLD GERALD.

BEATRICE. Madam, come forth—he's gone. *(Enter* ANGELICA.*)* Now, Madam, let us laugh while our sides ake. What would this old, stinking, fumbling fool, do with a sweet young Wife? When once love gets into an old man's head, it teaches him as many tricks, as a dancing Dog.

ANGELICA. They say he's very covetous: How did you get that money out of him?

BEATRICE. I tickled the old Trout in the right place; see, Madam, here are the merry Spankers, I'le warrant you, I'le do his business for him.

ANGELICA. You have engag'd me, Beatrice; instruct me how I shall come off with hime.

BEATRICE. Trouble not your self about it, leave that to my management: I must go and find young Mr. Gerald out, and Crispin too, they must help to carry on the work. You shall have nothing to do, but to laugh at his folly, and applaud our contrivance.

ANGELICA. I'le in, and expect th' event. *Exeunt Severally.*

Enter YOUNG GERALD, *and* CRISPIN.

CRISPIN. Well, Sir, what think you now of my Adventures?

YOUNG GERALD. Why truly, they were extraordinary.

CRISPIN. A dead man—a Doctor—an Astrologer.

YOUNG GERALD. You made your way thro many difficulties, but for my sake, you must once more go to the Doctor's House.

CRISPIN. Who, I, Sir?

YOUNG GERALD. Yes.

CRISPIN. I beg your pardon. What to be dissected, carv'd artifically Limb after Limb. No, Sir, I'le have no more Dissection, Amputation, nor Incision. You may go, and venture your self, Sir, if you please.

YOUNG GERALD. Should I go, and be seen there by the Doctor, I ruine our design, and lose my Mistress; he'll tell my Father that I am in Town.

You run no hazard, for he knows not you.

CRISPIN. No hazard! call you it, I hazard my Legs, Arms, Veins, Arteries, and Muscles; and in the Doctor's gibberish, I hazard Incision, Dissection, Amputation, and Circulation, thro the Systole and Diastole. Why, Sir, in such a case, a Physitian cuts up a man with as little remorse, as a Hangman carves a Traytor.

YOUNG GERALD. For all that, you must venture your pretious self once more. When I get my Mistress, I'le make thee ample satisfaction.

CRISPIN. Well, if I must, I must. I saw a Physitians Gown and Cap, hang up at a Broakers Shop, hard by, to be sold. Buy 'em, or hire 'em for me: I had rather appear before him, in the shape of a Doctor, than a dead Man. That habit, Pills, and impudence brought me off then, I'le think of some other remedy now.

YOUNG GERALD. While I secure the Habit, step to my Father's and secure the Money.

CRISPIN. I will, but first, Sir, tell me what is *Latin,* for I am a Doctor.

YOUNG GERALD. *Medicus Sum.*

CRISPIN. *Medicus sum, Medicus sum.*

YOUNG GERALD. You have it right.

CRISPIN. Very well, *Medicus sum.* Go about your business, I'le about mine. *Medicus sum, Medicus sum.* *(Exit* YOUNG GERALD.*)* Well, 'tis a fine thing to understand *Latin;* I must be sure not to forget *Medicus sum.* Now I'le to the old man: Ho! talk of the Devil and his Horns appear.

Enter OLD GERALD, *and* MARTIN.

OLD GERALD. O Crispin! where's your Master? tell me true.

CRISPIN. Where should he be? at the University.

OLD GERALD. Ay, he should be at the University—but where is he, ha?

CRISPIN. I warrant in his Chamber, hard at study: or else in the Schools chopping Logick. Please you to give me the Money, Sir, that I may return to him with speed.

MARTIN. Give you the Money? ha, ha, ha.

CRISPIN. What do you sneer at? ha.

MARTIN. Money! who's the fool then?

CRISPIN. Meddle with your own business, Sirrah, or I'le give you a douce o' the chaps—

OLD GERALD. Be quiet, Knave.

CRISPIN. A Jack—an—Apes—to interrupt me—

OLD GERALD. Have done, I say— how does your Master spend his time there?

CRISPIN. He studies all the morning. After dinner studies again, after Supper, he walks out and talks with the Students, and then they jabber Latin like the Devil. The best on't Sir, they'll dispute and wrangle so long, till they are almost choak'd with hard words. Then they go very lovingly together, and drink a chirping Cup, or two, and then to their Chambers in good time.

OLD GERALD. 'Tis very well: But several of my acquaintance tell me, they have seen him here, here in this Town.

CRISPIN. O abominable!

OLD GERALD. Sirrah, confess the truth, is he in Town?

CRISPIN. Medicus sum—he is not here indeed, Sir.

MARTIN. He equivocates—here? No, he is not here.

OLD GERALD. But, Slave, he is in Town.

is in: "in" supplied from 1722 edition.

CRISPIN. No.

OLD GERALD. I lye then, do I?

CRISPIN. Medicus sum.

OLD GERALD. What's that you mutter, Rascal?

CRISPIN. A word I learn'd at the University. Medicus sum; that is, I am a Doctor.

MARTIN. Yes, of the lying faculty.

CRISPIN. Sirrah, if I had you in another place, I would—

MARTIN. What would you do?

CRISPIN. I would dissect you, Rascal, run my Fist thro your Systole, and Diastole.

OLD GERALD. What gibberish is this?

MARTIN. You Thin-Gut.

CRISPIN. Yes, impudence, If I had you under my clutches, I would make you feel Dissection, Incision, Amputation, ay and Circulation too.

MARTIN. Come and you dare, let's see what you can do.

OLD GERALD. Sawcy Knaves, forbear. (They offer to fight, OLD GERALD holds his Cane betwixt 'em.)

CRISPIN. Sirrah, I'le rip up your Belly, from the Cartilage Ziphode, to the Os pubis, you dog.

OLD GERALD. The fellow's mad— be quiet or I'le cudgel both of you. Well, Crispin, since your Master's not in Town, return you to the University, tell him, next week I'le send the Money to him by the Carrier.

CRISPIN. But, Sir—

OLD GERALD. One word more, and my Cane shall fly about your Ears.

CRISPIN. Well, I know what I know.

OLD GERALD. What do you know?

CRISPIN. That I'le be reveng'd of that audacious Villain.

OLD GERALD. For what you, Rascal?

CRISPIN. Pray, Sir, what will you beat me for?

OLD GERALD. For a lying Rogue.

CRISPIN. And I would maul him, because he's a Fac-totum, and sets you against my young Master and me.

OLD GERALD. Sirrah, Sirrah, I could find it in my heart—

CRISPIN. Ay, strike if you think good.

OLD GERALD. Say you so; there's for you then. (OLD GERALD strikes at CRISPIN he ducks: OLD GERALD misses his blow, and falls. CRISPIN *gives* MARTIN *a Cuff and a Trip, throws him down, and runs off saying,* Medicus sum.*)*

MARTIN. Son of a Whore, he has lam'd me.

OLD GERALD. Help me up, good Martin.

MARTIN. Oh! oh! I want help my self, Sir. The Rogue has broke my Crupper.

OLD GERALD. The Villain has rumbled my clean Band too.

MARTIN. If ever I light on him—

OLD GERALD. Be patient, Martin.

MARTIN. I must, whether I will or no.

OLD GERALD. Go home, Martin; I have business another way. *Exeunt.*

Enter YOUNG GERALD *and* CRISPIN. YOUNG GERALD *helping* CRISPIN *to put on his Gown.*

YOUNG GERALD. So, now your Worship's fitted.

CRISPIN. Then you met, Beatrice, Sir.

YOUNG GERALD. I did.; there's work enough cut out for you, rub up your memory, you'll have occasion to make use of all the Jargon you can think on.

CRISPIN. Those damn't heathenish names will never out of my memory.

YOUNG GERALD. I see my Father coming; he's running like a Wood-cock into the snare.

CRISPIN. I care not if he meet me now; I'le outface him. *Medicus sum, non sum Dogus, non sum Rogus, Medicus sum.*

YOUNG GERALD. Come this way, that I may inform you fully of our design; the time is short.

CRISPIN. Hold, Sir, degrade me not, the Gown must have precedency, and take the upper hand too. *Exeunt.*

Enter OLD GERALD.

OLD GERALD. This is the hour, 'tis just 4 by my Watch; if Beatrice prevails, I am made for ever.

Enter BEATRICE.

BEATRICE. O, Sir, are you come? I have been peeping for you at the Window, a whole half hour.

OLD GERALD. Is the Coast clear? Where's my Angelica.

BEATRICE. No questions, but come in. *Exeunt.*

Enter YOUNG GERALD, *and* CRISPIN.

YOUNG GERALD. So, so, he's caught, run to the fore dore, when you hear me Thunder at this—

CRISPIN. I'le beat an alarm at that— I have my cue. *Exit.*

Enter OLD GERALD, *and* BEATRICE.

BEATRICE. I chose this Room on purpose for your meeting. Here are two doors you see; if my Master or Mistress come to one, I can slip you out at the other.

OLD GERALD. 'Twas wisely done.

BEATRICE. I see her coming; make good use of your time.

OLD GERALD. I warrant you. I have brought something to shew her, will sparkle like her Eyes.

Enter ANGELICA. *The Door claps after her.*

ANGELICA. O Beatrice What shall we do? The Door unluckily is lock'd, the Key is on the other side too.

BEATRICE. That's the mischief of all Spring Locks: There's no remedy now. Look here, Madam, here's Mr Gerald come to kiss your hands.

OLD GERALD. With your favour, Madam—*(Salutes her.)*

ANGELICA. I vow I am asham'd to see you, Sir.

OLD GERALD. Young Maids, I know are bashful; but when you are married, a loving Husband will teach you confidence.

ANGELICA. O Beatrice! if my Mother should find me here—

BEATRICE. Fear nothing, Madam; this door is fast; I'le lock the fore dore presently.

ANGELICA. Well, Mr Gerald, you see my Maid has prevail'd with me: She gives you great commendations too.

OLD GERALD. Ay, my sweet; I'le make 'em all good, I warrant you.

ANGELICA. I am young, and some say I am handsom too; I doubt not you'll love me: But, Mr Gerald, what reason is there for me to love a man in years, as you are?

OLD GERALD. I have many reasons for your Ear, more for your Eyes. Look here, my Queen, look here, my Cleopatra? Here's a Necklace of Pearl worth above 500 pounds; it will become that soft white Neck most rarely. Then here's a set of Bodkins for your hair, cost fourscore pounds: Ah how they sparkle like your pretty Eyes: Then here's a Croceat of Diamonds cost 300, an Ambrosie, worth above 400 more. How like an Angel you will look, when this is set under those white panting Bubbies!

ANGELICA. Indeed they're very fine, and very large.

OLD GERALD. Here are two Diamond Rings, one with 3 Stones besides the Sparks; and this has 5, one cost 50 pounds, the other above fourscore. Then here are Diamond Bracelets for your Arms. But here, my Jewel, here's the rarety, the Phoenix of 'em all. This Ring here with one Stone, 'tis a Diamond of the old first Water. I have refus'd, my Child, above four hundred. pounds for this one single stone.

ANGELICA. 'Tis beautiful indeed!

BEATRICE. Did not I tell you, Madam—

OLD GERALD. And then for Plate, old, and new fashion'd too, plain, gilt, and wrought; I have a Cedar Chest full. full.

BEATRICE. What young man could make you such fine Presents?

OLD GERALD. All, all shall be yours, my little Mouse, my Pigeon.

ANGELICA. O Heaven! some body knocks.

BEATRICE. I'le peep thro the Keyhole: O Madam, 'tis my Master and my Mistress.

OLD GERALD. Let me out at this door quickly.

BEATRICE. Ah, the Key's broke in the Lock! undone, undone for ever.

ANGELICA. I am ruin'd if my Mother finds me here.

BEATRICE. Ah, Madam, What will become of me.

ANGELICA. For Heaven's sake hide your self, do Mr Gerald, I'le love you dearly for it.

OLD GERALD. How? Where? I'le do any thing my dear will have me.

BEATRICE. Here's the Coffin the dead body was sent in from the Gallows, you may hide your self in that.

ANGELICA. Ay do, Mr Gerald, do.

OLD GERALD. How! Coffin me before I am dead, I beg your pardon; I can't endure the thought on't.

BEATRICE. Then strip your self to your Wastcoat, and your Drawers, and lye at your length, here on this Table, I'le tell my Master you're the dead body, sent in to be dissected.

ANGELICA. Quickly, Mr Gerald; if you love me deny me not. (Knocking all this while.)

OLD GERALD. Come then, I'le do any thing my Dear Commands me.

ANGELICA. Hark how they knock; I fear they'll break the door down. (Within. Ho! Beatrice, Beatrice.)

BEATRICE. Make haste, or we're undone. (They strip him.) (Within. Open the door! Why Beatrice, where are you?)

BEATRICE. So, so; what e're they say or do, be sure you stir not for your life.

OLD GERALD. Where will you hide my Cloaths?

BEATRICE. Here, here, I'le put them and my young Mistress into the Coffin. (Knock again.) I am coming presently.

OLD GERALD. So, so; I am as dead as a Herring.

BEATRICE. What ever happens, Sir, be not afraid. Come in.

Enter CRISPIN *like a Doctor.* YOUNG
GERALD *disguis'd like his man.*

I thought I heard my Master and my
Mistress.

CRISPIN. They come here presently;
but where, where be the dead Carcass
for dissection?

BEATRICE. Here, Sir.

CRISPIN. Ver—good—Mr Doctor, send
me to begin de *manuel operation* upon
de exterior, an den he will come hear
me read upon *de interior*—

BEATRICE. Are you the *German* Doctor, that was here this morning with
my Master?

CRISPIN. Yes, de-ver-same, me am
de *German* Doctor, *de Medicine, de
Physitien, de Operateur, de Anatomist,
de Chymist, de*—

BEATRICE. Very well, Sir, have you
any service for me?

CRISPIN. Stay one little time. Dis
be de Body, let me make de observation of the Visage—here be de ver ill
aspect—dis was one person of fair
Speech, but de fals Heart; covetous,
designing, letcherous; a Robber, a
Thief, a Cut-throat—Sacrament, hanging was too good for him, a Rogue,
a Villain—ah vat pleasure will dis be
to make de Dissection, de Incision,
and de Amputation, upon dis Body,
and rip open his Belly from de Cartilage Ziphode, quite along his Os-pubis.
Ah! vat be dis? his Heart pant still—
dis was the stubborn old Thief, was
but Mr Doctor here, just a now, I
would shew him de Circulation of de
Blood, thro de Systole, and Diastole.
Come I'le begin de Dissection while
de body be warm.

BEATRICE. What before my Master
comes?

CRISPIN. Yes indeed, dis be only de
Manuel Operation, me vil read de
Lecture ven he be here: vare be my
man, vare be de Instruments?

YOUNG GERALD. Here, Sir, here.

BEATRICE. Bless me! what's that
great Knife for?

CRISPIN. Dis be to cut de Troat,
from Jugular to Jugular; as thus.

BEATRICE. Hold Sir, I beseech you.
Fear nothing, Mr Gerald *(aside).*

CRISPIN. You shall see presently.

BEATRICE. 'Tis just like one of our
Butchers Knives: and then what is that
Ax for?

CRISPIN. Dis be de decolation Ax,
to cut off de head at one Chop; as
thus—

BEATRICE. Not yet Sir: What's that
there like a Wimble?

CRISPIN. Dat be to bore a hole in
de Scull; when any part of de Scull
be broke, and depress'd upon de
Brain, with dis we bore hole hard by
de fracture, as you shall see just-a-
now.

BEATRICE. No Sir, not now; I'll see't
anon.

CRISPIN. Den we put in de proper
Instrument, and raise de depressure up
to de proper place, and so make de
cure.

BEATRICE. But what is this terrible
Saw for?

CRISPIN. Dat be de dismembring Saw,
to Saw off de Leg, or de Arm: You
see me presentale Saw off de Bone of
dis Leg, and—

BEATRICE. Stay Sir; What's that
sharp crooked Knife for?

CRISPIN. Dis be de Amputation Knife,
to cut off de Leg or de Hand, just-a
in de Joynt. Ha! where be de Leg
and de Arm?—*(*CRISPIN *draws one
Leg from the other, and one Arm from
his Body, and* OLD GERALD *draws
'em close to him again.)* De Devil!
me lay one Arm here, and one Leg
here, to Saw off just in de middle,
and cut off just in de Joynt, for de
fine experiment; and de Arm, and de
Leg, be gone home to de Body.

Enter two Men.

1 MAN. Mr Doctor we come for the
Coffin we brought the dead Body in.

CRISPIN. Dere be de Coffin; be gone,
and give me no interruption; now I
open all de Breast. *(*CRISPIN *tears
open his Wastcoat.)* So, now with dis
Instrument, dis *(The men carry off the*

Coffin.) Knife, I will in one moment cut de Breast-bone, from de Ribs, and lay all open, dat you shall see how de Heart, de Lungs, de Liver, lie in dair place proper, and order natural. O de Devil, agen! de Body shrink! de Leg move; and de Arm too: vat strange Carcass have you in his Country?

BEATRICE. Oh! Sir, I have seen whole Bodies, after they have lain here a day or two, get up, and run away.

OLD GERALD. And so will I! I'll not stay to be butcher'd here. *(He leaps off the Table.)*

CRISPIN & BEATRICE. Ah, ah, ah.

OLD GERALD. Lose my Cloaths, my Life, and Jewels all at once!—Your Servant, Mr Doctor.

CRISPIN. Stop Thief, stop Thief. *(As OLD GERALD is running out, and CRISPIN after him, the DOCTOR and his WIFE enter. OLD GERALD runs against the DOCTOR, beats the DOCTOR and his WIFE down, and Exit.)*

DOCTOR. O murder, murder!

WIFE. Ay, murder, murder!

Enter SIMON, and Waiting Woman.

SIMON. Wounds! Where's this Dog of a Doctor? I'le knock the old Cheat's Brains out.

WOMAN. And if I can reach him, I'le claw his Eyes out.

DOCTOR. O I am bruis'd all over.

WIFE. And I am lam'd too.

WOMAN. O are you there?

SIMON. Wounds, Doctor, you have scour'd my Guts out, with a murrain to ye—

WOMAN. And I can hardly draw my Legs after me, for your Physick. But I'le clay you for't.

WIFE. Hold, Mistress, or I shall pluck a Crow with you.

DOCTOR. Be patient Wife—you are both mad. I never saw either of you before.

SIMON. O damn'd lying Doctor! did you not give me Pills? and I gave you a whole half Guinea?

WOMAN. And had not I some of your Rot-gut Pills too, and gave you 2 new Crown-pieces?

DOCTOR. You rave both, and must be sent to Bedlam.

SIMON. 'Sbud I'le have my money again—

WOMAN. And so will I,—or tear his Eyes out—

CRISPIN. Hold friends! pray moderate your angers, and don't affront a person of our faculty.

SIMON. Ah, ha! I was mistaken, this is the Doctor —

WOMAN. I this is he gave us the Pills. I beg your pardon, Sir.

CRISPIN. Beatrice, you must refund.

BEATRICE. There—

CRISPIN. Look you friends, 'twas a mistake. There's your Half Guinea, and your Crown-pieces too.

SIMON. O pox! this is something. *(Exeunt SIMON and Woman.)*

DOCTOR. What is the meaning of all this?

WIFE. Beatrice, what is the matter here?

DOCTOR. What strange out-cry was that we heard?

WIFE. I, and who threw us down?

DOCTOR. And what strange thing was that ran over us?

BEATRICE. Why, Sir, as I was shewing Mr Doctor here the dead Body that was sent you from the Gallows, he felt his pulse, and laying his hand upon his Breast, he found his Heart panted; then he took his Incision Knife, and before he could touch his naked skin, up started the dead Body, and ran away, just as you saw—

CRISPIN. All this is true, Sir, as I am a Member of the learned Faculty.

DOCTOR. I am amaz'd!

WIFE. Nay Husband, I have heard of such strange things: I warrant the poor man was hang'd wrongfully.

Enter OLD GERALD hastily.

OLD GERALD. O undone! undone!

WIFE & BEATRICE. Ah, ah, ah!

WIFE. He's come again, Husband, ha!

DOCTOR. In the name of goodness! What art thou?

OLD GERALD. Undone I say, undone.

DOCTOR. Art thou a Spirit? or Flesh and Blood? answer.

OLD GERALD. Give me my Cloaths, my jewels, Huswife—

BEATRICE. Avant, avant!

OLD GERALD. Where are they? Gipsy, speak.

BEATRICE. In the Coffin, in the Coffin.

OLD GERALD. I overtook the Coffin, and there's none of 'em. Where are they, and the Jilt too your young Mistress?

DOCTOR. Sure 'tis our Neighbour, Mr Gerald.

OLD GERALD. I am the same.

WIFE. You tell me wonders, Crispin.

CRISPIN. Step to your Daughter's Chamber, Madam; there the Riddle will easily be unfolded. *Exit* WIFE.

DOCTOR. What is the matter, Sir? why in this posture? and why this out-cry too?

OLD GERALD. That Baggage there, and the young Witch your Daughter, have contriv'd to abuse and cheat me, of two thousand pounds worth of Jewels, that were pawnd to me.

DOCTOR. Here they come then, who must give you satisfaction.

Enter WIFE *and* YOUNG GERALD, *leading in* ANGELICA, *dress'd in the Jewels.*

OLD GERALD. How! my Son here!

YOUNG GERALD. Yes, Sir, and my Wife.

WIFE. I found 'em shut up together in my Daughter's Chamber.

DOCTOR. Married say you.

YOUNG GERALD. Yes, Sir, contracted long since; and now confirm'd in private, as far as modesty would permit.

OLD GERALD. And Married too! then all is at an end.

YOUNG GERALD. Here are your Cloaths, Sir, Doctor Crispin can tell you how I came by 'em.

DOCTOR. Crispin!

OLD GERALD. My Rogue.

CRISPIN. *Non Rogus; Medicus sum;* that is, I am a German, or a Polish Doctor.

YOUNG GERALD. The Jewels, Sir, so well become my Wife, I think you cannot in conscience demand 'em back.

ANGELICA. They were his own free gift; he scorns to take what he has given me.

WIFE. Well, I am glad the Son has married my Daughter, and wish Joy to you both.

DOCTOR. Bless you together. Come Brother Gerald, 'tis your Son's Wedding Night; you must forgive 'em and be sociable: Let me prevail with you to give order for a good Supper, and we shall be very merry, Brother.

OLD GERALD. I had as good, I shall be laught at else. Sirrah, here has been fine practice, and my Son's marriage was your contrivance.

CRISPIN. I do confess it, Sir, and glory in the success.

DOCTOR. Come then, sit down, and listen to the Musick, and after Supper we'll hear at large the adventures of Doctor Crispin in this Affair.

CRISPIN. Beatrice and I will tell you the whole Story,
And as we snack'd the Fees, we'll share the Glory.

The Fourth and last Musical Entertainment. After that, the Curtain falls.

FINIS.

Entertainment: The text of Motteux' *Mars and Venus* scenes has been omitted.

H O B:

OR, THE

COUNTRY WAKE.

A

FRACE.

As it is Acted at the

THEATRE-ROYAL in *Drury-Lane*,

By His MAJESTY's Servants.

By Mr. DOGGET.

The Second Edition.

LONDON:

Printed: by D. Brown, near Fleet-street. 1715.
(Price Two Pence,)

Hob

Author

In spite of persistent efforts to connect *Hob: or The Country Wake* with the much more famous name of Colley Cibber, there would seem to be no sound reason for taking it away from Thomas Doggett, whose name stands on the title page and whose claim to the longer play from which it was directly taken has never been disputed.[1] Doggett was a native of Ireland but of such obscure origins that nothing is known of the exact place or date of his birth. He is said to have begun his career in Dublin but with so little success that he took to the road with a strolling troupe. Joseph Knight's statement in the *DNB* that he first appeared in London at Bartholomew Fair in a droll named *Fryar Bacon, or the Country Justice* has an authentic look but is unfortunately undocumented.[2] Our first records of his theatrical life come from his appearance in the early 1690's at Drury Lane, where he played a number of low comedy parts in plays by D'Urfey, Congreve, and others then writing for the United Company. His most famous role he created on a most famous occasion. He was the

---

[1]The most recent expression of an opinion is that of R. H. Barker, who, in his *Mr Cibber of Drury Lane* (New York, 1939), p. 266, still claims the play for Cibber and refuses to accept Genest's quite sound arguments against such an ascription. Barker thinks Chetwood, apparently the first to list it under the laureate, "too good an authority to be set aside on *a priori* grounds." While it would perhaps be uncharitable to go all the way with Isaac Reed in his sweeping condemnation of Chetwood in the introduction to the *Biographia Dramatica* (1782), we find it impossible to accept the entry Barker refers to. Chetwood simply sets down *The Country Wake*—no date, no statement to indicate that he refers to *Hob* rather than the earlier play—to round out the list of Cibber's plays at two dozen. Fifteen years later D. E. Baker followed Chetwood's lead and listed the farce under Cibber in *The Companion to the Play-House* (1764). His detailed account, which even confuses the stages of adaptation, has evidently carried so much weight that in spite of Genest the ascription to Cibber is still widely accepted.

[2]Summers, in the Addenda to his *Bibliography of Restoration Drama* lists under Doggett's name an undated droll called *Mad Tom of Bedlam* and what appears to be a playbill for *Fryar Bacon*, 1691. He does not give his sources. Ned Ward in his *London Spy* tells of seeing this droll at Bartholomew Fair in 1699. He does not mention Doggett by name, but his reference to him in the part of Ralph in the droll leaves no doubt who is meant.

original Ben in *Love for Love* on the memorable evening in 1695
when the seceders opened their new house in Lincoln's Inn Fields.
But Doggett was himself an inveterate seceder and shifted about during the next decade or so between the two theaters and between London and the provinces. Cibber tells us one of his very best stories
about Doggett's successful defiance of authority in 1697, when he
had run off to Norwich.[3] Miss Rosenfeld's account[4] of his activities
in that city lends a good bit of support to Colley's account, which
otherwise might be suspect. In fact, Doggett always found it difficult
to remain at ease in any circumstances, and the whole period from
his return to Lincoln's Inn Fields in 1701 to his death in 1721 is
checkered with quarrels and litigation and occasional withdrawals
from one theatre or the other. Again Cibber's account of how Doggett proved difficult as a co-manager at Drury Lane can be accepted
in the main, for we have any amount of supporting evidence for
such events as the storm caused by Booth's accession to a share in
the management. Doggett continued to act, somewhat intermittently,
up to 1717, but the last four years of his life he spent in retirement,
something he at least could well afford to do as he was always a man
of thrifty habits. We have some very fine tributes to his ability in
comic parts from Downes, Cibber, and others. He was also notable
for his staunch Whiggishness—witness his establishing of an annual
prize for oarsmen to celebrate the anniversary of George's accession—
and for a sturdy independence of character which proved sometimes
hard to distinguish from mere obstinacy.

Source

The source of Doggett's farce is his own play called *The Country
Wake* (1696). In the absence of any discovered source for that play
we must accept it as his own invention.[5] It is not at all a well con-
trived play, the best scenes in it being just those which survive in the

---

[3] *Apology* (ed. R. W. Lowe), II, 21–22.

[4] *Strolling Players*, pp. 43–46.

[5] Gildon admired Doggett's play, "nor do I know of any remarkable Thefts
from other Plays, unless the imitation of Shakespeare's Clowns, in the Character
of Hob, which I look on as a praise to Mr. Doggett, and no Fault." *Lives and
Characters*. Another principal character, that of Flora, may very well have been
patterned after the vivacious girl in Rhodes' highly popular *Flora's Vagaries*.

farce.[6] The Friendly-Flora intrigue is handled even less adroitly than in the one-act version. The affair between Woodvil and Lady Testy is far more natural, though depending on an excessive use of disguise and darkness, and so downright bawdy that it is difficult to sympathize with Doggett when, in his dedication of the play, he seems genuinely hurt by the charge that his play is a lewd one. The character of Lucia, introduced as a companion to her cousin Flora, wanders about rather aimlessly until she can be handed over to Woodvil at the end of the play. Of the scenes involving Hob there are two which were not used in the farce, one a "crowner's quest" scene in which Hob presides and a drunkard supposed dead serves as the center of attraction.[7] Doggett pretty certainly had the gravediggers' solemn but ludicrous debate over Ophelia's suicide in mind when he wrote this passage, though the very effective ending, when Hob stalks off at the end of the procession as chief mourner and therefore the eligible heir to the drunkard's clothing, is Doggett's own invention. The other scene, one in which Hob supposes he is dying from Sir Thomas's blows and takes sad leave of his parents and friends, is not so effective. The amusing scene of Hob's sousing in the well is a farcical addition not to be found in the earlier play.[8]

Stage History

In No. 189 of the *Spectator* there appeared an advertisement reading:

By His Majesty's Company of Comedians, at the Theatre Royal in Drury-Lane this present Saturday, being the 6th of October, will be presented a Comedy call'd the Chances. . . . To which will be added a Farce of one Act only, call'd the Country Wake, (revis'd with Alterations.) The Part of Hob by Mr. Dogget, Sir Tho. Testy by Mr. Bullock, Freindly by Mr. Pack, Flora by Mrs. Santlow, and all the other Parts to best Advantage.

---

[6]Genest on the contrary thought the original play superior to the pieces taken from it. He especially admired the Woodvil-Lady Testy scenes but out of modesty refrained from quoting from them. III, 352.

[7]Both the discarded scenes involving Hob and the main Woodvil-Lady Testy scenes were used in a farce by John Leigh called *Hob's Wedding*, Lincoln's Inn Fields, January, 1720, which was in turn made into a ballad opera called *A Sequel to the Opera of Flora*, "by the Author of *Flora*," Lincoln's Inn Fields, March, 1732. Neither of these concoctions of left-overs had any success.

[8]There is good reason to suppose that Doggett may have borrowed this scene from a piece called *She Ventures and He Wins*, produced at Lincoln's Inn Fields in the same season in which *The Country Wake* first appeared. In this play Squire Wouldbe, played by Doggett, is almost drowned in a cistern.

In its original form Doggett's play had been well received according to a contemporary witness,[9] but now as a one-act afterpiece it became even more popular. Between 1711 and the appearance in 1729 of the ballad opera version, of which we shall speak in a moment, there were over one hundred and thirty performances at the two regular London theatres according to our records. Outside of these theatres the account is, as usual, more obscure, but we have records of five performances in the provinces[10] and Scotland[11] and at least one record for Southwark Fair.[12] In addition to these there were performances of some parts of the play by Tony Aston, Doggett's old strolling companion.[13] After the opening of Rich's theatre in the 1714–15 season, *Hob* enjoyed about equal popularity at both theatres for about ten years and might conceivably have continued to hold its own for several decades more in its one-act form had it not been for the great vogue of pantomimes, especially at Lincoln's Inn Fields. In fact, after 1724 it had been passed up altogether at the latter theatre in favor of these new entertainments, which were forcing most of the farces with dialogue into the background.

The eventual rescue of Doggett's piece was due to that remarkable find of John Rich's, *The Beggar's Opera*. After the record-breaking run of Gay's piece in the spring of 1728 had set the fashion, the English theatre went ballad-opera mad. Numerous fresh pieces with airs set to familiar tunes appeared, but even more old ones were revived, furnished with songs, and rushed onto the stage before the fad could end. Among these latter was Doggett's farce. Someone in

---

[9]Gildon, *Lives and Characters*.

[10]Miss Rosenfeld gives the title for the farce four times, but the circumstances of the last entry make us suspicious that the ballad-opera is meant. She quotes a news-account of Rich's taking the piece down to entertain the royal family, but the date is for the summer of 1729, when *Flora* had been running in London since April. Surely Rich would not dare to present royalty with old-fashioned material when the town had the newest for its delectation. In her entry for *Hob in the Well* on p. 219, we cannot be sure who is at fault, but since the date is 1728, the farce must have been intended.

[11]Logan, p. 4.

[12]*Daily Post*, September 25, 1723.

[13]Tony was advertising his "Medley," consisting of various scenes from older plays, in the newspapers late in the fall of 1723. Among these was "the Humours of Hob in the *Country Wake*." The "Medley" was to be played in various taverns with especially quaint names, such as the Dog, the Three Tuns, the Bull-Head. *Daily Post*, November 1, December 13, 23.

Rich's company, presumably one of the leading low comedians, John Hippisley, reworked *Hob,* making some not very significant changes in the dialogue[14] and providing twenty-five new songs. In this new form Doggett's play, now called *Flora or Hob in the Well,* began life anew on April 17, 1729, and soon established itself as one of the half dozen favorite afterpieces in the English-speaking theatre. To give a brief abstract of sample records, it was performed twenty times by the end of the first summer, in spite of its appearing so late in the season. During the next five seasons it averaged better than thirty performances in London, even though Drury Lane apparently did not adopt the ballad-opera version within this period.[15] After that the London records fall off until there are only scattered performances, with an occasional burst of popularity, as shown by the twenty-two performances in the 1746–47 season, for example. Though Genest continues to give occasional records, even as late as June 18, 1823, the popularity of the farce in London had been pretty well dissipated by the end of the century.

In the provinces and especially in this country, *Flora* was also very successful. Miss Rosenfeld has ten entries of the ballad opera, some of these representing certainly more than one performance, and Genest gives performances at Bath and Liverpool, 1774 and 1775. Miss Stockwell provides a record for June 23, 1729, to show us how quickly the musical version caught on in Dublin; however, its subsequent history in Ireland is almost completely blank,[16] as usual. We have some five performances for Edinburgh,[17] where there is little more light in the recesses of theatrical history than in Dublin. The fortunes of *Flora* in America are better known and more impressive, for over here it began early and held its own very well.

---

[14]Hippisley, if he was the adapter, worked with both versions of Doggett's play before him. He retained the exact plot and virtually everything else from *Hob* but restored a number of sentences from the earlier play.

[15]Bills for Drury Lane as late as 1731 give the old form of the title, indicating that the farce without songs was still running there. The first bill with *Flora* as the title is for September 28, 1734.

[16]From Kemble's transcript of bills from the *Dublin Journal* in the Harvard Theatre Collection we learn of a performance on June 12, 1734; Genest gives one for Cork, September 14, 1764. X, 481.

[17]Dibdin gives two performances for 1734, one for 1754, pp. 44, 75; Logan gives two performances for 1758, pp. 22–23.

On February 18 [1735] "The Opera of Flora, or Hob in the Well," with the dance of the two Pierrots and the Pantomime of "Harlequin and Scaramouch" was an announcement of great American import, for it heralded to the country for the first time a musical play upon its shores.[18]

This performance was in Charleston, where there were a half dozen more by the end of the century. There were twice as many in New York, almost that many in Philadelphia, and single performances— or available records at least—for Annapolis, Baltimore, and Boston.[19] The last American performance that we have noticed was also in Charleston, taking place on March 5, 1806.[20]

Publication

The version printed here, the one-act farce without songs, saw just two editions, both of them appearing in 1715, four years after Doggett had made his alteration. The ballad-opera version went through ten times as many editions. In addition to these the songs from the opera appeared separately. The narrative verse rendering forty years after the opera first appeared hardly counts as an edition but serves to demonstrate the continued interest of the public in the story.[21]

Hob: or, The Country Wake. As it is Acted at the Theatre-Royal in Drury-Lane, By His Majesty's Servants. By Mr. Dogget. London: Printed for A. Bettesworth . . . and E. Curll . . . 1715.

Hob: or, the Country Wake . . . The Second Edition. London: Printed by D. Brown . . . 1715.[22]

Flora; an Opera. As it is now Acting at the Theatre Royal in Lincoln's-Inn-Fields. Being the Farce of the *Country-Wake,* alter'd after the Manner of the *Beggar's Opera.* Written by a Gentleman . . . London: Printed for T. Wood . . . 1729.

Flora . . . To which is Added, the Musick Engrav'd on Copperplates. Written by a Gentleman. London: Printed for T. Wood . . . 1729.

Flora . . . To which is Added, the Musick . . . The Second Edition. . . . London: Printed for T. Wood . . . 1729.

---

[18]Willis, p. 14.

[19]Seilhamer, *et al.*

[20]W. S. Hoole, *The Ante-Bellum Charleston Theatre* (1946), p. 71.

[21]*Hob in the Well: or, the Guardian Outwitted.* A Poem, Humorous and Moral. London: Printed for H. Roberts . . . and S. Gamidge . . . 1769.

[22]*Biographia Dramatica* (1782) gives an edition of *Hob* for 1720, but this is certainly an error for 1715.

Flora . . . The Third Edition . . . 1729.

Flora . . . The Fourth Edition . . . London: A. Bettesworth, 1731.

Flora . . . The Fourth Edition, Corrected . . . London: G. Weld, 1732.

Songs in the Opera of Flora . . . London: Sold by T. Cooper . . . and by Geo. Bickham . . . 1737.

Flora; or, Hob in the Well. An Opera. As it is now acting at the Theatre Royal in Drury Lane . . . By Mr. Hippisley . . . The Sixth Edition. London: Printed for W. Feales . . . 1748.

Flora . . . Dublin: Printed for George Faulkner, 1749.

Flora . . . Glasgow: Printed for William Duncan Junior, 1755.

Flora . . . The Seventh Edition. London: Printed for T. Lowndes, 1768.[23]

Flora . . . In Vol. V, 77–109, *The Dramatic Works of Colley Cibber, Esq.* . . . London: Printed for J. Rivington, *et al.*, 1777.[24]

Flora . . . London: Printed for Harrison . . . [1780].

Flora . . . In Vol. IV, 301–28, *Bell's Supplement*, London, 1784.

Flora . . . London, Printed for T. Sabine, 1787.

Flora . . . In Vol. IV, 301–28, *A Collection of the Most Esteemed Farces* . . . 1792.

Flora . . . Compressed by Mr. Hippisley into Two Acts . . . In Vol. II, *Parsons' Minor Theatre*, London, 1794.[25]

Flora . . . In Vol. V, 333–66, Inchbald's *A Collection of Farces*, London: Longman, *et al.*, 1809.

Flora . . . In Vol. V, 333–66, *A Collection of Farces and Other Afterpieces* . . . Selected by Mrs. Inchbald . . . London: Printed for Longman, *et al.*, 1815.

Analysis

In *Hob* we have a farce which differs from several of the others in this collection in that it owes little or nothing to foreign borrowing.

---

[23]This edition is listed in Grove's *Dictionary* under the composer William Bates, who is said to have composed, besides some glees, "Also 'Flora: or Hob in the Well,' ballad opera, 1768."

[24]It will be noted that this is the first time an edition has been ascribed to Cibber; previous editions of his works did not contain *Flora*. Baker had assigned the piece to Cibber thirteen years earlier, Chetwood nearly thirty years earlier.

[25]Here is a result, thirty years later, of Baker's confused account. It would be more accurate to say that Flora had been *expanded* to two acts, since *Hob* (1715) rather than *The Country Wake* (1696) formed the basis of the operatic version.

The character who gives both life and unity to the play, and the title as well,[26] is a sturdy native clown somewhat reminiscent of English drama of a century earlier, as Gildon was quick enough to perceive. His brothers are Bottom and Dogberry, rather than Harlequin and Mascarille.

In reworking the materials in his earlier play Doggett showed considerable judgment. The weakest element in *The Country Wake* had been the plot, which he very clearly did not know how to handle skillfully or was not sufficiently interested in. When he made his farce from the longer piece, he threw away most of the love intrigue, keeping enough merely to make the play hang together, and concentrated upon the scenes with Hob. The result is that the Friendly-Flora plot is almost negligible, the conflict being resolved in a twinkling at the proper time, and without the clumsily handled prison scene.

The scenes involving Hob, on the other hand, now dominate the whole piece. And these consist chiefly of noise and fun. In the first slight episode, in which Hob agrees to carry the letter, nothing happens, but we have a chance to get acquainted with our hero. His broad dialect, his fear of the dark and the law and Sir Thomas are matched by his independence: "Why, that's my Humour now; if I say I'll do't, I'll do't." And he would if Sir Thomas's vigilance were not so great and his own wits not so decidedly inferior to his resolution. The scene of detection shows how slow witted Hob really is. Where the Italian-French servant would have been prepared with witty answers Hob can only stammer, and protest that he wants no reward: "Not one Farthing, Sir, Sir: Mr. Friendly order'd me to the contrary." And so the scene ends in a noisy beating with the clown threatening Sir Thomas with the law—a truly English retort! The well scene, which had not been in Doggett's play originally, is the same kind of noisy slapstick, Hob taking a double sousing for good measure when his mother takes fright. The most direct borrowing from Shakespeare, the inquest scene, Doggett chose to omit from his one-act version, but he retained most of the fun of the ale-selling and cudgelling scenes, which show Hob off to the very best advantage. The rustic dancers in this scene doubtless added to the fun.

---

[26]It is interesting to note that in the advertisement in the *Spectator*, 1711, Doggett had not bothered to change the name of his play. By 1715, when he came to publish it, the title had inevitably become *Hob*.

The final bit in the play is a delightful one, bringing us for a moment into intimate touch with the theatre. Sir Thomas's refusal to be reconciled might seem to have demanded heroics, but the dramatic spell is quickly broken when Dick—obviously a character designed for Jubilee Dicky Norris—steps forward with: "Won't you? Why then, Mr. Pack give out the Play, and Mr. Newman let down the Curtain."

DRAMATIS PERSONAE.
MEN.

Sir Thomas Testy, Uncle and Guardian to Flora.
Friendly, a Gentleman in Love with Flora.
Dick, An impudent Fellow, his Man.
Hob. A simple Country Fellow.
Old Hob, his Father.
Three Servants to Sir Thomas.
Two Country-Men.

Mr. *Bullock, Senior.*
Mr. *Pack.*
Mr. *Norris.*
Mr. *Dogget.*
Mr. *Leigh.*

WOMEN.

Flora, Niece to Sir Thomas, in love with Friendly.
Betty, Her Maid and Confident.
Hob's Mother.

Mrs. *Santlow.*
Mrs. *Saunders.*
Mr. *Willis.*

THE COUNTRY WAKE

SCENE [1.] *A Chamber.*

Enter FLORA *and* BETTY.

FLORA. Betty!

BETTY. Madam.

FLORA. This is a strange Life I lead, Betty.

BETTY. Life's a sad thing any where Madam, to Lovers that are uncoupled.

FLORA. Wer't thou ever in love, Betty?

BETTY. O! most cruelly, Madam.

FLORA. And how do you find your self now?

BETTY. As most Folks do Madam, after the Loss of an old Lover.

FLORA. How's that?

BETTY. Ready for a new one.

FLORA. Ay, but my Mind's so set upon Mr. Friendly, that all Mankind else are no more than my own Sex to me.

BETTY. Then you must have him, Madam.

FLORA. Ay, but how to come at him, Betty?

BETTY. Run a Risque.

FLORA. Run a Risque: What's that?

BETTY. Run away with him.

FLORA. How is that [possible]? when my uncle locks me up as if I were his only Bottle of Brandy.

BETTY. But there are Ways to convey letters to him, for him to prepare the Means for your Escape.

FLORA. I dare not employ any one: I fear you are all in my Uncle's [Interest].

BETTY. If you please, Madam, try your humble Servant, for I pity you with all my Heart, and therefore swear my self wholly devoted to assist you, in freeing you from your old Tyrannical Uncle.

FLORA. Well then, Swear.

BETTY. By all my Hopes and Perquisites; By your Scarves that grow out of Fashion as soon as brought; By your Laced Shoes too beg, and those too little; By all your Heads, Hoods, and Furbelows; and that your last new Atlas may never be worn again, I Swear.

FLORA. That you will inviolably assist me in running away with Mr. Friendly.

BETTY. I Swear.

FLORA. Then I will trust thee: And, when I am married, every Article of thy Oath shall be perform'd. Here's a Letter I had just now writ to Mr. Friendly, wherein I have told him, if he will be ready with a Ladder, at the Garden Wall, about Twelve a Clock, I'll toss over my Band-box, venture

Note: The corrections in the dialogue indicated by brackets are taken from the first edition in the Huntington Library.

catching cold in the Dew, and seek my Fortune with him.

BETTY. Give me the Letter; theres Mettle in the Proposal: He shall have it in a Quarter of an Hour, tho' I carry it my self.

FLORA. But, dear Betty, take care, for I have no Mortal to trust, but thee.

BETTY. Nor no Mortal fitter to be trusted.   *Exit running.*

FLORA. So, now my Heart's at ease, I will have this Friendly, tho' my Uncle were as wise as a Bishop, and the Garden Wall as high as a Church-Steeple. Ah! *(Going to run off, starts and shrieks.)*

Enter SIR THOMAS TESTY.

SIR THOMAS. Why, how now, how now, Mrs Irreverence? Am I such a Hobgoblin that you start at the Sight of me?

FLORA. No, Sir; but when you come upon a Body unawares.

SIR THOMAS. Unawares! What, then I suppriz'd you, did I? Your Thoughts were full of Matters in Question, which, I suppose, that close Committee of the Flesh and the Devil, you're resolv'd shall be the Fundamental of your Constitution?

FLORA. Lard, Uncle, how you talk to one!

SIR THOMAS. Talk to you, you Malapert you! Why, who am I? Whom am I, Huzzy?

FLORA. Why, [you] are my Uncle by Relation, my Guardian by my Will, and my Jailour against it.

SIR THOMAS. Why then, as long as you are my Prisoner, how dare you take this [Liberty]?

FLORA. Because Liberty is the sweetest thing a Prisoner can take.

SIR THOMAS. Dare you own this to my Face?

FLORA. I think, in short, you ought to let me marry since I have a mind to't.

SIR THOMAS. Amazing! Go you out of my Sight: The Devil has harden'd

you, Huzzy. To your Chamber go, a dark room and Water-gruel. Discipline and Watergruel. Ye Gods! I wou'd not have you seen abroad in this Condition for—O Lud! Lud!

FLORA. Come, Sir, I see you have a mind to drive me to a hard Bargain; I'll tell you a Proposal shall fairly come up to the most you can make of me.

SIR THOMAS. What new Whim hast thou got in thy Head?

FLORA. Why, Sir, you know that I have Eight Thousand Pounds to my Fortune, and that, by my Father's Will, you are to have the sole Disposal of it till I am either marry'd, or of Age. For my Maintenance, which said Maintenance, by a modest Computation, may stand you in about some—Let me see— (for I have had no Cloaths but my Mother's) and about Seven or Eight Pounds a Year. Now, Sir, if you'll give me leave to marry the Man I have a mind to, I'll procure that he shall give his Consent for your throwing my fortune into the Publick fund, the Moment you throw me into his Arms; so that you shall have the Use of my Pence till I am of Age, as a Praemium for advancing to him the Use of my Person.

SIR THOMAS *(Aside).* Hum! the Girl begins to talk sensibly: But 'tis not yet Time to understand her. —Hark'ee, Child, when you can persuade your Lover to make good, under Hand and Seal, what you have promis'd, then I shall think you are equally mad for another; Till then, I shall advise you to your Chamber; from whence I shall allow you the lovely Prospect of the Garden. Go, Shu, Shu.

FLORA. You may chance to fret for this, my very wise Uncle.

SIR THOMAS. Shu, Shu, Shu, Shu.   *Exeunt.*

SCENE 2. *The Country.*

Enter FRIENDLY, *and* DICK *his Man.*

FRIENDLY. What a watchful old Rogue's this?

DICK. A very Dragon, Sir.

FRIENDLY. To use a young Creature so unkindly.

DICK. So unnaturally, Sir! To force her to the Extremity of [stradling] over a great Wall at Night, when he ought to lend her his Hand to bring her out of his great Gates to your Worship's Coach at Noon-Day; but the Rascal has no Breeding.

FRIENDLY. By Mercury, I'll be even with him.

DICK. Faith, Sir, you have Reason for it tho' I say it.—

FRIENDLY. That shou'd not say it.

DICK. She is a most lovely Piece of Temptation.

FRIENDLY. Hold your Peace, Sirrah; What's a Clock?

DICK. Why, Sir, by the Moon's Rising, it shou'd be about—about—past Ten.

FRIENDLY. Why, then, Sir, about—about—past Twelve.

DICK. You'll have one of her Blue Silk Stockings stradling over the Wall.

FRIENDLY. But where's this Fellow you engag'd should carry my Letter?

DICK. Who Hob, Sir, Here he comes; and if any Body suspects him for a Pimp, I have no Skill in the Science.

Enter Young HOB.

FRIENDLY. So, honest Hob; Canst thou carry this Letter for me to Sir Thomas Testy's, and bring me an Answer?

HOB. Yes, Sir, Yes.

FRIENDLY. And deliver it to Madam Flora.

HOB. Yes, Sir, Yes.

FRIENDLY. But, be sure, let no Body see you deliver it.

HOB. Noa, Noa, Sir: But must it be carry'd to Night, 'tis main dark!

FRIENDLY. To Night, Ay, Ay, immediately, Man.

HOB. Wou'dn't the Morning do as well, Sir? 'Tis main dark—I had rather carry it in the Morning, if I cou'd.

FRIENDLY. Prithee, why, honest Hob?

HOB. Why, you know, one of our Neighbours, being in a dispareing Condition, has gone and hang'd himself at the lower end of Sir Thomas's Orchard.

FRIENDLY. What then you are afraid?

HOB. No, not I, Sir, thank Mercy; I defie the Devil and all his Works.

FRIENDLY. Why don't you go then?

HOB. But you must know, Sir, that to Morrow the Crowner's Quest doth sit upon 'en; whereof, d'ye zee I am to be one. Now who knows but he may have something upon his Spirits to disburthen to me.

FRIENDLY. Well, if thou art not afraid; prithee make haste with my Letter.

HOB. Tho I must tell you,—I fear it will make a bad Day for some Body.—

FRIENDLY *(aside)*. Lord, Lord, how this Fellow tortures me!

HOB. For if Sir Thomas had kept his Fences whole, the Man had never gone into his Ground to have hang'd himself.

FRIENDLY. Pox on thee, prithee get thee gone.

HOB. Why, that's my Humour now; if I say I'll do't, I'll do't: Pray, Sir, be pleas'd to read the Subscription.
Exeunt.

Enter SIR THOMAS *and his ·Servants.*

SIR THOMAS. 'Twill be a hard matter to sink any of the [Principal]; so that if the Girl would engage her Lover to make good the Proposals, under Hand and Seal[,] I did not care how soon she was kiss'd black in the Face; 'till then, I'll put on a smoother look to the Girl, and show her a little of the Country Diversion from the Mount in the Garden: Rascals, look out sharp there, for this is the usual Hour that all your soft sighing Coxcombs come a Catterwauling.

SERVANT. Sir, Sir, here is some Body coming down the Field with a Light.

SIR THOMAS. Stand by and observe.

[Enter Young HOB *with a Lanthorn and Candel.]*

HOB. So this is the House. Now if this au'd Fox, Sir Thomas, shoald spy me, he'd maul me for zartain; but if he spy me, he shall have more Eyes than Two, I can tell 'en that: But now let's zee how I shall go about to do this same business; *(feeling in his Pockets,)* Ay, this is he; let me zee; vor, vor, Madam Flora. *(*SIR THOMAS *snatches the Letter out of his Hand.)*

SIR THOMAS. Where are you going with this Letter Sirrah.

HOB. Letter, Sir!

SIR THOMAS. Letter Sir! Ay, Letter, Sir; where were you carrying of it?

HOB. I dan't know where I was carrying of it.

SIR THOMAS. Who did you bring it from?

HOB. I dan't know who I brought it from.

SIR THOMAS. Where had you it, Sirrah?

HOB. I dan't know where I had it, not I.

SIR THOMAS. How came you by it?

HOB. I—, I found it in my Pocket.

SIR THOMAS. Found it in your Pocket! What did [it] grow there? What Business have you here at this Time o' Night?

HOB. I dan't know what I do here, not I; I'll go home; I wish your Worship good Night.

SIR THOMAS. No, No, I'll reward you before you go.

HOB. Not one [Farthing], Sir, Sir; Mr. Friendly order'd me to the contrary, [pray don't] you offer it.

SIR THOMAS. Yes, something I will give you. *(Beats him.)*

HOB. O Lud! O Lud! Here's fine doings: Fore-gad I'll take the Law an ye, an there be any Law in all the King's Kingdom.

SIR THOMAS. I'll Law you, I will; What are you their Letter-Carrier?

(Beats him again.) Lay hold of him whilst I read the Letter. *(A Servant holds the Lanthorn up.)*

Madam, The Proposals you mention in Case of Extremity will certainly do; but 'twould be a much pleasanter Piece of Justice to bite him for his Barbarity. *(Son of a Whore, he means me to be sure.)* The Ladder and all things shall be ready exactly at Twelve. *(Oons! What do I here?)* If you have any thing of Moment, this Fellow is honest, and will convey it safe to your eternal Lover,

TOM. FRIENDLY.

A very honest Fellow, truly; pray desire that honest Gentleman to walk down into the Bottom of that Well there.

HOB. O Lud! O Lud! I can't do it [as] I hope to be saved.

SIR THOMAS. Try, Try, in with him.

HOB. O Lud! O Lud! *(They throw* HOB *into the Well then Exeunt.)*

SCENE 3.   *A Chamber.*

Enter FLORA.

FLORA. Well, I'll swear this Love is a strange thing[,] my Heart flutters about like a Bird in a Cage.

Enter BETTY *running.*

BETTY. Undone! Undone! Madam.

FLORA. What's the Matter?

BETTY. Why your Uncle has intercepted Mr. Friendly's Answer to your Letter, and in his Passion has thrown the poor Fellow that brought it into the great Well.

FLORA. Let me [die, but] I thought 'twould come to this: It vexes me to the Heart.

BETTY. Don't vex your self, Madam, for John tells me 'tis a Thousand to One but [the Fellow] drownded.

FLORA. Psha, wou'd my Uncle were drown'd in his room.

BETTY. No, but he'll be hang'd.

FLORA. Do you really think so?

BETTY. Yes.

FLORA. Why then I'll marry in spight of his Teeth.

BETTY. Right, Madam; while he's in one Noose, you may slip into the other.

FLORA. Well, dear Betty, go see how 'tis [with] the poor Fellow; and if things go, as you know how,—ask when the Assizes begin.

SCENE 4. *The Well.*

Enter OLD HOB *and his* WIFE.

OLD HOB. Come Wife never troble thy Head; he will go a Roguing sometimes; he'll come home again I warrant 'en.

WIFE. I think in my Heart, 'tis no matter whether he does or no; a base Rogue to be out of the way at zuch a busie Time as thick. The Zun has been up this Hour and Quarter; and I warrant you he has not been in Bed. Prithee Husband, step and zee if he has not ben't a zotting at the Park gate, and I'll draw the Water in the mean time.

OLD HOB. Well, do ye, do ye then. *Exit.*

WIFE. The Boy's the Plague of my Life. I think 'twere more than time the Gammon were boil'd by now[;] the Volk will be come to the Wake before it be cold, and then it wo'n not be vit to be eaten.—A Jackanapes— when I bait 'en, and bait 'en, and pray'd 'en to stay, and he wou'd go, he wou'd go. *(Goes to draw Water at the Well, and sings.)*
Did you not hear of a Spanish Lady, How she woo'd an English Man?
Lud! Lud! 'tis main heavy. *(Sings again. When she had almost heav'd the Basket to the Top,* HOB *cries out.)*
O, the Devil! the Devil! a Ghost! *(Falls down in a Fright.)*

Enter OLD HOB.

OLD HOB. Hey Day! Is the Woman in her Tantr[am]s, trow?

WIFE. O! a Ghost! H[o]b's Ghost in the Bottom of the Well.

OLD HOB. Let me zee; if the Devil be in the Well I'll vetch 'em out again,

I warrant you that. I think the Devil *(Goes to the Well and heaves up.)* be in the Bucket. Hawd a bit, hawd a bit: now I have got 'en up half way, I'd vain know what zort of a Devil he be; for Ecod, if he ben't [ci]vil, I'll zous 'en, zop 'en to the Bottom again.

HOB *(in the Bucket).* Hawd fast Vather, 'tis I, 'tis I.

WIFE. There, there 'tis, again now.

OLD HOB. Hawd your peace, hawd your peace; the Devil can't put in a word for you, I think: who's there, Hob?

HOB. Ay, Ay; 'tis I, 'tis I; hawd vast Vather, hawd vast.

OLD HOB. Lends a Hand Mary, lends a Hand. *(She runs to the Well and helps him up.)*

HOB. O Lud! O Lud!

OLD HOB. O poor Hob! How cam'st thou there Boy?

HOB. Ask me no Questions, I am a Dead Man. 'Tis Sir Thomas has done this; but an there be Law in all the King's Kingdom, I'll have it next Hize prizee an it cost me Vorty Shillings.

WIFE. O poor Hob! I'll make thee a few Zugar-zops [to] comfort thy poor Bowels. Ah poor Boy! *Exeunt.*

Enter SIR THOMAS TESTY, *with* RALPH *his Man.*

SIR THOMAS. Ralph!

RALPH. Sir.

SIR THOMAS. Has any Body taken care of the poor Fellow that fell into the Well?

RALPH. No, Zir; you said he should stay there till your Worship was pleas'd to call for him.

SIR THOMAS. Why, you Rogue, you have not gone and drownded the poor Fellow, have you?

RALPH. Hawd ye, hawd ye, I drown 'en, 'twas you bad me; and if any Mischance come on't, you mun answer it: S'flesh! What have I to do with it?

SIR THOMAS. Why, you Rogue, wou'd you father your Villanies upon me?

Did not I see you lay violent Hands upon him? And an't I a Witness against you?

RALPH. Lud! Lud! Why, at this Rate one had better be a Gally slave than a Servant; for if one does not doe what one's bid, why one's Head's broke; and if one does, one's to be hang'd for't. But one Comfort is, the Gallows will hold Two.

SIR THOMAS. Keep your own [C]ounsel, Sirrah, and I'll try what I can do to save you.

RALPH. Nay, Sir, do for that as you zee cause; for let it go thick way, or that way, 'tis all a Case to me go which way it will—; one good Turn requires another.

SIR THOMAS. Hold your Peace, you Rogue you; —This surly Rascal is not to be frightned I find. (Aside.)

Enter a Servant.

SERVANT. Sir, here's a Letter for you.

SIR THOMAS. Who brought it?

SERVANT. Mr. Friendly's Man, Sir[.]

SIR THOMAS (Opens it and reads). "Sir, the Proposals your Neice mentioned to you, concerning her Liberty, if they concur with your desire, I am willing to ratify, whenever you'll do me Honour of a Meeting. Your's

TOM FRIENDLY.

Hum! 'Tis not yet Time to understand him. This Meeting may be to meet with my Neice, for ought I know: And that I do not understand him, shall be my Answer. Bid the Fellow stay till I have writ.

SERVANT. Yes, Sir.   *Exeunt.*

SCENE 5. *The Country.*

Enter OLD HOB and his WIFE, with a Table, a Stool, and Sign.

WIFE. Come Husband, now the Boy has gotten on his dry Cloaths, let 'en be stirring a little, wu't.

OLD HOB. Ay, Ay, there's nothing but the Zign to be put up, and then all's ready. (Puts up the Sign.) Zo,

he that wou'd drink good Ale, let 'en come [to] the Zign of the Pot-lid. Hob! Hob!

HOB (within). What zay you, Vather?

OLD HOB. Tap the Ale Boy Wu't?

HOB (within). Ay, Ay, Vather.

SCENE 6. *A Garden Wall.*

Enter SIR THOMAS TESTY, FLORA, and BETTY, as looking over the Wall. Enter several Country People.

SIR THOMAS. Well, Neice, if you have a mind to see the Country Sports, you may see them as well from hence, as below in the Crowd.

FLORA. I like it very well, Sir?

Enter FRIENDLY, like a Ballad-Singer, w[i]th his Man DICK.

DICK. Sir, I can't think what you propose by this.

FRIENDLY. Why, that Flora will know me by my Voice, and that her Wit will be consequently at work to come at me.

DICK. But of what Use can I be to you, Sir, for I can sing no more than I can dance.

FRIENDLY. What then you will serve to draw other gaping Fools about me.

DICK. O! there's something in that truly.

FRIENDLY. Well, *Ho this same is call'd*, &c. (The Original Song was, The Dragon of Wantly; but London is a fine Town, &c. is now most us'd.)

SIR THOMAS. Come, Neice, we shall have a Merry Ballad.

FLORA. A Ballad! Bless my Eyes! Betty, Is not that Friendly?

BETTY. The very same, Madam; but hush. (Here FRIENDLY sings a Song. After the Song he speaks to DICK.)

FRIENDLY. Do you think she knows me, Dick.

DICK. Know you; yes, Sir, I sold her a couple of your Ballads, and she gave me a Nod, as much as to say, Don't go till you hear from me.

FRIENDLY. Well, sit down, and call for a Mug of Ale, I'll but step and put on my Cloak, and be with you in an instant. *Exit.*

DICK. House! House! *(beating on the Table.)* What are you all dead here? House!

Enter FRIENDLY *and* HOB.

HOB. Good Morrow good Master Friendly. How d'ye do; How d'ye do Zir?

FRIENDLY. Thank thee honest Hob.

HOB. I should know this honest Gentleman too; Mr. Richard, I take it.

DICK. Ay. How dost do, honest Hob?

HOB. Thank you heartily, good Mr. Richard. Come, dear Zir, zit down a bit, and drink one Pot before [you] go.

FRIENDLY. Prithee let's sit down, or this Fellow's Impertinence will make us be observ'd. But Hob[,] what dost thou do with an Apron on, Man?

HOB. Why Zir, Vather will do as Neighbours does, and all the Volks in the Town zell Ale o' Vairday; but we zell zeveral other zorts of Liquors, and Wine too.

FRIENDLY. Wine!

HOB. Ay, all zort[s] of Wine.

FRIENDLY. Well, prithee let's have a Bottle of Claret then.

HOB. Claret, Zir! we have no Claret, 'tis against the Law to zell Claret; but you may have some Red Port, or White Port, or zuch zort of Stuff.

FRIENDLY. Well, prithee now, bring us such Stuff as thou hast then.

HOB. Yes Zir. *(Going.)* What think you of a little Zack, with zome Zugar, is main good.

FRIENDLY. Well, prithee bring such as thou lovest thy self; for I am sure it will please no Palate but thy own.

HOB. Yes Zir, Yes. *Exit.*

DICK. Sir, I can't perceive any great Product this Project of your's is like to bring.

FRIENDLY. No, nor I neither; for that old Dragon watches the Golden Fruit so carefully, that I almost despair. But I'll not quit the Place, for Fortune may do something for me unexpected.

Enter Young HOB, *with two Mugs of Beer, and a Trencher.*

HOB. Come Mr. Friendly, bite a bit, and I'll put a little Zugar in the Ale, and make it as good as I can.

FRIENDLY. Ay, but Hob[,] where's the Sack?

HOB. Zack!—I thought you said you loved Ale best. I confess that's much wholesomer for our English Stomachs. Come Zir[,] against you are dispos'd.

FRIENDLY. This Fellow's kindness will poison us.

DICK. Not at his rate of Tasting.

HOB. 'tis main good.

FRIENDLY. Prithee drink off this and fetch us two more.

HOB. Yes Zir, Yes. Ch'am coming, Ch'am coming. *Exit.*

SIR THOMAS. Come my merry Country-men, every Man take his Lass, and let's have a Dance; and then we'll have the Cudgels out.

COUNTRYMEN. Ay, an please your Worship, we are all ready. Come, strike up, *Scratch. (A Dance here.)*

In the midst of the Dance, enter HOB *with Beer.*

HOB. Ay marry, Well said Ralph; set too Joan; *(just at the End of the Dance.)* you are all out, you are all out.

COUNTRYMEN. How so, how so Hob?

HOB. Dick should have led up Moll, and Ralph shou'd have gone Back to Back with Joan; Joan should have turned round and Belly to Belly with Roger, and come into her own Place again, and so all had been right.

COUNTRYMEN. Well, we'll begin again.

OLD HOB *(within).* Hob! Hob!

HOB. Ch'am coming, Ch'am coming. *(As soon as they have began to dance again, enter* OLD HOB, *and pushes Young* HOB *almost down.)*

OLD HOB. Sirrah, why dan't you come in a Doors.

HOB. I wun't, so I wun't[;] What do you strike me vor?

OLD HOB. Yonders your poor Mother within a scawring and a scawring till she sweats again, and no-body to draw one Drop of Beer, Sirrah.

HOB. I dan't care, so I dan't.

OLD HOB. Sirrah, come you in, and dan't stand dancing here.

HOB. I wun't draw a Drop more, if you go to that and I'll dance and dance again, if that vexes you. *Dal de rol. (Sings and dances.)*

OLD HOB. O! thou art a wicked Boy; Mercy on me for [begetting] thee. Sirrah, come you in[,] do you.

HOB. I wun't—*Dal de rol. (Sings and dances.)*

Ent[e]r a [C]ountry-man, with Cudgels.

COUNTRYMAN. An like your Worship, here be the Cudgels, Wou'd you please to have us begin?

SIR THOMAS. Ay, Come here's a half-a-Crown for the first Somersetshire Man that breaks a Head; and he that breaks that Rogue Hob's Head, shall have another. Roger, fetch the Hat and Favour.

HOB. Shall he? Ecod he shall earn his Money, be he who he wull, I can tell 'en that; and here d'ye zee, I take up the v[i]rst Cudgel, let the best Man here take up t'other an he dare. I vight for Glocestershire, I dan't care who knows it.

SIR THOMAS. What will no body take him up? Neighbour Puzzlepate, do you take up t'other Cudg[el].

PUZZLEPATE. Not I, an like your Worship; I have had enough on 'en already, for he broke my Head but last Week.

SIR THOMAS. Roger[,] do you take it up, and thrash him; thrash him soundly, d'ye hear.

ROGER. I can't promise that, an like your Worship; I'll do the best I can;

I'll break his Head, an I can, in Love; and if he breaks mine, much good may do him.

HOB. Ecod, I'll zous thy Zomerset Cod for thee.

ROGER. I dan't much fear thee, Hob. *(HOB pulls off his Coat.)*

FRIENDLY. Dick, encourage Hob; if he shou'd chance to get the better, the old Testy Knight may be prov[o]k'd to come down; and then I may hope for something. Here, Hob, here's an Angel for thee, and if thou br[e]ak'st his Head, I'll give thee another.

HOB. Thank you, Zir.

DICK. Now, Hob, now for Glocestershire.

HOB. Come, come on. *(Here they take two or three Hits at Back-Sword; and at the End of the Hit, HOB breaks his Head.)*

OMNES. Fair, fair, fair.

SIR THOMAS. Foul[,] foul. *(HOB runs about the Stage with the Hat and Favour on his Head.)*

FRIENDLY. Hob, take care of your self, the Knight's coming down.

HOB. Ecod, let 'em come; I shall take no other than St. George's Guard for 'en, Ecod. An he meddle with me, I'll take 'en o'er the Sconce, an he were a Knight of Gould.

SIR THOMAS *(comes down).* Who says 'was fair? I say ['twas] foul.

HOB. I say 'twas vair.

SIR THOMAS. So is that and that. *(HOB and SIR THOMAS fight. HOB brakes his Head. SIR THOMAS draws his Sword. HOB runs.)*

OMNES. Well done, Hob.

SIR THOMAS. You Dogs, I'll be with you presently, ye Scoundrels.
Exit after HOB.

(FRIENDLY goes to the Garden Wall to FLORA.)

FRIENDLY. Now, dear Creature, if you wou'd free your self from eternal Bondage, fly into the Arms of Liberty. *(To DICK.)* Scout, scout, you Dog you.
Exit DICK.

FLORA. What wou'd you have me do?

FRIENDLY. Madam, the Door is open, and no Mortal to oppose your Flight.

FLORA. I am in a thous[a]nd Fears, least my Uncle should return.

BETTY. This is downright provoking, Sir, since you see there's no hopes of my Lady: If you can but settle the least Tip of your Heart upon your humble Servant, I'll be over in an instant.

FLORA. Hold, hold, rather than you shou'd break your Neck, I will venture; *(Comes out.)* —Well, and whether will you carry me now?

FRIENDLY. To a Doctor, my Dear, that shall cure thee of all thy Fears for ever.

FLORA. Ay; but what if he shou'd not be at home?

BETTY. What shou'd I do for something to be afraid of?   *Exeunt.*

Enter SIR THOMAS TESTY

SIR THOMAS. These Rustick Rogues, I have met with some of their S[c]ulls; I have notch'd their Noddles for 'em.— Ha! Me Garden-door's open! My Mind misgives me consumedly. Neice! Betty. Neice! Lost, gone, not to be found!

Enter DICK.

DICK. So here he is, and I must stop him: dear Sir, what's the Matter with you?

SIR THOMAS. Oons, Sir, what's that to you?

DICK. I am afraid your Brain is somewhat discompos'd, Sir.

SIR THOMAS. Stand you o[u]t of my way, or I'll run my Sw[o]rd into your Guts.

DICK. An 'twou'd be but a friendly Part of me to take care of you.

SIR THOMAS. You Rascal you, stand out of the Way, or I'll [cut] you over the Face.

DICK *(Presents a Pistol in one Hand, and Sword in t'other).* Will you? Nay then make your T[h]rust. Come Sir, come on; Why don't you come on?

SIR THOMAS. Oons, Sir, Who are you?

DICK. I am a Philosopher, Sir, and this small Pop is my Argu[ment].

SIR THOMAS. I [rather] b[e]lieve you to be a Highway-man, and that small Pop there your Livelihood.

DICK. You may be as scurrilous as you please, provided you pass not this way.

SIR THOMAS. Why what Business have you to hinder me.

DICK. Because I have no other Business at present, but to hinder you.

SIR THOMAS. 'Sblood, Sir, How come it to be your Business?

DICK. Because 'tis my Business to do my Master's Business and I have some modest Reasons to believe he and the Priest are now doing your Neice's Business.

SIR THOMAS. O the Devil! What do I here? Undone! Undone! Where are they, Sirrah?

DICK. Compose your self, Sir; they are here.

Enter FRIENDLY, FLORA, BETTY.

FRIENDLY. Your Blessing, Sir.

DICK. Does not this show ab[un]dance of good Nature now, to you, who are but his bare Uncle. Come, Sir, don't be as obstinate as an old Father at the latter end of a Comedy; you see the main Action is over; you had as good be reconcil'd.

SIR THOMAS. Zoons, Sir, I can't be reconcil'd, nor I won't be reconcil'd.

DICK. Won't you? Why then, Mr. Pack give out the Play, and Mr. Newman let down the Curtain.

NOTES

There was evidently a good deal of careless typesetting in the second edition of this play: punctuation marks were often turned, spaced incorrectly, or even dropped out, and occasionally a letter or word was omitted. These printer's errors have been rectified in the present text from the readings of the first edition.

Page 137. *Spanish Lady:* from "The Spanish Lady's Love," composed shortly after the affair at Cadiz in June, 1603, and printed in one of Deloney's *Garlands,* a printing of which was issued as late as 1709. The first edition of *Hob* contains two more lines of the song. It may be found in the *Roxburghe Ballads,* VI, 655.

Hize prizee: a corruption of the law term *nisi prius;* this form is cited from Somerset in Wright's *English Dialect Dictionary.*

Page 140. *Zomerset:* a considerable distinction between the use of dialect in *Hob* and the older *Country Wake* can be noticed at once. In the 1696 text Hob says only "Ch'am coming" and a few other dialect expressions. In the 1715 version the author gave Hob and his parents a heavy dialect, with a great many of the forms characteristic of the Somersetshire and Gloucestershire areas. Almost every initial *s* and *f* are voiced, and the word *thick* ("this") characteristic of this region is used. At first sight, then, it would seem that the author had attempted to give an authentic presentation of a local dialect, even going so far as to differentiate between the local people, who all say "Lud," and Flora, the city girl, who says "Lard" in the then-proper affected London style. However, a close examination shows that the speech is after all but stage-dialect, for there are many Scotch and other non-Southwestern dialect words used. It is interesting to note that over a century later when the play was revived on June 18, 1823, at Drury Lane, Knight was advertized as Hob "in the Somersetshire Dialect."

Page 141. *Rascal:* evidently the printer ran low on type, for most of the last page is set up in italic; we have reverted to the convention used in the first edition.

The text concludes with a song in eighteen stanzas in the old "poulter's measure" called "London City's Triumph" and sung by Pack; since it is not germane to the farce, we have omitted it.

THE
COBLER
OF
PRESTON.

As it is ACTED at the

THEATRE-ROYAL

IN

DRURY-LANE.

By His MAJESTY's Servants.

Written by Mr. *JOHNSON.*

The THIRD EDITION.

LONDON:

Printed by W. WILKINS, at the *Dolphin* in *Little-Britain*; and Sold by W. HUNCH-CLIFFE, at *Dryden*'s *Head* under the *Royal-Exchange.* 1716.

(Price One Shilling.)

The Cobler of Preston

Like a great many of his otherwise obscure contemporaries Charles Johnson earned himself an extra bit of fame by offending Pope and thereby finding a place in the *Dunciad*. Trained for the bar, he deserted law for drama as Ravenscroft had done a generation earlier. He had entered Middle Temple as a student in 1701, when he was twenty-two, but his friendship with Wilks providing an easy access to the theatre, he was soon turning out plays at frequent intervals, though not, as Pope said, one every season. By 1716, when he wrote *The Cobler of Preston*, he had produced ten plays, only two of them, *The Wife's Relief* and *The Country Lasses*, having enjoyed much success in the theatre. His political affiliations undoubtedly led to his including the satire on the Jacobites in the *Cobler*, for he was, as Professor Sutherland describes him in the Twickenham *Dunciad*, "a faithful member of the Button's group of Whig writers who paid court to Addison." His next play provided the occasion to offend Pope and insure himself a place in Pope's satire. In writing the prologue to *The Sultaness*, adapted from Racine, he jeered at Gay, Pope, and Arbuthnot for their attempt "to club a Farce by Tripartite-Indenture," that is, for combining their talents in the ill-fated *Three Hours after Marriage*, which had appeared at Drury Lane a few weeks earlier. None of the half dozen other plays he wrote during the remainder of his career as a dramatist have any great significance, with the possible exception of his last one, "the domestic *Caelia*," as Professor Nicoll describes it. After 1732 he seems to have retired to the easier life of tavern keeper. He died in 1748, according to the *Biographia Dramatica* of 1812. Johnson was actually up to or even a little above the level of the hack playwrights of the period, but he will doubtless be remembered, when he is remembered at all, as the fat and prolific plagiary of Button's coffee house.

Source

Johnson went to Shakespeare for his main idea and for a good many passages in the first act of his farce. His principal figure still retains the name of Shakespeare's drunken Christopher Sly though the tinker of Burton-heath has become the cobbler of Preston Heath, with an addiction to treasonable politics foreign to the first Sly. While he kept the name of the drunkard, Johnson did make some effort to make other alterations where he borrowed passages directly from Shakespeare, as when he substituted new names for the lord's hunting dogs. There are other Shakespearean borrowings in the play, for the whole scene in which Cicely brings her elaborate complaint against Kit to the constable was obviously written with *Much· Ado*, III, v, and IV, ii, open before the author. Having decided to make the hostess a malaprop, he found it easier to rifle Shakespeare than to create his own "epitaphs." There is no mistaking such echoes as Cicely's request "that he may be comprehended as an aspitious Person."

Johnson's use of the double metamorphosis which puts the butler into the cobbler's clothes could easily come from his desire to carry out the neoclassical principle of balance, but he was more likely just borrowing another idea from an older play, this time Jevon's *Devil of a Wife*. In support of this theory let us call attention to the scene in which a "countryman," whose name later turns out to be Gaffer Hobson, comes in to assist Joan in convincing Kit that he is really a cobbler and not a lord. In Jevon's play an unnamed "countryman" aids Jobson in convincing Lady Loverule that she is Goody Jobson.

Genest has suggested that "It seems probable that some Cobler had made himself conspicuous at Preston in the time of the rebellion," but the suggestion strikes us as being somewhat gratuitous. If it be granted that Johnson borrowed the drunkard and his adventures from *The Taming of the Shrew* and at least one idea from Jevon's play about a cobbler and that he set the scene at Preston to give point to his hero's rabid Jacobitism, then it will scarcely be necessary to go searching for historical Jacobite cobblers.

Stage History

Johnson must have felt the keenest sense of frustration over what happened when his farce was first brought on the stage, and it must be admitted that he had ample reason.[1] His plans had been carefully

---

[1]Though nothing is said in the printed version of the farce about the trick played on Johnson by the other house, we learn from Bullock's preface that the Drury Lane bills contained an advertisement announcing the coming of Johnson's piece and warning that "no other Company could have any part of the said

> I hear Alarms, and bloody Wars begin,
> 'Twixt haughty Drury-Lane, and Lincoln's Inn.
> Advertisements against Advertisements are toss'd,
> Bills fight with Bills, and clash on ev'ry Post;
> Coblers of Preston like two Socia's Rise.
> So like—they might deceive their Author's Eyes.

laid to capture public interest. Not only had he gone to a play by Shakespeare to get the lively scenes which were to provide the basis of his farce; he had also worked into his play numerous references to the stirring political events of the day. In the preceding November the Pretender's supporters had suffered an ignominious defeat at Preston, and a few days before Christmas the defeated generals Forster and MacIntosh with two hundred followers had been marched into London amid the hoots of the rabble, which, we are told, was especially incensed at the Scotch brigadier and his men in Highland cap and bonnet.[2]

With a view to making capital of the political ferment Johnson changed Shakespeare's Sly into a Jacobite cobbler of Preston, scene of the last stand in England of James' supporters. Unfortunately for him his fine plan got noised abroad, and Christopher Bullock of the rival Lincoln's Inn Fields theatre somewhat unscrupulously stole Johnson's thunder before he could bring it into use.[3] True, Bullock's hastily concocted piece omitted any allusion to politics, except for

---

Farce but the name." One of the quasi-dramatic political pamphlets of the time took notice of the rival plays. In the prologue to Phillips' *Pretender's Flight* (1716) we are told:

[2] Martin Haile, *James Francis Edward* (1907), p. 204.

[3] W. J. Lawrence, "A Player-Friend of Hogarth," *The Elizabethan Playhouse*, 2nd series (1913), pp. 215–26, retells a story of how Bullock acquired the information about Johnson's play, a story which he doubtless got from Akerby's *Life of Mr. James Spiller* (1729), though he neglects to give his source. It is indeed a colorful and highly circumstantial account of how Jemmy Spiller, the one-eyed comedian and close friend of Bullock, beguiled Pinkethman of Drury Lane into a drinking bout, picked his pocket of the script for the part of Sly, took it home to Bullock, and so on. Unfortunately it is difficult to take the story seriously, as Lawrence evidently did. All Bullock in his preface says he knew was that Drury Lane had a farce called *Cobler of Preston*—therefore obviously making use of recent political events—based upon Shakespeare's *Taming of the Shrew*, and he would have needed to know only so much to turn out the play he did. A comparison of the two farces reveals nothing, in addition to the title, that two writers borrowing from the same source could not have worked out in entire independence.

the purloined title, but it took off the edge of novelty by bringing
Shakespeare's story onto the London stage ten days before Drury
Lane was ready.[4] When Johnson's play did come out it had a not
quite solid run of thirteen days, so that Bullock's theft did not utterly
ruin his plans.

The subsequent history is not very splendid, however. There was
only one more performance in the spring of 1716, two more during
the next season, and little beyond that. It is not easy to be certain
about the scattered revivals of the two cobbler farces since the titles
are identical. However, when we can tell, by the *dramatic personae*
or other means, Bullock's play is usually indicated. We do know that
Johnson's piece formed the basis of a ballad opera *Cobler of Preston*
acted in Dublin in 1732.[5] We also have Genest's account of a revised
and revived version as late as September 29, 1817, still at Drury
Lane. It may be safe to assume that the one-act *Cobler of Preston*
produced at Drury Lane three years later represents the remains of
Johnson's farce.

Publication

In spite of the very limited success of this play in its first year and
the scarcity of performances in later years, it went through at least
eight editions, three of them in the first year. No doubt the political
allusions are accountable for this early popularity.

The Cobler of Preston. As it is Acted at the Theatre-Royal in Drury-
Lane. By His Majesty's Servants. Written by Mr. Johnson. London: Printed by W. Wilkins . . . and Sold by W. Hinchliffe
. . . 1716.

---

[4]Bullock was frank enough in admitting his motives in his prologue:

> Tho' this our Farce bears such a Name to-night,
> Some Heads, brim-full of Politicks, t'invite;
>
> .   .   .   .
>
> Indeed I can't deny—
> But th' Underplot was laid with a Design
> To please some Friends—and draw the Vulgar in.

[5]There are a few not very material differences between the accounts of this
piece given by W. J. Lawrence and Miss Stockwell. She says, for example that
Bullock's piece was the source of the ballad opera but she gives a *dramatis
personae* which could have come from Johnson's farce only. For his account
see *The Musical Quarterly*, VIII (1922), 397–412; for Miss Stockwell's, see her
Dublin Theatres, p. 325.

The Cobler of Preston . . . The Second Edition. London . . . 1716.[6]
The Cobler of Preston . . . The Third Edition. London . . . 1716.
The Cobler of Preston . . . Dublin: Printed by S. Powell, for George Risk, 1725.[7]

The Cobler of Preston . . . Dublin, 1767.[8]
The Cobler of Preston . . . London, 1775.
The Cobler of Preston . . . London: T. Rodwell, 1817.
The Cobbler of Preston . . . In Vol. XLII, *Cumberland's British Theatre* [c. 1838.]

Analysis

Genest's opinion that Bullock's reworking of *The Shrew* was superior to Johnson's is difficult to controvert. Though it is not necessary to agree with him that the political allusions do any great harm to the play, he is certainly right in condemning Johnson for returning Sly to his stall and then having the "Spanish" servants come and get him again. He is now, as Genest points out, sober; however, he may be said to be still somewhat overcome by delusions of grandeur which cause him to wish to escape from his sordid home and low calling. Johnson's difficulty apparently arose from his habits of composition. Shakespeare had deserted him in mid-career to begin the main business of *The Taming of the Shrew*, and Johnson had to look elsewhere for suggestions. Borrowing the idea of a double metamorphosis from Jevon, he prepared to put the intoxicated butler into Sly's place. But when he saw certain insuperable difficulties in the exchange— after all, intoxication proved inferior to magic in that it deceived only those who were intoxicated—he began to flounder. Almost completely abandoning the butler, he shifted the cobbler about, worked

---

[6]Talcott Williams, "A Bibliography of the 'Taming of the Shrew,'" *Shakespeariana*, V (1888), 452, misread the date of this second edition as 1786, and Jaggard reproduced the error in his *Shakespeare Bibliography*, p. 459.

[7]The copy of this edition at the Folger is made up as an interleaved prompt copy. On the interleaves are found the manuscript alterations and additions that provide the revised form of the play as produced in the nineteenth century. A new character, Marian, the daughter of Jolly, has been added to provide the romantic love interest to the play, as described by Odell, *Shakespeare from Betterton to Irving*, II, 130.

[8]We have not been able to locate a copy of this edition. By an odd coincidence the Bullock *Cobler of Preston* was republished the same year. Any possibility of confusion seems to be removed by the fact that one was issued in London and the other in Dublin, according to Nicoll and others.

in whatever political satire he could, and finally brought the piece to an end by frightening Sly into loyalty.

A few words about specific scenes or passages. Little comment is necessary about the scenes directly from Shakespeare, for these have long been familiar. The situation of the drunken tradesman awakening in a fine bed, surrounded by obsequious servants of whom he is much in awe, is bound to produce laughs. Kit's feelings are a mixture of fear and awe and bewilderment. He is just arrogant enough to suppose that it is really possible that his past history as a cobbler was only a dream; yet he is worried about his ignorance of decorum. Is his new wife to be addressed as "Alice Madam or Joan Madam"? But the awe wears off and by the time Joan appears he is capable of "strutting and roaring."

Johnson tried another well known farcical device when he doubled his transformation, just as Shakespeare had once doubled the twins he had borrowed from Plautus. But after putting the drunken butler into Kit's clothes and transporting him to the gutter, Johnson was at a loss to make further use of him so that for most of the play he remains a kind of off-stage effect.

A more successful use of repetition occurs in the scene of Kit's awakening at home. Here he moves in just the opposite direction from what he does in Act I, from arrogance and a patronizing air toward the "good woman" who professes to be his wife to reluctant acceptance of his old life. Then, after a kind of parabasis in which Kit steps out of character for a moment to pronounce the author's sentiments on the power of ale to turn "Fox-hunters into Statesmen" and so on, the servants reappear, Kit returns immediately to his former highflown manners, and they march out leading the cobbler, who cannot see the way for his ridiculous ruff.

The final scene of threatening Kit with blisters and bleeding and finally hanging until he agrees to change his principles would appear to have been more amusing to the partisan audience of that day than to us, but it is not a novel device on the stage. In fact, Johnson very likely borrowed much of it from Jevon's scenes with Noddy, the noncon parson who tries, without Kit's success, to change his allegiance in the end.

PROLOGUE,

Perform'd by Mr. WILKS.

Names that could never rise to Epic Verse,
May furnish out a Ballad, or a Farce.
Our Author has a Comick Rebel stole
To make you Mirth; a drinking, noisy Fool:
His Heimskirk Muse in Life's low Business plays,
And hopes in Laughter to receive your Praise.
If he wants Plot, consider, Sirs, he draws
These Scenes, from the worst Plot that ever was;
He paints not in big Verse those Hills of Snow,
Where Traitors breathe, and North-Winds ever blow,
We might be brought to pity Carles that live,
Where neither Tree, nor Beast, nor Man can thrive;
If pinch'd with Frost, and Famine, they aspire,
To taste a Lowland Meal, or smell a Seacoal Fire:
But 'tis amazing, that an English Cudden
Should quarrel with his honest Beef and Pudden;
And yet 'tis so;——And we contend with Knaves,
That only wish to Conquer,——to be Slaves.
To Night a plotting Cobler will appear,
He plots indeed, but still he plots in Beer;
The Man's a quiet Protestant when sober,
'Tis a most Popish Liquor that October;
Who knows how high his Courage had aspir'd,
If with French Claret, and French Pistols fired:
—But—may this Plot, and every Plot hereafter,
Produce but little Bloodshed, and much Laughter.
(He goes off, and returns with a Paper in his Hand.)
An Express just arriv'd from North-Britain, a propos.
(Reads.) From Perth, we hear, the Warriours all are Rubbing;
They wisely stay not for a second Drubbing;
That the Pale Hero with his Lady-Crown
Took Courage, and forsook his Bed of Down.
(To the Galleries.)
——Fair Ones, the Stripling has no Favour done you,
Poor joyless Youth, he turn'd his Back upon you,
And the keen Night-Air from the Mountains scorning,
North-Eastward gallop'd bold—at One i'th' Morning.

PERSONS OF THE DRAMA

SIR CHARLES BRITON, a Country Gentleman.   Mr. *Rian.*
CAPT. JOLLY, his Friend.   Mr. *Walker.*
Servants to SIR CHARLES BRITON, dress'd in Spanish
    Habits, by the Names of
LORENZO [PETER].
DIEGO [JOHN].
BARTOLINO [WILLIAM].
PEDRO [RICHARD].
Huntsman.
Constable.   Mr. *Leigh.*
Butler to SIR CHARLES.   Mr. *Birkhead.*
[HOBSON, a Countryman].
KIT SLY, a drunken Cobler.   Mr. *Pinkethman.*
BETTY, Chamber-Maid to SIR CHARLES, dress'd for a   Mrs. *Willis* the Younger.
    Spanish Princess.
CICELY GUNDY, a Country-Ale Wife.   Mrs. *Baker.*
JOAN, KIT SLY's Wife.   Mrs. *Willis.*
[ALICE.]

Scene, SIR CHARLES'S House, and the Road before it, with the Cobler's
Hovel, and the Constable's House.

Time of Action, from Nine in the Morning till Ten at Night.

ACT I. SCENE [1.]

The Road (Eight in the Morning).
The Cobler, CICELY GUNDY, *and*
ALICE.

KIT. Huzza, Huzza, a Mackintosh, a
Mackentosh; there is something now so
courageous, as it were, in the very
Sound of his Name—You are sure he
wears Whiskers as soon as you hear
him mention'd—I must be a Rebel,
and I will be a Rebel—I never saw a
finer Army of Sportsmen in my Life—
Hawks, Halloo my brave Boys—O'd,
here is my Guard, and thus will I
stand, do you see, firm to the Cause,
to the last Drop of Eale in Squire
Carbuncle's Cellar.

CICELY. Out you Knave! a pair of
Stocks, Sirrah! a Whipping Post, you
Rogue! a Whipping-Post!

KIT. You are a Baggage: Look'ee, say
what you will of me, but don't dis-
parage my Family.—The Sly's came in
with Richard the Conqueror; and so
let the World slide, *Sessa. (Fencing
with his Stick.)*

CICELY. Sirrah, Sirrah! will you pay
for the Mugs you have broke?

Sportsmen: from 1725 edition; text has "Sports-
ment."

KIT. No, not a single Farthing. I will
live upon Free-Quarter, Cicely, I am
free of all the Eale and Beef in England, you Housewife—I will have no
Reckonings paid at all—'Tis downright Abomination, Heresy—Your sober
Small-Beer Whey-beards, shall pay all
the Scot.—And I will Tax them at my
Will and Pleasure, Huzza—He that cannot Leap a Five Bar Gate, knows nothing of Generalship—

ALICE. Varsal, Father! what a Pickle
is he in!

CICELY. Well, Kit, I know my Remedy, Kit; I'll e'en fetch the Constable—

KIT. Give me some more Drink, you
old dry Puttock—Why, let the Constable come—I'll answer him by Law,
I'll not Budge an Inch; let him come—
What, are you for that Sport? Have
at you—*(Tumbles down.)* Well! you
have conquer'd me—I surrender—Here,
Cicely, Alice! a double Jugg; score it.
(falls asleep.)

Enter SIR CHARLES BRITON, *Squire*
JOLLY, *Huntsmen, Servants, &c. as
from Hunting.*

SIR CHARLES. I was never more disappointed in my Life; the Morning
promised us good Sport.

JOLLY. How thick the Mists fell, and puzzled the Scent!

SIR CHARLES. And yet, for all that, Bellman made it good at yon Hedge Corner in the coldest Fault.

JOLLY. I think Ringwood is as good a Dog as he, Sir Charles; for twice to Day, I observ'd him to pick out the faintest Scent—What's here! one Dead or Drunk! Look—Does the Fellow breathe?—

HUNTSMEN. Yes, Sir, he breaths—If he were not well warm'd within, this would be but a cold Bed this hazy Weather—Hah! why, Sir, this is our drunken Neighbour Kit—

SIR CHARLES. This Rascal is the greatest Politician, and the great Sot in our Parish, Mr. Jolly—His Head is perpetually confounded with the Fumes of Ale and Faction—

JOLLY. His Habit shews him a Cobler.

SIR CHARLES. Even so; but he has laid aside cobling of Shoes, to mend our Constitution—

JOLLY. Our Constitution has been too much handled by such Fellows as these, who have of late Years been the Journeymen to a Sett of merry Statesmen, that turned all Government into a Jest—

SIR CHARLES. This Fellow has fancy'd himself of some Consequence a great while, and has been extreamly troublesome and factious; there has been hardly any Iniquity committed in this Country, but this drunken Knave has had a Finger in it—What if we should take this Opportunity to punish him a little, and practice upon him for our Diversion?

JOLLY. As how?

SIR CHARLES. Suppose we should convey him thus drunk and senseless, as he is, to my House, and lodge him in the best Apartment; strip him of his Rags, change his Linnen, put him into a Down-Bed, and order him to be attended in every Respect as a Man of Quality: Will it not strangely amaze him when he awakes, to find his Condition so wonderfully alter'd?

JOLLY. It must surprize him, and make his Behaviour entertaining.

SIR CHARLES. We'll put the Project in execution this instant. John and William, do you take up that Corpse and bear it into the best Chamber—and do as I have said—I'll follow, and give further Directions.   *Exeunt.*

SCENE [2.] *The Hall in* SIR CHARLES's *House.*

PETER *and* RICHARD, *two Servants.*

PETER. To be sure the Butler is dead drunk, and fast asleep in the Pantry; how shall we get Things in Order against my Master comes home? For it has struck Ten.

RICHARD *(to* JOHN *and* WILL, *entring with the Cobler).* Hey Day!—What have we here, John?

JOHN. A sleeping Tun of strong Beer, Peter, that's all—

PETER. Whether do you carry him?

JOHN. Open the great Chamber, let the best Bed be sheeted; for here is your Lord and Master, Man, for this Day. [*Exeunt* JOHN *and* WILLIAM.]

PETER. My Lord and Master! what is the Fellow wild, tro'?

Enter SIR CHARLES *and Mr.* JOLLY.

SIR CHARLES. Aye, it shall be so; who waits there? Bid the Butler bring a Bottle of Wine.

PETER. Sir, he is a little indispos'd.

SIR CHARLES. Eternal Sot—Always drunk—Is it not so?

PETER. A little disguis'd, Sir.

SIR CHARLES. Where is he?

PETER. Asleep in the Pantry.

SIR CHARLES. Asleep, say you? Let me see; I have a Thought, Mr. Jolly, now strikes me: What if we should dress this drunken Butler in the Cobler's Cloaths, and lay him in the very Place where we found the Cobler?

JOLLY. It may improve our Mirth, and thicken our Plot with variety of Circumstances.

Enter WILLIAM *and* JOHN.

SIR CHARLES. Have you bestowed the Cobler, as I directed?

WILL. He is fast asleep in the best Bed.

SIR CHARLES. Harky', strip the Butler this Moment of his Livery, and dress him in the Cobler's Habit: When you have done this, carry him and lay him down gently in the very Place where we found Kit Sly—And, do you here, bid all your Fellow Servants come hither instantly.

Exeunt JOHN *and* WILL.

JOLLY. What a flattering Dream will this poor Fellow think has laid hold on him, when he wakes!

Enter several Servants.

SIR CHARLES. Where are those Spanish masking Suits I bespoke for last Christmas?

SERVANT. In the Wardrobe, Sir.

SIR CHARLES. Each of you instantly put on one of those Spanish Habits— and so disguise your Features, that you may not be readily discover'd.

SERVANT *(aside).* Hey day! what Gambols are we to play now?

SIR CHARLES. That done, place your selves all round the Cobler's Bed; perfume the Apartment where he lies; attend him as his Servants; wait upon him; obey all his Commands, and call him your Lord—. Let him have Musick, when he wakes; and Bid Betty, the Chambermaid, take the Spanish Princesses's Dress, and personate his Lady; and let her call him her Lord and Husband—

1st SERVANT. This will be pure Sport, Efackins!

2nd SERVANT. Adad, I shall never hold from laughing.

SIR CHARLES. Come, Mr. Jolly, while these things are preparing, we will walk in and refresh our selves.

[*Exeunt.*]

SCENE [3.] *The Road.*

The Butler in the Cobler's Cloaths dead Drunk.

CICELY, ALICE, *and* CONSTABLE.

CICELY. Ah! Mr. Constable, he is the most harlotry Knave alive! I warrant he is an infinitive thing, at least fourteen or fifteen Pence on my Score! Then he swaggers so, when he is in Eale; he beats my Customers, he breaks my Mugs; and, to be sure, is so untowardly about Steate Matters—

CONSTABLE. Well, well Woman, but what dost thou charge him with?

CICELY. It was but the last Fear Day, when he was bound over to the *Nisi Prizi,* about breaking Gaffer Dobbins Head with our Pewter Flaggon, d'ye see,—only because he call'd the Pope the Whore of Babylon; and you know Gaffer Dobbins cannot abide the Pope.

CONSTABLE. What have I to do with your Story of the Pope and Gaffer Dobbins? What do you charge him with, I say again?—

CICELY. Why, first, I charge him with Burgulary.

CONSTABLE. For what?

CICELY. For calling his good Worship, Sir Jeoffry Freeman, a Presbyterian, Schematick, and a Round Head—

CONSTABLE—Very well! this is *ad Rem*— What have you farther?

CICELY. Why then, I charge him with forswearing himself, and with Perjury, and bearing False Witness.

CONSTABLE. As how?

CICELY. Why, for knocking down Peter Turph—because honest Peter would not drink his abomination Healths: Besides, he is guilty of the Statue of Stabbing.

CONSTABLE. How Woman! guilty of the Statute of Stabbing, say you?

CICELY. Yes, I do say it; for being treacherously disposed towards my Daughter Kitty in the Hay-ricke—Will ye nill ye, I protest—Oh, he is a most Honey-suckle Villain—And so I preay ye, Master Constable, that he may be comprehended as an aspitious Person.

CONSTABLE. Well, well, he shall be forth coming. Here Richard Slough, take the Prisoner upon your back and carry him to my House—When he awaketh he shall be examin'd. *(Carry off the Butler.)* But you must make Oath of these things, Woman.

CICELY. Aye, that I will, take my Bible Oath on't.

CONSTABLE. Very well, very well: To morrow Morning, Woman, when this Cobler has recover'd his Understanding, that is, his Legs, I will translate him to Sir Charles Briton's, where he shall be examin'd, *solus cum solo*; and thou shalt be consol'd about the Fractures in thy Juggs, and the fourteen Pence that he is upon thy Score. *(Exeunt CICELY and ALICE.)* So, so, it behoveth a Magistrate to be sententious; and if so be, he is capable of seasoning his Wisdom with some smack of Mirth, he acts judiciously indeed.   *Exit.*

SCENE [4.] *An Anti-Room to a Bed-Chamber.*

SIR CHARLES BRITON *dress'd like a Spanish Doctor, and two Servants as Spaniards.*

SIR CHARLES. So, so, I see you are dress'd; are all the rest ready?

SERVANT. They are all now attending round the Bed. He just now lifted up his Eye-Lids and yawn'd—and then clos'd 'em again for another Nap—Will your Worship please to have the Door set open?

SIR CHARLES. By all means! but be sure you give him no Occasion by over-acting your Parts, or any unseasonable Laughter, to suspect the Deceit. *(The Doors open'd, the Cobler discover'd in a rich Bed; Servants on each side the Stage, some preparing Tea, others Chocolate, as against his Levee.)*

KIT *(Yawning).* Heigh Ho! a Pot of Small Eale, Joan, for Heaven's sake, a Pot of Small Eale—Why dost not come Woman? Hey day! what! Why certainly I am awake—Hah—What! I am most damnably frighted—I don't like these Fellows—Who are they? I dare not ask; no, not for the Soul of me— *(Enter LORENZO.)*

LORENZO. Is my Lord awake, Diego?

DIEGO. Softly Lorenzo, softly—He is asleep still—Heaven grant this sweet Refreshment may do him good.

LORENZO. His Majesty has sent to know how he rested last Night.

DIEGO. Better than usual truly, better than usual—He does not stir yet—How greatly the King honours him!

KIT. I am most horribly frighted. The King send to know how I rest—I am most damnably frighted; why, what is to be done here—*(DIEGO goes to the Bed, and KIT sneaks his Head under the Bed-cloaths.)*

DIEGO. He sleeps still; this Doctor will do Wonders: Well, if he recovers his Lordship, he will have a Gratuity of a Thousand Pound from the King for the Cure; besides the Honour of bringing back a Person of his Wisdom and Weight to the Service of the Public—

KIT. Humph—How! I cannot guess what the Devil they drive at.

DIEGO. 'Tis a thousand pities so fine a Gentleman should be thus disturb'd in his Head—

KIT. A fine Gentleman—

DIEGO. Ten to one, now, when he awakes, he will ramble and rave as he used to do, about the Story of the Cobler and his Wife—

KIT. How!—What!—a Cobler and his Wife; why, they can't mean me sure all this while—

LORENZO. Aye, how idly will he talk of his being a poor Cobler, and that his Wife Joan is the veryest Vixin in all Lancashire—

How came I here?—
DIEGO. 'Tis that Beer, Lorenzo, that damn'd English Strong Beer, that distracts him so, and fills him with base ignoble Thoughts.

LORENZO. 'Tis strange! No Advice can prevail with him not to drink it.

KIT. Aye! now 'tis plain they mean me—But what!—Why sure! Nay, now I am more amazed than ever—Humph—What Company am I got into?—What Business have I in this Bed?—

DIEGO. Order his Lordship's Band of Musick in the Anti-Chamber, gently to touch their Instruments, and awake him with the sweetest, softest Sounds of Harmony—

KIT. Musick! What the Devil are they about? Here is some cursed Blunder made; I shall be hang'd that is certain, I am got into a Lord's Bed-Chamber, I don't know how; Aye, and into his very Bed too.

DIEGO. I will venture to peep once more into his Curtains, and see if he stirs yet—

KIT. Ah Lord!—now I am taken in the Fact: What shall I do?

DIEGO (Softly at his Curtains). My Lord—My honour'd Lord—

KIT. What does your good Worship say? Here is no body here but I, an it please you—

LORENZO. Your Lordship's Gown— (They put on his Gown, and set him at the Feet of the Bed.)

DIEGO. Will your Lordship taste some Chocolate or Tea?

KIT. An it shall please you, you mistake me for some other Person to be sure.

LORENZO. Ah! Diego, Diego, he is still in the same unhappy Distraction!

KIT. What's that you say, good Sir? Upon my Word I don't know how I came here, I had no Design indeed.

DIEGO. What Cloaths will your Lordship please to wear to day?

KIT. Pho, Pox, what do you mean? I am Christopher Sly of Preston Heath. Nay, nay, do no' geam a body thus— Why, what?

DIEGO. Your English Brocade will be too hot, and the Persian too cool, I think your Genoa ash-colour'd Velvet will suit your Honour best to day.

KIT. Prithee now, Prithee indeed, an it shall please you, it is well known I have no more Doublets than Backs, nor no more Stockings than Legs, nor no more Shoes than Feet; nay sometimes more Feet than Shoes, or such Shoes as my Toes peep through the upper Leather.

DIEGO. Heaven, good Heaven, amend this idle Humour: Oh! that a Man so born—in such Esteem and Credit, of so clear a Judgment, and so sound an Understanding—shou'd be possess'd by such an evil Spirit.—

KIT. What wou'd you make me mad! Am not I Kit Sly? old Sly's Son of Wiggan—born a Pedlar, brought up a Card-maker, then turn'd into a Bear-herd—and now, as you see, translated into a Cobler—Ask Cicely Gundy, the fat Eale-wife of Preston, if she know me not; if she say I am not fourteen Pence on her Score for sheer Eale, score me up for the most Lying Knave in Christendom. What, I am not be-straught! here's!—

DIEGO. Oh! this it is that makes your Lady mourn.

LORENZO. Oh! this it is that makes your Servants droop.

BARTOLINO. Therefore your noble Kindred shun your House, As driven hence by this strange Lunacy. Behold your Servants all attend around, Each in his Office ready at your Nod.

KIT. Very well, very well, then you say I am a Lord, Hah!

DIEGO. You are a Lord—and you can draw your Lineage down from the Flood—so noble is your Name.

KIT. Oh, Hoh—but am I really, really a Lord?

LORENZO. Ah, my good Lord, why should you doubt your Worth? You have a Lady far more beautiful Than any Woman in this waining Age.

KIT. A Lady—Hah!—what, is she handsome? very handsome?

SIR CHARLES. Until those Tears, which she has shed for you, Like wasting Floods, o'er-ran her lovely Face, She was the fairest Creature in all Spain.

KIT. Spain! Am I a Lord? And have I such a Lady? Or do I dream? Or have I dream'd till now? I do not sleep, I see, I hear, I speak; I smell sweet Savours, and I feel soft Things: Oh Pox, it would be very rude and impertinent in me to doubt any longer.

Well, bring our Lady hither to our sight—And prithee, Friend, once more, a Pot of the smallest Eale.

LORENZO. Oh how we joy to see your Wits restor'd!
Oh that once more you knew but who you were!
These fifteen Years you have been in a Dream,
Or when you waked, so waked as if you slept.

KIT. Fifteen Years, dost thou say! a goodly Nap by my Faith. But did I never speak in all that time?

LORENZO. Oh yes, but very wild and idle Words.

KIT. Well! Heaven be praised for my good Recovery!

LORENZO. Amen, with all my Heart.

KIT. I thank thee; thou shalt not lose by it; I'll be good to thee.

Enter BETTY, *as his Lady, with Attendants.*

BETTY. How fares my noble Lord?

KIT. Marry I fare well—here's Chear enough—but pray where's my Wife?

BETTY. Here my good Lord—What is your Lordship's Pleasure?

KIT. Hah! a goodly Wench! a *Bona Roba* in troth;—Now shall I know whether this be a Dream, or no in a Moment. Are you my Wife, forsooth? My Men say, I am a Lord, and I am your good Man.

BETTY. My Husband and my Lord, my Lord and Husband. I am your dearest Wife in all Obedience.

KIT. Very well! I am glad to hear it, in Troth. What must I call her?

DIEGO. Madam.

KIT. Alice Madam, or Joan Madam?

DIEGO. Madam, and nothing else; so Lords call their Ladies.

KIT. Madam Wife, they say that I have slept and dreamt some fifteen Years, or thereabouts.

BETTY. Yes, and it seem'd a tedious Age to me, being all that Time abandon'd from your Bed.

KIT. Ha!—that's much! Servants, leave me and Madam alone, before I take t'other Nap.—Madam Wife, undress your self, and come to Bed now.

[SIR CHARLES.] My honour'd Lord, this wou'd endanger a Relapse; indeed your Blood must be gently temper'd by degrees, the possession of a Woman now wou'd cause a Tumefaction, which wou'd occasion an Inflammation, which might increase to a Conflagration, and thereby give Birth to a Schirrification, which must end in a Mortification, which is properly speaking, a Dissolution of Action, in consequence whereof the Springs of Life stand still—the Vulgar call it Death.
            ....(*Spoken very fast.*)

KIT. Zounds, Mr. Doctor, I'll venture all that, I am not to be directed by you in this Matter; let my Blood take its course, I warrant you I do well after it.—You're a pragmatical Fellow, I must tell you that, to meddle in this Business; come Madam Wife, if we give ear to this idle Rascal, I may fall into a Trangrum Dream again, and thou may'st lie fallow fifteen Years longer.—What!—

BETTY. Thrice Noble Lord, let me intreat of you,
To pardon me yet for a Night or two;
Or if not so, until the Sun be set:
For your Physitians all agree in this,
'Tis certain your Distemper will return,
If I consent not to refrain your Bed.
I hope this Reason stands for my Excuse.

KIT. Aye, it stands so—that I may hardly tarry so long. But I shou'd be loath to fall into my Dreams again, I will therefore tarry, for I am devilishly afraid of relapsing into a Cobler,—But hearky', you Whiskers, Don Diego, —What Countryman am I, pray?—

DIEGO. Ah, my good Lord, there's not a Conde in all Arragon can boast a Family so Ancient, or a more plentiful Inheritance.

KIT. An Arrogant Conde, what's that?

DIEGO. The King of Spain himself, whom we all serve, has not a nobler Subject.

KIT. What! then I am a Spaniard, am I? Prithee, my Friend, what Language de we speak now? Hah!

DIEGO. Truly, my Lord, I think we speak better Spanish here than they do at Madrid.

LORENZO. Ah! Alcantara has been always famous for the purest Spanish.

KIT. Ha, ha, ha, why these Mustachio, stiff-neck'd Sons of Whores, are a Pack of the most consumed Lyars—Hearky' Friend, 'tis in vain to argue this matter with you I find; but I do, between you and I now, positively assure you, that I cou'd never speak any other Language than plain English in my Life.

DIEGO. Why, how is it possible, my Lord, for me, who understand nothing but Spanish to answer you, if you spoke nothing but English?

KIT. Aye, why that is true, very true.

DIEGO. Ah, my good Lord, this cursed Distemper yet hangs about you, and clouds your Understanding.

KIT. Well, well, I will ask no further Questions, for they puzzle me consumedly.

DIEGO. My Lord, some Neighbours hearing of your Recovery, are come to entertain you with a Song, and chear your Heart with Mirth.

KIT. Hah! —this must be some damn'd Mistake or other at the bottom!—but I dare not ask Questions—well! let 'em come in, Diego.

A Dialogue SONG *between a Cobler and his Wife.*

I.

SHE. Goe, goe; you vile Sot!
    Quit your Pipe and your Pot:
Get home to your Stall, and be doing.
    You puzzle your Pate
    With Whimsies of State,
And play with Edge-Tools to your Ruin.

II.

HE. Keep in that shrill Note,
    Or I'll ramm down your Throat
This Red-hot black Pipe, I am smoaking.
    Thou plague of my Life!
    Thou Gypsie! Thou Wife!
How darest thou thy Lord be provoking?

III.

SHE. You riot and roar
    For Babylon's Whore,
And give up your Bible and Psalter:
    I prithee, dear Kit,
    Have a little more Wit,'
And keep thy Neck out of the Halter.

IV.

HE. Nay pr'ythee, sweet Joan,
    Now let me alone
To follow this Princely Vocation.
    I mean to be Great,
    In spight of my Fate;
And settle my self and the Nation.

V.

SHE. Goe, goe, you vile Sot!
HE. I matter Thee not?
SHE. Was ever poor Woman so slighted!
HE. Thy Fortune is made!
SHE. Goe follow your Trade!
HE. I tell Thee, I mean to be Knighted.

VI.

SHE. A Whipping-Post Knight!
HE. Get out of my Sight !
SHE. Thou Traytor, Thou! mark thy sad Ending.
HE. I'll new-vamp the State;
    The Church I'll translate:
Old Shoes are no more worth the mending.

KIT. Ha, ha, this is a very Commonty, Faith. That Fellow now is as like me, I mean in my Dreams—and my Wife too! —Well, well: Come, we have had Singing enough—For Godsake, let us have a Cup of Strong Beer—Nay, don't stare: for, by the Lord Harry, I will have it so, or I'll flea you all alive. How now! Aye, and you shall all sit down and drink Bumbers round, as fast as you can pour them down— Come, Diego, you are my first Minister; sit on my Right-Hand: So!—What is Madam Wife gone? be it so: for, to say the Truth, she is but a Temptation to me, since I may not use her—

[SIR CHARLES.] Might I presume, my Lord, that English Beer which you delight in, is too heavy for your Constitution.

KIT. What? are you giving your Advice again, Sirrah! you smutty muzzled Dung-Broker, pretend to tell me Strong Beer is not good for me! Lend me your Spit, Friend; I'll put that Dog to Death, this Moment. What, is he gone? 'tis well: What a Pox, if one did not pluck up a Spirit, I see—Come, Diego, all of you sit down—*(A Servant brings in a large Jugg of Strong Beer and a Country Horn.)* Aye, that is somewhat like! set it down, and place the Horn in my Right-Hand: bring Pipes and Tobacco; so!—Come—here's to all true Hearts and sound Bottoms!

DIEGO. Aye, this is a Loyal Health indeed!

KIT. Ah Diego! if we were not in Spain now, I cou'd drink such Healths as would set us all together by the Ears in a Moment!—Are you a Whig or a Tory?

DIEGO. I don't know what your Lordship means.

KIT. I am glad on't: Come, drink about: I have had the Devil to do in my Dreams about that Matter.

Enter JOAN.

JOAN. Oh the Vather! how they have dizen'd him! Why Kit, Kit! why dost let 'em play their Gambols with thee thus, Kit?

KIT. Aye, there she is, by the Lord Harry! before I have drank two Horns round—

LORENZO. Who, my good Lord?

KIT. Oons, you stiff-rump'd Pimp, my Wife: don't you see her?

JOAN. Goe, you eternal Sot! never well, but when you have a Pot and a Pipe at your Nose!—Goe, goe—And you may be asham'd, that you may, to keep a Woman's Husband here Ranting and Scanting, when he shou'd be pains-taking with his poor Wife at Home. *(They keep her from him.)*

KIT. Looky', Neighbours; I know the Woman well enough: She must be nointed; her Constitution requires it; one Ounce of Oil of Stirrop makes her as supple and tractable as a Lamb— This to me! This to me! *(Strutting and roaring)* What, am I not your Sovereign Redidary Lord and Husband? Hah!

LORENZO. Who is it you talk to, my Lord?

DIEGO. What troubles your Lordship thus?

[SIR CHARLES.] You hold Discourse e'en with the idle Air.

JOAN. Ah, what an Oaf they make thee, Kit, Come home you Sot! come home!

KIT. Will you help me, my Neighbours, to a Leather about an Ell long, such a one as your Coblers use; and let it be doubled, Do you hear? Let it be doubled in the Form of a Stirrop. You shall see what sort of Discipline I used to dream I gave to just such a sort of a Woman, when I was in my Trangrums, before I waked.

JOAN. Let me come at him! Let me come at him! I'll tear his Eyes out, a Rogue! *(She attempts to fly at him, and they force her out; as she is going LORENZO speaks to her aside.)*

LORENZO. What art thou mad, Woman, to disturb his Lordship in this manner, when you hear he is a little disorder'd in his Head? Thy Husband is now dead drunk, in the Possession of the Constable. Go, go to him, and satisfy thy self.

KIT. So! Heaven be praised, she is gone!

DIEGO. Who is gone, my Lord? Here was no body.

LORENZO. How his Imagination abuses him!

KIT. Why, what did you not see our Joan?

[SIR CHARLES.] This evil Spirit still haunts him.

KIT. Why, aye, it is true; this is an evil Spirit that always haunts me, Morning, Noon, and Night; I can tell you that—And so you say my Wife was not here? Hah!

DIEGO. Ay, my good Lord!—

KIT. Nay, nay, I only ask; 'tis very well—My Mind is very much disorder'd indeed! —I am in mighty whimsical Circumstances, Aye, very whimsical Circumstances.

DIEGO. My Lord, the Dancers attend, as you order'd 'em.

KIT. I order'd 'em! Nay, nay, it may be so! Let 'em come an they will: but a Pox on 'em! they shall not interrupt our Mirth. Come, my Boys! sit down, we'll drink till our Heads turn round as fast as their Heels—Ah! when all is done, this is the only true Pleasure of Life! *(While the Dance is performing, they drink fast about, and the Cobler is very Drunk.)* Dub—Rub, Dub a Dub! Rumps and Round-Heads, Rumps and Round-Heads! I'll be a

Rebel, down with the Rump, down with the Rump; and yet I do not Rebel, look'ee because I hate the Government—but because there should be no Government at all—Look'ye, I am for Passive Obedience and Non-Resistance; and so I will knock every Body down, and be subject to no Body. I am likewise for Liberty and Property; that is, declare for a Spunge and no Taxes: and in order to bring this about the more expeditiously, I pronounce my self a Doxy Member of that Church which can forgive all my Sins, past, present, and to come. And so Diego, good Night.   *(Falls asleep.)*

SIR CHARLES. Hah, hah—So his Lordship is finish'd—

JOLLY. He has perform'd beyond our Hopes.

SIR CHARLES. Well, now take his Lordship up, and convey him to his own dirty Hovel; lay him in his Bed—his Wife is abroad; she is now searching for him at the Constable's House: Let us see how we may yet work upon him, when he returns to his original Shape.

JOLLY. The Delusion is now so strong, I believe we may prolong it still.

DIEGO. Away with him. *(They take him upon their Backs and bear him off.)*

LORENZO. Come my Lord, to your Stirrop and Hammer once more.

SIR CHARLES. In the mean time let us not forget the Surloin of Beef I order'd to be ready by Three. That will be the chief of your Dinner, Mr. Jolly, with a Flask of spritely Burgundy, to drink his Majesty's Health, and all the Royal Family.

The End of the First Act.

ACT II.

SCENE [1.] *The Constable's House. The Butler in the Cobler's Cloaths, dead drunk.*

BUTLER *(raises his Head)*. Dick, Dick! lay the Cloath—whet the Knives: I cannot come; I am busie, very busie—

Enter CONSTABLE, *followed by* JOAN.

CONSTABLE. What a Howling is here? is the Woman wild tro!—There: there lies your Houshod-stuff: the Furniture of your best Chamber; but 'tis in a most filthy Pickle—Come, up with him; take your Government upon your Shoulders—Dame, march off with your Head upon your Back—You know his Weight.

JOAN. Ah, 'tis a filthy Pig! always wallowing in the Wash!—What the Dickens, did the Eale they gave me in the Buttery at the Hall-House, dazzle my Ears and my Eyes, so that I took a Lord there for our Kit?—and made such an Uproar, Efackins, I am asheam'd as it were—

CONSTABLE. Away with your Rubbish, I say; remove your Lumber, Dame.—

JOAN. Ah, 'tis our Kit sure enough! I'll ring 'en such a Peal, when he is sober, as it were—I pray ye now, Master Constable, let' him have his Nap out—and I'll borrow Neighbour Treddle's Wheel-barrow for 'en in the Morning, and roul e'n Home as well as I can.

CONSTABLE. Do so, thou Hoop of a Hogshead: for as thou art that Vessel's Rib, 'tis plain, thy whole Business is to keep a Tun of Beer tight only—Do so; and drive him Home in Triumph. Hear ye me, Good Woman! thy Husband is guilty of no Crime, but what Justice may wink at—for our whole County consists of walking Vessels of October; now to accuse one Vessel to another, for no other Crime but being full, would be downright false Heraldry.—I am a Magistrate, and have some Wisdom. Away!—Away!   *Exeunt.*

SCENE [2.] *A Cobler's Stall on one side of the Stage, and a little poor Bed on the other. KIT in Bed.*

KIT *(alone)*. Hey hoh!—where are my Servants? Here, some of you bring me a whole But of your English Small-Beer—Here Diego! Lorenzo! Bartolino! —Why, where are my Varlets?—I'll have the Dogs Liveries stripp'd over their Ears, and turn 'em all out to Grass—Tho' I must own I have a sort of a liking to Senior Diego, he took his Glass off *super Na-culum*—Hah!— What! why this is my old Flock Hammock! Aye, and there is my spacious Shop too, of a Yard long!—and those are my base Implements!—But where's Joan?—Aye, Mad as sure as a Gun— I am in my Trangrums again—Ho! Pox! I am always undervaluing my self: this is only now one of my old Quondaries they tell me of—Here; where are you? What, will no Creature come near me?—Now am I most consumedly puzzled, to know whether I Dreamt before, or whether I Dream now, or whether 'tis all a Dream from beginning to ending? whether I am my Lord what do y' call him, or Kit the Cobler? Some Body or No Body!— *(Enter* JOAN.*)* Hold! here comes one will interpret all my Dream, with a Vengeance —

JOAN *(Busie sweeping and setting the Room to right).* Was there ever such a Sot!—All our Neighbours cry Shame o'en —Wou'd he were here—I wou'd rattle him!—Good lack!—What a Litter this Shop is in!—We have a mort of Work, and not one Stitch set; there's Neighbour Clump's Boots to be liquor'd, there's Peter Hobson's Shoe'n to be tapp'd—besides Dame Goslin's Patins, and the Curate's Galoshoes that are to be lined with Swan Skin.— Oh Lud! Oh Thieves!—Thieves!— Murther!—Fire!

KIT. How now! what is the Woman Galliad, tro'!

JOAN. Thieves, Thieves!

KIT. Silence, I say—What has possess'd the Woman? Either take that abominable shrill Pipe of thine a Note lower—or I will—

JOAN. Who are you? What are you? How came you here? And what Business have you in this Place?

KIT. Hah!—

JOAN. Oh Lud! Kit! Why, I left thee just now fast asleep in the Constable's Kitchin; I staid but one Moment at Goody Tattles, to tell her to take her Cow out of the Lees—And see if thou hast not slipt home, and got into Bed before me!

KIT. Let us hear that again!—Hah! where didst thou leave thy Husband, good Woman, dost thou say?

JOAN. Why, I tell the[e] Kit, I left thee at the Constable's, drunk asleep; and I Marl how thou gottest home so soon!

KIT. Haud ye!—Haud ye!—Not so fast, Woman, I will take care thy Husband shall come to no Harm—he is an honest Man; he loves a Cup of Bale, I have heard; but that's a small Fault indeed—Go home—be easy, my Servants shall bring thee thy Husband.

JOAN. Thy Servants, Tom. Dingle!— Goody'e now! Goody'e, what in this Eale still, Kit? Come, Do'n thy Cloaths, and get thee to Work—What the Dickens!—

KIT. Good lack! good lack!—Why this is the Hag now that has plagued me in my Dreams thus for fifteen Years together! and so puzzled my Pate, that I have all along mistaken my self for a Cobler, and her for my Wife!

JOAN. Out you drunken Sot!—Why, Kit, what do you deny your lawful Wife, Kit? Adsnigs, I'll make you find your Senses, in good Faith, I will! Why Sirrah, Sirrah!—I'll fiegue your Trulls, Efaith!—I'll ferret out your Coneyboroughs! I'll teach you to Drink, and Wench, and come home and bely the Wife of your Bosom thus, I will!— *(Crying.)* Oh! Oh!—was ever poor Woman so us'd by a sawcy Knave, that had not a Shoe to his Foot, 'tis well known, nor a Rag to his Back, till I took him out of a Joal and cloath'd him!

KIT. Look thee Joan, that I do not use any Discipline to thee now, if I can guess at thy Husband's Temper, may be a Proof to thee, that I am not thy Husband—This Place, 'tis true, does appear to me to be a Cobler's Stall, neither better nor worse; and thou dost appear likewise, both by thy Words and Looks, to be a Cobler's Wife—But Joan, I know now most certainly, that all this is but a Dream—a base low Imagination, which I am always afflicted with when I sleep—But be peaceable, and presently too, or else I know, by some infallible Symptoms, that I shall Dream of strapping thee most confoundedly.

JOAN. Oh Lud, Oh Lud! to be sure our Kit is distraught; his Brains are quite addled!—What shall I do with 'en? —Come Kit, I won't be angry:—lye down in the Bed, do ye so, and I will get a Cardous Posset, and thou shalt sweat a little.

KIT. No, No, I will arise and consider this matter uprightly; Aye, and with much Wisdom.—But do not thou multiply Words; if thou art my Wife, be Obedient and Silent: Come, give me my Cloaths, Woman.

JOAN. Cloaths! Goody'e now! Goody'e! here are no Cloaths! Why Kit, what hast thou done with thy Cloaths, Kit?

KIT. No Cloaths!—No Cloaths!—Nay, I do not remember that I wore any Cloaths when I was your Spanish Lord yonder, neither.

JOAN. Oh Gemini—what is this, Kit? Oh the Father! what a fine silken Gown is here!

KIT. Aye, why there's it! now 'tis plain again! *(In a Rage.)* Answer me thou Witch of Endor—How came I hither? How did you steal me away? Where are your Imps? Restore me to my Lordship, my House, my Lands, my Servants, and my Cellar of strong Beer—

Enter a Countryman.

HOBSON. Odsnigs, Kit, give me my Sho'en done or undone. I'll stay no longer for 'en. Eale and Politicks will be the undoing of thy good Man; I foresee that now, Joan.

JOAN. Ah Gaffer! he has gotten into an Acquaintance, as one may say, with some of your Spanish Roysters, that lie yonder at Sir Charles Britons—and he is at last drunk for good and all—Lookee, where he struts in his silken Gown!—He reaves so! you never saw the peer o'en; he says he is a Lord, and denies me to be his lawful Wife! —Pray ye Gaffer, talk to 'en a little, and try to dispose 'en an ye con.

HOBSON. Why hearkee Neighbour, Neighbour Kit; why, what the good

Year! Why dost thou straddle about, and toss up thy Snout so, like one of your Actors in a Stage-Play?—Speak to me, Mon, give me thy Hond—What dost thou not know thy old Friend and Neighbour Gaffer Hobson.

KIT. You are somewhat sawcy, methinks, my familiar Friend.

HOBSON. Ha, ha, ha—Aye, 'tis all Pride and Idleness!—he wou'd always be meddling with your Cudgel-playings, and your State Affairs, and your Bull-baitings, and Randying all the Country over, and such like—see what 'tis come to! 'Tis true, he always bore a mind above his Means.

KIT. Thou Devil, in the Shape of a Clown, Avant—What hand have you had in this Journey-work? Did you help that Witch to unlord me; thus to steal me out of my self, and my own Spanish Country, and transform me into this rascally Cobler's Form that I now wear?

HOBSON. Lookee, my Lord, I do not come to preat with yee about your Politicks, and your outlandish Affairs. I bore in Head welly a Twelmonth ago, that ye would be mad, or be hang'd—Dono' dunder my Head with your Nonsense—I came in an honest way, as I may say, to pay yee the Thirteen Pence that I owe; and take my Sho'en, if they are soal'd and heel-pieced. And so, my Lord, if you pleasen, as they say'n, to wax one End of Thred, and handle your Awl for a Minute or two, you may be a Lord afterwards, and Welcome.—Ha, ha, ha.

KIT. Hah!—what!—Thirteen Pence dost thou say? Thirteen Pence is, indeed, a considerable Sum!—And seriously now, I do not find that my Lordship has any Mony at all. I suppose my Steward keeps my Cash—Aye, but where is he? the Scoundrels are all vanished—what shall I do?—I don't know, I think it may be proper however to try, whether I have Ingenuity enough to earn a Penny in an Honest Way—My Mind misgives me now, that I can soal a pair of Shoes by Instinct, as it were.—Od, I'll try—Joan! take the poor Fellow's Thirteen Pence, and fetch a double Flaggon of Goody

Gundy's Stingo—I think I heard of such an Ealewife among you, when I was in England.

JOAN. Heaven be thankful, his Brains begin to earn towards his Business again!—I'll fetch his Eale; we must not cross 'en in these Humours. *Exit* JOAN. *(KIT sits down to Work and Sings, after which he speaks.)*

KIT. Honest Kit, or my Lord, or my Lord or Kit, for which of you I speak to, I cannot tell at present, give me a patient Hearing: The Question then, between me and my self, is, Whether I am a dreaming Lord and a waking Cobler, or a dreaming Cobler and a waking Lord?—Yesterday my Servants were all Spanish Gentlemen; my Wife was a Lady; my Bed all silken; my House as big as a Church; my Meat so good, that I could not tell what it was; and my Booze as right as ever was tipp'd: All these things, I say, did then appear to these Eyes of mine, (if these Eyes of mine are mine, and were then open) to belong to me, their natural Lord and Master: And now this Morning, my fine Lady is turned into a scolding Vixen; my great House into a wretched Hovel; my spacious Chamber into a Cobler's Stall; and my Silken Down Bed into musty Flocks and filthy Woollen.—In short, all Things round me appear to be the Rascally Appurtenances of Kit the Cobler—I am horribly transmogrified from Day to Day!—Pho! Pox! it must be so; I am but a Cobler after all: at least I'll fix here now; 'tis better to be Somebody than Nobody; however—

Enter JOAN with a double Flaggon of Ale.

JOAN *(giving him the Flaggon).* So Kit, how dost thou do? What, art not out of thy Conundrums yet, Mon?

KIT. Ah, this is an old Acquaintance indeed! this proves me broad awake, and clears up all my Scruples at once: Welcome to my Arms once more: It makes me weep for Joy to see my old Friend and Acquaintance! What Wonders dost thou work? as Sir Charles used to say: Thou makest Men Plot without Brains, Fight without Courage, and Rebel without Reason: Thou turnest Libertines into Zealots, and Fox-hunters into Statesmen: To thee I owe my Briskness, when I Randy my fine Speeches at the Head of the Mobility; To thee, my dearest, I owe that I was a Spanish Lord last Night; and for thee I owe Cicely Gundy the Lord knows what!—and so, Neighbour Hobson, here's to you.

HOBSON. See, see, Joan, how he pulls! —what, is all out?

KIT. Aye, aye, an it were Ten Fathom deep—Come Joan, as I was a Lord of my own making, I unlord my self again, and acknowledge thee for my Lawful Spouse.—Nothing sticks on my Conscience, but this Harlotry Gown here— Od, I believe it was brought by the Fairies.

Enter Servants dress'd as before like Spaniards.

DIEGO. I was afraid his old Distraction wou'd return.
[*Servant.*] This is very Witchcraft!

LORENZO. Look, if he be not set down to Work like a poor Cobler!

DIEGO. Alas, my Lord, how is it with you?
[*Servant.*] How came your Lordship here?

LORENZO. Your faithful Servants have been seeking you this Hour and more.
[*Servant.*] My poor Lady refuses all Comfort.

DIEGO. And has charg'd us on pain of Death to find you out, and bring you back, once more, to your own Palace.

KIT. Hah!—What!—aye! 'tis my Old Friend Diego! Aye; and that is Lorenzo!—and there is that hatchet-faced Rogue, who deny'd me the use of Madam Wife last Night! I remember 'em all very well!

LORENZO. We have brought your Lordship's Cloaths.

DIEGO. Will your Honour please to Dress?

KIT. Aye, Aye, Dress me quickly,— quickly!—*(They dress him)* But Harkee, Varlets, Scoundrels! are you sure now, positively sure, that I am your natural Lord and Master? *I am devilishly afraid I am but a Pretender. (Aside.)*

DIEGO. Oh, my good Lord!

LORENZO. If your Lordship wou'd but confine your self to the Rules of your Physicians—

DIEGO. These vain Imaginations cou'd never prevail upon you.

KIT. Look thee, honest Diego, I hate Physick, I abominate Doctors: Talk not to me of Doctors.—I wou'd not deny my self the Enjoyment of Roast Beef and October, to be an Emperor.— What, the Pox! will the Fellow choak me. *(To a Servant putting on his Ruff.)* What is this, Friend!—What is this?

LORENZO. Only your Lordship's Ruff.

KIT. Rough indeed, I think!—Oons, you must provide me with a Dog and a String too,—or I shall break my Bones, I can tell you; for I cannot see one Inch of my Way.

JOAN. Oh Lud! Neighbour Hobson! what is the meaning of all this tro'?

HOBSON. Meaning? Oons, the People are aw wild, I think!—This is most certain now, some o' your Conjurations, or your Witchcrafts or Ghosts, as they sayn—Flesh, Ise' e'en ready to sink!—

KIT. Heark thee, thou Witch of Endor! If ever thou layest any Claim to my Person again—I'll have thy Wainscot Hide 'stripp'd over thy Ears, and tann'd to make Soals for Plowmen— What a stinking Hole is this?

DIEGO. Will your Lordship use your Mule, or your Chariot, or your Litter?

KIT. I cou'd walk well enough, Friend Diego, if I cou'd but see my Way.

LORENZO. We'll attend your Lordship—

KIT. Good Woman, Fare-you-well, commend me to your Husband; if he wou'd be sober, he is a special Workman, that is certain; I'll be his Customer, he shall mend my Shoes. *Exeunt omnes, but JOAN and Countryman.*

JOAN. To be sure, Neighbour Hobson, the World is turn'd topsy torvey!—

One cannot trust to one's own Eyes or Ears—

HOBSON. I think they have conjur'd thee out of try Husband, indeed—Odsfish, follow 'em Joan; for, be he Lord, or Squire, or Emperor, he is thy Husband, Woman still—

JOAN. Aye, so I thought last Night at the Hall-House, but they persuaded me out on't; And to be plain w'ye, Neighbour, to be sure I did see our Kit just afterwards, drunk in the Constable's House. He is indeed as like my Husband as if he were spit out of his Mouth; and yet I am partly persuaded I may be mistaken—Prithee, Robin, go w'me to the Constable's; to be sure I am in a terrible Quandary. *Exeunt.*

SCENE [3.] *The Hall-House discover'd; a spacious Room; the Cobler at a Table; Strong Beer upon it; his Servants waiting round him; and a Doctor at his Right Hand, offering him a Viol.*

KIT. Looky', Doctor, make as many damnable ugly Faces as you please, I'll not taste a drop of your Lixar.

[SIR CHARLES.] My Lord, with the most profound Submission, 'tis impossible to recover your Lordship without the Administration of Medicine—

KIT. Why then I will remain as I am—What, the Pox, wou'd the Fellow have?—Hearkee, Diego—tap a fresh Hogshead, I command you—this damn'd Fellow denies me the use of Madam Wife—my Roast Beef—and pretends to be my Friend!

[SIR CHARLES.] My Lord, 'tis absolutely necessary your Lordship shou'd bleed.

KIT. Hah!—Bleed!—

[SIR CHARLES.] It will qualify this unnatural Heat in your Blood, and make it circulate freely.

KIT. You are a Son of a Whore. *(Throws a Glass of Ale in his Face)* Leave my Presence—I am not able to bear the Sight of you.

[SIR CHARLES.] It is not you, my good Lord, who use me thus; but your

Distemper, which for that Reason, I am resolv'd to conquer. It will be proper therefore to shave your Head—After which we will make a Couple of Blisters incisional in the Nape of your Neck, which will draw down the Humours from the *Pia Mater* of your Brain; which Dreins must be kept open by two small Ventages, that may not improperly be called Back-Doors in your Body.

KIT. Back Doors!—thou most execrable abominable Spawn of a Clyster Pipe. Why, Diego! Vincentio! Lorenzo! what the Plague is to be done now?—What am I to be butcher'd here?—Aye, this is a Plot, a villanous Contrivance, I see it plain—You are all Rebels, arrant Antimarchial, Schematical Hereticks; and have a mind to destroy the Church: Oons what do you mean?

[SIR CHARLES.] My Lord, I shall act only according to the celebrated Prescription of that most learned Doctor in the Faculty, Seignior Palambrino Cento Galfrido Pedro de Mendosa—who was a Galenist.—

KIT. I did not care if Seignior Doctor —Mendosa Palfrey and you were both hang'd in a String—Sirrah, I dismiss you my Service; I'll have no more to do with you.

[SIR CHARLES.] Ah by poor Lord! —how sorry will he be when he comes to his Senses, for thus misusing his most faithful Servant!—Come, Diego, Lorenzo, hold him—This is the most proper time imaginable —the Moon is in the last Quadrant of the Eclyptick. *(They hold him, the Doctor draws his Incision Knife, while* KIT *struggles and cries out.)*

KIT. Dogs, Rogues, Villains, Low-Church Rebels! I'll have you hanged.— *(Enter a Servant running hastily, and in a great Fright—The rest quit the Cobler.)*

LORENZO. What's the matter you stare so wildly!

KIT. Aye, what's the matter, Friend?

SERVANT. Ah, my good Lord, a whole Troop of Dragoons have surrounded the House, they charge you with Treason,

and say, they have a Warrant to hang you upon one of the highest Elms before your Palace Gate.—

KIT. High Treason!—Hah!—I have been a little inclin'd to Rebellion, 'tis true, but sure that was when I was a Cobler only. What shall I do, Diego? Cou'd not you clap me into an empty Hogshead in the Cellar?—Do, Diego, do, and throw a Cheshire Cheese and a Peck Loaf or two after me; and I'll retire from this vile World, like a Peace-making Minister, and pass the rest of my Days in Solitude and Sleep—

DIEGO. Alas, my Lord! they'll put us all to the Torture, who can keep a Secret when a Sword is at his Throat?

KIT. Good lack!—good lack! This is worse than Senior Palfrey's Receit. Pray, Friend, what is your King's Name? for I have been in such Visions, my Memory is absolutely spoil'd.

LORENZO. Alphonso.

KIT. Oh Alphonso! Aye, why if they go to that then, Squire Blunder and I took the Oaths together to his Majesty at the Quarter Sessions.

LORENZO. Then you think taking the Oaths absolves you from every Thing for the future?

KIT. Aye, for when I have sworn I won't be a Rebel, what signifies what I do after, you know?

LORENZO. Right!

KIT. Why aye; there was Squire Clumsey, Squire Blunder, Nick Quicksett and Sir Tim. Dodypole, and I—used to Drink, and Roar, and talk Treason, it would do your Heart good! —What, mun one not be Fisky a little bit or so in this Country, Hah!

LORENZO. Nay, that I know not: But hark, I fear, my Lord, your Servants have capitulated—Aye, 'tis so! I see the Captain is coming in: He will take your Confession to be sure.

Enter Squire JOLLY *as a Captain of Dragoons, and Servants as Dragoons with him.*

JOLLY. My Lord, I am yours—I have a small Affair to dispatch here—Read this, my Lord, read this—

KIT. I cannot read, an it please your Honour.

JOLLY. Read it to him, Slaves.

DIEGO (reads). Captain, When Pedro Lorenzo, Conde of Alcantara, sees this, you are to Execute him forthwith, unless he shows good Reason to the contrary.
Alphonso.

JOLLY. If you have a Prayer or two ready made, huddle it over as fast as you can; for I am in haste.

KIT. In haste, Sir!

JOLLY. Oons Sir—yes, in haste! Come, come, be quick, or I'll Halter you, and put you out of your Pain in a Moment.

KIT. Give me leave, Sir, to say, I am not the Person you take me for; I am but a Cobler, Sir,—

JOLLY. Frederico, do your Office. (Puts the Halter about his Neck.)

KIT. Ah, dear Sir, my dear Sir, spare me but one Word: Recommend me to my Wife Joan; and tell his Majesty, that I ca-not help-ta-aking it ve-ry i-ill at his Hands.

JOLLY. Very well, my Lord! you expect to die like a Man of Quality—and I'll hold your Lordship a Thousand Pounds now this Fellow, simply as he looks here—takes off your Head—at one Blow!—Draw Pedro—I warrant you, he nicks the Joint!—Come, Kneel, kneel—

KIT. Oh, spare my Life, Captain, and I'll Peach; I'll tell you the whole Plot.

JOLLY. Well—you look so penitentially, I'll try you: if what you have to say will deserve a Reprieve, you shall have it.—Come, begin; but be very clear and full in your Discovery, without the least Prevarication.

KIT. Yes indeed, I will make a full and true Discovery.

JOLLY. Come then, begin—Was not you concerned in some or all of the Riots and Rebellions that have been in this Country?

KIT. I do not remember.

JOLLY. How came you among the Traitors?

KIT. I do not know.

JOLLY. Who sent you thither?

KIT. I cannot tell.

JOLLY. What are the Names of your Companions?

KIT. I have quite forgot.

JOLLY. Had you any Money or Strong Beer given you?

KIT. My Memory quite fails me of a suddain.

JOLLY. How this Rogue prevaricates! Sirrah, Sirrah, you learnt this of your Betters: Come, off with his Head; for he can have no farther use for it.

KIT. Ah, dear Sir, do not ye be so hasty, and I'll try to remember.

JOLLY. Quickly then, while you have Life to do it.

KIT. Imprimis then, I was drawn away, as they sayn, to Drink your Jacobite Papish Healths; which I did at first for the Love of the Beer only, as I am a Christian.

JOLLY. Well, go on.

KIT. Then, when I was very Boosie, I used to leave my Stall, and go a Rioting with Timothy Sprig the Tythingman, Edward Belfrey our Sexton, Patrick Quaver the Clerk, Dick Marrowbone, John a Geates, David Bullock.—

JOLLY. Well, and what then?

KIT. Why then we did beat and knock down all People who were soberly disposed; and we did likewise most abominably disuse both the King and Parliament.

JOLLY. Who encourag'd you to do all this?

KIT. The Honourable Sir Andrew Squib, the Worshipful Nicholas Quickmatch, Esq; and the Reverend Mr. Peter Pinacle.

JOLLY. What Reasons did they give you for it?

KIT. Money and Strong Beer.

JOLLY. O my Conscience, I believe thy Confession now is pretty honest—Fear has made thee speak Truth.

KIT. Aye, I have been wheadled and terrify'd too into this Plot, indeed Captain.—Why what cou'd a poor weak Sinner do? Our Parson frighted me with Fire and Brimstone, and the Squire tempted me with Beef and October; what could frail Flesh and Blood do in such a case?

JOLLY. Do you now promise to amend your Life for the future?

KIT. Most sincerely.

JOLLY. Then get thee Home, honest Kit; learn to Cobble thy Shoes, and let the Commonwealth alone.—Look upon those Spaniards, now their Whiskers are off.—Do you know 'em? *(The Servants pull off their Wigs and Whiskers.)*

KIT. Hah; what, is not that thy old Friend Peter Pimpernell?—and Diego, there is my dear Boy Jack, the Postilion of Blossom-Hall.

JOLLY. Aye, and that's your good Master, Sir Charles Briton; whose Advise, if you had follow'd, you wou'd never have fall'n into these Scrapes, Christopher.

KIT. Ah, good your Worship! I beg your Worship's Pardon for being so free in your House, as they sayn.

DIEGO. There's your Wife below, has seiz'd upon the Butler, and swears she will have him, since she has lost her 'tother Husband—

KIT. Why, let her make good her Title, and in Troth I'll serve Sir Charles in his stead, if his Honour pleases—A Butler's a snug Thing, as I may say. In troth I am heartily glad this Matter is settled; it is a most perplexing thing not to know who one is—I have been in very whimsical Circumstances in Troth—

SIR CHARLES. Aye, and we will transform you again, if you do not keep your Promise to amend your Manners for the future.

KIT. I will, I do promise most faithfully.

SIR CHARLES. Upon these Conditions my Cellar Doors shall be always open to you—

KIT. I humbly thank your Honour.

SIR CHARLES. Stand aside awhile and attend the Entertainment we prepared for your Lordship. You have a sort of Right to govern here today.

A Masque.

SIR CHARLES. Go, comfort thy Wife. Mend thy Life and thy Shoes. Be courteous to thy Customers, and mannerly to thy Superiors. Live soberly, and be a good Christian. And remember you are obliged to me for bringing you to the Knowledge of your self.

KIT. To be sure I shall never forget your Honour's Kindness. I'll from this Hour leave Sir Andrew Squib's Cellar, and be faithful to yours, and for the future mix Loyalty with my Liquor.
Our Squire, for Kit, may by himself Rebel,
To his mad Politicks I bid Farewell.
Henceforth I'll never Rail against the Crown,
Nor swallow Traytors Healths, in Bumpers down;
Nor sham Pretences of Religion forge,
But with true Protestants cry, Live King George.

FINIS.

Page 153. *Rian:* John Ryan.

Page 153. *Eight:* the text shows signs of the haste in composition. On the preceding page we are told that the time of action begins at "Nine in the Morning."

Page 158. [*Sir Charles*]: throughout this scene "Doctor" and "Sir Charles" are used interchangeably in the speech tags, but the stage direction after I, iv, clearly states "*Sir Charles Briton dress'd like a Spanish Doctor.*"

Page 164. *Enter:* the text is more confused here than at any other point. The reading in the source is "*Enter Squire Jolly's Servants dressed as before, like Spaniards,*" and one of the servants is given in the speech tag as "Ant." But the other two servants are named Lorenzo and Diego, Sir Charles's servants as before. Furthermore, in II, iii, Jolly's servants will enter as Dragoons. To eliminate confusion, we have omitted "Squire Jolly's" from the stage direction and have substituted "Servant," in brackets, for "Ant." in the speech tag.

Page 165. *Scene 3:* we have again regularly used "Sir Charles" in the speech tag where the text has "Doctor."

THE
DEVIL *to* PAY;
OR, THE
WIVES *Metamorphos'd.*
AN
OPERA

As it is Perform'd at the

THEATRE-ROYAL in *Drury-Lane,*

By His MAJESTY's Servants.

Written by the Author of *The Beggars Wedding.*

In nova fert animus mutatas dicere formas
Corpora ———   Ovid.

With the MUSICK prefix'd to each SONG.

LONDON,
Printed for J. WATTS at the Printing-Office in
Wild-Court near *Lincoln's-Inn Fields.*
MDCCXXXII.
Price One Shilling.

The Devil to Pay

Author

Since several authors were involved in the composition of this ballad farce, it will be necessary to treat all of them briefly. The one .chiefly responsible for both the framework and most of the dialogue was Thomas Jevon, author of the play from which *The Devil to Pay* was taken. Of Jevon we know little beyond the list of light-heeled and light-headed parts he filled in low comedies in the mid-Restoration period, often playing opposite the great comedian Leigh. He began his career as a dancing-master but became an actor in the early 1670's, when he was around twenty-one. His greatest successes came in the next decade in such parts as Harlequin in Mountford's *Faustus* and Mrs. Behn's *Emperor of the Moon*. He died in December 1688. His only play was *The Devil of a Wife*, first acted at Dorset Garden early in 1686.

From the detailed account in the list appended to *Scanderbeg* (1747) of the reworking of Jevon's farce into a ballad opera we learn a good bit about the division of labor. Charles Coffey did an act and a half; John Mottley, now usually accepted as the compiler of the *Scanderbeg* list, did the remaining act and a half. Then, when further revision seemed called for, Theophilus Cibber cut the piece down to a single act, his part of the task being much simpler than that of his collaborators. At any rate we have three more authors to account for.

Since Coffey's name became attached to the farce we may take his case first. We are told that he was a facetious hunch-back who got his start in Ireland, where his fairly successful ballad opera *The Beggars Wedding* was produced in 1729, a year before its initial appearance in London. Coffey's fortunes in London, to which he soon migrated, were changeable. After producing three more plays which had very indifferent success, he took part in the phenomenal triumph of *The Devil to Pay*. Then came three more failures. Even his last piece, *The Merry Cobler*, in which he tried to insure success by making it a sequel to *The Devil to Pay*, met with no approval. He died in 1745.

Of John Mottley we know a great many more details than it is necessary to repeat.[1] When he came to prepare the entry under his own name in the *Scanderbeg* list, he undertook to tell everything about himself. Of all these details we may extract a few essentials. He was the son of a Jacobite officer and was forced early in life to make his own way, which he did by various kinds of hackwriting. He tried playwriting but had no success with the four plays he wrote independently and very little with *Penelope*, in which he collaborated with Thomas Cooke. Only *The Devil to Pay* had any success. Besides plays, he worked on a revision of Stow's *Survey*, edited *Joe Miller's Jests*, wrote biographies of Peter and Catherine of Russia, and in general ground away at the trade of journalism without achieving either fame or financial success.

Theophilus Cibber achieved a great deal of notoriety, if not fame, and he must have made a good deal of money though he could never manage to hold onto it and spent part of his life dodging creditors. The son of the actor-manager-playwright-laureate Colley Cibber, he inherited most of his father's vanity without much of the latter's shrewdness. He also inherited many of his father's enemies but made more of his own. As an actor he fell considerably short of the elder Cibber's success but he managed to play a number of roles in practically every theatre in London and Dublin. He is best known as Ancient Pistol, largely because of the numerous satirical references to him in that part. He tried his hand at writing plays also, characteristically working in almost every manner with very meager success in any. Nicoll lists for him two tragedies, both alterations of Shakespeare, a comedy, a ballad opera, a farce, and a pantomime. Toward the end of his career he wrote, or lent his name to, two or three ventures into literary history and biography, and he engaged in several pamphlet wars, with Thomas Sheridan, Henry Fielding, David Garrick, and others. His most notorious conduct involved his conniving in and profiting from the infidelity of his second wife, the excellent actress Susannah Maria Arne. All in all, it may be doubted whether he left many to mourn for him when in 1758, at the age of fifty-four, he went down with a ship as he was crossing to Dublin to fill a theatrical engagement.

---

[1]For details on Mottley's career not given in his own account see P. B. Anderson, "Thomas Gordon and John Mottley, *A Trip through London*, 1728," *Philological Quarterly*, XIX (1940), 244–60.

Source

The Devil to Pay was taken directly from Jevon's *Devil of a Wife*, at a time when numerous hacks were composing new pieces "in the manner of *The Beggar's Opera*" or transforming old comedies and farces into ballad operas. Mottley describes the somewhat mechanical process in all frankness:

Forty-four Years after [Jevon's piece was composed], viz. in the Year 1730, Mr. Coffey and Mr. Mottley took each of them one Act and a half of this Farce, and altering some part of the Dialogue, and adding Songs, called it a Ballad-Opera, and gave it the name of *The Devil to Pay*.[2]

The source of Jevon's piece is something of a mystery, needlessly complicated by a careless error made two hundred and fifty years ago but still surviving in spite of several attempts to correct it.[3] Perhaps Langbaine by his remark that it was "founded on a Tale as well known as that of *Mopsa*" meant to suggest that it was founded not on any specific tale but on the popular tradition that the best way to have a wife was to rule a wife. At any rate we are unable to suggest any more definite source.[4]

Stage History

The Devil to Pay was first performed on August 6, 1731, at Drury Lane in the three-act version and was repeated on August 16 and

---

[2] Whincop, p. 199.

[3] Writing about *The Devil of a Wife* in his *Account* (1691), Langbaine had said simply that the piece "was founded on a Tale as well known as that of Mopsa, in Sir Philip Sidney's *Arcadia*." When Gildon brought out the revision of Langbaine, *Lives and Characters* (1699), he altered this to "Taken from the Story of Mopsa in Sir Philip Sidney's *Arcadia*."

[4] Several persons have professed to see the hand of Jevon's brother-in-law Thomas Shadwell in *The Devil of a Wife*. Mottley was apparently the first to make the suggestion in print, though he puts it in the form of a tradition. Under the entry for Coffey in the Whincop lists he says that "some People doubted if that [*The Devil of a Wife*], at the Time it first came out, was not partly wrote by his Brother-in-law, Shadwell. . . ." *The Companion to the Playhouse* (1764) repeated the suggestion, though it was not copied in the revisions of that work by Reed and Jones; but it remained for a modern student to examine the evidence. A. E. Richards, in "A Literary Link between Thomas Shadwell and Christian Felix Weisse," *PMLA*, XXI (1906), 808–30, offers an array of parallel passages and other pieces of evidence by which he at least was convinced that "Shadwell, and not Jevon, was the man behind the pen which wrote *The Devil of a Wife*."

again on August 20. It was not, however, very successful. Mottley, who was undoubtedly in a position to know, said that the part of the noncon parson did not please, though whether the audience disliked the satire, as several later commentators have assumed Mottley to mean, or merely Chark's callow performance is not altogether clear.[5]

In September the piece was acted at Lee and Harper's booth in Southwark Fair in what appears to have been a somewhat mutilated form, if we can assume that the cast given in the advertisements is a full one, as it appears to be.[6] The offending part of the parson— along with the actor who played it—has been dropped, some half dozen other members of the *dramatis personae* have also disappeared, and nearly a dozen airs have been deleted. The piece seems well on its way toward the shortened form which it was eventually to assume. Whether it pleased the audiences at Southwark any better than those at Drury Lane the preceding month is more than we can tell, but it may be significant that about September 20 Lee and Harper changed to *Whittington*.[7]

By the time the regular season at Drury Lane got under way, young Cibber had taken the play in hand and reduced it to one act, cutting the list of songs to less than half those in the original version. It

---

[5]Mottley's rather puzzling account reads, "It was performed in the Summer Season, in three Acts, but some Part of it not pleasing, particularly the part of a Non-Conforming Pastor, performed by Mr. Chark, who never acted any Thing before, it was cut short, that Part left out, and so reduced to one Act. . . ." *The Companion to the Playhouse* altered this passage to read, "It was performed in the Summer Season; but some Things in it giving Disgust, particularly the part of a Nonconforming Pastor . . . Theo. Cibber . . . reduced it to one Act. . . ." Nicoll confuses the account still more: "In 1732 [actually 1731], because of some offense given to the Nonconformists, it was cut down from three acts to one by Theophilus Cibber. . . ." p. 244.

[6]*Grub-Street Journal*, September 9, 16; *Fog's*, September 11, 18; *Daily Advertiser*, September 14, 18. There are slight variations in the bills, but most of them read like this one, from *Fog's:* "At Lee and Harper's Great Theatrical Booth, Behind the Marshalsea Gate, leading to the Bowling-Green, during the Time of Southwark Fair, will be presented, A New Opera never perform'd here before, call'd, The Devil to Pay: or, The Wives Metamorphos'd. Intermix'd with above 30 new Songs, made to old Ballad Tunes, and Country Dances . . . N. B. The right Book of the Droll is Sold in the Booth, and is Printed and Sold by G. Lee, in Blue-Maid-Alley, Southwark; and all other (not Printed by him) are false."

[7]On September 18, the *Daily Advertiser* carried two different bills for Lee and Harper's Booth.

was in this form, according to Genest, that the piece was offered at Drury Lane on October 2, after *Rule a Wife*.[8] From then on its course was set, so that Mottley's boast in 1747 that it "has been oftener acted than any one Piece on the Stage" is not too greatly exaggerated. Nor did its popularity wane. It held a place in the repertory at home and abroad for over a century, its popularity in this country possibly outlasting that in England, the earliest record being one for Charleston only five years after Coffey and Mottley composed it, the latest being for a revised version given in New York in 1852.[9]

On the Continent it was if anything even more successful, for it is credited with starting the vogue of the *Singspiel* in Germany. It was taken over, music and all, by the Germans as early as 1743 but its greatest vogue came in the third quarter of the century when Weisse's translation with music by Standfuss and, later, Hiller became

[8]Lowenberg says it was first given in the one-act version at Goodman's Fields, but offers no authority; the *Daily Advertiser*, however, shows it at Drury Lane first.

[9]It is impossible to give any very specific account here, but some idea of the popularity of the piece may be had from sample records or comments. Our own unpublished list, from contemporary newspapers and other sources, shows that for the first ten seasons there was an average for all London theatres combined of thirty performances, with a high of ninety for the 1731–32 season. MacMillan lists one-hundred forty-three for Drury Lane during Garrick's management. For the last fifty years before his final entry, for Covent Garden, May 9, 1828, Genest lists over fifty performances though his account cannot be considered exhaustive. Scattered records indicate that it was for generations the leading afterpiece in the provinces. The account for this country is no less impressive. Seilhamer, whose account of eighteenth-century American performances overlaps that of later scholars, lists fifty-one performances and describes the play as the leading afterpiece. Miss Willis and Pollock, surveying Charleston and Philadelphia for the same period, give eleven and twenty-one. Odell, covering the entire history of the New York stage, lists thirty performances, the last one being for an adaptation in 1849. James, giving records of a troupe playing in Philadelphia, Baltimore, and Washington for the first thirty-five years in the nineteenth century, lists thirty-nine. Wilson gives only five for Philadelphia during the next fifteen years. Hoole continues the account for Charleston with eleven performances between 1805 and 1836. Miss Smithers gives ten performances for New Orleans between 1820 and 1838. Finally, to go still farther afield, Wright gives two performances for Jamaica toward the close of the eighteenth century, and Loewenberg comes up with one for Capetown in 1802. The most recent performance to come to our attention was at the University of California at Los Angeles in 1945.

highly popular. Patu translated the piece into French in 1756, and
Sedaine adapted it for the French comic opera about the same time.
There were also Italian operatic versions. European audiences even
gave Coffey's sequel, *The Merry Cobler,* a much warmer reception
than it had in London.[10]

Publication

The great popularity of *The Devil to Pay* in the theatre led to its
being published again and again over a period of a century and a
half. We have examined more than forty editions of the play and
have noted several more which have eluded us, so that the total runs
to around forty-five. No doubt there are others of which we have no
knowledge.

The history of the earliest issues of the play is interesting enough,
and the accounts usually given inaccurate enough, to make some comment necessary. It seems to have been generally supposed that the
three-act version was printed at the time it was produced in 1731 and
that when this version proved unpopular on the stage it was reduced
to one act and printed in 1732, this second version forming the basis
of subsequent editions.[11] This account, as we shall try to show, is
greatly oversimplified.

The first edition of *The Devil to Pay,* in three acts, was published
on August 11 or 12, 1731, just short of a week after its *première.*[12]
What should perhaps be termed the second edition must have appeared a month later. This was "the right Book of the Droll . . .
Sold in the Booth and . . . Printed and Sold by G. Lee, in Blue-Maid
Alley, Southwark. . . ." Whether this was in one act or three we
cannot say as we have been unable to locate a copy. The third edition
appeared sometime before the end of the year, in one act with

---

[10]The best compact account of all these adaptations is to be found in
Loewenberg.

[11]In his handlist Nicoll gives an abstract of the history of early publication
in this fashion: "8° 1731 (3 acts); 8° 1732 (1 act; later edns. are reprints of
this); 12° 1732" and so on.

[12]*Gentleman's Magazine,* 1 (1731), 359; *Grub-Street Journal,* August 19, 1731;
from *Monthly Chronicle,* IV (1731), 163, we can be certain that this was the
three-act version because of the announced price. There are copies at New
York Public and Harvard.

sighteen songs, and this edition was reissued in 1732.[13] Again in 1732 appeared a fourth edition, in one act but with only sixteen songs. It was this edition which became standard for years to come. There were minor changes in airs in the later editions[14] and by the early nineteenth century some alteration of details in the text, such as the substitution of some less offensive terms for *cuckold* and *buttocks*.

For the first twenty-five years or so Watts retained control of the London issues of the play, except for one or two apparently pirated editions, and then assigned it to Lowndes, who brought out at least two editions. Shortly thereafter the first cheap collections of plays, such as those of Wenman and Bell, began to appear. In these *The Devil to Pay* almost invariably found a place unless the publisher was restricting himself to full-length plays.

We have discovered only one publication of the songs alone, six of them having been printed in a collection of popular songs published sometime toward the end of the eighteenth century.[15]

The Devil to Pay; or, the Wives Metamorphos'd. An Opera . . . .
   With the Musick prefix'd to each Song. . . . London, Printed
   for J. Watts . . . 1731. Price one Shilling and Six Pence.[15a]
[*The Devil to Pay: or, the Wives Metamorphos'd* . . . Printed and
   Sold by G. Lee, in Blue-Maid-Alley, Southwark . . . 1731][16]
The Devil to Pay; or, the Wives Metamorphos'd . . . London, Printed
   for J. Watts . . . 1731. Price One Shilling.
The Devil to Pay; or, the Wives Metamorphos'd . . . London, Printed
   for J. Watts . . . 1732 [18 songs as in preceding edition].
The Devil to Pay; or, the Wives Metamorphos'd . . . London, Printed
   for J. Watts . . . 1732 [16 songs in this and all editions up to
   1815].

---

[13]There are copies of the one-act, eighteenth-song edition of 1731 at the Library of Congress, New York Public, and Texas. Copies of the one-act, eighteen-song edition of 1732 are at Newberry and Harvard.

[14]Professor Walter Rubsamen of the Music Department of the University of California at Los Angeles is preparing an edition of *The Devil to Pay* in which the revisions of the music will be fully treated.

[15]In the New York Public Library there is an undated publication of popular songs called *The Busy Bee, or, Vocal Repository* in which six airs from *The Devil to Pay* are reproduced.

[15a]For a fuller description of these editions, see our article, "*The Devil to Pay: A Preliminary Check List*," *Univ. of Pennsylvania Library Chronicle*, XV (Spring, 1948), 15–24.

[16]This entry has been made up from the newspaper announcement; we know of no extant copies.

The Devil to Pay; or, the Wives Metamorphos'd . . . The Fifth Edition. London: Printed and Dublin Reprinted and Sold by George Faulkner . . . 1732.

The Devil to Pay; or. the Wives Metamorphos'd . . . 1733.[17]

The Devil to Pay; or, the Wives Metamorphos'd . . . Printed by E. Cook, 1736.

The Devil to Pay; or, the Wives Metamorphos'd . . . London, Printed for J. Watts . . . 1738.

The Devil to Pay: or, the Wives Metamorphos'd. An Operatical Farce. . . . [c. 1740].[18]

The Devil to Pay: or, the Wives Metamorphos'd . . . The Eighth Edition. Dublin, printed by E. Bate, for Joseph Cotter . . . 1746.[19]

The Devil to Pay; or, the Wives Metamorphos'd . . . London, Printed for J. Watts . . . 1748.

The Devil to Pay; or, the Wives Metamorphos'd . . . London, Printed by Assignment from Mr. Watts, for T. Lownds . . . 1758.

The Devil to Pay: or, the Wives Metamorphos'd . . . Glasgow, 1761.[20]

The Devil to Pay: or, the Wives Metamorphos'd. An Opera . . . London, Printed by Assignment from Mr. Watts, for T. Lownds . . . 1763.

The Devil to Pay; or, the Wives Metamorphos'd . . . London, Printed for the Proprietors . . . 1771.

The Devil to Pay; or, the Wives Metamorphos'd . . . London, Printed for T. Lowndes . . . 1771.[21]

The Devil to Pay: or, the Wives Metamorphos'd. By Charles Coffey . . . London: Printed for J. Wenman . . . 1777.

---

[17]From Professor Nicoll's list; we have not seen a copy dated 1733.

[18]The Folger Library has a copy of an edition without publisher's name or date. The title page bears the signature of H. Grimston. From the dates of other plays with this signature and a cast like that of the 1738 edition we assume that this edition may be dated around 1740. This and the 1736 edition printed by Cook appear to be piracies.

[19]There is a copy of this edition at the Clark Library of the University of California at Los Angeles. Professor Rubsamen has kindly called our attention to it. Both early Dublin editions, labeled "Fifth" and "Eighth," have sixteen songs but are evidently taken from the first one-act edition of 1731 rather than the sixteen-song version of 1732. In these Dublin editions, the list of sixteen songs is arrived at by dropping Airs 5 and 7 from the earlier list of eighteen songs.

[20]We do not list an edition possibly printed about this time in Belfast by Magee. He includes it in a list of plays printed and sold by him in an edition of *The Vintner Trick'd* (1766).

[21]In an edition of *The Stage Coach* which he brought out in 1766 Lowndes listed *The Devil to Pay* for sale in 8° at a shilling and in 12° at sixpence.

The Devil to Pay: or, the Wives Metamorphos'd . . . In Vol. I, 64–88, Bell's *Supplement*, 1784.

The Devil to Pay: or, the Wives Metamorphos'd . . . In *a Collection of the Most Esteemed Farces and Entertainments Performed on the British Stage.* Vol. I. 37–59. North Shields: Printed by and for W. Thompson, 1786.

The Devil to Pay; or, the Wives Metamorphos'd. An Opera . . . London: Printed for H. D. Symonds . . . [c. 1790].²²

The Devil to Pay: or, the Wives Metamorphos'd . . . By Charles Coffey, Esq. In Vol. II, 64–88. *A Collection of the Most Esteemed Farces,* etc. Edinburgh, 1792.

The Devil to Pay: or, the Wives Metamorphos'd. An Opera. By Charles Coffey . . . London: Printed for J. Barker. . . . [c. 1799]²³

The Devil to Pay; or, the Wives Metamorphos'd . . . In Vol. III, 33–43, *The British Drama* . . . London, Published by William Miller . . . Printed by James Ballantyne, Edinburgh, 1804.

The Devil to Pay; or. the Wives Metamorphos'd. A Farce . . . London: Printed by C. Whittingham . . . for John Sharpe . . . 1805. In *Sharpe's British Theatre,* Vol. XIV.

The Devil to Pay: or, the Wives Metamorphosed. In Vol. V, 107–137, Inchbald's *A Collection of Farces,* London: Longman, *et al.,* 1809.

The Devil to Pay, or the Wives Metamorphosed . . . London: Printed by and for J. Roach. [c. 1810]²⁴

The Devil to Pay; or, the Wives Metamorphosed . . . In Vol. V, 78–87, *The Modern British Drama.* London: Printed for William Miller . . . by William Savage . . . 1811.

The Devil to Pay; or the Wives Metamorphosed . . . In Vol. V, 107–137, *A Collection of Farces and Other Afterpieces* . . . Selected by Mrs. Inchbald . . . London: Printed for Longman, *et al.,* 1815.

The Devil to Pay; or the Wives Metamorphosed. A ballad Farce. By C. Coffey, Esq. . . . In Vol. III, Dibdin's *London Theatre.* Lon-

---

²²From the cast (Kelly, Williames, Benson; Moody, Mrs. Ward, Miss Davis, Miss Tidswell, Mrs. Jordan), we can date the printing between December 17, 1788, when Mrs. Jordan first played Nell, and 1791, when Williames' name no longer appears in the bills.

²³This is the date assigned by the New York Public Library; actually this printing may be much earlier.

²⁴Again the cast gives some help in the dating. It lists J. Smith, Miller, Maddocks, Sparks, West, Evans, Dowton, Mrs. Harlowe, Miss Tidswell, Mrs. Chatterly, and Miss Mellon (as Nell). Since Mrs. Jordan did not give up her role as Nell until 1809, and Miller and Smith began to act with the Drury Lane company about this time, and since Genest states that Mrs. Chatterly was with the company only when it was acting at the Lyceum after the fire (1809–1811), this edition may have been issued about that time.

don, Printed . . . By C. Whittingham, for Whittingham and Arliss, 1815.

The Devil to Pay; or, the Wives Metamorphosed . . . In Vol. XIII, *London Theatre*, 1816.

The Devil to Pay; or, the Wives Metamorphosed . . . A Farce . . . New York: D. Longworth, 1816.[25]

The Devil to Pay; or, the Wives Metamorphosed. A Ballad Farce . . . In Vol. XI, *The Cabinet Theatre*, London: Printed by and for D. S. Maurice. [c. 1819]

The Devil to Pay; or, the Wives Metamorphosed . . . In Vol. XIV, *English Theatre*, London: Printed by and for D. S. Maurice, sold by T. Hughes . . . [c. 1821]

The Devil to Pay: or, the Wives Metamorphosed. A Ballad farce . . . New York: Published by C. Wiley . . . 1824.

The Devil to Pay. A Ballad Farce. By C. Coffey, Esq. With Prefatory Remarks. In *Oxberry's Drama*, Vol. II. By W. Oxberry, Comedian. London. Published for the Proprietors, by W. Simpkin, *et al.* 1824.

Te Devil to Pay, or the Wives Metamorphosed . . . In Vol. I, 108–15, *The British Drama*, London: Jones & Company, 1824.

The Devil to Pay; or, the Wives Metamorphosed . . . In Vol. I, *The London Stage*, London, Sherwood, Jones, and Co. [1825].

The Devil to Pay; or, the Wives Metamorphosed . . . In Vol. V, *The English Theatre*, London, D. S. Maurice, [c. 1827].

The Devil to Pay; or, the Wives Metamorphosed. A Comic Opera, in two Acts. No. 44, *Lea's Illustrated British Drama* . . . London: Henry Lea [1827].

The Devil to Pay, or, the Wives Metamorphosed . . . In Vol. I, 108–15, *The British Drama*, Philadelphia: J. J. Woodward, 1832.

The Devil to Pay; or, the Wives Metamorphosed . . . In Vol. XXXVIII, *Cumberland's British Theatre*, London: John Cumberland [1838].[26]

The Devil to Pay . . . London: G. Vickers, 1847.

The Devil to Pay; or, the Wives Metamorphosed . . . In Vol. I, 108–15, *The British Drama*, Philadelphia: Thomas Davis, 1850.

The Devil to Pay; or, the Wives Metamorphosed . . . In Vol. I, 108–15, *The British Drama*, Philadelphia: J. B. Lippincott, 1859.

The Devil to Pay; or, the Wives Metamorphosed. In No. 2, *The British Drama*, London: J. Dicks, [c. 1870].

---

[25]First American edition. One Harvard prompt copy signed "Mrs. M. Garretson Phil" and another is interleaved and marked for production, with the word "fool" substituted for "cuckold."

[26]Also on the title page are the statements "Revised by Colley Cibber" and "Embellished with a fine Engraving, from a Drawing taken in the Theatre by Mr. R. Cruikshank."

Analysis

What remains of Jevon's piece is, in the light of its brevity and flimsiness, a farce but with some of the livelier slap-stick omitted. With the omission of the parson it is no longer possible to have the boisterous scene in which he is almost literally roasted and at the end of which his tormentors themselves are frightened away by the appearance of the actual spirits. However, there are some knock-about episodes left, as when Lady Loverule breaks the fiddle over the fiddler's head or when Jobson tames his unaccountably shrewish wife with his strap after she has thrown the bed staff at him. With the disappearance of most of the satire, particularly most of the jibes at nonconformity, the chief interest is in the transformation, and in the consequent mixup before the shrew is finally tamed. Two favorite motifs of farce can be seen in the beatings and the disguises, if the transformation may be so termed, but there is much less farce here than in most of the plays in this collection.

There have been attempts to account for the huge success of this play by pointing to the succession of excellent actors who played in it, with Harper and, much later, Munden in the part of Jobson or, even better, Mrs. Clive and Mrs. Jordan playing Nell. They were from every account excellent performers, but with all respect to their abilities we must insist that they could hardly have contributed to the triumph of *The Devil to Pay* in theatres where they had never appeared or in countries they had never visited. The success of the piece seems to have come from its having just the right combination of song and action to suit the times. Added to this is the sharp contrast of character and of domestic situation and, not an insignificant factor in popular drama, the happy ending which sees the virtuous rewarded and the vicious reformed.

PROLOGUE

Spoken by Mr. THEOPH. CIBBER.

In ancient Greece the Comic Muse appear'd,
Sworn Foe to Vice, by Virtue's Friends rever'd;
Impartial she indulg'd her noble Rage,
And Satire was the Business of the Stage:
No reigning Ill was from her Censure free,
No Sex, no Age of Man, and no Degree;
Whoe'er by Passion was, or Folly, led,
The laurel'd Chief, or sacerdotal Head,
The pedant Sophist, or imperious Dame,
She lash'd the Evil, nor conceal'd the Name.
How hard the Fate of Wives in those sad Times,
When saucy Poets wou'd chastise their Crimes!
When each cornuting Mate, each rampant Jilt,
Had her Name branded on the Stage with Guilt!
Each Fair may now the Comic Muse endure,
And join the Laugh, tho' at her Self, secure.
Link'd to a patient Lord, this Night behold
A wilful, headstrong, Termagant and Scold;
Whom, tho' her Husband did what Man cou'd do,
The Devil only cou'd reclaim like you;
Like you, whose Virtues bright embellish Life,
And add a Blessing to the Name of Wife.
A merry Wag, to mend vexatious Brides,
These Scenes begun, which shak'd your Fathers Sides;
And we, obsequious to your Taste, prolong
Your Mirth, by courting the Supplies of Song;
If you approve, we our Desires obtain,
And by your Pleasure shall compute our Gain.

DRAMATIS PERSONAE.

MEN.

SIR JOHN LOVERULE, An honest Country Gentleman, be-   Mr. *Stopelaer.*
lov'd for his Hospitality.

BUTLER,   ⎫   Mr. *Berry.*
COOK,   ⎬ Servants to SIR JOHN.   Mr. *Wetherelt, Jun.*
FOOTMAN,   ⎪   Mr. *Leigh.*
COACHMAN,   ⎭   Mr. *Gray.*
JOBSON, A Psalm-singing Cobler, Tenant to SIR JOHN.   Mr. *Harper.*
DOCTOR.   Mr. *Oates.*
[A Blind Fidler.]

WOMEN.

LADY LOVERULE, Wife to SIR JOHN, a proud, canting, brawl-
ing, fanatical Shrew.   Mrs. *Grace.*
LUCY,   ⎫   Miss *Oates.*
LETTICE,   ⎬ Her Maids.   Miss *Williams.*
NELL, JOBSON'S Wife, an innocent Country Girl.   Miss *Raftor.*
    Tenants, Servants.
    Scene, A Country Village.

SCENE 1. *The Cobler's House.*

JOBSON, *and* NELL.

NELL. Pr'ythee, good Jobson, stay with me Tonight, and for once make merry at home.

JOBSON. Peace, peace, you Jade, and go Spin; for if I lack any Thread for my Stitching, I will punish you by virtue of my Sovereign Authority.

NELL. Ay marry, no doubt of that; whilst you take your Swing at the Ale-house, spend your Substance, get drunk as a Beast, then come home like a Sot, and use one like a Dog.

JOBSON. Nounz! do you prate? Why, how now, Brazen-face, do you speak ill of the Government? Don't you know, Hussy, that I am King in my own House, and that this is Treason against my Majesty.

NELL. Did ever one hear such Stuff! But I pray you now, Jobson, don't go to the Alehouse To-night.

JOBSON. Well, I'll humour you for once, but don't grow saucy upon't; for I am invited by Sir John Loverule's Butler, and am to be Princily drunk with Punch at the Hall-Place; we shall have a Bowl large enough to swim in.

NELL. But they say, Husband, the new Lady will not suffer a Stranger to enter her Doors; she grudges even a Draught of small Beer to her own Servants; and several of the Tenants have come home with broken Heads from her Ladyship's own Hands, only for smelling strong Beer in her House.

JOBSON. A Pox on her, for a fanatical Jade! She has almost distracted the good Knight: But she's now abroad, feasting with her Relations, and will scarce come home To-night; and we are to have much Drink, a Fiddle, and merry Gambols.

NELL. O dear Husband: let me go with you, we'll be as merry as the Night's long.

JOBSON. Why how now, you bold Baggage: wou'd you be carry'd to a Company of smooth-fac'd, eating, drinking, lazy Serving-men; no, no, you Jade, I'll not be a Cuckold.

NELL. I'm sure they wou'd make me welcome; you promis'd I shou'd see the House, and the Family has not been here before, since you marry'd and brought me home.

JOBSON. Why, thou most audacious Strumpet, dar'st thou dispute with me, thy Lord and Master? Get in and spin, or else my Strap shall wind about thy Ribs most confoundedly.

Air 1. The Twitcher.

He that has the best Wife,
She's the Plague of his Life;
But for her that will scold and will quarrel,
Let him cut her off short
Of her Meat and her Sport,
And ten times a Day hoop her Barrel, brave Boys,
And ten times a Day hoop her Barrel.

NELL. Well, we poor Women must always be Slaves, and never have any Joy; but you Men run and ramble at your Pleasure.

JOBSON. Why, you most pestilent Baggage, will you be hoop'd? Be gone.

NELL. I must obey.   *(Going.)*

JOBSON. Stay! now I think on't, here's Sixpence for you, get Ale and Apples, stretch and puff thy self up with Lamb's Wool, rejoice and revel by thy self, be drunk and Wallow in thy own Sty, like a grumbling Sow as thou art.

He that has the best Wife,
She's the Plague of his Life, &c.

Exeunt.

SCENE 2. SIR JOHN'S.

BUTLER, COOK, FOOTMAN, COACHMAN, LUCY, LETTICE, &c.

BUTLER. I wou'd the blind Fidler and our dancing Neighbours were here, that we might rejoice a little, while our termagant Lady is abroad; I have made a most sovereign Bowl of Punch.

LUCY. We had need rejoice sometimes, for our devilish new Lady will never suffer it in her hearing.

BUTLER. I will maintain, there is more Mirth in a Galley, than in our Family: Our Master indeed is the worthiest Gentleman — nothing but Sweetness and Liberality.

FOOTMAN. But here's a House turn'd topsy turvy, from Heaven to Hell, since she came hither.

LUCY. His former Lady was all Virtue and Mildness.

BUTLER. Ay, rest her Soul, she was so; but this is inspir'd with a Legion of Devils, who make her lay about her with a Fury.

LUCY. I am sure I always feel her in my Bones; if her Complexion don't please her, or she looks yellow in a Morning, I am sure to look black and blue for it before Night.

COOK. Pox on her! I dare not come within her Reach. I have some six broken Heads already. A Lady, quotha! a She-Bear is a civiler Animal.

FOOTMAN. Heaven help my poor Master! this devilish Termagant scolding Woman will be the Death of him; I never saw a Man so alter'd all the Days of my Life.

COOK. There's a perpetual Motion in that Tongue of hers, and a damn'd shrill Pipe, enough to break the Drum of a Man's Ear.

Enter blind FIDLER, JOBSON, and Neighbors.

BUTLER. Welcome, welcome all; this is to our Wish. Honest old Acquaintance, Good Jobson! how dost thou?

JOBSON. By my Troth, I am always sharp set towards Punch, and am now come with a firm Resolution, tho' but a poor Cobler, to be as richly drunk as a Lord; I am a true *English* Heart, and look upon Drunkenness as the best part of the Liberty of the Subject.

BUTLER. Come, Jobson, we'll bring out our Bowl of Punch in solemn Procession; and then for a Song to crown our Happiness. *(They all go out, and return with a Bowl of Punch.)*

Air 2. Charles of Sweden.

Come, Jolly Bacchus, God of Wine,
Crown this Night with Pleasure;
Let none at Cares of Life repine,
To destroy our Pleasure:
Fill up the mighty sparkling Bowl,
That ev'ry true and loyal Soul
May drink and sing without controul,
To support our Pleasure.
Thus, mighty Bacchus, shalt thou be
Guardian to our Pleasure;
That under thy Protection we
May enjoy new Pleasure;
And as the Hours glide away,
We'll in thy Name invoke their Stay,
And sing thy Praises, that we may
Live and die with Pleasure.

BUTLER. The King and all the Royal Family, in a Brimmer—

Air 3.

Here's a good Health to the King,
And send him a prosperous Reign;
O'er Hills and high Mountains,
We'll drink dry the Fountains,
Until the Sun rises again; brave Boys,
Until the Sun rises again.
Then here's to thee, my Boy boon,
And here's to thee, my Boy boon;
As we're tarry'd all Day
For to drink down the Sun,
So we'll tarry and drink down the Moon;
brave Boys,
So we'll tarry and drink down the Moon.
(Omnes Huzza!)

(Enter SIR JOHN, and LADY.)

LADY. O Heaven and Earth! What's here within my Doors? Is Hell broke loose? What Troops of Fiends are here? Sirrah, you impudent Rascal, speak!

SIR JOHN. For shame, my Dear. As this is a time of Mirth and Jollity, it has always been the Custom of my House, to give my Servants liberty in this Season, and to treat my Country Neighbors, that with innocent Sports they may divert themselves.

LADY. I say, meddle with your own Affairs, I will govern my own House without your putting in an Oar. Shall I ask leave to correct my own Servants.

SIR JOHN. I thought, Madam, this had been my House, and these my Tenants and Servants.

LADY. Did I bring a Fortune to be thus abus'd and snubb'd before People? Do you call my Authority in Question, ungrateful Man? Look you to your Dogs and Horses abroad, but it shall be my Province to govern here; nor will I be control'd by e'er a hunting, hawking, Knight in Christendom.

Air 4. *(Set by Mr. Seedo.)*

SIR JOHN.

Ye Gods! you gave to me a Wife,
Out of your Grace and Favour;
To be the Comfort of my Life,
And I was glad to have her:
But if your Providence Divine,
For greater Bliss design her;
To obey your Wills, at any time
I am ready to resign her.

This it is to be marry'd to a continual Tempest; Strife and Noise, Canting and Hypocrisy, are eternally afloat.—'Tis impossible to bear it long.

LADY. Ye filthy Scoundrels, and odious Jades, I'll teach you to junket thus, and steal my Provisions; I shall be devour'd at this Rate.

BUTLER. I thought, Madam, we might be merry once upon a Holiday.

LADY. Holiday, you popish Cur! is one Day more holy than another? and if it be, you'll be sure to get drunk upon it, you Rogue. *(Beats him.)* You Minx, you impudent Flirt, are you jiging it after an abominable Fiddle? all Dancing is whorish, Hussy. *(Lugs her by the Ears.)*

LUCY. O Lud! she has pull'd off both my Ears.

SIR JOHN. Pray, Madam, consider your Sex and Quality; I blush for your Behaviour.

LADY. Consider your Incapacity; you shall not instruct me. Who are you thus muffled, you Buzzard? *(She beats 'em all, JOBSON steals by.)*

JOBSON. I am an honest, plain, Psalm-singing Cobler, Madam; if your Lady-ship wou'd but go to Church, you might hear me above all the rest there.

LADY. I'll try thy Voice here first, Villain. *(Strikes him.)*

JOBSON. Nounz! what a Pox, what a Devil ails you?

LADY. O prophane Wretch! wicked Varlet!

SIR JOHN. For shame! your Behaviour is monstrous!

LADY. Was ever poor Lady so miserable in a brutish Husband, as I am? I that am so pious and so religious a Woman:

JOBSON *(Sings).*

He that has the best Wife,
She's the Plague of his Life,
But for her that will scold and will quarrel.

Exit.

LADY. O Rogue, Scoundrel, Villain!

SIR JOHN. Remember Modesty.

LADY. I'll rout ye all with a Vengeance, I'll spoil your squeaking Treble. *(Beats the Fiddle about the blind Man's Head.)*

FIDLER. O Murder, Murder! I am a dark Man, which way shall I get hence?

Oh Heav'n! she has broke my Fiddle, and undone me and my Wife and Children.

SIR JOHN. Here, poor Fellow, take your Staff and be gone, There's Money to buy you two such; that's your way.

Exit FIDLER.

LADY. Methinks you are very liberal, Sir; must my Estate maintain you in your Profuseness?

SIR JOHN. Go up to your Closet, pray, and compose your Mind.

LADY. O wicked Man! to bid me pray.

SIR JOHN. A Man can't be compleatly curs'd, I see, without Marriage; but since there is such a thing as separate Maintenance, she shall To-morrow enjoy the Benefit of it.

Air 5. *Of all Comforts I miscarry'd.*

Of the States in Life so various,
Marriage, sure, is most precarious;
'Tis a Maze so strangely winding,
Still we are new Mazes finding;
'Tis an Action so severe,
That nought but Death can set us clear;
Happy's the Man, from Wedlock free,
Who knows to prize his Liberty:
    Were Men wary,
    How they marry,
We shou'd not be by half so full of Misery.

(Knocking at the Door.)

Here, where are my Servants? Must they be frighted from me?—Within there—see who knocks.

LADY. Within there.—Where are my Sluts? Ye Drabs, ye Queans—Lights there.

(Enter Servants, sneaking, with Candles.)

BUTLER. Sir, it is a Doctor that lives ten Miles off; he practises Physick, and is an Astrologer; your Worship knows him very well, he is a Cunning Man, makes Almanacks, and can help People to their Goods again. *(Enter Doctor.)*

DOCTOR. Sir, I humbly beg your Honour's Pardon for this unseasonable Intrusion; but I am benighted, and 'tis so dark that I can't possibly find my way home; and knowing your Worship's Hospitality, desire the Favour to be harbour'd under your Roof To-night.

LADY. Out of my House, you lewd Conjurer, you Magician.

DOCTOR. Here's a Turn! —Here's a Change! —Well, if I have any Art, ye shall smart .for this. *(Aside.)*

SIR JOHN. Ye see, Friend, I am not Master of my own House; therefore to avoid any Uneasiness, go down the Lane about a Quarter of a Mile, and you'll see a Cobler's Cottage, stay there a little, and I'll send my Servant to conduct you to a Tenant's House, where you shall be well entertain'd.

DOCTOR. I thank you, Sir, I'm your most humble Servant.—But as for your Lady there, she shall this Night feel my Resentment. *(Exit.)*

SIR JOHN. Come, Madam, you and I must have some Conference together.

LADY. Yes, I will have a Conference and a Reformation too in this House, or I'll turn it upside down—I will.

Air 6. *Contented Country Farmer.*

Grant me, ye Pow'rs! but this Request,
And let who will the World contest;
Convey her to some distant Shore,
Where I may ne'er behold her more;
Or let me to some Cottage fly,
In Freedom's Arms to live and die.

Exeunt.

SCENE 3. *The Cobler's.*

NELL, *and the* DOCTOR.

NELL. Pray, Sir, mend your Draught, if you please; you are very welcome, Sir.

DOCTOR. Thank you heartily, good Woman, and to requite your Civility, I'll tell you your Fortune.

NELL. O, pray do, Sir; I never had my Fortune told me in my Life.

DOCTOR. Let me behold the Lines of your Face.

NELL. I'm afraid, Sir, 'tis none of the cleanest; I have been about dirty Work all this Day.

DOCTOR. Come, come, 'tis a good Face, be not asham'd of it, you shall shew it in greater Places suddenly.

NELL. O dear Sir, I shall be mightily asham'd; I want Dacity when I come before great Folks.

DOCTOR. You must be confident, and fear nothing; there is much Happiness attends you.

NELL. Oh me! this is a rare Man; Heaven be thanked.

DOCTOR. To-morrow before Sun-rise you shall be the happiest Woman in this Country.

NELL. How, by To-morrow! alack-a-day! Sir how can that be?

DOCTOR. No more shall you be troubled with a surly Husband, that rails at, and straps you.

NELL. Lud! how came he to know that? he must be a Conjurer! Indeed my Husband is somewhat rugged, and in his Cups will beat me, but it is not much; he's an honest Painstaking Man, and I let him have his way. Pray, Sir, take t'other Cup of Ale.

DOCTOR. I thank you—believe me, To-morrow you shall be the richest Woman i'th' Hundred, and ride in your own Coach.

NELL. O Father! you jeer me.

DOCTOR. By my Art! I do not. But mark my Words, be confident, and bear all out, or worse will follow.

NELL. Never fear, Sir, I warrant you— O Gemini! a Coach!

Air 7. *Send home my long-stray'd Eyes.*

My swelling Heart now leaps with Joy,
And Riches all my Thoughts employ;
No more shall People call me Nell,
Her Ladyship will do as well,
Deck'd in my golden, rich Array,
I'll in my Chariot roll away,
And shine at Ring, at Ball, and Play.

Enter JOBSON.

JOBSON. Where is this Quean? Here, Nell! What a Pox, are you drunk with your Lamb's Wool?

NELL. O Husband! here's the rarest Man—he has told me my Fortune.

JOBSON. Has he so! and planted my Fortune too, a lusty pair of Horns upon my Head—Eh!—Is't not so?

DOCTOR. Thy Wife is a virtuous Woman, and thou't be happy.

JOBSON. Come out, you Hang-dog, you Juggler, you cheating, bam-boozling Villain, must I be cuckolded by such Rogues as you are, Mackmaticians, and Almanack-makers?

NELL. Pr'ythee Peace, Husband, we shall be rich, and have a Coach of our own.

JOBSON. A Coach! a Cart, a Wheel-barrow, you Jade—by the Mackin, she's drunk, bloody drunk, most confound-edly drunk.—Get you to Bed, you Strumpet. (*Beats her.*)

NELL. O Mercy on us! is this a Taste of my good Fortune?

DOCTOR. You had better not have touch'd her, you surly Rogue.

JOBSON. Out of my House, you Villain, or I'll run my Awl up to' the Handle in your Buttocks.

DOCTOR. Farewel, you paltry Slave.

JOBSON. Get out, you Rogue. *Exeunt.*
Scene 4. [C]*hanges to an open Country.*

DOCTOR, *solus.*

Air 8. *The Spirit's Song in Macbeth.*

My little Spirits now appear,
Nadir and Abishog draw near;
The time is short, make no Delay,
Then quickly haste and come away:
Nor Moon, nor Stars afford their Light,
But all is wrapt in gloomy Night:
Both Men and Beasts to rest incline,
And all things favour my Design.

SPIRITS (*Within*).

Say, Master, what is to be done?

DOCTOR.

My strict Commands be sure attend,
For ere this Night shall have an end,
You must this Cobler's Wife transform,
And to the Knight's the like perform:
With all your most specifick Charms;
Convey each Wife to diff'rent Arms;
Let the Delusion be so strong,
That none may know the Right from Wrong.

SPIRITS (*Within*).

All this we will with Care perform,
In Thunder, Lightning, and a Storm.

(*Thunder.*) *Exeunt.*

[SCENE 5.]

Scene changes to the Cobler's House.

JOBSON *at work.* *The Bed in view.*

JOBSON. What Devil has been abroad To-night? I never heard such Claps of Thunder in my Life. I thought my little Hovel would have flown away;

but now all is clear again, and a fine Star-light Morning it is. I'll settle my self to Work. They say Winter's Thunder is Summer's Wonder.

Air 9. *Charming Sally.*

> Of all the Trades from East to West,
> The Cobler's past contending,
> Is like in time to prove the best,
> Which ev'ry Day is mending.
> How great his Praise who can amend
> The Soals of all his Neighbors,
> Nor is unmindful of his End,
> But to his Last still labours.

LADY. Heyday! What impudent Ballad-singing Rogue is that, who dares wake me out of my Sleep? I'll have you flead, you Rascal.

JOBSON. What-a-Pox, does she talk in her Sleep? or is she drunk still? *(Sings.)*

Air 10. *Now ponder well, ye Parents dear.*

> In Bath a wanton Wife did dwell,
> As Chaucer he did write
> Who wantonly did spend her Time
> In many a fond Delight.
> All on a time so sick she was,
> And she at length did die,
> And then her Soul at Paradise
> Did knock most mightily.

LADY. Why, Villain, Rascal, Screech-Owl, who makes a worse Noise than a Dog hung in the Pales, or a Hog in a high Wind. Where are all my Servants? Some body come and hamstring this Rogue. *(Knocks.)*

JOBSON. Why, how now, you brazen Quean! You must get drunk with the Conjurer, must you? I'll give you Money another time to spend in Lambs-Wool, you saucy Jade, shall I?

LADY. Monst'rous! I can find no Bell to ring. Where are my Servants? They shall toss him in a Blanket.

JOBSON. Ay, the Jade's asleep still; the Conjurer told her she should keep her Coach, and she is dreaming of her Equipage. *(Sings.)*

> I will come in, in spite, she said,
> Of all such Churls as thee;
> Thou art the Cause of all our Pain,
> Our Grief and Misery.
> Thou first'st broke the Commandment,
> In honour of thy Wife
> When Adam heard her say these Words,
> He ran away for Life.

LADY. Why, Husband! Sir John! will you suffer me to be thus insulted?

JOBSON. Husband! Sir John! what-a-pox, has she Knighted me? and my Name's Zekel too; a good Jest, Faith.

LADY. Ha! he's gone, he is not in the Bed. Heaven! where am I? Foh! what loathsome Smells are here? Canvase Sheets, and a filthy ragged Curtain; a beastly Rug, and a Flock Bed. Am I awake, or is it all a Dream? What Rogue is that? Sirrah! Where am I? Who brought me hither? What Rascal are you?

JOBSON. This is amazing, I never heard such Words from her before. If I take my Strap to you, I'll make you know your Husband. I'll teach you better Manners, you saucy Drab.

LADY. Oh astonishing Impudence! You my Husband, Sirrah? I'll have you hang'd, you Rogue; I'm a Lady. Let me know who has given me a sleeping Draught, and convey'd me hither, you dirty Varlet?

JOBSON. A sleeping Draught! yes, you drunken Jade, you had a sleeping Draught with a Pox to you. What, has not your Lambs-Wool done working yet?

LADY. Where am I? Where has my villanous Husband put me? Lucy! Lettice! Where are my Queans?

JOBSON. Ha, ha, ha, what does she call her Maids too? The Conjurer has made her mad as well as drunk.

LADY. He talks of Conjurers; sure I am bewitch'd. Ha! what Cloaths are here? a Lindsey-woolsey Gown, a Calicoe Hood, a red Bays Petticoat, I am removed from my own House by Witchcraft. What must I do? What will become of me? *(Horns wind within.)*

JOBSON. Hark! the Hunters and the merry Horns are abroad. Why Nell, you lazy Jade, 'tis break of Day; to Work, to Work, come, and spin, you Drab, or I'll tan your Hide for you: What a Pox, must I be at work two Hours before you in a Morning?

LADY. Why, Sirrah, thou impudent Villain, dost thou not know me, Rogue?

JOBSON. Know you, yes, I know you well enough, and I'll make you know me before I have done with you.

LADY. I am Sir John Loverule's Lady; how came I here?

JOBSON. Sir John Loverule's Lady! no, Nell, not quite so bad neither; that damn'd, stingy, fanatick Whore plagues every one that comes near her, the whole Country curses her.

LADY. Nay, then I'll hold no longer; you Rogue, you insolent Villain, I'll teach you better Manners. *(Flings Bedstaff and other things at him.)*

JOBSON. This is more than I ever saw by her, I never had an ill Word from her before. Come, Strap, I'll try your Mettle; I'll sober you, I warrant you, Quean. *(He straps her, she flies at him.)*

LADY. I'll pull your Throat out; I'll tear out your Eyes; I'm a Lady, Sirrah. Oh Murder! Murder! Sir John Loverule will hang you for this; Murder! Murder!

JOBSON. Come, Hussy, leave Fooling, and come to your Spinning, or else I'll lamb you, you ne'er were so lamb'd since you were an Inch long. Take it up, you Jade. *(She flings it down, he straps her.)*

LADY. Hold, hold, I'll do any thing.

JOBSON. Oh! I thought I should bring you to your self again.

LADY *(Aside)*. What shall I do? I can't Spin.

JOBSON. I'll into my Stall; 'tis broad Day, now. *(Works and sings.)*

Air 11. *Come, let us prepare.*

Let Matters of State
Disquiet the Great,
The Cobler has nought to perplex him;
Has nought but his Wife
To ruffle his Life,
And her he can strap if she vex him.
He's out of the Pow'r
Of Fortune, that Whore,
Since low as can be, she has thrust him;
From Duns he's secure,
For being so poor,
There's none to be found that will trust him.

Heyday, I think the Jade's Brain is turn'd. What, have you forgot to Spin, Hussy?

LADY. But I have not forgot to run. I'll e'en try my Feet; I shall find somebody in the Town, sure, that will succour me. *(She runs out.)*

JOBSON. What, does she run for it? I'll after her. *(He runs out.)*

[SCENE 6.]

Scene changes to SIR JOHN'S *House;* NELL *in Bed.*

NELL. What pleasant Dreams I have had To-night! Methought I was in Paradise, upon a Bed of Violets and Roses, and the sweetest Husband by my Side. Ha! bless me, where am I now? What Sweets are these? No Garden in the Spring can equal them; not new blown Roses with the Morning Dew upon them. Am I on a Bed? The Sheets are Sarsenet sure, no Linen was ever so fine. What a gay, silken Robe have I got? Oh Heaven! I dream! Yet if this be a Dream, I would not wish to wake again. Sure, I died last Night, and went to Heaven, and this is it.

Enter LUCY.

LUCY. Now must I wake an Alarm that will not lie still again till Midnight, at soonest; the first Greeting, I suppose, will be Jade, or Whore. Madam! Madam!

NELL. Oh Gemini! who's this? What do'st say, Sweetheart?

LUCY. Sweetheart! Oh Lud, Sweetheart! the best Names I have had these three Months from her, have been Slut, or Whore.—What Gown and Ruffles will your Ladyship wear To-day?

NELL. What does she mean? Ladyship! Gown! and Ruffles! Sure I am awake; Oh! I remember the Cunning-Man, now.

LUCY. Did your Ladyship speak?

NELL. Ay, Child, I'll wear the same I did Yesterday.

LUCY. Mercy upon me! Child! Here's a Miracle!

Enter LETTICE.

LETTICE. Is my Lady awake? Have you had her Shoe or her Slipper flung at your Head yet?

LUCY. Oh, no, I'm overjoy'd; she's in the kindest Humour! go to the Bed and speak to her, now is your time.

LETTICE. Now's my Time! what, to have another Tooth beat out Madam?

NELL. What dost say, my Dear? —O Father! what would she have?

LETTICE. What Work will your Ladyship be pleas'd to have done To-day? Shall I work Plain-work, or go to my Stitching?

NELL. Work, Child! 'tis Holiday; no Work To-day.

LETTICE. Oh Mercy! am I, or She awake? or do we both dream? Here's a blest Change!

LUCY. If it continues, we shall be a happy Family.

LETTICE. Your Ladyship's Chocolate is ready.

NELL. Mercy on me! what's that? Some Garment, I suppose. (Aside.) Put it on then, Sweetheart.

LETTICE. Put it on, Madam! I have taken it off, 'tis ready to drink.

NELL. I mean, put it by, I don't care for drinking now.

Enter COOK.

COOK. Now go I like a Bear to the Stake, to know her Scurvy Ladyship's Commands about Dinner. How many rascally Names must I be call'd?

LETTICE. Oh, John Cook! you'll be out of your Wits to find my Lady in so sweet a Temper.

COOK. What a Devil, are they all mad?

LUCY. Madam, here's the Cook come about Dinner.

Nell (Aside). Oh! there's a fine Cook! He looks like one of your Gentlefolks. —Indeed, honest Man, I'm very hungry now, pray get me a Rasher upon the Coals, a piece of one milk Cheese, and some white Bread.

COOK (aside). Hey! what's to do here? my Head turns round. Honest Man! I look'd for Rogue or Rascal, at least. She's strangely changed in

her Diet, as well as her Humour. —I'm afraid, Madam, Cheese and Bacon will sit very heavy on your Ladyship's Stomach, in a Morning. If you please, Madam, I'll toss you up a white Fricasee of Chickens in a trice, Madam; or what does your Ladyship think of a Veal Sweetbread?

NELL. E'en what you will, good Cook.

COOK. Good Cook! good Cook! Ah! 'tis a sweet Lady. (Enter BUTLER.) Oh kiss me, Chip, I am out of my Wits; we have the kindest sweetest Lady.

BUTLER. You shamming Rogue, I think you are out of your Wits, all of ye; the Maids look merrily too.

LUCY. Here's the Butler, Madam, to know your Ladyship's Orders.

NELL. Oh! pray Mr. Butler, let me have some Small Beer when my Breakfast comes in.

BUTLER (aside). Mr. Butler! Mr. Butler! I shall be turn'd into Stone with Amazement. —Would not your Ladyship rather have a Glass of Frontiniac or Lacryme?

NELL (aside). O dear! what hard Names are there; but I must not betray my self. —Well, which you please, Mr. Butler.

Enter COACHMAN.

BUTLER. Go, get you in, and be rejoiced as I am.

COACHMAN. The Cook has been making his Game I know not how long. What do you banter too?

LUCY. Madam, the Coachman.

COACHMAN. I come to know if your Ladyship goes out To-day, and which you'll have, the Coach, or Chariot.

NELL. Good lack-a-Day! I'll ride in the Coach, if you please.

COACHMAN. The Sky will fall, that's certain. *Exit.*

NELL. I can hardly think I am awake yet. How well pleased they all seem to wait upon me. O notable Cunningman! My Head turns round; I am quite giddy with my own Happiness.

Air 12. *What tho' I am a Country Lass.*

Tho' late I was a Cobler's Wife,
    In Cottage most obscure—a,
In plain-stuff Gown, and short-ear'd Coif,
    Hard Labour did endure—a;
The Scene is chang'd, I'm alter'd quite,
    And from poor humble Nell—a,
I'll learn to dance, to read, and write,
    And from all bear the Bell—a.

Exit.

Enter SIR JOHN, *meeting his
Servants.*

BUTLER. Oh, Sir! here's the rarest
News!

LUCY. There never was the like, Sir;
you'll be overjoy'd and amaz'd.

SIR JOHN. What, are you mad?
What's the matter with ye? How now!
here's a new Face in my Family; what's
the Meaning of all this?

BUTLER. Oh, Sir! the Family is
turn'd upside down. We are almost distracted; the happiest People!

LUCY. Ay, my Lady, Sir, my Lady.

SIR JOHN. What, is she dead?

BUTLER. Dead! Heaven forbid; O!
she's the best of Women, the sweetest
Lady!

SIR JOHN. This is astonishing! I
must go and enquire into this Wonder.
If this be true, I shall rejoice indeed.

BUTLER. 'Tis true, Sir, upon my Honour. Long live Sir John and my Lady!
Huzzah!   *Exit* SIR JOHN.

Enter NELL.

NELL. I well remember the Cunning-
Man warn'd me to bear all out with
Confidence, or worse, he said, wou'd
follow. I am asham'd, and know not
what to do with all this Ceremony:
I am amaz'd, and out of my Senses. I
look'd in the Glass, and saw a gay
fine thing I knew not; methought my
Face was not at all like that I have
seen at home in a piece of Looking-
Glass fasten'd upon the Cupboard. But
great Ladies, they say, have flattering
Glasses, that shew them far unlike
themselves, whilst poor Folks Glasses
represent them e'en just as they are.

Air 13. *When I was a Dame of Honour.*

Fine Ladies with an artful Grace,
    Disguise each native Feature;
Whilst flatt'ring Glasses shew the Face,
    As made by Art, not Nature:
But we poor Folks in home-spun Grey,
    By Patch nor Washes tainted,
Look fresh and sweeter far than they,
    That still are finely painted.

LUCY. O Madam! here's my Master
just return'd from Hunting.

Enter SIR JOHN.

NELL. O Gemini! this good Gentleman my Husband!

SIR JOHN. My Dear, I am overjoy'd
to see my Family thus transported with
Exstasy which you occasion'd.

NELL. Sir, I shall always be proud to
do every thing that may give you Delight, and your Family Satisfaction.

SIR JOHN. By Heaven! I am
charm'd; dear Creature, if thou con-
tinuest thus, I had rather enjoy thee
than the Indies. But can this be real?
May I believe my Senses?

NELL. All that's good above can witness for me, I am in earnest. *(Kneels.)*

SIR JOHN. Rise, my Dearest. Now am
I happy indeed—Where are my Friends,
my Servants? call 'em all, and let
them be Witnesses of my Happiness.
Exit.

NELL. O rare sweet Man! he smells
all over like a Nosegay.—Heaven preserve my Wits.

NELL.

Air 14. *'Twas within a Furlong, &c.*

O charming Cunning-Man! thou hast been
    wond'rous kind,
And all thy golden Words do now prove true
    I find;
        Ten thousand Transports wait,
        To crown my happy State,
            Thus kiss'd, and press'd,
            And doubly bless'd
    In all this Pomp and State:
    New Scenes of Joy arise,
    Which fill me with Surprize;
        My Rock, and Reel,
        And Spinning-Wheel,
    And Husband I despise;
    Then Jobson, now adieu,
    Thy Cobling still pursue,
For hence I will not, cannot, no, nor must
    not buckle to.

Exit.

SCENE [7.] JOBSON'S *House.*
Enter LADY.

Was ever Lady yet so miserable? I can't make one Soul in the Village acknowledge me; they sure are all of the Conspiracy. This wicked Husband of mine has laid a devilish Plot against me; I must at present submit, that I may hereafter have an Opportunity of executing my Design. Here comes the Rogue; I'll have him strangled; but now I must yield.

Enter JOBSON.

JOBSON. Come on, Nell, art thou come to thy self yet?

LADY. Yes, I thank you, I wonder what I ail'd; this Cunning-Man has put Powder in my Drink, most certainly.

JOBSON. Powder! the Brewer put good store of Powder of Malt in it, that's all. Powder, quoth she! Ha, ha, ha!

LADY. I never was so all the Days of my Life.

JOBSON. Was so, no, nor I hope ne'er will be so again, to put me to the trouble of strapping you so devilishly.

LADY *(aside)*. I'll have that right Hand cut off for that, Rogue. —You was unmerciful to bruise me so.

JOBSON. Well, I'm going to Sir John Loverule's; all his Tenants are invited; there's to be rare Feasting and Revelling, and Open House kept for three Months.

LADY. Husband, shan't I go with you?

JOBSON. What the Devil ails thee now? Did I not tell thee but Yesterday, I wou'd strap thee for desiring to go, and art thou at it again, with a Pox?

LADY. What does the Villain mean by Strapping, and Yesterday?

JOBSON. Why, I have been marry'd but six Weeks, and you long to make me a Cuckold already. Stay at home and be hang'd, there's good cold Pie in the Cupboard, but I'll not trust thee any more with strong Beer, Hussy. *Exit.*

LADY. Well, I'll not be long after you; sure I shall get some of my own Family to know me, they can't be all in this wicked Plot. *Exit.*

SCENE [8.] SIR JOHN'S.

SIR JOHN *and Company enter.*

Air 15. *Duetto.*

SIR JOHN.

Was ever Man possest of
So sweet, so kind a Wife!

NELL.

Dear Sir, you make me proud:
　Be you but kind,
　And you shall find
All the good I can boast of
　Shall end but with my Life.

SIR JOHN.

Give me thy Lips,

NELL.

First let me, dear Sir, wipe 'em;

SIR JOHN.

Was ever so sweet a Wife!

(Kissing her.)

NELL.

Thank you, dear Sir!
　I vow and protest,
　I ne'er was so kist;
　　Again Sir!

SIR JOHN.

Again, and again, my Dearest;
　O may it last for Life!
What Joy thus to enfold thee!

NELL.

What Pleasure to behold thee!
　Inclin'd again to kiss!

SIR JOHN.

How ravishing the Bliss!

NELL.

I little thought this Morning,
　'Twou'd ever come to this.

(Da Capo.)

Enter LADY.

LADY. Here's a fine Rout and Rioting! You Sirrah, Butler, you Rogue.

BUTLER. Why how now! Who are you?

LADY. Impudent Varlet! don't you know your Lady?

BUTLER. Lady! here, turn this mad Woman out of Doors.

LADY. You Rascal, take that, Sirrah. *(Flings a Glass at him.)*

FOOTMAN. Have a Care, Hussy, there's a good Pump without, we shall cool your Courage for you.

LADY. You, Lucy, have you forgot me too, you Minx?

LUCY. Forgot you, Woman! why, I never remember'd you, I never saw you before in my Life.

LADY. Oh the wicked Slut! I'll give you Cause to remember me, I will, Hussy. *(Pulls her Headcloths off.)*

LUCY. Murder! Murder! help!

SIR JOHN. How now! what Uproar's this?

LADY. You. Lettice, you Slut, won't you know me neither? *(Strikes her.)*

LETTICE. Help, help!—

SIR JOHN. What's to do there?

BUTLER. Why, Sir, here's a Madwoman calls her self my Lady, and is beating and cuffing us all round.

SIR JOHN *(To* LADY*).* Thou my Wife! poor Creature, I pity thee; I never saw thee before.

LADY. Then it is in vain to expect Redress from thee, thou wicked Contriver of all my Misery.

NELL. How am I amaz'd! Can that be I, there in my Cloaths, that have made all this Disturbance? And yet, I am here, to my thinking, in these fine Cloaths. How can this be? I am so confounded and affrighted that I begin to wish I was with Zekel Jobson again.

LADY. To whom shall I apply my self, or whither can I fly? Heaven! What do I see? Is not that I, yonder, in my 'Gown and Petticoat I wore Yesterday? How can it be! I cannot be in two Places at once.

SIR JOHN. Poor Wretch! she's stark mad.

LADY. What, in the Devil's Name, was I here before I came? Let me look in the Glass. Oh Heav'ns! I'm astonish'd, I don't know my self! If this be I that the Glass shews me, I never saw my self before.

SIR JOHN. What incoherent Madness is this?

Enter JOBSON.

LADY. There, that's the Devil in my Likeness, who has robb'd me of my Countenance. Is he here too?

JOBSON. Ay, Hussy, and here's my Strap, you Quean.

NELL. O dear! I'm afraid my Husband will beat me, that am on t'other side the Room there.

JOBSON. I hope your Honours will pardon her, she was drinking with a Conjurer last Night, and has been mad ever since, and calls her self my Lady Loverule.

SIR JOHN. Poor Woman! take care of her; do not hurt her, she may be cur'd of this.

JOBSON. Yes, and please your Worship, you shall see me cure her presently. Hussy, do you see this?

NELL. O! pray Zekel, don't beat me.

SIR JOHN. What says my Love? Does she infect thee with Madness too?

NELL. I am not well, pray lead me in.

(Exeunt NELL *and Maid.)*

JOBSON. I beseech your Worship don't take it ill of me, she shall never trouble you more.

SIR JOHN. Take her home, and use her kindly.

LADY. What will become of me?

(Exeunt JOBSON *and* LADY.*)*

Enter FOOTMAN.

FOOTMAN. Sir, the Doctor who call'd here last Night, desires you will give him leave to speak a Word or two with you, upon very earnest Business.

SIR JOHN. What can this mean? Bring him in.

Enter DOCTOR.

DOCTOR. Lo! on my Knees, Sir, I beg Forgiveness for what I have done, and put my Life into your Hands.

SIR JOHN. What mean you?

DOCTOR. I have exercis'd my Magick Art upon your Lady; I know you have too much Honour to take away my Life, since I might have still conceal'd it, had I pleas'd.

SIR JOHN. You have now brought me to a Glimpse of Misery too great to bear. Is all my Happiness then turn'd into Vision only?

DOCTOR. Sir, I beg you, fear not; if any Harm comes on it, I freely give you leave to hang me.

SIR JOHN. Inform what you have done.

DOCTOR. I have transform'd your Lady's Face so that she seems the Cobler's Wife, and have charm'd her Face into the Likeness of my Lady's; and last Night when the Storm arose, my Spirits convey'd them to each other's Bed.

SIR JOHN. Oh Wretch! thou hast undone me, I am fallen from the Height of all my Hopes, and must still be curs'd with a tempestuous Wife, a Fury whom I never knew Quiet since I had her.

DOCTOR. If that be all, I can continue the Charm for both their Lives.

SIR JOHN. Let the Event be what it will, I'll hang you if you do not end the Charm this Instant.

DOCTOR. I will this Minute, Sir; and perhaps you'll find it the luckiest of your Life; I can assure you, your Lady will prove the better for it.

SIR JOHN. Hold, there's one material Circumstance·I'd know.

DOCTOR. Your Pleasure, Sir?

SIR JOHN. Perhaps the Cobler has— you understand me!

DOCTOR. I do assure you, No; for ere she was convey'd to his Bed, the Cobler was got up to work, and he has done nought but beat her ever since, and you are like to reap the Fruits of his Labour. He'll be with you in a Minute; here he comes.

Enter JOBSON.

SIR JOHN. So Jobson, where's your Wife?

JOBSON. And please your Worship, she's here at the Door, but indeed I thought I had lost her just now; for as she came into the Hall, she fell into such a Swoon, that I thought she would never come out on't again; but a Tweak or two by the Nose, and half a Dozen Straps did the Business at last. Here, where are you, Housewife?

Enter LADY.

(BUTLER *holds up the Candle, but lets it fall when he sees her.*)

BUTLER. O Heaven and Earth! is this my Lady!

JOBSON. What does he say? my Wife chang'd to my Lady!

COOK. Ay, I thought the other was too good for our Lady.

LADY. *(To* SIR JOHN.*)* Sir, you are the Person I have most offended, and here confess I have been the worst of Wives in every thing, but that I always kept my self chaste. If you can vouchsafe once more to take me to your Bosom, the Remainder of my Days shall joyfully be spent in Duty, and Observance of your Will.

SIR JOHN. Rise, Madam, I do forgive you; and if you are sincere in what you say, you'll make me happier than all the Enjoyments in the World without you could do.

JOBSON. What a Pox! am I to lose my Wife thus?

Enter LUCY *and* LETTICE.

LUCY. Oh, Sir! the strangest Accident has happen'd, it has amaz'd us; my Lady was in so great a Swoon, we thought she had been dead.

LETTICE. And when she came to herself, she prov'd another Woman.

JOBSON. Ha, ha, ha! a Bull, a Bull.

LUCY. She is so chang'd, I knew her not! I never saw her Face before: O Lud! is this my Lady?

LETTICE. We shall be maul'd again.

LUCY. I thought our Happiness was too great to last.

LADY. Fear not, my Servants. It shall hereafter be my Endeavour to make ye happy.

SIR JOHN. Persevere in this Resolution, and we shall be blest indeed, for Life.

Enter NELL.

NELL. My Head turns round, I must go home. O Zekel! are you there?

JOBSON. O Lud! is that fine Lady, my Wife? I'gad I'm afraid to come near her. What can be the meaning of this?

SIR JOHN. This is a happy Change, and I'll have it celebrated with all the Joy I proclaim'd for my late short-liv'd Vision.

LADY. To me 'tis the happiest Day I ever knew.

SIR JOHN. Here Jobson, take thy fine Wife.

JOBSON. But one Word, Sir.—Did not your Worship make a Buck of me, under the Rose?

SIR JOHN. No, upon my Honour, nor ever kist her Lips till I came from Hunting; but since she has been a Means of bringing about this happy Change, I'll give thee Five Hundred Pounds home with her; go buy a Stock of Leather.

JOBSON. Brave Boys! I'm a Prince, the Prince of Coblers. Come hither and kiss me, Nell, I'll never strap thee more.

NELL. Indeed, Zekel, I have been in such a Dream, that I'm quite weary of it. [*To* LADY] Forsooth, Madam, will you please to take your Cloaths, and let me have mine again.

JOBSON (*aside*). Hold your Tongue, you Fool, they'll serve you to go to Church.

LADY. No, thou shalt keep them, and I'll preserve thine as Reliques.

JOBSON. And can your good Ladyship forgive my Strapping your Honour so very much?

LADY. Most freely. The Joy of this blessed Change sets all things right again.

SIR JOHN. Let us forget every thing that is past, and think of nothing now but Joy and Pleasure.

Air 16. *Hey Boys up go we.*

LADY.

Let ev'ry Face with Smiles appear,
   Be Joy in ev'ry Breast,
Since from a Life of Pain and Care,
   We now are truly blest.

SIR JOHN.

May no Remembrance of past Time,
   Our present Pleasures soil,
Be nought but Mirth and Joy a Crime,
   And Sporting all our Toil.

JOBSON.

I hope you'll give me leave to speak,
   If I may be so bold;
There's nought but the Devil, and this good
    Strap,
   Could ever tame a Scold.

FINIS.

NOTES

The chief omission from the 1732 text has been the deletion of the musical scores for the airs. The dedication (to Lionel Cranfield, Duke of Dorset) and the table of airs have also been excised. Scene numbering, after scene iv, has been supplied. Two consecutive speeches by Nell on the last page of the text have been joined together. One or two stage directions have been added, always bracketed.

The text of *The Devil to Pay* experienced a number of changes in the different printings. The first one-act version (1731) has eighteen songs, four of which are different from the songs in the present edition. Sir John is called Sir Richard at the end of scene vi. There was also some additional dialogue upon Sir John's return from the hunt. These changes made, the 1732 octavo remained the source for most of the later editions of the London printers.

Page 187. *Jobson:* Following Harper, many prominent low comedians played this role. Among those noted for the part were Turbutt, Moody, and Dowton at Drury Lane, the latter playing the part for a thirty-year period, and Dunstall, Edwin, and Munden at Covent Garden, the latter enacting the part for at least twenty-five years.

Doctor: American newspaper bills often list "the Sorceror," but we have seen no textual authority for this change.

Miss Raftor: the inimitable Mrs. Kitty Clive. She played the part from 1831 to 1766, acting the role fifty-six times in the first season and from ten to twenty times for many years thereafter. At Covent Garden Jane Hippisley and Mrs. Isabella Mattocks took the part for many seasons. Miss Pope and Mrs. Arne followed Mrs. Clive at Drury Lane, but the role was really revived by Mrs. Jordan, who acted the part for about twenty-five years with great success. Later on the role was taken by Miss De Camp, by Miss Farren, and then by Madame Vestris.

Lady Loverule: The great Siddons once deigned to take this part, but her name really has no place here as she couldn't play farce—she wouldn't let Jobson beat her.

Page 188. *Punch:* in the Oxberry edition Jobson plays a game with the servants and engages in a *lazzo* of stealing wine from the punchbowl.

Page 189. *Beats the Fiddle:* by 1786 the whole sequence of the beating of the blind fidler is printed with inverted commas denoting, of course, that the passage was no longer represented on the stage. The text, however, remains in the later printings.

Page 191. *Awl:* one forceful expression of the age of the Stuarts (and the projectors of *The Devil to Pay* took it direct from Jevon) remained in the text as late as 1824. Oxberry cuts the line to "I'll run my awl—quit the building." The most amusing purification appears in the Cumberland edition. The version there is "I'll run my awl up to the handle in your heart:"

THE
STROLERS
PACQUET OPEN'D.

CONTAINING SEVEN
Jovial DROLLS OT FARCES,

Calculated for the Meridian of
Bartholomew and *Southwark* FAIRS.

Reprefenting the COMICAL HUMOURS of

Defigning *Ufurers*, Sly *Pettifoggers*, Cunning
Sharpers, Cowardly *Bullies*, Wild *Rakes*,
Finical *Fops*, Shrewd *Clowns*, Tefty *Maf-
ters*, Arch *Footmen*, Forward *Widows*,
Stale *Maids*, and Melting *Laffes*.

LONDON:

Printed and Sold by A. JACKSON in *Clare Court, D'rury
Lane*; and moft Bookfellers and Pamphlet Shop*
in Town and Country.

[Price bound 2 s. few'd in blue Paper 1 s. 6 d.]
MDCCXLII.

The Bilker Bilk'd

Author

It is possible to say of this little farce that it had no author at all
or that it was produced by a whole club of authors. Just who prepared the version reproduced here there seems to be no way of knowing. The person chiefly responsible for the actual form of most of the
dialogue was Christopher Bullock, for the droll was taken directly
from his *Woman's Revenge* (1715). Since Bullock was only refur-
bishing borrowed materials, however, perhaps it would be wiser to
begin nearer the beginning and retell briefly the whole story of the
composition of the play.[1]

The first appearance in English drama of the vintner story was
around 1590, when William Percy borrowed the plot from Painter[2]
and used it as a minor incident in *Cuck-Queanes and Cuckolds Errants.*
It was then taken up about 1604 by John Marston, who added the
shaving episode[3] and used the whole story as a subplot to his loosely
woven *Dutch Courtezan.* A droll writer in the interregnum purloined
Marston's entire subplot, renamed it *The Cheater Cheated*, and offered
it in surreptitious productions sometime before the Restoration. True
we have no records of its having been so performed, but it appears
in *The Wits* of 1673 as one of the drolls played by Cox and his fellow
actors.

During the Restoration a playwright, probably Mrs. Behn,[4] returned to Marston's play, rewriting it in five acts to suit the taste of
audiences in 1680 but keeping most of the farcical underplot in the
form Marston had left it. In this form it was acted some twenty-five

---

[1]For a fuller account of the history of the several versions, see our article
"Some Theatrical Adaptations of a Picaresque Tale," *Studies in English* (Austin,
Texas, 1945–1946), pp. 98–114.

[2]Painter had taken the story from Masuccio, *Il Novellino*, ii, 17.

[3]Marston may have borrowed the shaving trick from Edwards' *Damon and
Pithias* or from Whetstone's *Promos and Cassandra.* It also appears in some
French farces.

[4]*The Revenge* has also been attributed to Betterton. See W. Van Lennep,
"Two Restoration Comedies," *Times Literary Supplement*, January 28, 1939, pp.
57–58.

years[5] before it passed into the hands of Christopher Bullock, who adapted it in three acts as *Woman's Revenge; or, a Match in Newgate*. This play formed the basis of at least four subsequent versions: A ballod opera, *Love and Revenge* (1729), made use of Bullock's double-plotted play in its entirety. A two-act farce called *Trick Upon Trick; or, the Vintner Out-witted* (1742) by a strolling actor in the York company, Joseph Yarrow, and two one-act farces, *The Bilker Bilk'd* and *The Vintner Trick'd; or, The White Fox Chas'd*, took only the farcical scenes.[6]

Source

As has been said, the direct source of *The Bilker Bilk'd* seems to have been Bullock's three-act play. There is no indication that the droll-writer bothered to consult earlier versions. However, he does not take Bullock's scenes word for word, as Yarrow virtually does in his version of the story. In fact the dialogue is frequently improved by the use of more vigorous and more colloquial diction. There is also a tendency to increase the importance of the trickster's role by lengthening his speeches, as when details are added to the already elaborate story of the white fox.

Stage History

The Bilker Bilk'd itself has almost no discoverable stage history. Miss Rosenfeld has found a record of one performance in the provinces. Beyond that we know nothing definite. Perhaps most disappointing is the absence of records for the London fairs for which the droll collection is said to have been intended.

The various rival versions of the story had somewhat better success though none created any sensation, or even equalled the London per-

---

[5]The last known performance took place on October 8, 1705, at the old theatre in Lincoln's Inn Fields, under a slightly altered title, the bill in the *Daily Courant* reading "*A Match in Newgate, or, The Vintner Trick'd.*" The original list of actors for *The Revenge* contains two items of interest to students of the theatre: first, it is printed before the *dramatis personae*, reversing the standard practice, and next the part of Ample could be played by "Anybody."

[6]There are some indications however that the author of *The Vintner Trick'd* drew upon *The Revenge* as well as upon Bullock's alteration. The goldsmith in Bullock's play is called Burnish, as in Marston's account; in *The Vintner Trick'd* he is called Glisten, after the name used in *The Revenge*. Ward's farce differs from *Trick upon Trick* and *The Bilker Bilk'd* in retaining the character Padwell and the fairly long prison scene found in both Bullock's play and *The Revenge*.

formances of Bullock's play, which stayed in the repertory for some twenty-five years. The ballad opera had an initial run of six nights in November, 1729, and only ten performances altogether.[7] A panto-mime called *Trick for Trick: or, An Odd Affair between Harlequin, His Associates, and the Vintner of York* could achieve nothing higher than a performance at Tottenham-Court Fair in August, 1739.

Though the version printed here is not recorded at the fairs, some of the others were. In August–September, 1734, a version which was apparently never printed was performed at a booth in Bartholomew Fair by Hippisley, Bullock, and others of John Rich's company; this is *The Impostor, or The Biter Bit.*[8] The most popular of the rival versions at the fairs, if we may depend upon the titles, was Yarrow's. It was performed at the fairs and at the "New Theatre, Bowling Green, Southwark" in 1743, 1747, and 1749.[9] It was performed at Drury Lane at least once, in 1740. Ward's version was performed at least once at Drury Lane in 1746 and several times at Twickenham and Richmond in the same year. The title *Trick Upon Trick* was in the bill for December 22, 1789, at Drury Lane.

Outside of London the account is hard to follow, the various titles being used indiscriminately it would seem. Miss Rosenfeld has entries for what appears to be Yarrow's version in Norwich and Kent, 1755 and 1757. On the Edinburgh stage the titles *Trick Upon Trick* and *Vintner Trick'd* shift about in haphazard fashion so that we can merely call attention to the existence of five recorded performances for 1757–58.[10] The story in this country is similar. Seilhamer and

---

[7]These performances have been supplied by Emmett L. Avery from his examination of papers in the British Museum.

[8]"At Hippisley, Bullock and Hallam's Great Theatrical Booth, over-against the Hospital-Gate in Smithfield, During the Time of Bartholomew-Fair, will be perform'd the True and Antient History of Fair Rosamund . . . To which will be added a new Ballad-Opera, call'd The Impostor, or the Biter Bit, with the comical Humours of Vizard the Biter, Mixum the Vintner, and his Drawer Balderdash. . . ." *Daily Advertiser*, August 21, 1734.

[9]It is not at all certain that the *Trick for Trick* performed at Bartholomew Fair in 1743 is our piece, but there is little uncertainty about the *Trick upon Trick* at Bartholomew Fair six years later or about the entries for the same title at the theatre in Bowling Green, Southwark, on September 24, 1747, and January 26, 1749.

[10]W. H. Logan, *Fragmenta Scoto-Dramatica*, p. 22.

the others give records of a dozen productions under a variety of titles.

The end of our story takes us back to London. Genest records a performance at the Haymarket on July 13, 1808: "never acted there, Cheats of Scapin—with alterations, and additions from old Farce of Trick upon Trick, or the Vintner in the Suds . . . Cheats of Scapin several times."

While none of these latter records are for performances of the exact droll printed here, they do indicate the wide and lasting popularity of almost identical versions of the same story.

Publication

Only one edition of this droll has come to our attention. It appeared along with six other plays in *The Strollers Pacquet open'd* . . . London: Printed and Sold by A. Jackson . . . 1742.

Analysis

In our collection of farces this is the only piece which has been called a *droll*. Even here the alternate term *farce* is used on the title page of *The Strolers Pacquet*, sufficient indication that both terms were loosely applied. If the term has any special significance, it refers to the circumstances under which the piece is intended to be performed, not to the nature of the play itself. That is, a droll is frankly designed for the lowest level of production, for strollers acting in booths at fairs, in barns in the provinces, before the least critical of audiences. It may be farcical and often is pure farce, but it may be tragic or at least melodramatic, or it may be a mixture of forms. This one happens to be a farce and therefore not essentially different from the other pieces here.[11]

---

[11]Since they were frequently unpublished, these eighteenth-century drolls are not easy to find. Of those which we have been able to see, perhaps the *Wat Tyler and Jack Straw* performed at Pinkethman and Giffard's booth in Bartholomew Fair in 1730 will serve as an example. There is no farce at all in this droll. The main plot is simply a quasi-dramatic reproduction of the historical events, or of the events as an unsympathetic writer imagined they might have happened. Combined with this is a sentimental love story of the Lord Mayor's son and the daughter of the Earl of Suffolk. These drolls had much in common with plays of a much earlier day in the English theatre, such pieces, for example, as the highly popular sixteenth-century *Mucedorus*.

All of the four episodes here had originally been taken from widely scattered sources and put into dramatic form—actually the first is still a narrative—with the traditional clever rogue serving to unite them.

The first episode was left in narrative form by Marston and by all his followers even though it has dramatic possibilities, being just another trick at Mixum's expense. Left in nondramatic form it serves chiefly as exposition. We learn a great deal about the relationship between sharper and vintner, and from the way he tells his sad tale, we learn that Mixum does not deserve the sympathy he is asking for. In other words, we are on the side of the clever rascal before we even meet him, in contrast to Marston's version where a rogue is a rogue.

The second episode, the first actually dramatized, is a version of the old barber trick very cleverly handled. The development of this scene through the several adaptations is an interesting one. Beginning with some bits of extravagant descriptions of monsters to keep the victim beguiled, the sharper develops his imaginative account until, in Bullock's version and those based on it, he is telling a tall tale about the white fox bigger than a large Flanders mare, the monstrous hasty-pudding, and all the rest. We have no evidence of the stage business with which all this was accompanied, but the opportunities for farce properties and for slapstick are obvious enough.

No great changes were made in the bowl and salmon episode borrowed originally from Masuccio. Perhaps most remarkable is the boldness of the rogue in returning to secure the salmon; however, poor Mrs. Mixum is so naïve and so susceptible to Vizard's flattery that the venture is not so hazardous as it might at first seem. Here in this episode is an excellent example of the repetition, or what might perhaps be called the *accretion*, device. No sooner has the trickster committed one theft, with the result of driving the vintner into a violent rage at his poor gullible wife, than he returns to repeat an almost identical one so that Mixum is driven to the point of contemplating suicide.

The last episode is the weakest of the lot. In the earlier plays in which the revenge story formed the principal plot it was better motivated, simply providing a lighter side to the prison scenes. Here it gives the clever rogue merely one more chance to vex his enemy, and the actor one more opportunity for comical disguise, and then the story closes in melodramatic fashion as everyone forgives everyone else, and the vintner's daughter is offered up as a kind of sacrificial victim to commemorate the peace-making.

THE BILKER BILK'D.

Persons who speak in the Bilker Bilk'd.

FREEMAN, A Gent.
MIXUM, a Vintner.
VIZARD, a Sharper.
[SOLOMAN SMACK.]
Drawers, Boys, etc.

Keeper of Newgate.
[Fidler.]
[Constable.]
MRS. MIXUM, the Vintner's Wife.

SCENE 1, a Tavern.

Enter FREEMAN and MIXUM.

FREEMAN. Hey day! here's a clutter of Curses against Rogues and Cheats! why thou rails with as hot a Zeal against Villany, as a demure Whore against Lewdness.

MIXUM. O, Sir, this is such a Piece of Roguery,—not of my own, Sir, no, no, of Vizards, that Root and Branch of all Villany: Hear me, Sir, this same Vizard, who I verily believe could cheat a Jesuit, and make an Ass of the Devil, comes into my House last Night, with a fine Female; says he, in a Whisper, Mixum, my Fortune is made, this is a Lady of Rank and Riches, whom I have this Day married; upon which I was full of Respect, o'course; he bespoke an elegant Supper; in a trice the Table smoak'd with Wild Fowl, they soon devour'd the first and second Course, Wine in Abundance drank, I was jocund; then he slips a twenty Pound Bill into my Hand, and bids me take my Reckoning; I suspecting nothing, return'd him full Change for his Bill, and retir'd to make mine; sends in a blind Harper to detain them longer, he cries "Musick is the Food of Love, play on," the Harper tunes up, my Drawer is beckon'd to withdraw, and you know when there is a Woman in Company it is Sam's Place to wink and vanish.

FREEMAN. Doubtless, Sir, that was but civil.

MIXUM. Well, Sir, this precious Pair, being left in the Room with the Harper, whose Eyes Heaven had clos'd, from beholding such Villany, silently opens the back Casement, quietly packs up my Plate, cleverly thrusts the Woman out of the Window, dextrously conveys himself after; the eyeless Harper plays on still, till Sam enters with,

D'ye call, Sir? but out, alas, the Birds were flown, and Nest of Plate also; then Lamentations rent the Air, the Drawer made the House ring, my Wife bawls, and all of us curse the blind Harper to the Devil: In this Confusion, I bethink myself of the twenty Pound Bill, and scour away to the Bankers to secure the Cash, but O ye cruel Fates, the Bill was forg'd, I was seiz'd, Vizard not to be found, I brought in guilty of Forgery, and got villify'd and pillory'd and pelted with rotten Eggs, and all for being cheated; but tho' he 'scapes me now, yet I still comfort myself with seeing him hang'd, in Hemp of his own beating. *Exeunt.*

SCENE 2, *the Street.*

Enter VIZARD.

VIZARD. A plague confound all Gaming, I think the Devil's in the Dice, what I get like a Rogue, I lose like a Fool; let me see, this Nest of Plate that I bilk'd Mixum, that Rogue of a Vintner, of, fetch'd me thirty Pounds, and lasted me just three Hours at Hazard, and this single Simon my whole Estate. O yonder comes a Barber, his Implements may fetch me a Dinner.

Enter SOLOMAN.

VIZARD. Well met my Lad, where art going.

SOLOMAN. I am a going to shave Mr. Mixum, Sir.

VIZARD. I am glad I met thee, I was just a going to thy Master's.

SOLOMAN. I believe you mean my Father's, Sir.

VIZARD. Ay, Ay, thy Father's, thou art a very pretty Boy, I have heard my Friend Mixum commend thee.

SOLOMAN. He is my Godfather.

VIZARD. He is so, and thy Name is —odso, that I should forget—

SOLOMAN. Soloman, my Name, Sir, is Soloman Smack.

VIZARD. Ay, Solomon, I knew it was some wise Name, I was just going to my Friend Smacks to borrow his Bason, Ball, and Razor, for I laid a Wager I could shave Mr. Mixum, and he not know it; a Frolick, my Lad, nothing but a Frolick, so I'll take thy Things, and in the mean Time, prithee call a Coach; for thy Godfather, and I, shall go to receive some Money, as 'soon as I have shav'd him; and here's Sixpence for thee to stay with the Coach till we come.

SOLOMAN. I thank you, Sir, but what shall I do for my Things?

VIZARD. I will leave them at thy Godfather's. *(Exit SOLOMAN.)* This is lucky; if I could cheat this Rogue Mixum six Days in a Week, I should keep my °Inclination wholly to remember him on the seventh. If I don't shave him in more Senses than one, I shall think my Wit as dull as the Back of my Razor.   *Exit.*

SCENE 3, *a Tavern.*

Enter MIXUM *and his* WIFE.

WIFE. Here's the Money, I am sure it is right, Forty two Pounds. *(Lays down the Bag.)*

MIXUM. Well, I must go taste some Wines that are just landed, and I'll call at Mr. Burnish's, and send home the Punch-bowl.

WIFE. In truth Husband, I am tired of the Trade we drive, when I call to mind how abominably we cheat, truly it afflicts my Conscience.

MIXUM. Conscience! what a devil have we to do with Conscience, don't we keep a Tavern, go, go, mind your Business, you had best, and to mend the matter, score double in the Devil's Name; talk of Conscience when we have got an Estate—

Enter VIZARD.

VIZARD. Sir, I am come to shave you, I am Mr. Smack's Man.

MIXUM. But where is my Godson, he us'd to shave me.

VIZARD. Sir, he's gone to shave Mr. Spintext the Lecturer, but my Master thought you might be in Haste, so sent me to shave you.

MIXUM. What's your Name Friend?

VIZARD. Timothy Perigrine, Sir, —Will you please to sit down. *(He sits,* VIZARD *puts the Cloth round his Neck.)*

MIXUM. How long have you been a Barber, Friend?

VIZARD. About a Year, Sir.

MIXUM. What then you serv'd no time to it.

VIZARD. No indeed Sir, I am glad to do any thing for an honest Livelihood; a wagging Hand you know, Sir, is getting a Penny. *(Raises a Lather.)*

MIXUM. What business was you brought up to.

VIZARD. The Sea, Sir, to plow the Ocean.

MIXUM. And how came you to leave the Sea faring Life?

VIZARD. Ill Fortune, Sir, that often attends the Industrious.

MIXUM. What was it? let's hear; these Sea Voyages are diverting.

VIZARD *(Aside).* Are they so? then faith I'll try if I can make one for you. —Why Sir, in my first unfortunate Voyage we was chac'd by three Algerine Pirates, and being deep laden found it impossible to escape; now I having heard what a miserable thing it was to be a Slave, chose rather to venture the Sea than be took Prisoner; with this Resolution, I prevail'd on the Cooper of our Ship to barrel me up in a Cask, clap a sound Cork into the Bunghole, and fling me overboard; no sooner said but done, there was I in the vast Ocean toss'd about for nine Days successively, till I was like to perish with Hunger, for I eat nothing all that time, but six Bisquets which I luckily had in my Pocket before we saw those terrible Pirates: Well, while I was in this Condition, a Dutch Man of War sail'd along, and spying a Barrel floating, they hoisted out their Boat and brought me aboard, I was not able to speak, but I heard them disputing what it should be that was in the Barrel; one said it was Butter, another said Beef, and some said it was Oatmeal, but to be satisfied they call'd the Cooper to strike out the Bung; when the Bung was out, there issued such a Fume, that they all agreed it stunk like the Devil: At length, one unfortunate Fellow more daring than the rest, thrust his Hand in to feel what it was, I snatch'd his Fore-finger and Thumb in my Mouth, and whipt 'em clever off in an Instant, (for I was consumed hungry) with that the Fellow bellow'd out, and swore it was the Devil, ram'd the Bung into the Barrel again, and toss'd me overboard.

MIXUM. Ods my Life, that was very ill Luck indeed! —how didst thou escape at last?

VIZARD. Providence preserv'd me, Sir; I roll'd upon the Billows in this Barrel twelve Days longer, and had no Sustenance but the Dutchman's Fore-finger and Thumb—hold up your Head, Sir—

MIXUM. Twelve Days, O the Devil, that could never be, Tim.

VIZARD. 'Tis true, upon my Honesty, well, at length my faithful Barrel was flung ashore, so I pondering with myself that I might as well be drown'd as famish'd (for by this time I had not so much as a Nail of the Man's Finger left) I bursts out the Bung, and putting my Head out for the Benefit of fresh Air, I saw I was cast ashore in Greenland, for casting my Eyes round I spy'd a huge white Fox, come scowering down the Sea-side, at a monstrous Rate; with that I skulk'd my Head into my Barrel again, knowing it to be a Beast of Prey—

MIXUM. A huge white Fox! how big might this Fox be?

VIZARD. Something, bigger than a large Flanders Mare, Sir— well he came thundering down to the Barrel, and smelling me out, he began to roar like a Lion, but by good Providence, that very Moment, a Fly as big as a Partridge, stung him on the Buttocks, he whisks round to rub himself against the Barrel, his Tail got a-cross the Bung-hole. I clap't fast hold on't with both my Hands; the Fox in a terrible Fright, fell a galloping as if the Devil was at his Tail, and hurried the Barrel with me in it, for three and twenty Miles over Hedges and Ditches, through Marshes and Woods, overturning all before him; till at last running full Speed between two Trees, that stood pretty close together, the Barrel stav'd all to pieces.

MIXUM. So, that was good Luck; then you got quit of the Fox.

VIZARD. No, Sir, no; my Hands, with grasping the Fox's Tail so violently all this long Journey, was clench'd so fast, I could not possibly open them. Well, away the Fox scower'd faster than ever, now he was lighten'd of the Barrel, and in an Instant dragg'd me twelve Miles and a half further. When he arrived at the Brink of a vast deep River, he plunges in directly, and fell a swimming with me at his Tail. Now a lucky Thought came into my Head, to be revenged on him for leading me this Dance; so when he was just got to the middle of the River, I suddenly plunged down to the very bottom, and calmly sate me down at my Ease, with his Tail in my Hand. He pants and struggles to get loose, but all in vain, I held him down while there was any Signs of Life.

MIXUM. O Tim! this must be a Gun.

VIZARD. Every Word true, or may this Shaving be my last. So, Sir, up comes I, swims ashore, and gets to a Port, where I found an English Ship, and came over to England in her.— Shut your Eyes, Sir, or my Ball will make em smart.

MIXUM. Ay, ay —Why, Tim, I find you have been a great Traveller: Was you never in the Popish Countries?

VIZARD. Yes, Sir, I have been in most Parts. In Italy I was once treated very handsomely, by a Monk of Loretto, with a delicious Hasty-pudding, made of the Milk of St. Luke's Cow, thicken'd with a Pound of the Chaos.

MIXUM. Psha! a pox Tim, you talk like a Traveller now.

VIZARD. Why, Sir, I hope you don't think I lye.—O dear, Sir, there are a Multitude of venerable Reliques in all their Churches.—I myself saw the very identical Shoes in which St. Ignatius walk'd barefoot to Jerusalem. Nay, Sir, I saw the Horse-shoe that was wore by the Horse, that fed with the Mare, that foal'd the Foal, that became the Horse, that begot the Mare, that was Dam of the Colt, that grew the Steed, that brought the Boy, that knew the Woman, that had seen the Man, that his Father told, that he saw the Lady of Loretta's Chappel fly from Judea into Italy.

MIXUM. Ha, ha, ha, What a Beadroll of Men, Horses, Mares, and Horseshoes, hast thou sputter'd forth!

VIZARD. O Sir, I assure we these are great Curiosities. Why, Sir, this was the very first Horse-shoe that ever kept Witches out of Houses; —Take Time by his Forelock of Hair, he is bald behind, says the wise Man, —I must leave the Vintner in the Suds. (Aside, takes the Bag, and exit.)

MIXUM. O Plague, Tim, this must be a devilish Lie. Come, make haste tho';— thou hast got a damn'd strong Memory, sure, to retain such a Heap of Lies, and pour 'em forth off Hand so pat; Ha, ha, ha; there's thy Barrel and white Fox, thy Hasty-pudding thicken'd with the Chaos, and blended with the Milk of St. Luke's Cow; and then the Genealogy of thy Horse shoe; Why what a Devil, dost thou take me to be such an Ass to believe all this,— Ha, ha, ha. —But come, why don't you shave me? —Why Tim, I shall be blind with winking.—Tim, why Tim, why dost not speak. —O Lord! my Heart misgives me! —Gone! —O the Devil! my Money! —Wife! —Wife! —why Wife! —

Enter WIFE.

WIFE. Hey day! What a Noise you make, Husband? What ail you?

MIXUM. Where's this curs'd Barber?

WIFE. Why he's just gone out.—Are you not trim'd then?

MIXUM. Trim'd! Yes, yes, I am trim'd, with a Vengeance: —Did you take the Money off the Table?

WIFE. I take the Money? No, indeed, not I.

MIXUM. O the Devil! I have wink'd to a fine Purpose.

Enter SOLOMAN.

SOLOMAN. Give me your Blessing, pray Godfather.

MIXUM. My Blessing! the Devil broil thy Heart, Where's your Father's Man?

SOLOMAN. My Father keeps no Man, Godfather.

MIXUM. Godfather! thou Devil's Son! who was it trim'd me?

SOLOMAN. Lord, Sir, I don't know the Gentleman; he borrow'd my Bason and Razors, as he said, for a Frolick.

MIXUM. Frolick! —My Money, my two and Forty Pounds gone in a Frolick!—It must be that cursed Vizard; Who the Devil would have suspected him in a Barber's Skin? Zoons! if I catch him, I'll strangle him with my own Hands—

WIFE. Nay, prithee Honey sweet Husband, have Patience.

MIXUM. Patience, with a Vengeance! Yes, a Plague on you, you could cry Patience, sweet Honey, when I caught Jack Rakish and your patient Ladyship upon the blue Squab Couch, in the red Room.

WIFE. Good Husband, take Heart; I'll play the Devil, but I'll recover this Loss; I'll score double and trebble for a Month, with a good Conscience.

MIXUM. Who the Plague could have suspected such ill Luck to Day? I got out of Bed backward too this Morning.—Well, I'll cast up my Accounts, make myself merry, and then fairly go and hang myself. The Devil take the Barber, and his white Fox together.

Exeunt.

SCENE 4, *the Street.*

Enter VIZARD.

VIZARD. Well, there is certainly a Fate attends those of my Profession: I that am so great a Master of the Art of Circumvention, am nevertheless bilk'd by every Bawd, and over-reach'd by tawdry half-witted Whores.

Enter MIXUM, and a Goldsmith's Boy, with a Silver Punch-Bowl.

MIXUM. Now Jervas, be sure you give this Bowl into my Wife's own Hands; let no Trick, nor Wile, prevail on you to part with it to any other. I am in continual Fear of that confounded Vizard; but if ever I catch him, Zoons! I'll play the Devil with him.

(Exit ambo.)

VIZARD. Curses fattens the Fox. —Friend Mixum, you want trimming again; my Mouth waters at that Punch-Bowl; to bite this Vintner, I hold meritorious, and will proceed to plot for his Plate, not having the Fear of Tyburn before my Eyes. *Exit.*

Enter MRS. MIXUM, with the Punch-Bowl, and the Goldsmith's Boy.

WIFE. 'Tis very well, Jervas; my profound Respects to your Mistress; I acknowledge the Receipt of this. —Profound Respects!—There's an Expression! This 'tis to have a fine Education, to be brought up in a Tavern: I let them see that I keep as good Company as any She within *London* Walls. —Fare thee well, Jervas.

Exit JERVAS.

Enter VIZARD, like a Goldsmith's 'Prentice, with a Jole of Salmon.

VIZARD. A fair Hour to you, Madam.

WIFE. A fine Compliment that! —I'll set it down—A beautiful Thought to you, Sir.

VIZARD. Madam, Mr. Burnish, my Master, has sent you a Jole of Salmon, and designs to come home with your Husband, to Supper, to season your new Bowl; and your Husband, Madam, desires you would send the Bowl back by me, to have his Arms engraven on it, which he forgot before.

WIFE. By what Token, Friend?—Nay, I have a Wit—

VIZARD. By the Token he was left in the Suds this Morning.

WIFE. An ill Token, but a true one.— Here, take the Bowl, and tell them, I expect 'em with Impatience. *(Exit VIZARD.)* Sam, Sam, why Sam, are you deaf?

Enter SAM.

SAM. Here, here, Mistress.

WIFE. Quickly, quickly, lay the Cloth and Napkins, and bring the Knives and Forks and Plates, and get every Thing ready.—There, there, that's well; the Company will soon be here. *(Enter MIXUM.)* O are you come, Husband? Where are they?

MIXUM. Hey dey! Hey dey! What's here? a Feast going forward, and in my best Parlour? Whose Treat, Peg? Whose Treat?

WIFE. Prithee leave fooling: Are they come?

MIXUM. Come, who come?

WIFE. Lord, how strange you make it?

MIXUM. Strange! What's strange? Is the Woman mad?

WIFE. What, you know of no Body that sent us a Jole of Salmon, do you? and said, they'd come to Supper?

MIXUM. Ha! Salmon! Hush, not I, hush, they have mistaken the House; let's eat it up quickly, before they return; come, come, sit down, Wife; —some good Luck yet.—Faith, I never relish'd Salmon better in my Life; —'tis delicious Feeding, freecost. *(Eating greedily.)*

WIFE. Husband, are you mad? Won't you stay till Mr. Burnish comes? Don't you know he sent the Fish?

MIXUM. No, I say no. *(Still eats fast.)*

WIFE. And that his Man, who brought it, said he would be here to supper?

MIXUM. I say, no, no, no, no. *(ats greedily.)*

WIFE. And hansel my new Bowl?

MIXUM. No, no, no. *(Eats still.)*

WIFE. And did not you order him to fetch the Bowl back?

MIXUM. *(Starts, and lays down his Knife.)* Ha! back?

WIFE. That your Arms might be engraved on't?

MIXUM. O Lord!

WIFE. By the Token you was left in the Suds this Morning?

MIXUM. O! O! O!

WIFE. And so I sent it back.—Nay, if I bear the Blame.

MIXUM. O I am shot! And is the Bowl gone, departed, defunct? ha?

WIFE. Gone? yes sure, 'tis gone.

MIXUM. I will never pray more, abandon all Remorse; on Horror's Head, Horrors accumulate. Hear me, thou Plague to Mortal, thou Wife thou; if I have not my Bowl again, I will send thee to Hell, and then go to a Conjurer, and if he fails to get it again, I'll have the Devil raised, before I lose it.   *Exit.*

WIFE. Bless me! how fearfully he talks.—

Enter VIZARD.

VIZARD. I must have my Salmon again, I cannot afford this old Rogue so nice a Bit, 'twill season my Punch rarely. Now for a Master-piece.—Fair Mistress.—

WIFE. O Sir! have I caught you? Sam, fasten all the doors—

VIZARD. Softly, softly, good Mistress, you shall know all. A very good Jest, I'faith; I warrant you was sadly frighted; your Husband's a Wag; he's gone to our House, laughing till he's ready to burst. The Bowl's safe enough, and brim full of Punch. Come away presently, and give me the Salmon, to carry before: You are to sup at our House.

WIFE. Praise the Powers 'tis no worse; but he did ill to fright me so; he has put every Part about me into a Constellation. Here take the Salmon. *(Exit VIZARD.)* Well, I was never so fluster'd in my Life: How my Heart beats yet! —Here, Sam, send Betty with my

Hood and Scarf and Gloves, quickly, quickly.

Enter BETTY, and puts on her Scarf and Hood, & then enter MIXUM.

MIXUM. How now? Whither are you jaunting, ha?

WIFE. Psha! pray leave your Fooling; you might have made one miscarry.

MIXUM. What unaccountable Devil has possess'd this Woman?

WIFE. Come, pray Devil me no Devils; Will you go?

MIXUM. Whither must I go? Is the Woman indeed possess'd?

WIFE. Whither? why, to eat the Salmon at Mr. Burnish's: I hate this Foolery.

MIXUM. Your Meaning, ye senseless Jade, your Meaning?

WIFE. Now Heaven bless your Wits, what a shallow Memory you have got! Did not you send for me and the Salmon, by the same Fellow that fetch'd the Bowl?

MIXUM. 'Tis mighty well, 'tis wond'rous well; And have you your Senses, you lunatick Jade?

WIFE. Nay, if you think to make me an Ass, I'll be sure to make you an Ox, I'll tell you that for your comfort.   *Exit.*

MIXUM. Well, I'll never pray again, that's certain: If Heaven prosper Knaves, the City's like to thrive. I'll go hang myself out of Revenge. *Exit.*

SCENE 5, *the Street.*

Enter VIZARD.

VIZARD. Ha, no Business stirring; sure the Devil's very busy; He used to give me Opportunity, as often as I had Inclination to be wicked.—O yonder comes a Fellow, by his Cloak he should have Money in his Pockets; I must knock at his Pate, before I can enter his Breeches.

Enter a FIDLER Cloak'd; VIZARD knocks him down.

FIDLER. O Murther! Murther!

VIZARD *(Searching his Pockets).* What a Devil have we here? a Fidler, with his Rosin and Cat-gut? Only a single Sixpence. Well, however, here's a Cloak for my Knavery. *Exit.*

FIDLER. Stop Thief! stop Thief. *Exit.*

Enter MIXUM, *meeting* VIZARD *in a Cloak.*

MIXUM. So, that is the Rogue paramount, Vizard.—Have I caught you at last? Sirrah, you shall hang for't. *(Takes hold of the Cloak,* VIZARD *slips it on his Shoulders.)* Odso, the Serpent has slipt his Skin; but however, I have got a good Cloak by the Bargain. *(He wraps himself in the Cloak.)*

Enter FIDLER, CONSTABLE, *and Watch.*

FIDLER. Stop Thief. O Mr. Constable, he has got my Cloak on his Back.

CONSTABLE. Seize him.

MIXUM. How now, Gentlemen, what's the matter?

CONSTABLE. No Harm, Friend, only carry you to *Newgate* for a Street Robber.

MIXUM. Why sure the Fellow's a Fool.

FIDLER. No, Sir; but he's a Constable, and that's all one. I'll take my Oath, that Cloak's mine, and that you came behind me, knock'd me down, and run away with it; and so Mr. Constable, I charge you with him.

MIXUM. Now shall I be hang'd for that Villain's Roguery. *Exeunt.*

SCENE 6, *Newgate.*

Enter KEEPER, MR. MIXUM, MRS. MIXUM, *and* VIZARD, *like a Fanatick Parson.*

MIXUM. Is there no Hopes of a Reprieve for me?

KEEPER. No, Sir, no; but here's a Parson come to prepare you for t'other World.

MIXUM. Alas! alas! then I'm in a bad way indeed.

VIZARD. Friend, I come from Zachariah Zealous, to be, as it were, a Staff to thee, whilst thou takest a great Leap—as it were—thou know'st not whither.

WIFE. Well, Husband, this is a Comforter, —this holy Man,—he is for the Soul. But, Friend, my Husband owes his Goldsmith Forty Pounds; and suppose now, when he is going to Execution, he should be so unneighbourly to set a Sergeant on his Back, might not that stay Execution?

VIZARD. I'll warrant his Back; but for his Neck, *Plinius Secundus,* and *Marcus Tullius. Cicero,* tell us in their Works, that a three-fold Cord is hardly broken.

MIXUM. A very learned Man, this!— Well, I am not the first honest Man that was hang'd, and I heartily pray to Heaven, I may not be the last.

WIFE. Ah, dear Husband, little did I think, when you swore the last Parson out of his Change, that you should have Occasion to think of Heaven so soon. —Oh!—If you had been hang'd deservedly, it would never have vex'd me: Many an honest Man has been hang'd deservedly, but to be cast away for nothing, Oh! Oh!

VIZARD. Comfort thyself, good Woman, grieve moderately, 'tis decent; you will shortly be a young Widow, I will visit you, and give you Christian Comfort.

WIFE. Thank you very kindly, Sir, you shall be heartily welcome to my House, by Day or by Night. *(Turning to her Husband.)* My Dear, do they, or we, the Halter find?

MIXUM. They, to be sure; this Government is kind.—O Woman! Woman! Why dost thou ask such a Question? thou may'st be sure they find the Halter.

WIFE. Alas, I could not tell, and so I brought one along with me.—O Robin! thou hast been a dear, dear Husband to me, and I was not willing thou shouldst want any Thing I could help thee to. *(Pulls a Halter out of her Pocket.)*

MIXUM. O my Dear, I thank thee, thou art so kind now.—

WIFE. My Neighbor Thong put it into my Hands upon his Word, and told me, he could not have made a stronger, if it had been for his own Wife.

MIXUM. I am mightily beholden to all my Friends; how ready they are to serve me at this Time!

WIFE. O dear Husband! I can't bear the Loss of you, I shall break my Heart. —O! I wish I were to be hang'd in your room.

MIXUM. I wish you were with all my Heart, that would be a Happiness; but I poor Sinner can't expect such a Mercy. —Well, I am but a dead Man.—And to die with a clear Conscience. If I owe any Man any thing, I here heartily forgive him; and whoever owes me any thing, let them pay my Wife.—Here Peg, here are the Writings to that Rogue Vizard's Estate; he has brought me to this untimely End; they are dear Writings to me. —And now, dear Wife, take Leave of thy doleful Husband.

WIFE. No, no, my Dear, I'll stay and see thee hang'd, and please the Lord. O dear! if the Rope should break, I shall break my Heart.

VIZARD. The Writings of my Estate! one Trick to recover them is worth all that ever I play'd.—Good Woman, the Rope will prove a trusty Rope, trouble him not with thy Fears, in this his Hour of Tribulation. *(Picks her Pocket of the Writings.)*

MIXUM. Wife, Wife, the sanctified Rogue has pick'd thy Pocket.—Some Comfort yet,—the Parson will be hang'd with me.—Ha!—as I live, 'tis Vizard! O Rogue! Rogue! why thou Villain! Didst thou come here to let me be hang'd for thy own Roguery?

VIZARD. Why faith, Mixum, thou hadst the Conscience to put me into the Con-

dition of hanging or starving, and thou art the Occasion of all the Tricks I have play'd; and is it Twenty to One, that I should rather have seen thee hang'd, than myself.

Enter KEEPER.

KEEPER. Mr. Mixum, here is a Pardon come at last for you.

MIXUM. Ah, Heaven be praised! How my Heart leaps for Joy! Well, Rogue, I shall not die this Time; and I am so light-hearted, and over-joyed, that I am resolved to show the same Mercy I have received, and forgive this Rogue this Time; tho' I foresee he will be hang'd at last.

VIZARD. Sir, I thank you, but I shall disappoint you, I hope; for I design to marry, as the lesser Evil of the two, and see what that will do.

MIXUM. Say you so? Why then, to make you Amends for the Wrong I have done you, and encourage you to be honest, I'll give you my Daughter to Wife, and a Thousand Pounds to maintain her; and as Earnest, there's the Mortgage of your Estate, to bind the Bargain.

VIZARD. What, sweet Nancy? a lovely Girl, faith! and Sir, I accept your Proposal, and thank you heartily. And now for Reformation, and a new life. Come Father, let's take our last Leave of this Hellish Place.

Farewell ye Whores and Dice, and Follies all;

Reason returns, and I attend her call.

Exeunt omnes.

FINIS

A

COLLECTION

OF THE MOST ESTEEMED

FARCES

AND

ENTERTAINMENTS

PERFORMED ON THE

BRITISH STAGE.

(PRINTED VERBATIM FROM THE LAST EDITIONS)

WITH THE

CORRECTIONS

OF THEIR

RESPECTIVE AUTHORS.

VOL. III.

NORTH-SHIELDS:

Printed by and for W. Thompson. 1787.

The Brave Irishman

Author

Although the title page of the first dated edition of *The Brave Irishman* says merely "Supposed to· be Written by T——S S——N, Esq;" there is little reason to question the traditional ascription to Thomas Sheridan, godson of Swift and father of one of England's most popular dramatists.

Sheridan was born in Dublin in 1719, his father being the schoolmaster Thomas Sheridan, long an intimate friend of Dean Swift. It was at Trinity College, from which he was graduated in 1739, that Sheridan is said to have written this farce, though in its original form it must have been rather different from the printed version.[1] Sheridan appeared at Smock Alley in 1743, and his success there and at Drury Lane the following year determined him to make a career in the theatre. From London he returned to Dublin to assume the management of Smock Alley. His insistence on certain reforms in the Irish theatre led to numerous improvements but, unfortunately for him, to several occasions of violence. These constitute a whole chapter in theatrical history and an interesting one.[2] In 1747 he married Frances Chamberlaine, minor novelist and playwright. After the most violent of the riots in Sheridan's house, in 1754, he quit Dublin for a few years and joined the Covent Garden company, with which he enjoyed fair success. Another attempt to resume the management of the Dublin theatre, in 1756, was abandoned, largely because of growing competition. Sheridan again returned to England, this time to a career as public lecturer at London, Bristol, Bath, and other principal cities. Never having been especially provident, he was forced to seek refuge from creditors on the continent for a few years,

---

[1] "It was written by Mr. Sheridan when a mere boy at college; but the original copy being lost, it was supplied from the memory of the actors, who added and altered in such a manner, that hardly any part of the original composition remains." *Biographia Dramatica* (1782). This information was added, presumably by Isaac Reed, to what Baker has to say in *The Companion to the Playhouse* (1764).

[2] Miss Stockwell gives a carefully documented account in her *Dublin Theatres and Theatre Customs* (1637–1820), Kingsport, Tennessee, 1938.

but the greater part of his later life he spent in London and Bath, the recipient of several honors and the center of some mild storms over his theories of education. Boswell has told of his friendship and estrangement with Dr. Johnson. He died in 1788.

Source

The main source of Sheridan's farce is *Monsieur de Pourceaugnac* by Molière, though the English farce is far from a close rendering of the French one, the ending being altogether different from Molière's. It is possible that Sheridan was influenced by some of the earlier English adaptations of *Pourceaugnac,* but his work is so different from both French and English versions that detailed comparisons are out of the question. Perhaps a brief account of the principal earlier adaptations would not be out of place here as it would serve to emphasize the independence of Sheridan's play.

Within two or three years after its first appearance in Paris, 1669, Molière's farce, or at least part of it, was transferred to the English stage. Ravenscroft borrowed from both *Pourceaugnac* and *Bourgeois gentilhomme* for his lively *Citizen turn'd Gentleman.* He remained fairly close to his French sources in this play. When he did depart we may be sure it was not in the direction of a more genteel or less farcical rendering. Ravenscroft appropriated parts of *Pourceaugnac* again in 1673 for his *Careless Lovers.*

Shortly after the turn of the century Molière's play was again translated, appearing on the stage and in print in 1704, but the circumstances are not as clear as they might be. The story has been told, in part at least, elsewhere.[3] For the present we may note merely the end result, so far as publication is concerned, the anonymous *Monsieur de Pourceaugnac, or, Squire Trelooby,* which is scarcely more than a fairly close translation of Molière.

In 1720, about the time of Sheridan's birth, there appeared in London a collection of five plays by Charles Shadwell, son of the Whig Laureate, with the descriptive phrase "As they are acted at the Theatre Royal in Dublin." In the very brief preface to his play called *The Plotting Lovers: or, The Dismal Squire, a Farce,* Shadwell describes the piece as "a translation from Moliere's *Monsieur de*

---

[3]See Montague Summers, *Complete Works of William Congreve,* I, 57–59, 76; W. C. Ward, *Sir John Vanbrugh,* I, l–lii; J. C. Hodges, "The Authorship of Squire Trelooby," *RES,* IV (1928), 404–13.

Pourceaugnac," but even a casual comparison of *The Plotting Lovers* and the *Squire Trelooby* of 1704 will reveal that "translation" must have been a very simple matter indeed, for Shadwell simply copied the earlier English version.

James Ralph, friend of Benjamin Franklin and collaborator with Henry Fielding, also had a hand in keeping *Pourceaugnac* before the English public, though he describes his *Cornish Squire* of 1734 as simply a delayed publication of the translation by Vanbrugh, Congreve, and Walsh which had been acted, but not published, in 1704. Not everyone has been disposed to accept the story Ralph tells in his preface of the long-neglected acting copy which by some mysterious means fell into his hands thirty years after it was written. Again a comparison of Ralph's play with the translation published in 1704 raises more than a little suspicion that his source was not so mysterious after all.[4]

What is notable about all these early eighteenth-century versions— perhaps *version* would be more accurate—is that Molière has been brought onto the English stage with few significant changes. Sheridan on the other hand borrowed only the main idea and some of the earlier farcical scenes. Since his principal character was to be from a region other than Limoges or Cornwall and since he was to be more hero than booby, not much of the dialogue and virtually none of the later scenes were useful to Sheridan.

The reader of Sheridan's farce will have no difficulty in recognizing the source of another brief scene, the one in which O'Blunder triumphs over the cringing Frenchman and forces him to eat the potato. Here Sheridan doubtless had the Fluellen-Pistol scenes from *Henry V* in mind.

Stage History

For no other play in this collection are there so many indications of success in the theatre with so few specific records. Genest records

---

[4]Another play which appeared in 1734, James Miller's *Mother-in-Law: or, the Doctor the Disease,* borrows some scenes from Pourceaugnac but devotes more time to other matters, especially material from another of Molière's plays, *Le malade imaginaire.*

but two, vossibly three, performances: the first for Goodman's Fields, 1746, a possible second one for Covent Garden, 1755,[5] and a third for Drury Lane, 1770. *The Daily Advertiser* lists performances at Bartholomew Fair in 1746. Add to these a couple recorded performances in the provinces,[6] about as many in Dublin,[7] a dozen in America,[8] and the story is told so far as available records go. Some supporting evidence is to be found in the title pages of the various editions: "As it is acted" at Dublin or Edinburgh.[9] But for the most part we have to depend upon contemporary accounts. The editor of *The Companion to the Playhouse*, 1764, tells us: "This farce has always met with great approbation in Ireland; on account of the favourable light in which the Irish gentleman . . . appears to stand." O'Keefe gives us a more circumstantial account:

Thomas Sheridan wrote a piece called "The brave Irishman," (the plot from the French) in which he worked up a very high character for Isaac Sparkes: it had a powerful effect, and was played very often. There were many signs of Sparkes in this same Captain O'Blunder. One day he was walking under one of these,

---

[5]The title recorded by Genest is *Irishman in London*, which he thinks was "in all probability . . . Sheridan's Brave Irishman." *The Larpent Catalogue* lists this piece as *The Brave Irishman; or, The Irishman in London* but adds that a comparison of the manuscript with the 1754 edition of Sheridan's farce shows such great differences that the Covent Garden piece "seems to be a different play based on the same source. . . ."

[6]Miss Rosenfeld lists performances for Bath, 1751–52, and for York, 1755–56.

[7]Professor Nicoll lists a performance for Aungier-street, February, 1737, but with only the date and the title *The Honest Irishman; or, The Cuckold in Conceit* to go by we are forced to doubt that this is the same play; this title suggests an Irish adaptation of *Sganarelle* rather than *Pourceaugnac*. J. P. Kemble transcribed records of a performance for July 7 and another for November 17, 1743 (Ms. in Harvard Theatre Collection). Miss Stockwell, pp. 154–55, quotes a letter in which the writer speaks of a performance in Dublin around 1775. Macklin is given as the author, but Sheridan's piece is probably meant; the fact that Macklin's *Love-a-la-Mode* borrows from Sheridan's piece has caused the confusion.

[8]Seilhamer, Miss Willis, Odell, and Pollock list twelve performances between 1765 and 1796. Though there were at least a few performances in the 1760's on March 17 for Irish organizations, the play did not survive the eighteenth century in this country.

[9]The Edinburgh editions invariably reproduce the cast given in the first (1755) Scottish edition, not quite invariably as there is some difficulty over the spelling of Keasberry's name.

when a chairman looking first at him with great admiration, and then up at the sign vociferated, "Oh there you are, above and below!"[10]

From the records transcribed from the Dublin *Journal* we know that the part of O'Blunder may not have been originally designed for Sparks, for in 1743 it was being played by Morris. However, the essential facts may be correct enough; Sparks is down for the part in the early editions an'd was still playing it when the farce was produced at his Drury Lane benefit, May 14, 1770.

Publication

Publication of *The Brave Irishman* seems to have been delayed until the play had established itself in the Dublin repertory. It may well be that Sheridan himself was indifferent toward the little farce and therefore required some prompting before he had it brought out. In fact, he may never have had anything to do with the original publication of the play.[11] Evidence in support of this suggestion can be found on the title page of what appears to be the first edition, Dublin, 1754. First, there is the announcement that the songs here printed are "not in any other Edition." Ordinarily such a statement would seem to look back to previous publications, but in the absence of any known record of earlier editions, the phrase would seem to look forward to possible rivals which could be forestalled.[12] Equally

---

[10]*Recollections of the Life of John O'Keeffe, Written by himself* (London, 1826), pp. 356–57. Genest in several places speaks of O'Keeffe's unreliability with dates, but perhaps we may give some credence to this colorful bit of theatrical lore.

[11]The compiler of *The Thespian Dictionary* (1802) repeats Isaac Reed's account of Sheridan's school-boy composition and the loss of the original copy and then adds that the frequent performances were "never, as Mr. Sheridan used to declare, with his consent." Just where he got this amazing bit of information he does not say. Walter Sichel, in his biography of the younger and more famous Sheridan, casts doubt on the whole business of the lost manuscript and to prove his case cites a letter by young Richard Brinsley in which he speaks of mislaying his father's manuscript. The account of piecing the play together from the actors' memories is rather implausible, but it is not at all clear how R. B. Sheridan's mislaying a manuscript years after the play was first printed can be used to refute the story.

[12]Unfortunately the other early Dublin edition, published by Corcoran, is undated, so that we have no way of knowing whether it preceded or followed the one of 1754. It too professes to have the genuine songs. It is virtually identical with the dated edition and is usually dated early, 1754 or 1755. Nicoll lists a 12° edition of 1754; it is not clear whether he has in mind this or the preceding edition, actually 8°, or some other which we have not seen.

puzzling and even more interesting is the next item on the title page: "Supposed to be Written by T——S S——r, Esq; and Revised . . . by J——n P——st—n." The first name here is of course that of Thomas Sheridan. The second requires a little more guesswork, but there is every reason to suppose that the name is John Preston. Who Preston was may be inferred from an entry in *Biographia Dramatica* which lists a John Preston, "an itenerant actor, who published in Dublin one piece, called The Rival Father. F. 8 vo. 1754." We learn further, from the entry in *Biographia Dramatica* for the play itself, that *The Rival Father* was considered too weak even to deserve a trial in the theatre but that its acknowledged author had it published anyway, in the same year that *The Brave Irishman* appeared.

Now it was early in this year that Sheridan had his second and major quarrel with the Dublin theatregoers. On March 2, 1754, there was a riot and the theatre was torn up. This time Sheridan did not stand his ground, as he had done in the Kelly affair of 1746, but closed the theatre, leased it to Victor and Sowden in May, and some-time in the summer went over to London, where he took his place in the Covent Garden company in the fall. It is not at all unreason-able to suppose, then, that the untalented but aspiring John Preston simply commandeered a prompt copy of Sheridan's successful farce and brought it out as at least partly his own.

The history of the publication of *The Brave Irishman* continues to be difficult to follow both because of other undated editions and because of the rarity of several editions. There would seem to have been some twelve editions between 1754 and the end of the century. The play was ignored by the editors of the large nineteenth century collections of popular drama.

The Brave Irishman: or, Captain O'Blunder. A Farce. As it is Acted at the Theatre-Royal in Smock-alley: with the genuine Songs, not in any other Edition. Supposed to be Written by T——s S——n, Esq; and Revised with Several Corrections and Additions by J——n P——st—n. Dublin: Printed, and Sold by R. Watts, Bookseller, at the Bible in Skinner-row MDCCLIV. (Price Three-pence)

The Brave Irishman: or, Captain O'Blunder. A Farce. As it is Acted at the Theatres in Crow-Street and Smock-Alley. With the Genuine Songs. Dublin: Printed for Bart. Corcoran on the Inns-Quay, near the Cloysters. [n.d.]

The Brave Irishman. A Farce. As acted at the Theatre in Edinburgh
 . . . MDCCLV.[13]
The Brave Irishman . . . 1756.[14]
The Brave Irishman. A Farce. As acted at the Theatre in Edinburgh.
 Edinburgh: Printed for J. Baillie and Company. [n.d.][15]
The Brave Irishman: or, Captain O'Blunder. Supposed to be Written
 by . . . Dublin, 1759.[16]
The Brave Irishman. A Farce. As it is acted at the Theatre in Edin-
 burgh. Glasgow: Printed in the year MDCCLXI.
Captain O'Blunder: or, The Brave Irishman. A Farce. As it is acted
 at the theatres in London, Dublin, and Edinburgh. Written by
 Mr. Sheridan. London: Printed in the year MDCCLXXI.
The Brave Irishman . . . [Belfast]. 1773.[17]
The Brave Irishman. By Thomas Sheridan. In Vol. III, 195–213,
 Bell's Supplement, 1784.
The Brave Irishman. By Mr. Thomas Sheridan. In Vol. III of *A Col-
 lection of the Most Esteemed Farces and Entertainments* . . .
 North Shields . . . 1787.
The Brave Irishman. By Mr. Thomas Sheridan. In Vol. III, 195–213,
 of *A Collection of the Most Esteemed Farces* . . . Edinburgh,
 1792.

Analysis

In *The Brave Irishman* both old and new are combined in interesting fashion. The piece begins with a stereotyped intrigue—the cir-
cumventing of a boorish rival who has a father's approval—combined
with some outworn satire—on the familiar stage Irishman combined
with Molière's provincial booby. But the outcome is far from conventional. The intrigue does not turn out according to the old pattern,
with the boor driven back to his native wilds or married off to some

---

[13]From the *British Museum Catalogue*; we have not seen this edition.

[14]*British Museum Catalogue*; we have not seen this edition.

[15]This seems to be the edition dated [1757] in the *British Museum Catalogue*
and elsewhere. The copy we examined at the Library of Congress is marked up
for a prompt copy. The title page is a cancel, with type different from that
used elsewhere in the book. Beside the printed cast for the Edinburgh theatre
is written a cast that suggests both Drury Lane actors, Lewis, Parsons, Aickin,
and Staggledoir being among the names, and a rather late date in the century,
possibly 1780–1788.

[16]*British Museum Catalogue*; we have not seen this edition.

[17]Nicoll's handlist; we have not seen it. There may have been an even earlier
issue in Belfast. In a Harvard copy of *The Vintner Trick'd* published by James
Magee at Belfast, 1766, appears a list of books printed and sold by Magee,
among them being *The Brave Irishman*.

trollop in disguise; instead, he plays the part of sentimental hero, rescuing the old homestead and winning the girl. The satire must change accordingly. The provincial booby is ridiculous at first with his broad dialect, outmoded dress, and ignorance of civilized manners; but he soon reveals traits not ordinarily associated with satirical figures: he is brave and patriotic, tenderhearted and magnanimous. No wonder the play succeeded so well with the Irish, who had been represented on the stage by generations of Teagues.

The play consists of four or five episodes, with the necessary exposition and links. First there is the "gulling" scene, taken from Molière but substituting for many of Pourceaugnac's speeches some Irish bulls, such as the one about the wind's turning. Then comes the comic duel, not in Molière but very nearly as old as the cart of Thespis itself. It may be noted that in spite of the fact that Ragou is reported dead, nothing further is really made of the danger to Phelim, except to provide a link with the next scene by having him seek refuge in Cheatwell's house, actually the madhouse. In this next episode we return to Molière, with some "improvements" in the dialogue to make it coarser but with the original *commedia dell'arte* ending, the pursuit with clister pipes. The last episode is somewhat disappointing as farce. The Captain and his servant having dressed themselves up in ridiculous fashion to go courting, we may expect some buffoonery of the usual sort. Instead we get the brief business of forcing Ragou to eat the potato—highly satisfying to Irish audiences no doubt—and then the scene goes off quite sentimentally.

A final word about alterations in the edition printed here from the earliest printed versions. There are numerous slight changes but no really significant differences. The changes may be grouped under four heads: 1. There are a few deletions of topical items, such as references to the Marriage Act and to the Blue Posts tavern. 2. There are some attempts to rid the play of offensive material, though a nineteenth-century editor would have had to remove still more passages. 3. A few thrusts at the Irish have disappeared. 4. The greatest number of changes consist of elaborations of O'Blunder's bulls and ridiculous stories.

THE BRAVE IRISHMAN.

By Mr. Thomas Sheridan.

DRAMATIS PERSONAE.

MEN.

	Edinburgh.
CAPTAIN O'BLUNDER.	Mr. *Kennedy.*
TRADEWELL, a merchant.	Mr. *Salmon.*
CHEATWELL.	Mr. *Davenport:*
SCONCE.	Mr. *Keasberry.*
SERJEANT.	Mr. *Lancashire.*
DR. CLYSTER.	Mr. *Wright.*
DR. GALLYPOT.	Mr. *Stamper.*
MONSIEUR RAGOU.	Mr. *Heyman.*

WOMEN.

LUCY, daughter to TRADEWELL.	Miss *Wells.*
BETTY.	Miss *Hamilton.*
Mob, Keepers, &.	

Scene [1], *a Chamber.*

Enter LUCY and BETTY.

LUCY. 'Tis not the marriage, but the man, we hate;
'Tis there we reason and debate;
For, give us but the man we love,
We're sure the marriage to approve.
Well, this barbarous will of parents is a great drawback on the inclinations of young people.

BETTY. Indeed, and so it is, Mem. For my part, I'm no heiress, and therefore at my own disposal; and if I was under the restraint of the act, and kept from men, I would run to seed, so I would.—But la! Mem, I had forgot to acquaint you, I verily believes that I saw your Irish lover the captain; and I conceits it was he, and no other, so I do;—and I saw him go into the blue postices, so I did.

LUCY. My Irish lover, Miss Pert! I never so much as saw his face in all my born days, but I hear he's a strange animal of a brute.—Pray, had he his wings on? I suppose they saved him in his passage.

BETTY. Oh! Mem, you mistakes the Irishmen. I am told they are as gentle as doves to our sex, with as much politeness and sincerity as if born in our own country.

Enter CHEATWELL.

CHEATWELL. Miss, your most humble and obedient—I come to acquaint you of our danger; our common enemy is just imported hither, and is enquiring for your father's house thro' every street.—The Irish captain, in short, is come to London. Such a figure! and so attended by the rabble!

LUCY *(aside).* I long to see him; and Irishmen, I hear, are not so despicable; besides, the captain may be misrepresented. Well, you know my father's désign is to have as many suitors as he can, in order to have a choice of them all.

CHEATWELL. I have nothing but your prepossessions and sincerity to depend on. O, here's my trusty Mercury. *(Enter SCONCE.)* Well Sconce, have you dogged the Captain?

SCONCE. Yes, yes. I left him snug in the Blue Posts, devouring a large dish of potatoes and half a surloin of beef for his breakfast. He's just pat to our purpose; easily humm'd, as simple and as undesigning as we would have him. Well, and what do you propose?

CHEATWELL. Propose, why to drive him back to his native bogs as fast as possible.

LUCY. Oh! Mr Cheatwell—pray let's have a sight of the creature.

CHEATWELL. Oh! female curiosity—Why, child, he'd frighten thee;—he's above six feet high.

SCONCE. A great huge back and shoulders—wears a great long sword, which he calls his *sweetlips.*

LUCY. I hear the Irish are naturally brave.

SCONCE. And carries a large oaken cudgel, which he calls his *shillela.*

LUCY *(aside).* Which he can make use of on occasions, I suppose.

SCONCE. Add to this a great pair of Jack-boots, a Cumberland pinch to his hat, an old red coat, and a damn'd potatoe-face.

LUCY. He must be worth seeing, truly.

CHEATWELL. Well, my dear girl, be constant, wish me success; for I shall so hum, so roast, and so banter this same Irish captain, that he'll scarce wish himself in London again these seven years to come.

LUCY. About it—Adieu—I hear my father.   *Exeunt severally.*

Scene [2], *a Street.*

Enter CAPTAIN O'BLUNDER *and* SERGEANT.

O'BLUNDER.

Tho' I will be dying,
For captain O'Brien,
In the county of Kerry;
Tho' I would be sad,
I'll be very glad
That you will be merry.

Upon my shoul, this London is a pretty sort of a plaash enough. And so you tells me, Chergeant, that Terence McGloodtery keeps a goon.

SERGEANT. Yes, Sir.

O'BLUNDER. Monomundioul! but when I go back to Ireland, if I catches any of these spalpeen brats keeping a goon, to destroy the shentleman's creation, but I will have 'em shot stone-dead first, and phipt thorrow the regiment afterwards.

SERGEANT. You mean that they shall be whipped first, and then shot.

O'BLUNDER. Well, isn't it the same thing? Phat the devil magnifies that?

'Tis but phipping and shooting all the time; 'tis the same thing in the end sure, after all your cunning; but still you'll be a wiseacre. Monomundioul, there ishn't one of these spalpeens that has a cabbin upon a mountain, with a bit of a potatoe-garden at the back of it, but will be keeping a goon; but that damn'd McGloodtery is an old poacher, he shoots all the rabbits in the country to stock his own burrough with—But Chergeant, don't you think he'll have a fine time on't that comes after me to Ballyshans Duff.

SERGEANT. Why, Sir?

O'BLUNDER. Why, don't you remember that I left an empty hogshead half full of oats there?

SERGEANT. You mean, Sir, that you left it half full, and it is empty by this time.

O'BLUNDER. Phat magnifies that, you fool? 'tis all the same thing, sure. But d'ye hear, Chergeant, stop and enquire for Mr Tradwell's the merchant,—at the sign of the—Oh! Cangrane, that's not it, but it was next door—Arrah, go ask phat sign my cousin Tradwell lives at next door to it.

Enter a Mob, who stare and lough at him.

1 MOB. Twig his boots.

2 MOB. Smoke his sword, &. &.

O'BLUNDER. Well, you scoundrels, you sons of whores, did you never see an Irish shentleman before?

Enter SCONCE.

SCONCE. O fie, gentlemen! are you not ashamed to mock a stranger after this rude manner?

O'BLUNDER *(aside).* This is a shivil short of a little fellow enough.

SCONCE. If he is an Irishman, you may see by his dress and behaviour that he is a gentleman.

O'BLUNDER. Yesh, you shons of whores, don't you see by my dress that I am a shentleman? And if I have not better cloaths on now, phat magnifies that? sure I can have them on tomorrow. By my shoul, if I take my shillela to you, I'll make you skip like a dead salmon.

SCONCE. Oh, for shame, gentlemen, go about your business: the first man that offers an insult to him, I shall take it as an affront to myself. *Mob exeunt.*

O'BLUNDER *(to* SCONCE*)*. Shir, your humble servant; you seem to be a shivil, mannerly kind of a gentleman, and I shall be glad to be gratified with your nearer acquaintance. *(Salute.)*

SCONCE. Pray, Sir, what part of England come you from?

O'BLUNDER. The devil a part of England am I from, my dear; I am an Irishman.

SCONCE. An Irishman! Sir, I should not suspect that; you have not the least bit of the brogue about you.

O'BLUNDER. Brogue! No, my dear; I always wear shoes, only now and then when I have boots on.

Enter CHEATWELL.

CHEATWELL. Captain O'Blunder! Sir, you're extremely welcome to London—Sir, I'm your most sincere friend, and devoted humble servant.

O'BLUNDER. Arra then! how well every body knows me in London—to be sure they have read of my name in the newspapers, and they know my faash ever since—Shir, I'm your most engaging conversation. *(Salute.)*

[*Exit* SCONCE.]

CHEATWELL. And, Captain, tell us how long are you arrived!

O'BLUNDER. Upon my shoul, I'm just now come into London.

CHEATWELL. I hope you had a good passage.

O'BLUNDER. Passage d'ye call it? Devil split it for a passage. By my shoul, my own bones are shore after it—We were on the devil's own turnpike for eight-and-forty hours; to be sure we were all in a comical pickle.— I'll tell you, my dear: We were brought down from Rings-end in the little young ship to the Pool-pheg, and then put into the great ship—the horse—ay, ay— the Race-horse they call'd it. But I believe, my dear, it was the devil's own posthorse; for I was no sooner got into the little room down stairs, by the corner of the hill of Hoath, but I was taken with such a head-ache in my stomach, that I thought my guts would come out upon the floor; so, my dear, I call'd out to the landlord, the captain they call him, to stop the ship while I did die and say my prayers: So, my dear, there was a great noise above; I run up to see what was the matter.— Oh hone, my dear, in one minutes time there wasn't a sheet or blanket but phat was haul'd up to the top of the house—Oh, kingrann, says I, turn her about and let us go home again; but, my dear, he took no more notice of me than if I was one of the spalpeens below in the cellar going over to reap in harvest.

CHEATWELL. No, Captain? —the unmannerly fellow! And what brought you to London, Captain?

O'BLUNDER. Fait, my dear jewel, the stage-coach; I sail'd in it from Chester.

CHEATWELL. I mean what business?

O'BLUNDER [*aside*]. How damn'd inquisitive they are here! but I'll be as cunning as no man alive.—By my shoul, my jewel, I am going over to Wirginny to beat the French—they say they have driven our countrymen out of their plantations: By my shoul, my jewel, if our troops get vonse among them, we'll cut' them all in pieces, and then bring them over prisoners of war besides.

CHEATWELL. Indeed, Captain, you are come upon an honourable expedition—But pray, how is the old gentleman your father? I hope you left him in good health?

O'BLUNDER. Oh, by my shoul, he's very well, joy; for he's dead and buried these ten years.

CHEATWELL. And the old gentleman your uncle?

O'BLUNDER. I don't believe you mean that uncle, for I never had one.

CHEATWELL. No! I'm sure—

O'BLUNDER. O, I'll tell you who you mean; you mean my chister's husband; you fool you, that's my brother in law—

CHEATWELL. Ay, a handsome man—as proper a man—

O'BLUNDER. Ha, ha, a handsome man! Ay, for he's a damn'd crooked fellow; he's bandy-shoulder'd, and has a hump on his nose, and a pair of huckle-baks upon his shins, if you call that handsome, ha, ha!

CHEATWELL. And pray is that merry joking gentleman alive still—he that used to make us laugh so—Mr—Mr—A—

O'BLUNDER. Phugh, I'll tell you who you mean; you mean Sheela Shagnassy's husband, the parson.

CHEATWELL. The very same.

O'BLUNDER. Oh, my dear jewel, he's as merry as he never was in his life. Phin I'm by, he's sometimes pretty smart upon me with his humbuggs—But I told him at last, before Captain Flaharty, Miss Mulsinin, and Miss Owney Glasmogonogh—Hark ye, Mr parson, says I, by my shoul, you have no more wit than a goose. Oh hone! he was struck at that, my dear, and hadn't a word in his cheek. Arra, my jewel, I'll tell you the whole story. We took a walk together; it was a fine calm morning, considering the wind was very high; so, my dear, the wind 'twas in our backs going, but by my shoul, as we came back, 'twas in our faash coming home; and yet I could never persuade him that the wind had turn'd—

CHEATWELL. Oh the fool!

O'BLUNDER. Arra, so I told him, my jewel. Pugh, you great oaf, says I—if the wind blows in your back going, and blows in your faash coming, sure the wind is turn'd—No, if I was to preach, and to preach till last Patrick's day in the morning, I could not dissuade him that the wind was turn'd.

CHEATWELL. He had not common sense—Well, and does the old church stand where it did?

O'BLUNDER. The old church—the devil a church I remember within ten miles of us—

CHEATWELL. I'm sure there was an old building like a church or castle.

O'BLUNDER. Phoo, my jewel, I know what you call a church.—By my shoul, 'tis old lame Will Hurly's mill you mean—the devil a church—indeed they say mass in it sometimes. Here, Terence, go to that son of a whore of a taylor, and see whether my cloaths be done or no. *Exit* TERENCE.

CHEATWELL. Sure I should know that sergeant of your's, his name is—

O'BLUNDER. Wiseacre, my dear: He's the best recruiting-sergeant in all Ireland; and, my dear, he understands riding as well as no man alive; and he was manured to it from his cradle. I brought him over to see if I could get no preferment for him at all: If I could get him now to be a riding-master to a regiment of marines, he would be very well; for I gave him a word of advice myself. Hark ye, Terence, says I—

CHEATWELL. Terence!

O'BLUNDER. Ay, that's his name—Hark ye, Terence, says I, you have a long time lain under the computation of being a Papist; and if ever you come into the field of battle, it will be encumbered upon you, to stigmatize yourself like a shentleman; and I warrant, let him alone, I'll warrant he plays his part, if once they come to dry blows. *Enter* SCONCE, *with Monsieur* RAGOU. *Talk apart.*

SCONCE. Consider, Monsieur, he's your rival, and is come purely and with an intent to rob you of your mistress.

RAGOU. Is he? *Le fripon—le grand fripon! Parblieu!* me no indure dat—*Ici l'epee*—my vat you call—my sword—*Est bien assuré*—me no suffer dat.

SCONCE. And he's the greatest of all cowards—tho' he carries that great swaggering broad-sword—Believe me. Monsieur, he would not fight a cat—he'd run away if you drew upon him.

RAGOU. *Etez vous bien assuré*, are you well assur'd, *mon ami*, that he be de grand coward—*Eh bien*— Vel ten—I will have his blood. *(Aside.)* My heart go pit-a-pat,— *Je n'ai pas le courage*, I have not de good courage.

SCONCE. Tut, man, only affront him—go up to him.

RAGOU. Me sall shew him de bon address—*Helas*—(*goes up to the Captain*) *Monsieur le Capitaine, vous etes le grand fripon.*

O'BLUNDER. Well, gelun a gud, have you any Irish?

RAGOU. Ireland! me be no such outlandish contre; you smell of de potatoe.

O'BLUNDER. Do I? —By my shoul, I did not taasht a pratty since I left Ireland. (*To* CHEATWELL) May be he has a mind to put the front upon me?

CHEATWELL. It looks very like it, very like it, Captain.

O'BLUNDER. Fait, my jewel, I don't know a more peaceable companion than sweet-lips here (*putting his hand to his sword*); but if he's provok'd, he's no slouch at it—Do you mean to front me, you French boogre?—Eh—

RAGOU. Affront—You be de Teague— de vile Irishman—de potatoe-face—Me no think it vort my vhile to notice you—*Allez vous en*—Get you gone, Sir—go along about your business—go to your own hottontot contre.

O'BLUNDER. Hot and trot! Oh ho, are you there? Take that, you French son of a whore. (*Gives him a box on the ear.*) Here, my dear, take my shillela. (*Gives his cudgel to* CHEATWELL.)

SCONCE (*aside to the Frenchman*). Draw, for he won't fight.

RAGOU. He be de terrible countenance—he be *fort enragé*, devilish angry! Ala, Monsieur, me demand satisfaction. (*Draws.*)

O'BLUNDER. Come on, you soupmaigre. (*They fight, Monsieur falls.*) After that you are easy—Who smells of pratties now, you refugee son of a whore?—Affront an Irish shentleman! Ah, long life to my little sweet-lips, it never miss'd fire yet.

SCONCE. The man is dead.

O'BLUNDER. Is he?—Phat magnifies that?—I killed him in the fair duelling way.

CHEATWELL. But, Captain, 'tis death by the law to duel in England; and this is not a safe place for you—I'm heartily sorry for this accident.

O'BLUNDER. Arra, my jewel, they don't mind it in Ireland one traween.

CHEATWELL. Come, Captain, safe's the word—the street will be soon alarmed—You can come to my house till the danger's over, and I will get you bail.

O'BLUNDER. By my shoul, I believe 'tis the best way, for fear of the boners. So farewel, Mr Shatisfacts. *Exeunt* CHEATWELL *and* O'BLUNDER.

SCONCE. Are you dead, Monsieur?

RAGOU. Ay, quite dead, quite run thro' the body, begar; dead as a doornail.

SCONCE. Why, you have no wound; you are not hurt.

RAGOU. Am I not hurt, do you say? —Begar, I am glad he be gone. *Parbleu! il avait* de long rapier—He be de terrible Irishman; 'tis vel me fall in time, or he make me fall so dat me never *resusciter*, never get up again. Get you into my scabbard; and if ever I draw you again, may de horse-pond be my portion; may I be drown'd in soup-maigre. Come, Monsieur, come along, Sir. *Exeunt.*

Scene [3], *a Mad-house.*

Enter O'BLUNDER *and* CHEATWELL.

CHEATWELL. This is my house; I'll go and get proper things for your accommodation; but you had best give me your sword, for fear of suspicion. (*Takes his sword and cudgel. Exit.*)

O'BLUNDER. Ay, and take shillela too for fear of suspicion. (*Sings*)

> Of all the fish in the sea,
> Herring is king,
> Huggermenany, &.

(*Looks about.*) Fait, my cousin's house is a brave large place—'tis so big as a little town in Ireland—tho' 'tis not so very well furnished—but I suppose the maid was cleaning out the rooms— So—who are these now?—Some acquaintances of my cousin's, I suppose.

Enter Dr CLYSTER *and* Dr GALLYPOT. *Both salute the Captain.*

O'BLUNDER. Shentlemens, being my friend's friend, I am your most humble sharvant—But where's my cousin?

CLYSTER. His cousin! What does he mean?

GALLYPOT. What should a madman mean? He's very far gone.

O'BLUNDER. No, my dear, he's only gone to see whether the fellow be dead that I kilt.

GALLYPOT. Sir, we come to treat you in a regular manner.

O'BLUNDER. O dear shentlemen, 'tis too much trouble—You need not be over regular—A single joint of meat, and a good glass of ale, will be a very good treat, without any needless expence.

CLYSTER. Do you mind that symptom—the canine appetite!

O'BLUNDER. Nine appetites—No, my jewel; I have an appetite like other people; a couple of pounds will serve me if I was ever so hungry—Phat the devil do you talk of nine appetites? *(aside)* do they think I'm a cat, that have as many stomachs as lives?

GALLYPOT. He looks a little wild, brother.

O'BLUNDER. Phat, are you brothers?

BOTH. Pray, Sir, be seated; we shall examine methodically into your case. *(They sit—the Captain in the middle—they feel his pulse—he stares at them.)*

O'BLUNDER. Phat the devil do you mean by taking me by the wrists? May be 'tis the fashion of compliment in London.

GALLYPOT. First, brother, let us examine the symptoms.

O'BLUNDER. By my shoul, the fellows are fools.

CLYSTER. Pray, Sir, how do you rest?

O'BLUNDER. In a good feather-bed, my jewel—and sometimes I take a nap in an arm-chair.

CLYSTER. But do you sleep sound?

O'BLUNDER. Fait, my dear, I snore all night; and when I awake in the morning, I find myself fast asleep.

GALLYPOT. The cerebrum or cerebellum is affected.

O'BLUNDER. The devil a Sir Abram or Bell either I mind.

GALLYPOT. How do you eat?

O'BLUNDER. Width my mouth—How the devil should I eat, d'ye think?

CLYSTER. Pray, Sir, have you a good stomach? d'ye eat heartily?

O'BLUNDER. Oh, my dear, I am no slouch at that; tho' a clumsy beef-steak, or the leg and arm of a turkey, with a griskin under the oxter, would serve my turn.

GALLYPOT. Do you generally drink much?

O'BLUNDER. Oh, my jewel, a couple of quarts of ale and porter would not choke me. But phat the devil magnifies so many questions about eating and drinking—If you have a mind to order any thing, do it as soon as you can, for I am almost famished.

CLYSTER. I am for treating him regularly, methodically, and *secundum artem.*

O'BLUNDER. *Secundum sartem*—I don't see any sign of treating at all. Arra, my jewel, send for a clumsy beef-steak, and don't trouble yourselves about my stomach.

CLYSTER. I shall give you my opinion concerning this case—Brother, Galen says—

O'BLUNDER. Well, Gelun agud?

CLYSTER. I say, that Galen is of opinion, that in all adust complexions—

O'BLUNDER. Well, and who the devil has a dusty complexion?

CLYSTER. A little patience, Sir.

O'BLUNDER. I think I have a great deal of patience—that people can't eat a morsel without so many impertinent questions.

CLYSTER.

Qui habet vultum adustum,
Habet caninum gustum.

O'BLUNDER. I'm sure 'tis a damn'd ugly custom to keep a man fasting so long after pretending to treat him.

GALLYPOT. Ay, brother; but Hippocrates differs from Galen in this case.

O'BLUNDER. Well, but, my jewels, let there be no difference nor falling out between brothers about me; for a small matter will serve my turn.

CLYSTER. Sir, you break the thread of our discourse. I was observing, that in gloomy, opaque habits, the rigidity of the solids causes a continual friction in the fluids, which, by being constantly impeded, grow thick and glutinous; by which means, they cannot enter the capillary vessels, nor the other finer ramifications of the nerves.

GALLYPOT. Then, brother, from your position, it will be deducible, that the *primae viae* are first to be cleared, which must be effected by frequent emetics.

CLYSTER. Sudorifics.

GALLYPOT. Cathartics.

CLYSTER. Pneumatics.

GALLYPOT. Restoratives.

CLYSTER. Corrosives.

GALLYPOT. Narcotics.

CLYSTER. Cephalics.

GALLYPOT. Pectorals.

CLYSTER. Styptics.

GALLYPOT. Specifics.

CLYSTER. Caustics.

O'BLUNDER. I suppose these are some of the dishes they are to treat me with. How naturally they answer one another, like the parish-minister and the clerk! —By my shoul, jewels, this gibberish will never fill a man's belly.

CLYSTER. And thus, to speak *summatim & articulatim*, or categorically to recapitulate the several remedies in the aggregate, the emetics will clear the first passages, and restore the viscera to their pristine tone, and regulate their peristaltic or vermicular motion; so that from the oesophagus to the rectum, I am for potent emetics.

GALLYPOT. And next for sudorifics; as they open the pores, or rather the porous continuity of the cutaneous dermis and epidermis, thence to convey the noxious and melancholy humours of the blood.

CLYSTER. With cathartics to purge him.

GALLYPOT. Pneumatics to scourge him.

CLYSTER. Narcotics to doze him.

GALLYPOT. Cephalics to pose him.

O'BLUNDER. The devil of so many dishes I ever heard of in my life. Why, my jewels, there's no need for all this cookery. Upon my shoul this is to be a grand entertainment—Well, they'll have their own way.

CLYSTER. Suppose we use phlebotomy, and take from him thirty ounces of blood.

O'BLUNDER. Flea my bottom, d'ye say?

GALLYPOT. Or, brother, suppose we use a clyster?

O'BLUNDER. Upon my shoul, I find now how it is: I was invited here to a feast, but it is like to be the backward way.

GALLYPOT. His eyes begin to roll— call the keepers. *(Doctors call, and enter Keepers with chains.)*

O'BLUNDER. Flea my bottom!—Oh, my andraferara and shillela, I want you now!—But here's a chair—Flea my bottom, ye sons of whores—ye gibberish scoundrels! *(Takes up a chair, and knocks one of the Keepers down. Doctors run off.)* Oh this son of a whore of a cousin of mine, to bring me to these slaves to flea my bottom! If I meet him, I'll flea his bottom. *Exit.*

Scene [4], *a Street.*

Enter SERGEANT.

SERGEANT. I have been seeking my master every where, and cannot find him; I hope nothing has happen'd to him:—I think that was one of the gentlemen I saw with him.

Enter SCONCE

SERGEANT. Sir, Sir, pray did you see the Captain, my master? Captain O'Blunder, the Irish gentleman?

SCONCE. Not I indeed, my friend—I left him last with Mr Cheatwell—I suppose they are taking a bottle—Oh no, here's the Captain.

Enter the Captain, running.

O'BLUNDER. Oh, my dear friend, I had like to be lost, to be ruinated by that scoundrel my cousin; I ran away with my life from the thieves: But take care there is no doctor or clyster-pipes or divel-dums among ye.

SCONCE. Why, what's the matter?

O'BLUNDER. That's the thing, my dear—You know you left me at my cousin's house—Well, I walk'd about for some time; to be sure, I thought it an odd sort of a house when I saw no furniture—there I expected my cousin every moment; and, my dear jewel, there came in two bird-like sons of whores with great wigs—they look'd like conjurers and fortune-tellers—So, my dear, one shits down on this side of me, and t'other shits down on this side of me; and I being the turd person, they made me shit down in the middle—So one takes hold of one of my wrists, and the other catches hold of my other wrist, I thought by way of compliment; then they fell a-chattering gibberish, like a couple of old baboons; and all this discourse was conchearning me: They talk'd at first of treating me, and ask'd me if I had a good stomach—One of them said I had nine appetites—But at length, my jewels, what should come of the treat, but they agreed before my faash to flea my bottom—Oh, if I tell you a word of a lie, I'm not here—My dear, they call'd in the keepers to tie me—I up with the chair, for I had given my shillela and my andrefarara to my cousin—I knock'd one of them down on his tonneen, and runs out, and they after, crying out to the people in the street, Stop the madman, stop the madman—Oh hone, my jewel, the people took no notice of them, but ran away from me as if the devil had been in the inside of them: And so I made my escape; and here I am, my dear; and am very glad I have found you, my dear friend.

SCONCE. I am sorry to see that your cousin has behaved so rudely towards you; but any thing that lies in my power—

O'BLUNDER. Oh, Sir, you are a very worthy shentleman: But Chergeant, I must go to see my brother Tradewell the merchant and his fair daughter—Has the taylor brought home my cloaths?

SERGEANT. Yes, Sir, and the old gentleman expects you immediately; he sent a man in livery for you.

O'BLUNDER. Come, my good friend, I won't part with you—I'll step to my lodgings, and slip on my cloaths—that I may pay my due regards to my mistress. *Exeunt.*

Scene [5], *a Mad-house.*

Enter CHEATWELL, CLYSTER, *and* GALLYPOT.

CHEATWELL. I am sorry for this accident.

CLYSTER. In troth, Mr Cheatwell, he was the most curious madman that I ever met with during the whole course of my practice.

GALLYPOT. I'm now surprised how he sat so long quiet.

CHEATWELL. He'll run riot about the streets; but I hope he'll be taken—Oh, here's Sconce. *(Enter* SCONCE.*)* Well, what news of the Captain?

SCONCE. I just ran to let you know of his motions; he is preparing to dress, in order to pay a visit to Miss Lucy, and to pay his respects to Tradewell—But I have worse news for you; 'tis whisper'd upon 'Change that Tradewell is broke.

CHEATWELL. If it should fall out so, I shall easily resign my pretensions to the Captain. 'Twas Lucy's purse, and not her beauty, that I courted.

SCONCE. I must run back to the Captain, and keep in with him to serve a turn: Do you at a distance watch us, and proceed accordingly. *Exit.*

CHEATWELL. Well, gentlemen, I shall take care to acknowledge your trouble the first time I see you again. So adieu.   *Exit. Doctors exeunt.*

Scene [6.] *The Captain's Lodgings. Enter Captain and Sergeant.*

O'BLUNDER. Arra, but who do you think I met yesterday full butt in the street, but Teady Shaghnassy!

SERGEANT. Well, and how is he?

O'BLUNDER. Arra, stay, and I'le tell you; he wash at t'oder side of the way; and phen I came up, it was not him.— But tell me, dosh my new regimentals become me?

SERGEANT. Yes, indeed, Sir, I think they do.

O'BLUNDER. This pocket is so high, I must be forced to stoop for my snuff-box.

Enter SCONCE.

SCONCE. Ha! upon my word, Captain, you look as spruce as a young bridegroom.

O'BLUNDER. All in good time; and dosh it shit easy?

SCONCE. Easy, Sir! it fits you like a shirt.

O'BLUNDER. I think 'tis a little too wide here in the sleeve; I'm afraid the fellow hasn't left cloth enough to take it in; tho' I can't blame him neither, for fait, I was not by when he took the measure of it. Chergeant, here, take this sixpence-halfpenny, and buy me a pair of phite gloves.

SERGEANT. Sir, I have been all about the town, and can't get a pair under two shillings.

O'BLUNDER. Two tirteens!

SERGEANT. Two tirteens, Sir.

O'BLUNDER. Two tirteens for a pair of gloves! monomundioul, but my hands shall go barefoot all the days of their lives before I'll give two tirteens for a pair of gloves—Come, come along; I'll go with 'em, my mistress will excuse it.   *Exeunt.*

Scene [7.] TRADEWELL'S House.

Enter TRADEWELL and LUCY.

TRADEWELL. Well, daughter, I have been examining into the circumstances of Cheatwell, and find he is not worth sixpence; and as for your French lover, he is some runaway dancing-master or heir-cutter from Paris: So that really, amongst them all, I cannot find any one comes up to your Irish lover, either for birth, fortune, or character.

LUCY. Sir, you're the best judge in disposing of me; and indeed I have no real tender for any one of them—as to the Irish Captain, I have not seen him yet.

TRADEWELL. You'll see him presently; I sent to his lodgings, and expect him every moment—Oh, here comes Monsieur. *(Enter Monsieur RAGOU.)* Well, Monsieur, I have been trying my daughter's affections in regard to you; and as she is willing to be guided by me in this affair, I would willingly know by what visible means you intend to maintain her like a gentlewoman?

RAGOU. Me have de grand acquaintance with the *beau monde;* and, *si vous plaira,* if you sal please, Sir, to do me de honour of making me your son-in-law, me vill transact your negociations vid all possible care *et belle air.*

Enter Captain O'BLUNDER and BETTY.

TRADEWELL. You are welcome, Sir, to my house—this is my daughter—this, child, is Captain O'Blunder, whom I hope you will receive as he deserves.

O'BLUNDER. Fairest of creatures, will you gratify me with a taste of your sweet delicate lips? *(Kisses her.)* By my shoul, a neat creature, and a good bagoorah girl; she's as fair as an image in Leislip, Egypt I mean—Phat's here? the little fellow that I kilt just now! 'pon my shoul, I have a pratty ready for him now.

RAGOU. *Oh le diable!* —he spy me now—me better go off vile I am vell.

O'BLUNDER *(goes up to Monsieur).* I tought, Monsieur Ragou, that you were ded: Do I smell of the pratty now, you soup-maigre son of a French boogre?

TRADEWELL. The Captain has a mind to be merry with the Frenchman.

O'BLUNDER. By my shoul, my jewel, I have got a pratty for you now! here, eat it—eat this.

RAGOU: Oh! *pardonnez moi*, pardon me, Sir; I cannot, begar.

O'BLUNDER. Och ho! come out then, my little sweetlips! *(Draws.)* Eat that pratty this minute, or I'll run my sword up thro' your leg, and thro' your arms, and spit you up, and roast you like a goose, you tawny-faced son of a whore; sure 'tis better nor your garlic or ingyons in France. *(RAGOU eats it.)*

Enter a Servant to TRADEWELL.

SERVANT. Oh, Sir—there are certain accounts come, that—But these letters will better inform you.   *Exit.*

TRADEWELL *(reads)*. —O Captain, I'm ruin'd—undone—broke—

O'BLUNDER. Broke! what have you broke?

TRADEWELL. Oh, Sir, my fortune's broke—I'm not a penny above a beggar.

RAGOU. Oh, den me be off de amour—Me have no dealings with beggars; me have too many of de beggar in my own contre; so me better slip away in good time. *Votre serviteur*—servant, Sir.   *Exit.*

O'BLUNDER. March, march, you son of a whore: Arra, get out.

TRADEWELL. Now, Captain, you see I have not conceal'd my misfortune from you; so you are at liberty to choose a happier wife,—for my poor child is miserable.

O'BLUNDER. I thought your ribs was broke. I am no surgeon; but if 'tis only a little money that broke you, give me this lady's lily-white hand, and I'll take her stark-naked, without a penny of money in her pocket, but the cloaths upon her back—and as far as a good estate in land and stock will go, I'll share it with her—and with yourself. Arra, never mind the tieves, my jewel—I'll break their necks before they shall break your little finger. Come, honey, I'll give you a song I made upon this dear creature.

Wherever I'm going, and all the day long,
Abroad and at home, or alone in a throng,
I find that my passion's so lively and strong,
That your name, when I'm silent, still runs in my song.
    Ballynamony, ho, ro, &.
Since the first time I saw you, I take no repose,
I sleep all the day to forget half my woes;
So strong is the flame in my bosom that glows,
By St. Patrick, I fear it will burn thro' my cloaths.
    Ballynamony, ho, ro, &.
By my shoul, I'm afraid I shall die in my grave,
Unless you'll comply, and poor Phelim will save;
Then grant the petition your lover doth crave,
Who never was free till you made him your slave.
    Ballynamony, ho, ro, &.
On that happy day when I make you my bride,
With a swinging long sword, how I'll strut and stride!
In a coach and six horses with my honey I'll ride,
As before you I walk to the church by your side.
    Ballynamony, ho, ro, &.

Enter CHEATWELL.

CHEATWELL. Gentlemen, I beg pardon for this intrusion.

O'BLUNDER. He! Phat's here! my friendly cousin, that bid the old conjurers flea my bottom.

CHEATWELL. Sir I beg your pardon in particular, and hope you'll grant me it. Nothing but necessity was the cause of my ungentle behaviour—This lady I had an esteem for; but since things have turn'd out as they have, my pretensions are without foundation; therefore, Captain, I hope you'll look upon me in the light of an unfortunate rather than a bad man.

O'BLUNDER. Fait, my dear cousin, since love is the cause of your mourning, I shall forgive you with all my heart. *(Shakes hands.)*

CHEATWELL. Sir, I shall always esteem your friendship as an honour; and hope that you'll look on me as a poor, unfortunate young fellow, that has not a shilling, nor the means of getting one, upon the face of the earth.

O'BLUNDER. Oh! upon my shoul, then, cousin Cheatwell, I pity your condition with all my heart; and since things are so bad with you, if you'll take a trip with me to my Irish plantation along with my dear creature here, I'll give you 500 l. to stock a farm upon my own estate at Ballymascush-lane in the county of Monaghan, and the barony of Coogafighly.—Fait, and here's Betty, a tight little girl; and since you cou'd not get the mistress, if you'll take up with the maid, my dear here shall give her a couple of hundreds to fortune her off.

BETTY. Captain, I'm very much oblig'd to you for getting me a husband; if Mr Cheatwell has any tenders for me, I have a thousand pound left me as a legacy, which is at his service.

O'BLUNDER. Arra, what's that, my dear! a servant-maid with a tousand pound!—by my shoul there is many a lady in my country, that goes to plays, and balls, and masquerades, that has not half the money, and scorns to make her own smock.

CHEATWELL. I should be blind to my own interest not to accept of such valuable proposals, and with gratitude take your hand, promising for the future to lead a life which shall be a credit both to myself and benefactor.

O'BLUNDER. Well then, without compliment, I am glad I have made one poor man happy; and since we have made a double match, hey for Ireland, where we will live like Irish kings.

LUCY. This generosity amazes me, and greatly prejudices me in the honesty and goodness of the Irish.

O'BLUNDER. Oagh, my dear little charmer, I've another song just à propos.

Of all the husbands living, an Irishman's the best,
    With my fal, lal, &.
No nation on the globe like him can stand the test,
    With my fal, lal, &.

The English they are drones, as plainly you may see;
But we're all brisk and airy, and lively as a bee.
    With my fal, lal, &.

Appearance is againſt Them.

A

F A R C E,

IN TWO ACTS,

AS IT IS ACTED

AT THE THEATRE ROYAL,

COVENT GARDEN

———

L O N D O N·

PRINTED FOR G. G. J. AND J. ROBINSON, PATER-
NOSTER ROW, 1785

Appearance Is Against Them

Author

Though her works are now largely forgotten, Elizabeth Inchbald at one time held a commanding position in the world of letters, especially in view of the fact that women were then just beginning to claim their rightful place in the arts. No small part of her success—and of her subsequent decline in popularity—was due to her being temperamentally fitted to turn out the sentimental plays and novels then so much in vogue.[1]

She was born Elizabeth Simpson in Suffolk in 1753. Quite early in life, it would seem, she demonstrated an independence of character hardly to be expected of ladies of her day. An older brother having turned to the stage for a living, Elizabeth determined to try her fortunes in the theatrical profession, though a confirmed habit of stuttering, which she never shook off, and a total lack of "connections" would seem to have made the attempt almost foolhardy. With characteristic determination she ran away to London when she was nineteen and after various adventures, among which may be included her marriage to the actor Joseph Inchbald, then nearly forty, she began her career on the provincial stage. After eight years in the provinces she succeeded in capturing a place in one of the London companies in 1780. Having by now discovered that she could never attain the fame and security of leading roles, she began to write for the theatre, her initial offering being the topical farce *A Mogul Tale* (1784). Within her first six years as a writer she turned out nine plays.

Mrs. Inchbald quit the stage in 1789 to devote her time to writing. A novel upon which she had been at work for some time, *A Simple*

---

[1]A. H. Thorndike, *English Comedy*, p. 463, makes a very interesting suggestion concerning Mrs. Inchbald's work. Discussing the place accorded, or not accorded, a sense of humor in late eighteenth-century plays, he remarks, "Mrs. Inchbald seems to have compromised on a distinction similar to the famous romanticist separation of fancy and imagination. Fun and merriment might be given rein in such trivial and fanciful pieces as farces and petite comedies, but should have only a slight and secondary place in the works of the imagination extolling, as the sentimental plays assuredly did, 'scrupulous purity of characters and refinement in sensations.'"

Story, was published in 1791. Another novel, *Nature and Art*, appeared in 1796. Meanwhile she kept busy with plays, turning out some ten more before she virtually gave up writing, except for some editing of popular collections of plays, around 1805.

During her mature years she formed a number of important friendships, among the most notable with Kemble, Holcroft, and Godwin; but her sharp tongue made her a difficult friend, and quarrels were numerous and lasting. Toward the end of her life she shut herself off more and more from the world, though never ceasing to live in or near London, and turned more and more to religion. She died on August 1, 1821.

Sources

The story of the sources of *Appearance Is against Them* can be told in the briefest terms. "*A Mogul Tale* and *Appearance is Against Them* : . . are probably original efforts in all respects; at least no sources have been suggested nor is there anything in the plays to suggest adaptation."[2] If this statement is sound, as it seems to be, Mrs. Inchbald's farce would appear to be an exception to the general rule. Unlike the run of farce writers, she hit upon a clever idea and chose to develop it without assistance from others.

Stage History

On its initial performance, October 22, 1785, *Appearance Is against Them* made a very promising beginning. A critic writing in *The European Magazine* for this month had high hopes of its success.

This farce is the production of Mrs. Inchbald, author of *The Mogul Tale* and *I'll Tell You What*, a farce and a comedy produced with success at Mr. Colman's theatre in the Haymarket. The latter the reader will recollect was exceedingly popular, and if the public have not lost their good taste, we have no scruple to say the present piece will prove equally popular. . . .[3]

---

[2]G. Louis Joughin, *The Life and Work of Elizabeth Inchbald*, unpublished Harvard thesis, 1932, p. 143.

[3]Not everyone was so sanguine. James Boaden tells us that Colman, who had produced her first two plays with success, had turned this one down. Harris was "charmed" with the piece, however, and produced it at once. *Memoirs of Mrs. Inchbald* (1833), I, 223–24. Oulton also hints of pessimism over the play's success, as he says that *Appearance Is against Them*, "contrary to the green-room expectation, was very well received." *The History of the Theatres of London* (1796), I, 145–46.

For a few weeks this prediction seemed sound enough. By November 15 the piece had been acted nine times. The following night, Wednesday, November 16, the performance was "By Command of Their Majesties," and on Friday the command bill was repeated "by Particular Desire." But after this high point the play languished rapidly, seeing only one or two more productions the first season and virtually dying out after that.[4] The list is even scantier for this country. Quite recently M. S. Shockley has discovered a record of a performance in Richmond for October 6, 1792;[5] Miss Willis lists two performances for Charleston for February, 1793, and one for March, 1795. These four performances tell the story of American production.

Explaining the poor success of a play much superior to the usual run of eighteenth-century farces is no easy task. One possible explanation is that it was much better suited for a main piece than an afterpiece. Since much of its appeal lies in the dialogue it may have required more attention than an audience already wearied from seeing a five-act play would give it. Song or slapstick would at this point have been much more acceptable. It is difficult to believe that any considerable number of spectators would have agreed with the objection voiced by a reviewer in the *Monthly Review* during the play's first season. After a few not especially acute observations he closes,

Ladies are observed, by malicious wits, to have a remarkable *pruriency* in their writings: *appearances, are against them.* As we may fairly say of Mrs. Inchbald, what Pope has said before of Mrs. Behn,

> The stage how loosely does Astraea tread,
> Who fairly puts all characters to bed.

---

[4]Harvard has six of the playbills for the run, including those for November 16 and 18; the last of the six is for December 8, marked as the twelfth time. Isaac Reed records having seen the piece on September 18, 1786, on one of his jaunts to Stourbridge Fair.

[5]"First Performances of English Plays in Richmond before 1819," *Journal of Southern History*, XIII (1947), 91–105. Shockley is in error in giving the first London performance, misreading Nicoll's 1785 as 1765. He is also apparently unaware that the play was renamed a time or two, for he says there are no records of other performances in this country. Miss Willis's records for Charleston show that the farce had become *Adventures of a Shawl* over here; Genest's last record, for Covent Garden, May 1, 1804, is for *Mistake upon Mistake: or, Appearance Is against Them.*

Publication

Since *Appearance Is Aaginst Them* met with no continued success on the stage, few editions were called for. Its being published at all in the following century is no doubt due to the fact that later editors recognized its excellence and reprinted it even in spite of its early demise.

Appearance Is against Them . . . London: printed for G. G. J. and J. Robinson, Paternoster Row, 1785.

Appearance Is against Them . . . Dublin: Printed by W. Porter, for the Company of Booksellers, MDCCLXXXVI.

Appearance Is against Them . . . London: Published for the Proprietors, by Sherwood and Co. [n.d.] In Vol. IV of *The London Stage* [1824–1827].

Appearance Is against Them . . . London, Docks [n.d.] No. 237 in *Dicks' Standard Plays* [1883, etc.][6]

Analysis

Whereas most farces are at a disadvantage when judged by a reader rather than by a spectator, *Appearance Is against Them* strikes us today as a brisk and clever piece of stage business. Trivial though it may be, its very triviality is appropriate to the set of circumstances and characters involved. The title given it on its revival, *The Adventures of a Shawl*, is most appropriate.

The characters are not especially original. We have met most of them before: the old maid eager to get a husband, the crotchety and confirmed bachelor, the flighty man-about-town. Yet the author has done very well with them within the limits of two short acts. Of course there had to be a heightening to give the audience the key to various characters quickly, but the results do not seem too forced. Take the speech of Lady Mary: "Little did I think, when I heard of those dreadful wrecks, and many souls that perished, that I had a shawl at sea; if I had, I should have suffered a martyrdom!" Or Mr. Walmsley: "I vented my rage—in kissing the lady; and won her heart without further trouble. It's impossible I could have won her so soon, but by my being in that violent rage. . . ." Even the servants, Fish and Humphry, have their points.

---

[6]We have not seen a copy of this edition of the play. Joughin lists one for the British Museum. *An Inchbald Bibliography*, The University of Texas *Studies in English*, No. 14 (1934), p. 61.

As everyone who has commented on the play has acknowledged, and as the above quotations may indicate, the strength of the play lies in its dialogue. Many of the speeches are turned with as much care and with the same intent as in some of the earlier comedies of manners. Among many possible examples we may choose the epigrammatic retort to Fish's question about the possibility of old women's replacing young ones in fashion: "As soon as the vulgar lay hold of anything, the people of ton leave it off. Such is the case with young women: the vulgar have laid hold of them, and they are quite out." Or to take one of Humphry's frequently clever remarks: "You can't be at a loss for words while you are courting. Women will always give you two for your one: I know my wife did; and, egad! though we have left off courting, so she does now." Or take the clever retort when Mr. Walmsley fancies he has his nephew trapped and will not accept "accident" as sufficient excuse; Lord Lighthead turns his uncle's previous recital back upon him: "My servant had just lost me a favourite spaniel; and had the rascal been in the way, I should have broken every bone in his skin; but, happening to meet with this poor girl, I vented my rage upon her."

Having seen the author do so well, one wishes she had continued to do so throughout the play, but it must be admitted that through neglect or hurry she does not always make the most of a scene. A writer in the *Critical Review* of 1785 found a number of things for commendation; among them, he thought "the equivoque in the second act, where a simple clown and lady Margaret are at cross purposes, in consequence of an error into which they have been eventually led, is extremely diverting." To the present-day reader the possibilities of the scene would seem to be far from exhausted. A radio script writer would have rung the changes on the equivoque for half the program. But perhaps the comparison only reveals the superior judgment of Mrs. Inchbald.

DRAMATIS PERSONAE.

Mr. WALMSLEY.
LORD LIGHTHEAD.
CLOWNLY.
THOMPSON.
Servant to LORD LIGHTHEAD.
Servant to LADY MARY.
HUMPHRY.
LADY MARY MAGPIE.
LADY LOVEALL.
MISS ANGLE.
MISS AUDLEY.
BETTY.
FISH.

Mr. *Quick.*
Mr. *Palmer.*
Mr. *Kennedy.*
Mr. *Thompson.*
Mr. *Swords.*
Mr. *Ledger.*
Mr. *Edwin.*
Mrs. *Webb.*
Mrs. *Bates.*
Mrs. *Morton.*
Miss *Stewart.*
Mrs. *Davenett.*
Mrs. *Wilson.*

APPEARANCE IS AGAINST THEM.

ACT I. SCENE 1.

MISS ANGLE *and* FISH *discovered.*

MISS ANGLE. There's somebody at the door, Fish—'tis Lady Mary Magpie—let her in—even her ridiculous vanity is more supportable than the reflection on my own.

FISH. Lady Mary, ma'ah.

(Opens the door.)

Enter LADY MARY.

MISS ANGLE. Good-morrow, dear Lady Mary.

LADY MARY. Nay, sit still—and, Mrs. Fish, do you stay.—I have brought something to show your mistress, and you may see it too, if she will give you leave.

MISS ANGLE. Certainly.—Fish, you may stay.

LADY MARY. There! *(Opening a shawl.)* What do you think of that? —A present from Mr. Walmsley—a shawl, worth at a moderate valuation, no less than a hundred and fifty guineas. —He gave it to me this minute—it came over but last night from India— has been on the seas seven months— was in that terrible storm of October last.—Little did I think, when I heard of those dreadful wrecks, and the many souls that perished, that I had a shawl at sea: if I had, I should have suffered a martyrdom! —Now is not it pretty?—Beautiful? He assures me, his correspondent writes him word, "There is but one more such in all India."

—And I'm to wear it the first time on my wedding-day.

MISS ANGLE. It is very beautiful indeed.

LADY MARY. An't you well, my dear?—You don't seem to understand it's value.—What do you say to it, Mrs. Fish?

FISH. Oh madam!—I like it of all things!—

LADY MARY. I dare say you do.—But come, my dear Miss Angle, what's the matter with you? Since you first came to town, you are the most alter'd creature I ever saw!—

FISH. Your Ladyship does not think my mistress has lost any of her beauty, I hope?—

LADY MARY. As for that, Mrs. Fish, I dare say your Lady has made observation enough to know, that beauty is of little weight here;—of no signification at all!—Beauty in London is so cheap, and consequently so common to the men of fashion, (who are prodigiously fond of novelty) that they absolutely begin to fall in love with the ugly women, by way of change.—

FISH. And does your Ladyship think old women will ever come into fashion?—

LADY MARY. They are in fashion— they have been in fashion some time.— Girls, and young women, have made themselves so cheap, they are quite out.—

MISS ANGLE *(Aside).* I believe so.—

LADY MARY. As soon as the vulgar lay hold of any thing, the people of ton leave it off.—Such is the case with young women.—The vulgar have laid hold of them, and they are quite out.—

FISH. Oh dear me!—

LADY MARY. But come, my dear Angle, pluck up your spirits, against you know when—you are to be one of my bridemaids you know—O how I long to be away from lodgings, and in a house of my own.—Mr. Walmsley says, he shall invite you to stay a day or two with us.—He likes you (stranger as you are to us both) very much I assure you.—He is a great admirer of virtue, in us females; and, notwithstanding his little oddities, would do anything for a woman of character; and your refusing that vile Lord's odious addresses (which I inform'd him of) has interested him in you exceedingly. Well, heaven bless you—I can't stay—he'll be quite impatient. *(Going)* I may tell him you like the shawl I suppose?

MISS ANGLE. Beautiful, beyond measure!

LADY MARY. And you, Mrs. Fish?

FISH. Charming, ma'am.

LADY MARY. Did I tell you there was but one more such in all India? *(Coming back.)*

MISS ANGLE. You did.

LADY MARY. Only think of it's being in that storm!   *Exit.*

MISS ANGLE. Would I had been in the storm, and had fallen it's victim!—

FISH. Dear madam!—

MISS ANGLE. Oh Fish, that woman's nonsense, at which you laugh'd, was graced with sentiments of the strictest truth!—Young women are no longer thought of here.—How rashly did I give credit to our foolish country people!—They told me, that, "Tho' only admired by them, in London I shou'd be adored—that beauty here was rare—that virtue"—

FISH. Well, madam, and that is rare, every body knows!

MISS ANGLE. But is it valued?— No.—As soon as I gave Lord Lighthead

proofs of my possessing it, what was the consequence?—I have neither seen nor heard of him since.—

FISH. That's very odd!—For my part I thought him so much in love!—And sometimes I thought you looked a little.—

MISS ANGLE. That I felt a warmth— a something like tenderness for him, I own; but that it was the effect of love I will not pretend to say—It was perhaps the effect of hope—Pride too, had a great share in the agitation of my heart—and gratitude might have confirm'd the whole sensation love.—But, in the moment gratitude shou'd have been inspired, resentment, indignation, took possession—and I am now left solely to shame and disappointment.

FISH. Well!—it's very odd that a man should give himself so much trouble to come here after you, so many times as he did, and then all of a sudden never to come near you for a whole month.—I should not mind losing him, either, if some duke or other great man would come instead of him; or even that strange young man we met on the road, as we came to town, and that was so kind to us when our chaise broke down.

MISS ANGLE. Honest creature!

FISH. Well, as sure as ever I was in love in my life, that young man and his servant were both as deep in love—

MISS ANGLE. With me?

FISH. No: the master with you, and the man with me.—But we, I thought, were coming to town to make our fortune, and so I was above making it on the road.—For notwithstanding that young man looked so countrified, and had hardly a word to say for himself, he's worth thousands! — And poor Humphry, his servant, persuaded me to give him our direction; that his master and he might come after us to London— And yet, to see the fickleness of man! we have heard nor seen nothing of them.—But, dear madam, his Lordship runs most in my head—Perhaps he is sick?

MISS ANGLE. No—he visits the drawingroom, constantly; as we read in the papers.—I wonder what he wou'd say if he was accidently to meet me?—

FISH. He'd fall in love with you as much as ever.—Suppose, madam, you was to write to him?—

MISS ANGLE. For shame!

FISH. Dear madam, I know a few lines from you wou'd cheer his heart, and he would be as dying for you as ever! —Oh! when I have given him a letter from you, how he has jumped for joy! how he has kiss'd it! and how he has kiss'd me!—

MISS ANGLE. Cou'd I write to him with any appearance of prudence—for instance; upon any business—I shou'd have no objection: it wou'd at least remind him of me, and bring matters to a decision.

FISH. Then do, madam, contrive to write to him about some business.

MISS ANGLE. What business can I pretend?

FISH. Dear madam! if you had a handsome piece of silk for a gown, or a diamond pin, or something of that kind, you might return it him back again.—

MISS ANGLE. Return it him again! What do you mean?

FISH. Why, madam, you might send it him back—as if you had received the present from a person unknown: and concluding that it *must* come from his Lordship, you had thought proper to return it—and so you might send him, with it, a fine long virtuous letter, that "you wou'd not receive a present from a king, that had evil designs upon you," and so on—and so on—and so on.— This, I am sure would make him ten times fonder of you than ever—for he would think some rival had been sending you the present in that ananymous manner, which had made you think it was him—and I know he wou'd.—

MISS ANGLE. I protest there is something in that scheme which pleases me.

FISH. Do it, madam—do it.

MISS ANGLE. But how can I?—I have nothing of value—nothing that I cou'd

suppose he wou'd send for a present, and which I could think of consequence enough to return.

FISH. What's your watch, madam?

MISS ANGLE. An oldfashion'd thing!

FISH. Lord! I have thought of something! The finest thing!—

MISS ANGLE. What?—

FISH. Lady Mary Magpie's shawl— You know ma'am, 'tis the finest thing in the world—There is but one more such in all the universe.

MISS ANGLE. But the shawl is not mine!

FISH. No ma'am—but I dare say I know where her ladyship has laid it, and I can get it. *(Going to the door.)*

MISS ANGLE. For shame!

FISH. Dear madam, do you think I'd steal it—It cou'd do no harm to be a few hours at his Lordship's—He'd send it back directly: you may depend upon that—and then such a fine thing?—It would make him think that some great man indeed had taken a fancy to you— and he'd be so afraid of losing you.—

MISS ANGLE. Well!——I protest—— if I thought——

FISH. I can get it, ma'am, with all the ease in the world—I dare say.
(Runs out.)

MISS ANGLE. What will become of me?—Where will my folly end?

Enter FISH.

FISH. Yes—yes—ma'am, I can get it— her Ladyship has spread it on the bed in the blue chamber, and is gone out for the whole evening; and will sleep at her coursin's, Lady Beach's—her maid told me so in the morning.

MISS ANGLE. But suppose his Lordship should not return it?

FISH. Laud ma'am: do you think his Lordship will keep it, when he'll know he did not send it you?—His Lordship is not a thief, I suppose—You'll have it back, ma'am, I'll answer for it in an hour or two, and himself with it.— The person shan't leave it ma'am, if his Lordship is not at home; and then you'll be sure to have it in an hour or two—I'll go steal it—I'll go steal it. *(Going.)*

MISS ANGLE. Steal it!—

FISH. Take it, ma'am—not steal it.
                                              Exit.

MISS ANGLE. This scheme will at least renew our acquaintance—and that is all I want—for if, on the renewal, he appears cold, I will leave London instantly—if, on the contrary, he is as much in love as ever—

Enter FISH *with the Shawl.*

FISH. I have got it—I have got it—here it is.—Now, madam, come into your bed chamber and write a very affecting letter, while I do it up, and send for a porter.

MISS ANGLE. I protest I am frighten'd—tho' we take it but to return again.

FISH. Dear madam! I am sure it is not in half the danger as when it was in the great storm! *(Pulling her off.)*
                                              Exeunt.

SCENE 2. *A Chamber at* LORD LIGHTHEAD'S.

Enter MISS AUDLEY *and* THOMPSON.

MISS AUDLEY. What!—his Lordship is gone to see Lady Loveall, thus early, I suppose? or rather has staid with her thus late!

THOMPSON. You are just, like her Ladyship, ma'am, for she is ever accusing my Lord of being with you—But I assure you, ma'am, his Lordship slept at home—*(a loud rap)*. There he is madam.   *Exit.*

MISS AUDLEY. Yes—I have heard of her Ladyship's jealousy—and that she sometimes searches this whole house to find me.

Re-enter THOMPSON.

THOMPSON. Dear madam, I hear Mr. Walmsley's voice—my 'Lord's uncle, madam!—they are coming here—what shall we do, madam? My master will murder me if his uncle should see you! —a cross old man, madam—knocks

every body down that he does not like—and he has a great dislike to a fine lady—and, if he should see you here, such a life my Lord will have of it!

MISS AUDLEY. Oh! you need tell me no more.—I know Mr. Walmsley's character well.—Where can I go? I would sooner jump out of the window than meet him—a cruel, unfeeling—piece of ice.

THOMPSON. Here's madam, step into my Lord's bed-chamber.

[MISS AUDLEY.] His bed-chamber! Well, the creature won't stay long?

THOMPSON. Not above ten minutes, I dare say. *(She goes into the chamber.)*
                                              Exit Serv[ant.]

Enter MR. WALMSLEY *and* LORD· LIGHTHEAD.

WALMSLEY. Don't tell me, my Lord—you are a bad man—a very bad man—you say in excuse for your vices, they are fashionable—but I, being out of the fashion, can call 'em only wicked.

LORD LIGHTHEAD. What vices, Sir?

WALMSLEY. Why, you are a fellow that falls in love with every face you see; and yet admire your own more than any one of them.—You are a man whose purse is open to every gambler and courtezan, and is never shut, but to objects of real distress.

LORD LIGHTHEAD. But how are you informed of this?

WALMSLEY. Hear it!—told it by every body!—Do you think any thing but conviction would have forced me to the rash step I have taken?—Wou'd any thing but a certainty that you were unworthy to be my heir, have forced me to the desperate resolution of marrying, notwithstanding my natural aversion to opposition?

LORD LIGHTHEAD. I hope, Sir, when you marry—

WALMSLEY. Hope! Pshaw!—I know well enough what marriage is—'Tis a poesy of thorns—nobody knows where to lay hold of it—'Tis a stormy sea, where nothing is to be expected but squalls, tempests and shipwrecks!—One cries, "Help"—another, "Lord have mercy upon us"—a third, " 'Tis all over with us"—and souse they all go into the ocean of calamity.

LORD LIGHTHEAD. Then, for heaven's sake, Sir, if this is your opinion, decline your intention of marrying.

WALMSLEY. I can't—'tis too late— my word is pass'd.—Your indiscretions put me in a passion, and I took a rash step!—a step I never intended to take. —I offered a lady to marry her, in the heat of anger, and she took me at my word, before I had time to grow cool and recant.

LORD LIGHTHEAD. How unfortunate!

WALMSLEY. I was not aware she would be so sudden!—but I was in such a violent passion;—all against you for your follies—I was devilish hot! I don't remember that I was ever in such a heat in my life! I strutted— and fretted—and walk'd—and talk'd— all in anger against you; which she took for love to her, and so was overcome in less than ten minutes.

LORD LIGHTHEAD. Dear Sir, had I been present—

WALMSLEY. Why, then I should have broken every bone in your skin!—But as it was—I vented my rage—in kissing the lady; and won her heart without farther trouble.—It's impossible I could have won her so soon, but by my being in that violent rage; for she's a particular, prudent, discreet, reserv'd, middle-aged woman; and nothing but my great violence cou'd have had that effect upon her.

LORD LIGHTHEAD. But, Sir, is it possible that you should pay attention to a rash promise in a moment of anger?

WALMSLEY. My word!—My word is as dear to me as my honor—It is my honor—and I cannot keep one without keeping both.

LORD LIGHTHEAD. But now you are cool, Sir.

WALMSLEY. Yes, I am cool—but now the lady is in a passion—and I must keep my word with her, tho' I am afraid she'll never find me *warm* on the subject again.

LORD LIGHTHEAD. Dear Sir? And all this to revenge yourself on me? A man whose greatest faults arise merely from the report of malicious enemies.

WALMSLEY. Enemies! — Pshaw! — That's always your excuse!—But have not I enemies as well as you? And yet, I dare say, you never heard of my being caught gallanting my neighbour's wife?—Or walking arm-in-arm with a milliner? Or following fine ladies home to their lodgings?—Nor did you ever hear me accused of destroying a beautiful young woman's peace of mind—Did you?

LORD LIGHTHEAD. I can't say I ever did, Sir.

WALMSLEY. Then don't pretend to deny the reports I have heard of you.— Don't I know that you were caught with Lady Loveall and—

LORD LIGHTHEAD. I own, Sir, I have been very unfortunate as to Appearances — Appearances, and those alone, have been the ruin of my reputation;—accidents so strange, that no human wisdom cou'd prevent or avoid them—I have been found, for instance, with a female, whom I never had the smallest familiarity with, in the most suspicious situations; and only by mere accident.—

WALMSLEY. And pray was that an accident when I caught you kissing my house-keeper's daughter, as if you'd devour her?

LORD LIGHTHEAD. Yes, upon my word, Sir, that was an accident—entirely an accident—My servant had just lost me a favorite spaniel, and, had the rascal been in the way, I shou'd have broken every bone in his skin; but, happening to meet with this poor girl, I vented my rage upon her.

WALMSLEY. Then, I have only to say, you have lost my estate by your accidents.

Enter Servant.

SERVANT. Lady Loveall, Sir, is in the parlour.

WALMSLEY. Is that an accident?

LORD LIGHTHEAD (*Aside to the Servant*). Blundering—

SERVANT. I did not see Mr. Walmsley, Sir!——A fine life I shall have for this! *(Aside, and Exit.)*

WALMSLEY—This is another accident! —How dares that imprudent woman visit you?—My blood runs cold at the thought of her—for she was the cause of this rash step I have taken!—It was hearing of your intrigue with her that hurried me to the rash step of marrying. —Let me get out of the house—she's poison to me; and she knows it too, and speaks to me, wherever I meet her, on purpose to insult me.—Let me get away.—*(Goes to the door)* Zounds she's coming here!—I won't see her!—I shall be in one of my passion's if I do!— Where shall I go?—Put me somewhere.

LORD LIGHTHEAD. Here, Sir,—step into my bed-chamber—I'll take her Ladyship to another room immediately —and you may avoid her.

WALMSLEY. Oh, damn your accidents!—But, thank heaven, you are no heir of mine—you are out of my will.—*(He goes into the bed-chamber.)*

LORD LIGHTHEAD. And therefore may now offend you without fear.

Enter THOMPSON.

THOMPSON. Where's Mr. Walmsley, Sir?

LORD LIGHTHEAD. In my bed-chamber.—What did you want with him?

THOMPSON. Oh, dear Sir! Oh dear! —Miss Susan Audley is there, Sir!—I cramm'd her in, when I heard your Lordship and Mr. Walmsley on the stairs, for fear he should see her.—

LORD LIGHTHEAD. Zounds!—but no matter!—I'm struck out of his will, and may defy him.—But I don't hear him—*(list'ning)* he can't have seen her?

THOMPSON. Perhaps, Sir, she's crept under the bed?

LORD LIGHTHEAD. Very likely—for I know she would rather meet a tyger. What's become of Lady Loveall?

THOMPSON. William is trying to prevent her coming up, Sir:—for she says, it is not your uncle that you have with you, but a lady; and she will see her.

Enter LADY LOVEALL.

LADY LOVEALL. So, my Lord.— What's the reason I am not to be admitted?—You've no company, neither! —Oh, you have been hiding, I perceive!

LORD LIGHTHEAD. This way—come this way—I'll tell you who it is. Don't speak so loud.

LADY LOVEALL. None of your arts, my Lord. I will see who you have hid in your bed-chamber.

LORD LIGHTHEAD. I assure you 'tis my Uncle.—Hush!—Come this way.

(Leading her off.)

LADY LOVEALL. My Lord, you'll pardon me—but I can't.—

LORD LIGHTHEAD. Hush! Hush!

Exeunt, forcing her off.

SCENE 3. *A Bed-chamber,* WALMSLEY *discovered listening at the door.*

WALMSLEY. Now I'll steal out—No— she's coming again.

LADY LOVEALL *(Without).* I will see who you have in your bed-chamber —my curiosity shall be satisfied.

WALMSLEY. Shall it!—Then there must be neither closet nor cupboard in the room.—*(Goes to the closet.)* The devil take it, it's lock'd.

LADY LOVEALL *(Without).* I will see who you have here.

WALMSLEY. You won't.—I'll get under the bed first.—Hold, I can't stoop— no matter—I'll hide myself under the counterpane—and madam shall be disappointed.—*(He gets in and pulls the clothes over his head.)* Now find me if you can!—I believe you'll be bit.

Enter LADY LOVEALL *and* LORD LIGHTHEAD.

LADY LOVEALL. Why here's no one here!

LORD LIGHTHEAD. Now, I hope you are satisfied.—Where the devil is my Uncle? *(Aside.)*

LADY LOVEALL. Did you not tell me your Uncle was here?

LORD LIGHTHEAD. Yes—but you expected to find somebody else.

LADY LOVEALL. And there is somebody else—*(Goes to the curtain and discovers MISS AUDLEY)* A Lady! Oh you deceitful!—*(Sits down on* MR. WALMSLEY, *shrieks, and runs across, while* WALMSLEY *rises up in the bed.)* —Ah! Ah! Ah! *(shrieking)* I shall never recover the shock.

WALMSLEY. Why!—Why!—What is all this!—What a strange accident!—

LADY LOVEALL. I say accident, indeed!—

LORD LIGHTHEAD. Accident! Uncle!

LADY LOVEALL. The severe, puritanical Mr. Walmsley!

LORD LIGHTHEAD. Upon my word, Uncle, such a thing in my house—

LADY LOVEALL. Oh! Oh! Oh!

WALMSLEY. Oh! Oh! Oh!—Deuce take your Oh's.—My Lord, you used to have faith in accidents.—

LORD LIGHTHEAD. But you convinced me there were no such things.— And indeed, Uncle, tho' you may think lightly of this affair, I am very much concerned at it.—My reputation, as well as yours, is at stake—Such a thing to happen in my house.—Rat me, if I would have had it happened for the world—

WALMSLEY. What has happened? *(To* MISS AUDLEY.*)* Nothing has happened!

LADY LOVEALL. Oh heavens!—My Lord, I ask your pardon for all my former suspicions of you and this Lady.

MISS AUDLEY *(Goes up the stage).* I must cry for vexation—for 'tis in vain to attempt to clear myself.

LADY LOVEALL. See the Lady in tears, Mr. Walmsley!——Oh! what a treat to teize him. *(Aside.)*

LORD LIGHTHEAD. I beg that every means may be taken to put a stop to this affair getting abroad.—For my part, I declare never to breathe the

circumstance to a mortal—and I dare say we may so far prevail on Lady Loveall.—

LADY LOVEALL. No, indeed—I am bound to no secrecy.—Mr. Walmsley has never been sparing of my reputation, nor will I of his—the world shall know it.

WALMSLEY. Why then, Nephew, upon my soul!—I wish I may die!—I wish I may never speak again!—I wish—

LADY LOVEALL. Wish!—you used to pretend you had no wishes.

WARMSLEY. I don't speak to you— *(To* MISS AUDLEY.*)* Pray, madam, be so good as to tell me how you came into that bed?

MISS AUDLEY. 'Tis in vain to say— nobody will credit me.   *Exit.*

LADY LOVEALL. Well, Mr. Walmsley, I'll bid you good morning—and, though I know you to be no friend of mine, yet permit a poor weak woman to give you this counsel—that now you are about to enter the married state, you will not suffer these depraved inclinations, (even in youth a reproach) to ruffle that tranquillity which ought ever to attend on the honourable marriage-bed.   *Exit.*

WALMSLEY. Zounds! I have not patience!—Honourable marriage bed! Why her calling it honourable, would alone, have made me shudder at it, if I had not before.—That woman is the worst of all human—

LORD LIGHTHEAD. Dear Sir!—

WALMSLEY. Why you know, my Lord, if it had not been for her, you wou'd have own'd that—that gipsey was put there to meet you—but this woman is my bane wherever I go—or whatever I do.—Oh! that I could but once be reveng'd of her.—But I dare say I shall!

LORD LIGHTHEAD. No more on this subject, Sir—I hope the Lady you are going to marry, may prove of a more amiable disposition—and that you will like her.

WALMSLEY. Why since I found I must have her, I've been trying night and day to like her—but I can't say I make much progress.—However, I'm tolerably civil, and give her a vast number of presents, as a cover for my want of affection.—She's expecting me now to go a shopping with her; so good morning—you'll come to the wedding? *(Sighing.)*

LORD LIGHTHEAD. Certainly! — when is the happy day, Sir?

WALMSLEY. How dare you call it the *"happy* day?"—You just heard me say it was the most wretched, miserable affair I ever had to do with in all my life, and now you are calling it the "happy day."—

LORD LIGHTHEAD. The *day* then, Sir—when is the day?

WALMSLEY. Thursday *(sighing)*—the day after to-morrow — the 21st of December. *(LORD LIGHTHEAD bows.)* Oh! damme, the shortest day and the longest night. *Exit.*

Enter Servant.

SERVANT. Sir, this parcel was left about half an hour ago, to be deliver'd into your Lordship's own hands, as soon as you were at leisure.

LORD LIGHTHEAD. What is it?—Is that the bill?

SERVANT. This is a letter, Sir. *Exit.*

LORD LIGHTHEAD. A letter!—*(Reads.)*—"My Lord, altho' your Lordship has had the delicacy not to avow yourself the presenter of this valuable gift, yet, something whispers me, it can be none but your Lordship to whom I am indebted for so generous an intention.—But, my Lord, the intention only —permit me to remain obliged to you for.—The gift itself—honour, delicacy, and a thousand struggling sensations force me to return—and to add, that my residence in London has not yet so entirely eradicated those principles imbibed in the country, as to render a gaudy bait, even an allurement, but in its being a proof, that your Lordship sometimes honours with a thought, the humble, but contented,

LOUISA ANGLE."

Angle! Angle!—Which is that? The girl at St. James's, or the girl at Westminster?—Oh! the girl at St. James!—

I don't remember sending her a present!—but now I suppose I did, while I was mad for her—and now I have recovered my senses, I have forgot it.—What is it? *(Opens the parcel)* Zounds! but it is very handsome! and the very thing to present to Lady Loveall.—It will reconcile her to me immediately—for I am afraid she suspects me, notwithstanding her behaviour before my Uncle.—How came I to be such an extravagant puppy, as to send that little gipsey such a present, and she to return it, now she finds I have given over my pursuit?—Faith, I'm very glad she did.—Richard—*(Enter Servant.)* Bring me pen, ink, and paper. *(Exit Servant.)* I certainly ordered some of my people to send this thing, but it has slipt my memory.—*(The servant brings in the pen and ink—his Lordship writes and gives him the letter.)* Here—do up that parcel, and take it, with this letter, to Lady Loveall, directly.

SERVANT. Yes, Sir. *Exit.*

LORD LIGHTHEAD. Egad, it came back at a very lucky time!—Her Ladyship doats upon a present! and such a present as that!—Such a shawl!—Oh yes—the shawl will make her friends with me at once. *Exit.*

SCENE 4. *An Inn.*

CLOWNLY *discovered.*

CLOWNLY. What a journey have I and poor Humphry taken! and all perhaps for nothing! for if he should even find her, she may not be glad to see me.—*(Enter HUMPHRY.)* Why, Humphry, I thought you were lost?

HUMPHRY. Ay, master, and you may think yourself well off I was not.

CLOWNLY. Well—but have you found where Miss Angle lives?

HUMPHRY. Yes—I have found her out—but such a time I was about it!—Why, Sir, she lives up by St. James's, or St. Giles's, I forget which!—but 'tis all the same.—And such a thing happen'd to me as I went along!—

CLOWNLY. What?

HUMPHRY. Why just as I got to what they call the P. H'es, (a pretty place)—just as I got under cover, three or four, or five or six, (or egad, there might be a dozen) fine ladies met me; and one of them did give me such a slap in the face; the water came into my eyes again.—

CLOWNLY. What did she do that for?

HUMPHRY. I can't tell for the life of me!—For I pull'd off my hat, and made them a civil bow—but faith, as soon as I felt the blow, I forgot my manners, for after madam I ran, and gave her such a shake—

CLOWNLY. You did not?

HUMPHRY. But I did—and that was not the worst of it neither.—I made a sad mistake—for when I came to look, the lady had got a blue gown on, and she that gave me the blow was in red!

CLOWNLY. How cou'd you make such a blunder?

HUMPHRY. Why, tho' their gowns were different, their faces were exactly the same colour.

CLOWNLY. But about Miss Angle— have you seen her, or her maid?

HUMPHRY. Yes—I have seen Mrs. Fish; and she says, that her Lady has done nothing but talk of you since you left her on the road—and she desires you will go and see her Lady directly.— And she says too, that she'll get us a lodging in the same house before night; but that is to be kept a secret from her mistress.

CLOWNLY. I am very much obliged to Mrs. Fish for her contrivance; and I shall give her a very handsome present to satisfy her.

HUMPHRY. Lord, Sir, there is no occasion for that—I shall kiss her now and then, and I dare say that will be quite satisfaction enough. But come, Sir, we must go directly.

CLOWNLY. Do you know, Humphry, that my heart misgives me.

HUMPHRY. What! now you are so near seeing the Lady! Come, come, master, be merry.

CLOWNLY. Ah! Humphry; if I had continued poor—if I had never been your master, I might have been merry.

HUMPHRY. "Never been my master" —How can you talk so? Why, there are people in the world would give any money to be my master.—Why now, there's my wife—she'd give every farthing she has to be my master; but I tell her, No—No Jane, says I, you shall never be my master.

CLOWNLY. Oh, if I thought I should get Miss Angle—

HUMPHRY. I'll forfeit my head if you don't.—Have you not every thing to get her with? Fine clothes, in your box there, and plenty of money.—I never heard of a woman that cou'd not be got with fine clothes and plenty of money; nay, often without either money or clothes.

CLOWNLY. But, I tell you, that won't do with her—there is something more required.—I can't talk to her—I am at a loss for words.—

HUMPHRY. You can't be at a loss for words, while you are courting!—Women will always give you two for your one.— I know my wife did—and egad, tho' we have left off courting, so she does now.

CLOWNLY. Come—I'll set off.—Call a coach. *Exit.*

HUMPHRY. Ay, Sir, and I'll ride behind it, for fear I should get struck again.—'Tis very odd that any lady should wish to strike me. *Exeunt.*

ACT II. MISS ANGLE'S

Apartments.

Enter MISS ANGLE *and* FISH.

FISH. Dear Madam, let me persuade you to put on your other gown, for now his Lordship has kept it thus long, I dare say he'll bring it home himself.

MISS ANGLE. I begin to be uneasy.— Did the porter say, he was sure his Lordship was at home?

FISH. Quite sure, Ma'am—so we may expect him every minute; for he wou'd certainly have sent it back before now, if he had not intended to have brought it himself.—Do, Madam, change that ugly gown.—And what do you think of your other cap?—Your becoming cap? —Hark!—No—that's only a single rap.

—The deuce take him, he has sent it home by a porter, perhaps?

MISS ANGLE. I don't care how, so I get it again—for I begin to be alarmed, left by some accident— *(FISH looks out of the window.)* Is it that?

FISH. No, Ma'am, 'tis the milk-woman. —Perhaps, Ma'am, his Lordship may'nt call with it 'till the morning.

MISS ANGLE. Well, thank heaven, her Ladyship sleeps from home, you say; so she can't miss it to-night; and then, if we have heard nothing from him, you shall go after it, Fish—for as soon as her Ladyship comes home in the morning—

FISH. And the worst of it is—I am not sure she is to stay out all night!—

MISS ANGLE. You told me she was.

FISH. I did it for your good.—I knew you wou'd not have sent it to his Lordship, if I had not said so.

MISS ANGLE. Ridiculous!—And I still worse to listen to you.

FISH. Dear Ma'am, don't fret about it,—but think of Mr. Clownly.—I am sure he looks very beautiful; and so does his man, Humphry! And pray, ma'am, did not you see, by his master's looks, that he is in love with you?

MISS ANGLE. Pshaw!—

FISH. Nay, madam, you need not sneer at him; for if his Lordship shou'd never send back the shawl—

MISS ANGLE. Heavens!

FISH. We shall stand in need of a rich friend to make it up with Lady Mary. *(A loud rap.)* There's his Lordship!—That's his rap!—I know it so well; I cou'd swear to it at any time.— Now, madam, how do you look? vastly well, I declare!—Lord, how well I know his rap!—*(Goes to the door.)* I wish I may die if it is not Lady Mary!—

MISS ANGLE. Oh! I shall faint!

FISH. The first thing she does, will be to look at her shawl.

MISS ANGLE. Run, fly—take a coach, and fly to Lord Lighthead's, with my compliments—I made a mistake—he did not send it—but another person—who

now has claim'd it—and I must return it immediately.

FISH. Well, ma'am,—I'll do all I can.

Enter LADY MARY.

LADY MARY. Oh! Mrs. Fish!— Where are you going in such a hurry?

FISH. A little way, my Lady,—on— a little business. *Exit.*

LADY MARY. My dear Angle! I have been shopping.—*(Sits.)* Well, marriage is an expensive thing.—'Tis well it comes but once in one's life.

MISS ANGLE. With some people, Ma'am, it comes oftner.

LADY MARY. And with some, not at all—Now that was very near the case with me, 'till I struck Mr. Wamsley!— By the bye, he grows more and more attentive.—He has been taking me to the jeweller's—and see there!—All these are his presents.

MISS ANGLE. How profuse!—

LADY MARY. But my dear, you know all this is nothing to the shawl!—That, to be sure is the genteelest—most elegant present—as I live, here is the generous donor!

Enter WALMSLEY.

WALMSLEY. Ladies, I presume, I don't intrude?—Miss Angle, how do you do?—I beg pardon for not having called on you lately—I should—but I don't know—one is always happening of one accident or another, to prevent one's designs.—

LADY MARY. Very true.

WALMSLEY. Has your Ladyship been shewing Miss Angle any of your purchases?—

LADY MARY. Yes—and she's quite in love with your generosity!

WALMSLEY. Pshaw! — Pshaw! — No generosity at all.—Have you seen the shawl, Miss?—

MISS ANGLE. Yes, Sir.

LADY MARY. Yes—yes—I told you, you know, how much she admired it.— And even poor Fish seem'd to know its value.

WALMSLEY. Why, that shawl—

LADY MARY. I'll go fetch it.

MISS ANGLE *(Holding her).* Dear Madam, don't trouble yourself.

LADY MARY. What, would not you wish to see it again?

MISS ANGLE. Yes—Indeed, I would. —But—

WALMSLEY. Are you sure you have seen it?—

MISS ANGLE. Yes, Sir,—very sure.—

WALMSLEY *(To* LADY MARY*).* Why then sit still.

LADY MARY. No, Mr. Walmsley, the tea is waiting.—Miss Angle, you must come and drink tea with Mr. Walmsley and me.—We came on purpose to fetch you.

WALMSLEY. Your Ladyship will excuse my stepping to a friend's in the next street.—I'll be back instantly.

LADY MARY. Certainly.—Come, Miss Angle—

MISS ANGLE. I'll wait on your Ladyship in a moment.

WALMSLEY *(Sighing).* Will your Ladyship honour me with your hand?

LADY MARY *(Curtsies and smiles).* The honour is done to me, Mr. Walmsley.

WALMSLEY *(Aside).* So I think. Heigh ho! Heigh ho! *(Leads her off.)*

MISS ANGLE. Their civility distracts me!—How impatient I am for the return of Fish?

Enter FISH, *out of Breath.*

MISS ANGLE. You have not been!

FISH. Dear Madam, I met with his Lordship in the street, going out with a heap of noblemen.—Oh! Madam, we are undone. *(Begins to cry.)*

MISS ANGLE. How? What? Don't keep me in suspense.

FISH. Why, Madam, I called his Lordship on one side; and do you know he had the impudence to say, he did give you the shawl—and he was much oblig'd to you for returning it.—

MISS ANGLE. Oh heavens!

FISH. And then when I cry'd, and took on—he offered to pay me for it— and what do you think he offer'd me?—

MISS ANGLE. I don't know!—

FISH. Five guineas.—He said, he had no more about him—so I thought I should get nothing else—and so I had better take that. *(Shewing the money.)*

MISS ANGLE. You did not?—

FISH. Yes, ma'am—for I thought it might help to hire counsel to plead for us at the bar; for we shall certainly be taken up. *(Cries.)*

MISS ANGLE. Heavens!—Conceal your uneasiness.—I must go to Lady Mary directly—she expects me to tea.

FISH. Oh! How shall I ever look Lady Mary in the face?

MISS ANGLE. What distress—

FISH. No, Ma'am—now for it *(List'ning at the door.)* I hear her in her chamber, and now she'll miss it.

MISS ANGLE. Stay with me, Fish, or I shall faint!

FISH. Dear Ma'am, don't look so frighten'd!—If you do, indeed I shall go into fits!—indeed I shall!—For I know Mr. Walmsley is such a cruel man, he'll hang us both, notwithstanding we are two such poor, little, innocent lambs.

MISS ANGLE. Be more on your guard.—

FISH. Ay, madam, we must put a good face on it, for if we don't she'll suspect us.—I won't cry any more I am determined.

Enter LADY MARY.

LADY MARY. My dear Angle, and my dear dear Fish, I am terrified out of my life! do you know I laid my shawl on the bed—spread it on with my own hands—turn'd and look'd at it again as I went out of the room, and saw it safe—and now 'tis gone—nor can I find it high nor low.

MISS ANGLE. Your Ladyship does not think it is lost?

FISH. Lost, ma'am!—that's likely indeed?—We have no thieves in this house, I am sure.—You, *(To MISS ANGLE.)* I suppose ma'am, wou'd not steal it?—And I don't know what a poor servant, like me, should do with a shawl.—I cou'd not wear it if I had it. —Besides, my character—

MISS ANGLE. Hush, Fish!—

LADY MARY. I suspect no one, Mrs. Fish.—Heaven forbid I shou'd—but the thing is gone.

FISH. Dear me, what a pity!—

MISS ANGLE. Is your Ladyship sure you laid it on the bed?

LADY MARY. Sure—just as I told you.

FISH. How my Lady was it?—The long ways on the bed, or the cross ways?—Thus! *(Folding her handkerchief.)*

MISS ANGLE. Has your Ladyship enquired below?

LADY MARY. Of every creature.— But no one comes into my Apartments, but my own servant, and she is just stept out.

FISH. Then she knows where it is I dare say, ma'am.

LADY MARY. If she does not, I don't know what I shall do—I believe I shall lose my senses! *(Sitting down.)*

MISS ANGLE. Deam madam! altho' it was certainly a most valuable thing! yet consider—

FISH. Ay, madam, consider it was saved from the storm as it came over.— You ought to bless yourself you got it at all—tho' to be sure you have not had it long.

LADY MARY. Oh! if I had never seen it, I had been happy!—I shou'd not then have known my loss.

MISS ANGLE. But, madam, you are not certain you have lost it—stay till you see your woman.

LADY MARY. I know she has not removed it.—I charged her not to touch it.—Oh! 'tis gone! 'tis gone! 'tis gone! *(Rising.)*

FISH *(In the same tone).* Oh! that I did but know who had got it!

LADY MARY. Come hither Betty— *(Enter BETTY)* you never saw your poor Lady in such distress in your life.—Did you touch my shawl?

BETTY. No, my Lady—I never touch any thing.

LADY MARY. I told you so.—And did you let nobody into my bedchamber?

BETTY. No, my Lady—but I saw Mrs. Fish come out there this morning.

FISH. Oh! Oh! Oh!

BETTY. Indeed, Mrs. Fish, I did.

FISH. Oh dear! Oh dear! Oh dear!

LADY MARY. What do you cry for, child? If you took it, confess, and I'll forgive you.

FISH. I took it, ma'am?—no ma'am— that's not what I cry for.—'Tis because I am sure I shan't live long.—For if she saw me come out of your Ladyship's room, it was my apparition; and you never live long after your apparition has been seen to walk.

MISS ANGLE. But were you there? —Do you know any thing of it?

FISH. No more than you do, ma'am.

Exit BETTY.

LADY MARY. Well! I pity poor Mr. Walmsley.—It is a hard thing to say— for it will be a great disappointment to him—but I don't think I'll marry if I have lost it.—No, if I have lost it I won't be married—

Enter MR. WALMSLEY.

WALMSLEY. Ladies, I come to tell you—

LADY MARY *(Walking in a rage).* Don't teize me—don't argue with me— don't attempt to shake my resolution.— I won't marry you.

WALMSLEY. Did I hear right?—Or did my ears deceive me?—You won't marry me?

LADY MARY. No.—

WALMSLEY. The bells shall ring, *notwithstanding.*—The poor ringers shan't lose their fee! —And I'll give a dinner too—a very good dinner—a better dinner than I intended.

LADY MARY. Sir!

WALMSLEY. Here's an accident!—*(Aside.)* Why it will make me more than amends for that unlucky one in the morning!

LADY MARY. What does he say?

WALMSLEY. I was saying, I must give a very elegant entertainment on Thursday, notwithstanding the match is broken off.—And I believe I shall write to my tenants and have a bullock roasted.

LADY MARY. There!—Do you hear him!

MISS ANGLE. Dear Mr. Walmsley, her Ladyship has been only in joke.

WALMSLEY. And 'tis the best joke I ever heard.—Miss Angle, I never asked her to have me but once.—I happened to be in a violent passion, and I did ask her once.

LADY MARY. There!—He owns his violent passion.

WALMSLEY. But it was not for you. —However, I was in a passion, and she snap'd me up.—You took me at my word, and now I take you at yours; and we have done with each other.

LADY MARY. Cruel savage!—I dare say he has stolen the shawl himself, on purpose to break off the match.

WALMSLEY. What shawl?

FISH. Why, Sir, the fine grand one you were so good as to give her Ladyship: some wicked wretch has been making free with.

LADY MARY. Yes—'tis lost—'tis gone.—Don't you pity me?

WALMSLEY. No.—I am vastly glad.

LADY MARY. Oh! Heavens!—This is the man that is to be soon my husband—The partner of all my joys! and all my sorrows!

WALMSLEY. No.—Your Ladyship's sorrows are too violent—and if your joys had proved the same, egad, I don't know which would have been the most insupportable.

MISS ANGLE. Dear Sir, her Ladyship was so much agitated merely because it was a present from you.

WALMSLEY. Well, Miss—but where the deuce is it?—Who has been in the house?

MISS ANGLE *and* LADY MARY. No creature.

FISH. The Rats carried away one of my shoes last night, and eat a great hole in my apron.

WALMSLEY. I will find out what Rat has got it—I'll go to Bow-street directly.—You are sure nobody has been here to-day?—Who was that countryman I met on the stairs this morning?

FISH. A Mr. Clownly, Sir.—A gentleman that call'd to see my mistress, because we all happened to be fellow travellers on the road.—Laud! sure he did not take it?

WALMSLEY. I'll be damn'd if he did not!

MISS ANGLE. Dear Sir!

WALMSLEY. Write me down his name, Mrs Fish, (or at least the name he goes by) and where he is to be found, if you know.

FISH. Oh yes, Sir.

MISS ANGLE. Heavens! Dear Sir, you judge wrong.—I am sure he did not take it.

FISH. Now I have some little reason to think he did—Here's his direction, Sir.

LADY MARY. The country gentleman you told me of—Do you suspect him, Miss Angle?

MISS ANGLE. No, ma'am—no.— *(Aside.)* What can I do? I dare not confess.—Lord Lighthead may justly say I sold it him.—What will become of me?

WALMSLEY. Well, Miss Angle, I can do this gentleman no harm in having him taken up, and hearing what he has to say for himself—and I'll about it directly.—Her Ladyship has had one loss already, in losing me, and I don't think 'tis right she should have another. —Besides, I have now a value for the thing.—Who wou'd have thought that little shawl wou'd have turned out of such consequence? Providence preserved it from the storm at sea, to save me from a worse storm on land. *Exit.*

LADY MARY. I'll be as gentle as Zephyrs.—Plead for me, speak for me, dear Miss Angle.

MISS ANGLE. I will, Madam.—It is my duty.—Depend upon it I will reconcile you.

Enter BETTY.

BETTY. Dear my Lady, as Mr. Walmsley went out, he bid me observe if I should see the country gentleman, or his man, who were here this morning; for that he believed they were both no better than two highwaymen; and so, Madam, the servant is just come up to the back door;—and so I'm come to let your Ladyship know.

LADY MARY. I'm sorry Mr. Walmsley is gone.

BETTY. Shall I go for a constable, Ma'am?

LADY MARY. No—we'll proceed by fair means first.—Fish, you know the servant, go you and call him in; and I'll question him.

FISH. Dear, my Lady! A poor ignorant creature!—He knows nothing!—You won't understand him, nor make him understand you.

LADY MARY. Oh, that ignorance may be pretended—put on for the time. Call him in.—Why don't you go?

FISH *(Going)*. What can I say to him? If she should call him a thief, he'll perhaps serve her as he did the woman in the Piazza. *Exit.*

MISS ANGLE. These harmless creatures are no thieves.

LADY MARY. Dear Miss Angle, I wish to do them no injury—for if I could but secure Mr. Walmsley once more, I did not care if every thief in London was set at liberty.—Here the man comes.—What a hanging look he **has?** —I hope he has not got pistols about him.—Let us draw this way.

(They retire.)

Enter FISH and HUMPHRY.

FISH. Lady Mary, my mistress's particular acquaintance, wants to ask you a few questions.—What shall I say to him? *(Aside.)* She is a comical kind of woman!—You must know she has been out to dinner—and whenever that is the case, she always—you understand me—*(Putting her hand up to her mouth as if she were drinking.)* and then she comes home in such an ill temper, there is no peace or quietness for her.

HUMPHRY. That is so like my wife!

FISH. She'll ask you a heap of foolish questions, but don't you mind her—only say, Yes; and No; and so on.

HUMPHRY. Ay, that just suits me.—I can say Yes; and No; and am never at a loss.—But, harkye, she don't fight in her cups, I hope; I've had one blow already you know.

LADY MARY *(Coming forward, aside)*. So Mr. Humphry. What shall I say to him? Your name is Humphry, I think?

HUMPHRY. Yes, Madam—I'm much oblig'd to you.

MISS ANGLE. This is insupportable. *Exit.*

LADY MARY. And pray, how do you like London?

HUMPHRY. Very well, I thank you, Madam; pray how do you like it?

LADY MARY *(Aside)*. This folly is put on. Pray, Mr. Humphry, have you any acquaintance in town?

HUMPHRY. None: except your honour.—I have no acquaintance to give me a drop of any thing to drink.—And, you know, your Honour, that's a sad thing.

LADY MARY. I do know it—and you shan't want for something to drink.—*(Aside.)* Better prevail on him by kindness, and he may discover all. *(Gives him money.)* Here is something for you to drink.

HUMPHRY. Thank your Honour.—*(Aside.)* Well, I declare your staunch drinker's have more generosity than any people in the world!

LADY MARY *(Aside)*. I am at a loss how to accuse this man, tho' I am sure either he or his master is guilty.—— Mr. Humphry, I am very sorry—

HUMPHRY. Your Honour!—

LADY MARY. I say, I am very sorry, very sorry, indeed—

HUMPHRY. Oh! Madam, never be sorry about it.—For my part, I should hardly have found it out, if I had not been told of it.—Besides, nobody has any thing to do with it, but yourself;— and if they had, you are such a good companion *(Looking at his money)* nobody can be angry with you.

LADY MARY. What do you mean?— No cross-purposes—but answer me directly.—Do you know any thing of my shawl?

HUMPHRY. Your what, Ma'am?— your shawl? Ha, ha, ha, ha!—Oh! you'll have a fine headach for this to-morrow morning.

LADY MARY. What?

HUMPHRY. I would not be so ill as you'll be for five guineas.

LADY MARY. The fellow is laughing at me!—Fish, call a constable; I'll have him taken up.

HUMPHRY. Take me up!—Lord, Ma'am, do you lie down—only for half an hour—only just for half an hour—you can't think how refresh'd you'll be.—It will clear all this away; *(Pointing to his head)* and you'll be quite another woman.

LADY MARY. What do you mean?

HUMPHRY. Nay, I know a nap is of vast consequence to me, at these times— especially when my liquor makes me ill-tempered.

LADY MARY. The man's mad—I'll have him secured directly.—Call a constable.

HUMPHRY. Do, your Honour, let me persuade you to take a bason of camomile tea.—

Enter MISS ANGLE.

LADY MARY. Miss Angle, come hither.—Did you ever hear such an insult?—Fish—Fish—Call all the people of the house.—Who's there? Come and secure this robber.—My anger is rouz'd, and I'll be reveng'd.—

HUMPHRY. How like my wife!

MISS ANGLE. Dear Madam—

Enter CLOWNLY.

CLOWNLY. What's the matter?

MISS ANGLE. Mr. Clownly, I rejoice to see you!—Lady Mary has had some altercation with your servant, but I believe he has not been to blame.

HUMPHRY. How her poor head will ach for this! *Exit. taking off* FISH.

CLOWNLY *(To* LADY MARY*)*. Dear Madam, have the goodness—

Enter WALMSLEY.

WALMSLEY. I have done the job.— The thief is taken—and who do you think it is?—The very person in the world!—By Jupiter! I wou'd not have lost the pleasure of taking her up for fifty times the value of the thing.—I caught her just as she was going into Covent Garden theatre, with the goods upon her.—So with the help of one of the playhouse constables, I handed her (in spite of her squalling) into a coach, and have brought her here that she may be properly exposed.

LADY MARY *and* MISS ANGLE. What can this mean?

WALMSLEY *(Speaking loud)*. Desire the constable to bring up the woman in custody.—Sir, *(To* CLOWNLY*.)* whoever you are, I beg your pardon— you are not a thief, that I know of— if you are, that's best known to yourself.—I'm a little busy, Sir, at present— you'll excuse me!—Constable, bring up the prisoner!—Why don't you come?— Surely there never was such an accident!

Enter CONSTABLE *with* LADY LOVEALL.

WALMSLEY. There!—You see the goods are upon her!

LADY LOVEALL. Insupportable!— Have not I affirmed, that it was presented to me by Lord Lighthead?

MISS ANGLE *(Aside)*. I am tortured!

LADY LOVEALL. It is not to be borne?—Sir, you know 'tis mine.—This is only a scheme, on purpose to distress me, in revenge for what I discovered this morning!

WALMSLEY. Ay, you were vastly pleased at that.—And now 'tis only evening, and I have discovered something that pleases me.

LADY LOVEALL. Very well—go on.—But I have sent my servant to Lord Lighthead, to inform him of this affair, and I am certain the moment he has found him, his Lordship will come and clear me!

WALMSLEY. There wants no clearing!—Every thing is clear enough!

Enter LORD LIGHTHEAD.

LORD LIGHTHEAD. Dear Uncle!—Dear Lady Loveall! What's the matter?—Just as I was stepping into my coach, a summons came to me, to attend you upon life and death.—What's the matter?

WALMSLEY. No, —no death in the case.—I believe nothing more than hard labour on the Thames.

LORD LIGHTHEAD. Sir, altho' you are my Uncle, this insult to a Lady with whom I have the honour to be acquainted, is not to be suffered.—I presented the Lady with that shawl.—It was sent to me by this Lady, *(Pointing to* MISS ANGLE*)* and a few hours after she sent it, her servant received five guineas for it.

MISS ANGLE. 'Tis true.—I confess it.—Guilt and shame overpower me!

WALMSLEY *(To* MISS ANGLE*).* Why the devil did you confess? Nobody would have seen it in your face!—Besides, you have robb'd me of the pleasure of conducting her Ladyship to a prison; and damn me, if I ever met with so great a disappointment.

MISS ANGLE. Conduct me, Sir—I am ready to attend you.

LADY MARY. She has destroyed my peace—and I shall see her go to prison without a sigh.

CLOWNLY. But I would not, without losing my life.—Madam, I'll satisfy you for whatever loss you may have sustained by this Lady.

LADY MARY. You can't satisfy me.—I've lost Mr. Walmsley.

WALMSLEY. Ay, now ask her, what she demands for me.

LADY MARY. I shall take nothing less than the gentleman himself.

WALMSLEY. Well—I like her for that—she does not undervalue me.

MISS ANGLE. Mr. Clownly, while you imagine you are giving your protection to a thief only—you are protecting a more despicable character.—Had poverty seduced me to the crime of which I am accused, less wou'd have been my remorse, less ought to have been the censure incurred—But vanity —folly—a a mistaken confidence in that gentleman's honour, and my own attractions, prompted me to avail myself of a contemptible scheme, in order to regain his acquaintance, which (admitting what he profess'd to me real) he himself wou'd have rejoiced at.—But the event has proved and discovered both our hearts—nor can I reproach him with the cruelty of his, while I experience the most poignant reproofs of an inward monitor for the guilty fault of my own.

LADY LOVEALL. And so this was only a scheme for the Lady to procure a husband.—Here, Lady Mary, is your beloved shawl.—Take it, and take care—

WALMSLEY. Yes, do you take care of that, and I'll take care of myself.—Yet, I don't know, perhaps I may have her; but if I may judge by appearance—

LORD LIGHTHEAD. On that witness, who in company has not, throughout the adventures of this day, appeared culpable?

WALMSLEY. Very true.—Even I myself at one time made no very innocent figure.—These adventures shall then be a warning to us, never to judge with severity, while the parties have only appearances against them.

FINIS.

NO SONG NO SUPPER:

AN

OPERA,

IN TWO ACTS:

WITH ADDITIONAL SONGS.

As performed with great applause by the Old Ame-
rican company of Comedians.

※※※※※※※※※

SECOND PHILADELPHIA EDITION.

※※※※※※※※※

PHILADELPHIA:

FROM THE PRESS OF MATHEW CAREY.

JAN. 14,—M·DCC·XCIII.

No Song No Supper

Author

No great amount of significant information is known about Prince Hoare. Yet he managed, with very moderate talents in two or three branches of art and some fortunate acquaintanceships, to derive about as much fame as was due him. Born in Bath in 1755, son of a highly successful portrait painter in that fashionable resort, he was trained from boyhood to be a painter. He spent nearly five years in Italy under various masters, only to discover, by five more years of trial in London, 1780–85, that more than fortunate circumstances of birth were requisite for success in art. Giving up his exhibiting he returned home to Bath in 1785 to stay until 1788 when he departed for Lisbon in poor health. It was more than likely during this stay in Bath that he met his collaborator-to-be, Stephen Storace, for the young composer had thrown up his operatic work in London about this time and retired to Bath to study art. Like Storace, Hoare ventured into another field and during his stay in Lisbon sent home a tragedy, *Such Things Were*, to be acted at Bath and, some years later, Drury Lane. The even partial success of his first trial encouraged him to try again, and in April, 1790, he had the satisfaction of seeing *No Song No Supper* launched on a promising career at Drury Lane. His name seems not, however, to have appeared in any of the early announcements. Instead, the name of the musical composer was given prominence, the management no doubt wishing to capitalize on the success scored earlier in the season by Storace's *Haunted Tower*. The popularity of *No Song No Supper* provided Hoare with the necessary credentials for dramatic authorship, and he began turning out a succession of plays in the last decade of the century, nearly all of them musical pieces and most of them with the assistance of Storace or Michael Kelly. All run to farce or sentiment; none seem to have achieved quite the acclaim of his first success, though a few, notably *My Grandmother*, had considerable popularity. Shortly after the turn of the century he was made an honorary secretary of the Royal Academy and devoted much of his time to art, more or less as a gentleman amateur. He died at Brighton in 1834.

Source

Most of the episodes of *No Song No Supper* derive ultimately from folklore, for three distinct motifs occurring frequently in ballad and fable are used in the play. It is quite possible, however, that Hoare found the main one in theatrical literature and picked up the others from casual reading.

The main episode, the farcical business of the mock-magician's disclosure of the lover hiding in the sack, is quite old. Perhaps best known in modern times in the Grimms' "Little Farmer" or Anderson's "Great Claus and Little Claus," it may be traced back to various far more remote sources.[1] Hoare could very easily have found it close at hand in Ravenscroft's *London Cuckolds*, which had survived the first half of the eighteenth century but proved too salacious for the later period. In fact the contrast in moral tone between the 1681 version of the story and that of 1790 is quite revealing. Ravenscroft draws the would-be violator as a typical young and rakish gentleman, the intended cuckold as a dull citizen, the mock-magician as a young man whose intentions and principles are no better than those of the person he brings out of hiding. Hoare comes far closer to the moral level of the fairy tales we know so well. The lover is ridiculous, the husband is a bit gullible perhaps but on the whole sympathetically portrayed, the magician more or less neutral but on the sympathetic side. Moreover, the dramatist's respect for the sensibilities of his audience leads him to rather absurd lengths. If Dorothy has been as upright in her conduct with Endless as we are assured she has been, one wonders why she ever permitted herself to get into so horribly compromising a situation.

Two other motifs from folk literature have been worked into the main episode of the mock-magician. The first of these, the "air-castles" theme, is perhaps best known in La Fontaine's tale of Perette.[2] Little is made of the episode except to furnish a bit of dialogue. The Crops fall to arguing over what they will provide for the table if and when they win their lawsuit. Hoare fails to develop a situation which will

---

[1] See Bolte and Polívka, *Anmerkungen zu der Kinder und Hausmärchen des Brüder Grimm* (1913–32).

[2] Baskerville, *The Elizabethan Jig* (1929), pp. 303 ff, discusses the use of this and similar themes in English jigs and German *Singspiele*. The Grimms also used the theme in their stories of "Lazy Heinz" and "Skinny Bess"; Bolte and Polívka give possible sources and analogues.

permit the familiar dramatic catastrophe with which the story commonly ends, and the argument trails off inconclusively with the entrance of Louisa. He took greater pains with the second, the door-closing motif, running the story out to its familiar climax. No doubt he had become acquainted with the story in the ballad version of "Get up and Bar the Door," which had appeared in collections edited by David Herd in the 60's and 70's and in the collection of John Pinkerton published in 1783. Some of the non-British analogues listed in Child's *English and Scottish Popular Ballads* parallel Hoare's version more closely than the ballad in that the wife rather than the husband loses the contest. There seems to be scant reason, however, for supposing that our dramatist had to range very far for his story.

Stage History

Considerable interest attaches to the *première* of this little comic opera, for in it we find some interesting, though somewhat indirect, connections with one of the giants of eighteenth-century music, Wolfgang Amadeus Mozart. The composer of the music for *No Song No Supper*, Stephen Storace, had wound up his twelve-year tour of the Continent with a prolonged residence at the court of Emperor Joseph in Vienna, where Mozart was hard at work on his own early operas. From letters and recollections of the persons involved we are assured that the two composers were more than chance acquaintances, so that when Storace left Vienna in 1787 headed home to London he carried with him not only a recollection of the greater musicians's works but a letter of introduction to old Leopold Mozart in Salzburg as well.[3]

But this is getting ahead of our story. Along with Storace at the Emperor's court were other English musicians, most notably his sister Nancy and the Irish tenor Michael Kelly. And with this pair our connections with Mozart become even closer, for these two creators of leading parts in *No Song No Supper* were also involved in the memorable *première* of *Il Nozze di Figaro* on May 1, 1786, Nancy Storace as Susanna, Kelly doubling in Basilio and Don Curzio.

---

[3]The *Reminiscences of Michael Kelly* (1826) are always interesting though not reliable in every detail. The letters of Mozart and his father mention the English group. See especially Letter No. 545 in Miss Anderson's *Letters of Mozart and His Family* (London, 1938).

The first performance of *No Song No Supper* was not, however, attended with all the glory these circumstances may suggest. In fact, Kelly tells us that the proprietors of Drury Lane turned the piece down and he was forced to request it for his own benefit, April 16, 1790. It seems to have caught on rapidly and soon became a staple item in the repertory.[4] Genest records some twenty performances in his far from exhaustive lists.[5] Hoare's piece was perhaps even more successful in this country. For the period 1793–1853 Odell lists nearly fifty specific performances without attempting to give all. Miss Willis gives thirteen for Charleston during the last decade of the century and Hoole adds forty-three more down to 1841. In their accounts of Philadelphia theatres Pollock lists fourteen, James nineteen, and Wilson twenty-nine performances, all combined covering the period 1792–1851. Miss Smithers lists forty-six for New Orleans, 1820–42. Ranging still farther, Loewenberg cites appearances in Hamburg and Capetown and a revival in Manchester as late as 1870.[6]

Publication

The *Biographia Dramatica* of 1812, commenting on Hoare and this particular comic opera, remarks that the "Songs only [were] pub-

---

[4] If we may depend once more on Kelly, we see how popular Hoare quickly became. He tells of the serious mishap at a command performance in the Haymarket, February 3, 1794, in which sixteen people were killed. "Their Majesties, on that night, had commanded three pieces,—'My Grandmother,' 'No Song, No Supper,' and 'The Prize,' all written by my friend, Prince Hoare." Genest does not give the bill but speaks of the accident. On one occasion, at least, and that an important one here, Genest corrects Kelly, whose memory told him that Nancy Storace played "her favorite part of Margaretta" at her farewell performance. He does not correct Kelly, however, when the latter tells of his own use of *No Song No Supper* in saying goodbye to London audiences for the last time. Isaac Reed's diary gives us sufficient evidence of the play's catching on. He saw it at Drury Lane on May 3, a little over two weeks after its opening; he saw it a second time at the theatre at Yarmouth on August 4 following.

[5] Though Genest lists only eight London performances during the period from 1790–98, playbills at Harvard show seventeen additional performances, and there are numerous bills in the newspapers of the day. We do not say this in disparagement of John Genest, let us hasten to add. Without his remarkable account generations of students of the English stage would have wandered in darkness.

[6] Seilhamer's thirty-eight performances and Sonneck's fifty-two overlap those already given, though they account for a few cities not covered by the other authorities.

lished (except piratically), 8vo. 1790." However, the exception seems to have been an extensive one, for there were several editions within a few years in widely scattered cities. They continued to appear for close to a century.

Songs, Duets, Trio, and Finales, in *No Song No Supper.* As performed at the Theatre-Royal, Drury-Lane. The Music chiefly composed by Mr. Storace: the rest selected from Pleyel, Gretry, Dr. Harington, Giordani, Gluck, etc. 1790.

Songs, Duets, Trio, and Finales . . . The rest selected from Pleyel, Gretry, Giordani, etc. 1790.

No Song No Supper: an Opera, in two Acts . . . Dublin: P. Byrne . . . 1792.

The Opera of *No Song No Supper:* in two Acts. As performed at the Theatre-Royal, Smoke-Alley, 1792.

Songs, Duets, Trio, and Finales. . . . 1792.

No Song No Supper . . . As performed with great Applause by the Old American Company of Comedians. Second Philadelphia Edition. Philadelphia: Mathew Carew, 1793.[7]

No Song No Supper . . . Third American Edition, with Additions. New York: J. Harrisson, 1793.

No Song No Supper . . . As performed at the Theatre in Boston. Printed at the Apollo Press in Boston, for William P. Blake, 1794.

No Song No Supper . . . London: Longman & Broderip, [c. 1795].[8]

No Song No Supper . . . London: Printed for the Curious in Dramatical Performances, and not sold by the Booksellers in General, [c. 1795].

No Song No Supper . . . The Fourth Edition . . . London, 1795.

No Song No Supper . . . London: C. Rapson, 1818.

No Song No Supper . . . New York: David Longworth, 1819.

No Song No Supper . . . New York: Charles Wiley; H. C. Carey & J. Lea, and McCarthy & Davis, Philadelphia; Saml. P. Parker, Boston, 1824.

No Song No Supper . . . In Vol. IV, *The London Stage*, London; Sherwood and Co., [1827].

No Song No Supper . . . In Vol. IV, *Lea's British Drama*, London, [c. 1827].

No Song No Supper . . . In Vol. XXIV, *Cumberland's British Theatre*, London, [1830].

[7]We have been unable to discover any first Philadelphia edition.

[8]The Yale Library has a copy of the words and music for a single air, Margaretta's "With Lowly Suit and Plaintive Ditty," also published by Longman & Broderip.

No Song No Supper . . . London: The Music Publishing Company,
[c. 1830].

No Song No Supper . . . London: Thomas Richardson, [c. 1830].

No Song No Supper . . . London, Sherwood & Bowyer, 1845.

No Song No Supper . . . In Vol. IV, 1266–74, *The British Drama*,
London: John Dicks, 1865.

No Song No Supper, Comic Opera, the Words by Prince Hoare, the
Music by Storace, the Text revised by John Oxenford, with new
Symphonies and Accompaniments by J. L. Hatton. Boosey & Co.,
London and New York, [c. 1880].

No Song No Supper . . . In Vol. 89, *Lacy's Acting Edition of Plays,*
London: Thomas Hailes Lacy, (n.d.)

Analysis

No Song No Supper represents a fairly successful combination of
farce and sentiment. The main thread of the plot is concerned with
the distresses of not one but two pairs of lovers in distress; yet most
of the scenes, particularly the big final scene, are devoted to two or
three farcical episodes, and the love stories are allowed to drift
along toward the happy climax with which love stories always close—
that is, in the theatre.

The big farce episode with which the play closes is prepared for
early, in the second scene, and the others are included within it.
The first, the quarrel over what the Crops will feast upon when they
win their suit, hardly reaches the level of farce since the playwright
did not provide the circumstances necessary for the usual climax.

The second, the one involving the wrangle over shutting the door,
is played out to the end. It is, however, wholly extraneous. Like
Dorothy, in her speech at the beginning of the episode, the audience
may wonder why Crop has come drifting back onto the scene with no
discernible purpose, but then too critical an attitude toward motiva-
tion is scarcely conducive to the enjoyment of farce.

Scene 3, carrying us into the real beginnings of the mock-magician
episode, is notable chiefly for the mixture of song and sentiment
with which the leading singer is introduced and for the Mozartian
ensemble at its close where each singer states his hopes and fears.

The final scene is cleverly handled, except perhaps for melodramatic climaxes to the love affairs. The use of the mealsack as a
hiding place instead of the more conventional chest is no doubt due
to Hoare's wish to get as many laughs as possible. The terrified
lawyer, reduced to such indignities, with wig and finery all spoiled,

must have created a ludicrous figure indeed. Since this is all in fun, however, the lawyer is not so terrified that he ceases his execrable puns. In some of the later versions he even adds to the slapstick by returning to the scene after his discovery to throw flour on the others.

In a few versions also there was an extra scene of pathos involving a Welsh harpist and providing a more dramatic reunion for Frederick and Louisa than the more common version.

DRAMATIS PERSONAE

	Drury Lane:	Philadelphia:
FREDERIC.	[Mr. *Kelley.*	Mr. *Chambers.*
ROBIN.	Mr. *J. Bannister.*	Mr. *Hodgkinson.*
CROP.	Mr. *Dignum.*	Mr. *Prigmore.*
ENDLESS.	Mr. *Suett.*	Mr. *Martin.*
WILLIAM.	Mr. *Sedgwick.*	Mr. *Robins.*
THOMAS.	Mr. *Alfred.*	Mr. *Ryan.*
MARGARETTA.	Signora *Storace*	Mrs. *Hodgkinson.*
LOUISA.	Mrs. *Crouch.*	Miss *Brett.*
DOROTHY.	Mrs. *Bland.*	Mrs. *Pownall.*
[DEBORAH.]	Mrs. *Booth.*	
NELLY.	Miss *Hagley.*]	Mrs. *Rankin.*

Sailors, Messrs. BISSET, WEST, HAMMOND, *and* DURANG.
Drury Lane: The original cast is supplied from the first Dublin edition, 1792.

NO SONG NO SUPPER
ACT I. SCENE 1.

A view of the Sea on the Coast of Corn-wall; ROBIN *discovered asleep;* FREDERIC *enters from a part of the Rock.*

FREDERIC.

The lingering pangs of hopeless love, condemn'd
Unpitied—unpitied to endure;
Ah! hapless fate! by flight I strove
To soothe the pain I could not cure.
Sease, ocean, cease, cease thy angry strife,
Or here thy whelming billows pour: I ask, I ask
But this, oh! take, oh! take my life,
Or bear me to some distant shore.

Cruel destiny! to be driven ashore on this spot, which I had resolved to fly from forever: but all things conspire to counteract my designs; I had scarcely embarked, when a conspiracy was formed among the crew to deprive me of my life, which was happily preserved by the generosity of an English sailor; who, I fear, has perished, with all his honest companions. —*(Sees* ROBIN.*)* Good heav'ns! Is it possible, my generous preserver lives? Robin—what, ho! —Robin.

ROBIN, *(waking and starting).* No, we won't drown. Courage, my lads; lay hold of that plank, master Frederic.

FREDERIC. Honest spirit—careful of me, even in his dreams.

ROBIN *(Rises, takes tobacco, and stares at* FREDERIC*).* Where the deuce am I?

Deborah: supplied from the first Dublin edition, 1792.

FREDERIC. Don't you know me, my friend?

ROBIN. Master Frederic! —egad, then we are alive yet,—I thought we had been both in Davy Jones's locker.

FREDERIC. I assure you, I may sincerely say, that I rejoice more for your safety than my own.

ROBIN. Reef your compliments a little, and I'll believe you. Where are we, think you?

FREDERIC. Alas! I am but too well acquainted with the place. We are on the coast of Cornwall, not far from Penzance.

ROBIN. Say you so? Never droop then; we could not have made a better port. I have friends here will take care of us, all as one as if we were at home.

FREDERIC. Friends here!

ROBIN. Aye, if this storm has not carried them into the sea; I have a brother-in-law hard by, whom indeed I have not seen for some years; but he was alive when I last heard.

FREDERIC. What was his name?

ROBIN. Crop—an honest farmer.

FREDERIC *(aside).* Good heav'n! my Louisa's father.

ROBIN. He married a sister of mine, when I was a boy; she died some years ago, and left him a daughter; who, they say, is grown a fine girl; and now he's spliced to another mate.

FREDERIC. Well, Robin, we shall have no occasion to trouble your brother at present. I have an estate in the neighbourhood, where you shall be welcome; for your generosity has twice preserved my life.

ROBIN. Look ye, master Frederic, I have been from my country these three years; but I haven't so far forgot Old England, as not to stand by a man who fights against odds.

FREDERIC. You risked your own life for me.

ROBIN. That's no concern to a British sailor; he holds his life in keeping for his king, his country, and his friends; and for them he will cheerfully lay it down, whether scorching beneath the line, or freezing under the north pole—but look, some of our messmates heave in sight.

Enter WILLIAM and Sailors.

ROBIN. What cheer, my lads? Any part of the wreck saved? What! all ashore? What's become of the boat?

WILLIAM. Ah! Robin, she went down just after we left her, with all that we had on board.

ROBIN. So much the worse. I thought I had been rich enough to have taken Margaretta in tow for life; but now all's afloat again.

FREDERIC. You shall go home with me, my friends.—*(aside.)* I have a strong desire to see Louisa: what if I accompany Robin?

ROBIN. Thank you, sir; but some of us will look out, and see if the sea should heave ashore any of the cargo.

FREDERIC. I'll go with you, Robin, to your brother-in-law.

ROBIN. With all my heart; do you, William, keep a good look out from the top of the rock, till it is dark, and the rest keep watch on the beach.

WILLIAM. So we will, Robin; come along, my lads. *Exeunt WILLIAM and sailors.*

FREDERIC. Now, Robin, I have a secret to entrust to you.

ROBIN. Well, let it be a short one then; for a long one always sets me to sleep.

FREDERIC. You must know, Robin, that I quitted England on account of the fairest of women.

ROBIN. Why, that is something of my case; a shark of a lawyer bore down upon me, and carried off some property that I design'd for my mistress; and I was not willing to make her a beggar; and so I went to sea again.

FREDERIC *(aside).* How nearly allied in principles to my Louisa!—Know, then, Robin, the fairest of women I mean, was Louisa, your niece.

ROBIN. My niece! Give me your hand, master Frederic; if she is not married, you shall have her tomorrow: but what the devil made you bear away, and leave her tho'? Did you run foul of a lawyer too? You seem'd to have cash enough.

FREDERIC. Yes, Robin; but I was determined to prove her love for me, without acquainting her with my circumstances; I therefore gave out I was a poor scholar—this had'nt altogether the desired effect; for she, fearing to distress my friends by our union, refus'd me.

ROBIN. That was taking to the long boat, when you might have been safe in the ship.

FREDERIC. I shall not immediately inform her of my circumstances: therefore, Robin, promise not to betray me.

ROBIN. Nay, if it's your fancy—but, believe me, 'tis a foolish one. Well, if I had a thousand guineas, the greatest pleasure they could give me, would be to count them into Margaretta's lap.

FREDERIC. You won't disclose my secret.

ROBIN. What do you take me for? If this is all, step forward—I'll just give a look out, and see if any part of our little wreck remains above water, and come up with you presently.

A Sailor's life's a life of woe,
  He works now late, now early,
Now up and down, now to and fro.
  What then? he takes it cheerly.
Bless'd with a smiling can of grog,
    If duty call,
    Stand, rise or fall,
  To fate's last verge he'll jog;
    The cadge to weigh.
    The sheets belay,
He does it with a wish;
    To heave the lead,
    Or to 'cat-head
  The pond'rous anchor fish.
For while the grog goes round,
All sense of danger's drown'd,
  We despise it to a man:
We sing a little, and laugh a little,
And work a little, and swear a little,
And fiddle a little, and foot it a little,
  And swig the flowing can.
If howling winds and roaring seas,
  Give proof of coming danger,
We view the storm our hearts at ease,
  For Jack's to fear a stranger.
Bless'd with the smiling grog we fly
    Where now below
    We headlong go,
  Now rise on mountains high;
    Spite of the gale,
    We hand the sail,
  Or take the needful reef;
    Or man the deck,
    To clear some wreck,
  To give the ship relief:
Though perils threat around,
All sense of danger drown'd
  We despise it to a man:
      We sing a little, &c.
But yet think not our case is hard,
  Though storms at sea thus treat us.
For coming home, (a sweet reward!)
  With smiles our sweet-hearts greet us,
Now too the friendly grog we quaff,
    Our am'rous toast,
    Her we love most,
  And gaily sing and laugh;
    The sails we furl,
    Then for each girl,
  The petticoat display;
    The deck we clear,
    Then three times cheer,
As we their charms survey:
And then the grog goes round,
All sense of danger drown'd,
  We despise it to a man.
      We sing a little, &c.

                    Exeunt severally.

[SCENE 2.] *A room in* CROP'S
                 house.

   Enter CROP *and* DOROTHY.

CROP. But I tell you, wife, you are
wrong.

DOROTHY. Don't tell me, George; I
am sure it's your own fault.

CROP. My own fault, Dorothy!
Zounds! I wish the devil had the

SCENE: supplied from stage direction in *London
Stage*, 1827.

lawyer and the law-suit together, for
my part.

DOROTHY. Indeed, George, I can't
guess the reason why you should be
cross with me; I can't help it, you
know; and yet you always quarrel
with me.

    Go, George, I can't endure you;
    You wrong me, I assure you.
    I wonder why I love you,
    Why I love you still.
      Are women for no use meant
      But merely man's amusement,
    To teize and torture, as he will, and torture as
        he will?
    No, if you lov'd me true, you'd other means
        pursue.
    No, that you don't 'tis plain. I tell you so again.
    No, no, no, no, no, no, you ne'er could bear to
        use me so.
    No, no, &c.
        What see you, pray, about me,
        Thus still to scold and flout me?
      Such treatment yet was never heard;
        I ne'er must speak, (good gracious)
        I am sure 'tis quite vexatious;
        I never now must speak a word.
      No, if you lov'd me true, &c.

CROP. Why isn't it enough to make
one cross, to be kept dilly dally so
long after what's my right? I am sure
I wish I had never disputed about it,
though it is my right.

DOROTHY. What, you wish to give
up the legacy, do you? Though mr.
Endless assures you it will be settled
next week.

CROP. Aye, so he has said this long
time past. I have had plague enough
about it; and now I must neglect my
work, to go in search of Grist, the
miller, to answer for my character; he
must be brought up, forsooth, fooling
to mr. Endless.

How happily my life I led, without a day of
    sorrow
To plough and sow, to reap and mow, no care
    beyond the morrow,
  No care beyond the morrow!
  In heat or cold, in wet or dry,
  I never grumbled, no, not I.
  My wife, 'tis true, loves words a few,
  What then, I let her prate;
  For sometimes smooth and sometimes rough,
  I found myself still rich enough,
  In the joys of an humble state.
  For sometimes smooth, &c.
  But when with law I craz'd my head,
  I lost both peace and pleasure—
  Long says to hear, to search and swear,
  And plague beyond all measure.
  One grievance brought another on,
  My debts increase, my flock is gone;
  Wy wife, she says, our means 'twill raise.
  What then? 'tis idle prate.
  For sometimes smooth, &c.

DOROTHY *(cries)*. Ah! George, you don't care any thing about me: there's farmer Trotman's wife can have a silk cloak, and a dimity petticoat, and go dress'd like a lady; aye, and have a joint of meat every day; and I'm sure we hav'nt a joint above once a month, that we hav'n't.

CROP. Well, wife, don't be so uneasy; things have gone badly of late, to be sure; but have a good heart; when I have gain'd my law-suit, I'll live like a gentleman; I'll never have any small beer in my house. I'll drink nothing but wine and ale, and we'll have a joint of roast pork for dinner, every Sunday.

DOROTHY. I don't like pork; I say it shall be lamb.

CROP. But, I say, it shall be pork.

DOROTHY. I hate pork; I'll have lamb.

CROP. Pork! I tell you.

DOROTHY. I say, lamb; you don't know what's good.

CROP. Zounds! It shan't be lamb; I will have pork.

Enter LOUISA.

LOUISA. For ever contending! Will you never be at peace.

DOROTHY. What's that to you? Why do you interfere with what doesn't concern you? Leave your father and me to settle matters.

LOUISA. I only spoke because I wished you to have comfort.

DOROTHY. Comfort, indeed! Why, when you see every body happy in the house, you go moping and pining about like a sick turkey polt; you ought to be ashamed of yourself, to let your head be running on a young man— you ought—

CROP. Fie, fie, wife! an't you contented to have forc'd her to leave the house, but you must always be tormenting her? Come, Louisa, I am going to your cottage, and will walk with you. I shall be back presently.

LOUISA. Alas! why should you accuse me of loving Frederic, when you know I refus'd him, because I wou'd not add one to a poor family who hadn't means to support them? Alas! how little did I know my own heart.

> I thought our quarrels ended,
> And set my heart at ease,
> 'Tis strange you're thus offended;
> You take delight to teize;
> Yes, yes, you take delight to teize.
> Dear sir, decide the strife,
> Betwixt your child and wife;
> Alas! the grief I feel,
> I dare not to reveal.
> I know that you believe,
> For Frederic's loss I grieve.
> Psho! psho! psho! psho! very well, very well, as
> you please,
> Very well, very well, think as you please.
> In vain I'm always striving,
> To make our diff'rences cease,
> If you're disputes contriving,
> And will not live in peace,
> No, no, you will not live in peace.
> I'm vex'd, dear sir, for you;
> But say, what can I do?
> To none I can complain.
> I know that you believe, for Frederic's loss, &.

Exit LOUISA *with* CROP.

DOROTHY. A trumpery, saucy baggage. Nelly! *(calls* NELLY.*)*

Enter NELLY.

NELLY. Here, mistress.

DOROTHY. You heard what George said, Nelly?

NELLY. Yes, I heard him say he would be back again presently.

DOROTHY. It is not dark yet?

NELLY. No, it is not near night yet.

DOROTHY. Don't you know what I mean, Nelly?

NELLY. Yes, you expect mr. Endless to see you.

DOROTHY. Yes, I hope George won't meet him, because, as he don't know of mr. Endless's coming, he might be angry. The supper will be in time, Nelly?

NELLY. Yes, I shall take care to have the leg of lamb ready; and you know there is a nice cake that we baked yesterday will do for after supper; but what shall we do for wine?

DOROTHY. O! Mr. Endless promised to send some wine; he is a charming man, and talks so prettily; my sweet Dorothea, he calls me. I wish George would learn about manners from him; but I declare he drives me about like his sheep and oxen; and I haven't had the last word not once this week. *(Exit NELLY.)* Heighho! I've been a wife long enough to find out, that there's a dev'lish deal of difference between before and after marriage.

When Cupid, sly little rogue, blooming, fair
    and young,
First wounds the lover's heart, how sweet a
    woman's tongue!
We rob the bees of honey, whene'er we speak
    or sing,
But when the knot is tied, each word becomes
    a sting,
'Tis all clack, clack, clack, whate'er we say,
Both jarring, night and noon,
We ring the changes every day,
Like sweet bells out of tune.

Exit.

SCENE 3. *The outside of* CROP'S *house.*

Enter MARGARETTA *with ballads.*

With lowly suit and plaintive ditty,
I call the tender mind to pity,
My friends are gone, my heart is beating,
And chilling poverty's my lot,
From passing strangers aid intreating,
I wander thus alone forgot.
Relieve my woes, my wants distressing;
And heaven reward you with its blessing.
Here's tales of love and maids forsaken,
Of battles fought, and prizes taken,
The jovial tar so boldly sailing,
Or cast upon some desart shore;
The hapless bride his loss bewailing,
And fearing ne'er to see him more.
Relieve my woes, my wants distressing;
And heaven reward you with its blessing.

My old father little thinks where I am; 'ecod its all his own fault; for if he wou'd have let me marry Robin, I should not have run away; but he wanted me to marry a stupid old figure like himself, only because he was rich; but what are riches, when compared to love? I hated him, and woudn't have had him, if his skin had been stuck all over with diamonds. Besides, I knew it was on his account the law-suit was commenced against Robin, which made him leave me.—If I was fond of riches, I might have been rich long ago. Hav'n't I refused a great many offers? aye! and would again; for I love nobody but Robin: and to have him, I'd run away from fifty fathers. I think no one can know me in this disguise; however, I'll throw by my ballad-singing dress now, and seek some honest service, 'till I hear

of Robin's return: but my basket is empty, and 'tis high time to look out for a night's lodging—here's a cottage—that's fortunate—I'll try here. *(She knocks at the door.)*

Enter NELLY, *then* DOROTHY, *who with* MARGARETTA, *join in Trio.*

NELLY.

Knocking at this hour of day,
What's your business, mistress, pray?

MARGARETTA.

A stranger at your friendly door,
I shelter from the night implore.

NELLY.

This begging is a sorry trade,
I fear you'll find but little aid;
But stay. I'll ask and let you know.

MARGARETTA.

Alas! too sure, I fear 'tis true,
A beggar finds a beggar's due.
Tho' oft unfeign'd the tale of woe,
A beggar finds a beggar's due.

DOROTHY.

You must be gone, we're left alone;
And harbour here can give you none.

MARGARETTA.

My aching feet no more suffice;
A little straw is all I crave.

DOROTHY.

Not two miles hence the village lies;
I wonder what the wench wou'd have.

NELLY.

Not two miles hence, &.
I wonder what, &.

MARGARETTA.

Hapless lot! must I go hence? —Oh! pity
me.

DOROTHY.

Go, get you packing, gypsy, hence;
We told you that you cou'd not stay—

NELLY.

I wonder at your impudence;
Begone, you baggage; march away.

MARGARETTA.

Oh! let me stay; for poverty is no offense;
And 'tis too late to find the way.

(NELLY and DOROTHY go into the house.)

(sola.)—Now, as I'm a woman, here's some mischief a-foot, two women left alone, and refuse the company of a

third, only for the sake of being alone;
O! impossible, I'll find it out before
I go—who comes here? some men—
I'll step aside, and see if they are as
uncharitable to coat and waistcoat, as
they are to petticoats. *(retires.)*

Enter THOMAS *with a basket; knocks
at the door.*

THOMAS. Mrs. Nelly, mrs. Nelly.

NELLY *(enters from house).* Well,
Thomas, what do you want?

THOMAS. My master has sent the
wine, and —

NELLY. Hush! speak softly, Thomas.

THOMAS. My master will be here
himself presently.

NELLY. Oh! very well, walk in and
see what we have prepared. *(THOMAS
and NELLY go into the house.)*

MARGARETTA *(comes forward).* —
So, as I suspected; but let me see,
(goes and looks in at the door) one,
two, three, four bottles of wine; well
said, mr. Steward, very pretty pro-
vision, indeed! the cake in the closet
is for after supper, I suppose. The
boiled lamb is the gentleman's choice,
I imagine. O! mr. Thomas seems coming out; I'll step aside again, for I'll
see the end on't it, I'm determined.
(Retires.)

THOMAS *comes from the house
and exit.*

MARGARETTA *(coming forward).*
Egad! Thomas said true enough, for
here his master comes, I believe—I
shall see more.

Enter ENDLESS.

ENDLESS. 'Egad! this was finely contriv'd; while this law-suit of mine
turns my simple farmer *out* of his
house, I turn *in;* a good turn, faith—
Ha! one good turn deserves another.

MARGARETTA *(aside).* —Sure I
shou'd know that face and voice.

ENDLESS. This dress, I think, cannot fail of attracting Dorothea's heart;
but the best of the joke is, she fancies
I am in love with her—ha! ha! ha!
I doubt, whether I shine most in carrying on a sham action, or a counter-

feit passion, I am *Marti quam Mer-
cutio.*

MARGRETTA *(aside).* —As I live,
it is that wicked rogue, Endless, who
commenced an action against Robin,
took from him all he had, and drove
him to sea.

ENDLESS. If I can but compass my
suit, and prevail on her to consent to
my wishes, for she has always refus'd
me hitherto.

MARGARETTA *(aside).* I must plague
him a little—but hold, I had best de-
camp; for if he should know me, he'll
certainly carry me back to my father,
and have me married—I'll not venture
that. *(Crosses the stage and exit,
singing the last line of her song, looking at* ENDLESS.)

ENDLESS. This is unlucky; that girl
is watching me, I dar'n't go into the
cottage—I'll turn back again, 'till she
is out of sight—that I will.   *Exit.*

SCENE 4. *The inside of* CROP'S
house.

Enter CROP, *with a large basket hanging on a stick over his shoulder,
which appears heavy; he puts it on
the table, then enters* DOROTHY.

DOROTHY. So, George, you're come
back: where have you been?

CROP. Why about my business, and
heartily tir'd I am *(brings a chair near
the front of the stage, and sits down.)*

DOROTHY. Well, but where have you
been?

CROP. Go and shut the door, which
I perceive I've left open, and I'll tell
you.

DOROTHY. Not I indeed; I go shut
the door! No, go and shut the door
yourself; why did you leave it open?

CROP. Because my hands were full.

DOROTHY. So you want to give me
the trouble to shut the door, because
your hands were full. Indeed I shall
not. *(Brings a chair and sits down near
CROP.)*

CROP. Now, wife, go shut the door,
and don't be obstinate.

DOROTHY. I obstinate! upon my word! I obstinate indeed! I don't choose to shut it, sir.

CROP. Why then let it stand open.

DOROTHY. With all my heart, so it may.

CROP. Now, why can't you go and shut it?

DOROTHY. I don't choose it, and there's an end on't.

CROP. Come, I'll make a bargain with you, wife, whoever speaks the first word, shall go and shut the door.

DOROTHY. Agreed.

Duet.

CROP.

I think, I'll venture to surmise,
I know who'll speak the first.

DOROTHY.

You think, no doubt, you're wond'rous wise;
Before I speak, I'll burst.

CROP.

Depend upon't,

DOROTHY.

Depend upon't,

BOTH.

Depend upon't, You'll have the worst.

CROP.

Can you your tongue keep in?

DOROTHY.

Yes, when shall we begin?

CROP.

Agreed; agreed, and now take heed,
When I hold up my thumb;

DOROTHY.

Agreed, I'm silent, mum, mum, &.&.

(They turn their backs to each other, and sit mute.)

ROBIN *(without)*. Yo hoa! Messmates, what! doors open at this time of night? *(Enters.)* Ha! brother Crop, I'm heartily glad to see you. *(Shakes hands with CROP, who seems pleased to see him.)* I've a few friends hard by, who came to beg a night's lodging of you: we have been cast away, and saved nothing but our lives: I have promised them a hearty welcome, my boy, *(looks at CROP for an answer.)* What! are you deaf? Why, don't you know me! I never took you for one that would be dumb to a friend in distress. What the devil's the matter? Have you lost your speech since I saw you? That's a damn'd bad job, *(crosses to DOROTHY.)* Pray how long has poor brother Crop been on the doctor's list? What! a dumb wife too! I wish you joy, brother Crop. Which quarter is the wind in now?

Enter FREDERIC.

FREDERIC. So, Crop, where's your daughter? Why don't you answer me?

ROBIN. It's all in vain, not a breath stirring.

FREDERIC. Why do you shake your head? Why don't you speak, Crop?

ROBIN. There's an embargo laid on words, and you see the port is shut.

FREDERIC. Answer me, I beg. Where's Louisa?

ROBIN. Speak to him in some foreign lingo, master Frederick, for he seems to have forgot the use of his own tongue; he has lost his English. *(To DOROTHY.)* Do you always discourse together in this manner?

FREDERIC. I suppose this is some new quarrel.

ROBIN. No, it must be an old one; for they have had no words of late.

FREDERIC. I'll go and seek an answer elsewhere. *Exit.*

ROBIN. A quarrel would never produce such a dead calm. How the devil shall I get an answer! What's the matter with you both? *(bawling.)* Dam'me, he's as deaf as the mainmast: I might as well talk to the Gorgon's head under our bowsprit. Can you hear or not?

CROP *(Nods)*.

ROBIN. Can you speak?

CROP *(Nods)*.

ROBIN. Will you speak?

ROBIN. Dam'me, but if we had you aboard the Gorgon, we wou'd set your tongue afloat; a good ducking at the yard-arm, and a round dozen, wou'd put your jawing tacks aboard, and be well employed on you; wou'dn't it, mistress?

DOROTHY *(very eagerly).* Aye! that it would—O dear!—I forgot.

CROP. Go and shut the door.

Exit DOROTHY.

ROBIN. Shut the door!

CROP. Aye, she spoke first.

ROBIN. Why, you hadn't quarrelled about shutting the door, had you? a good joke, o' my conscience. Well, George, now your door's shut and mouth open, let me know if you can give us a night's lodging.

CROP. Aye! and welcome, but I fear I can't be your host to night, for I must go as far as Grist's the miller, on some business.

ROBIN. I'll go with you, and look after my messmates.

Enter FREDERIC.

FREDERIC. Prithee, Crop, tell me where she is?

CROP. Where who is?

FREDERIC. Louisa.

CROP. At her grandmother's, hard by, where she has been some time; and I assure you, Frederic, she has never had a smile on her countenance since you left her; therefore, make none of your fine speeches to her, or you'll break the poor girl's heart. Od's hearts, Robin! I'm so happy to meet with you again— I can't tell you how glad I am to see you.

ROBIN. No more you could, just now: your joy was so great, it seem'd to be past speaking.

Exeunt CROP and ROBIN.

FREDERIC. What have I heard? Is it possible my Louisa loves me still? I'll go to her immediately, and this night shall decide my fate.

Exit FREDERIC.

SCENE 5. *The outside of CROP'S house.*

Enter CROP, ROBIN, WILLIAM, and FREDERIC from the house, who begin the Finale. In the course of which, MARGARETTA, DOROTHY and NELLY enter, the two latter from the house, the former from the side wing. End of the Finale, DOROTHY and NELLY go into the house; CROP, ROBIN, WILLIAM and FREDERIC, exeunt on the right hand, MARGARETTA on the left. The stage very dark during Finale.

FINALE

CROP.

How often thus I'm forc'd to trudge!
I own this useless toil I grudge!

ROBIN.

Cheer up, and let your heart be light.

CROP.

Tho' long and tiresome is the way,
I must be back by break of day,

ROBIN.

Your gain the labour shall requite.

FREDERIC.

I'll think on what you said.

CROP.

Aye! aye! be careful, Fred.

MARGARETTA.

Lost in the dark, perplex'd I rove,
And know not where I stray;
Some kindly star, a friend to love,
Direct me on my way.

DOROTHY.

I'll see if yet the coast be clear;
Hold, hold, not yet, they still are here.

FREDERIC and CROP.

But if at last my suit should fail?

ROBIN and WILLIAM.

'Psha! never stand to quake and quail.

FREDERIC.

To night good fortune be our guide,
We'll take the best that may betide.

MARGARETTA.

Hope a distant joy disclosing,
Balmy comfort can impart;
Anxious doubt, in Hope reposing,
Fancy calms the tortur'd heart.

DOROTHY, FREDERIC, CROP, WILLIAM.

Hope, &.

MARGARETTA.

My weary toil success repay,
And fortune guide us on our way.

DOROTHY, FREDERIC, CROP, WILLIAM.

My weary, &.

ACT II. SCENE 1.

A view near the sea.

Enter WILLIAM and Sailors.

WILLIAM.

From aloft the sailor looks around,
    And hears below the murm'ring billows sound;
Far off from home, he counts another day,
Wide o'er the seas the vessel bears away.
    His courage wants no whet,
    But he begins the sail to set,
With a heart as fresh as rising breeze of May,
And, caring nought, he turns his thought
To his lovely Sue or charming Bet
Now to Heav'n the lofty topmast soars;
The stormy blast like dreadful thunder roars;
Now ocean's deepest gulps appear below,
The curling surges foam, and down we go.
    When skies and seas are met,
    They his courage serve to whet,
With a heart as fresh as rising breeze of May,
And dreading nought, &.

Enter CROP and ROBIN.

CROP. And is your heart still set on Margaretta?

ROBIN. Aye! 'as true as the wind blows; and if Margaretta's heart does but hold as steady as mine, I don't fear bringing all to bear. How goes it, lads? *(To sailors.)*

WILLIAM. Cheerfully, Robin! the tide has thrown ashore some of our property, which we have put safe under the rocks.

ROBIN. As the tide ebbs so fast, my boys, perhaps my keg may be left on the beach. Egad there's something dev'lish like it—Bye, brother Crop.

Exeunt ROBIN and sailors.

CROP. Why then, I must go to Grist's by myself. *Exit CROP.*

SCENE 2. *A wood.*

Enter MARGARETTA.

MARGARETTA. O! dear, what will become of me? I am quite benighted. I have led the lawyer a fine dance, faith! he may now follow his own schemes as much as he likes, so he does not spoil mine. Hey! sure I heard a rustling among the bushes; as I live,

here's a man coming this way; O Lord! I am frighten'd out of my wits; there are so many paths, that I am at a loss to know which takes me to the village.

Enter CROP.

CROP. Egad, its well I happen'd to meet with my neighbour Trotman, or I should have had a long walk, to no purpose; for he informs me poor Grist is dead.—Poor fellow! well, death can neither be seen or prevented; so there's an end of that. *(Sees MARGARETTA.)* Who goes there?

MARGARETTA. A poor girl, sir, who wants a night's lodging, and has lost her way.

CROP. Where did you want to go to, my girl?

MARGARETTA. To the next village, sir.

CROP. You are out of the way, indeed; however, come with me, I'll provide you with a night's lodging.

MARGARETTA. Lord, sir, I hope you don't intend me any harm.

CROP. Harm, indeed! no, not I, my girl. Do you see yonder cottage, where the smoke rises through the trees? I am the owner of it: and I trust its doors were never yet shut to charity.

MARGARETTA. Are you the owner of that cottage?

CROP. I am; there's an honest housewife who will use you kindly, who is melancholy enough—poor soul!—I dare say, at being left alone.

MARGARETTA *(aside).* Very melancholy, indeed. Well, some of you men

men: commas setting off "men" have been deleted, in accordance with the reading in Lacy's edition.

are really good creatures; and I could find in my heart to do you a piece of service, honest farmer.

CROP. Come, my girl, don't be afraid, I'll take care of you.

MARGARETTA. Heav'n bless you for your kindness: I think I shall have it in my power to reward you, or I am very much mistaken.

Exeunt CROP *and* MARGARETTA.
Enter FREDERIC.

FREDERIC. Thanks to fortune, this night makes me happy with my Louisa: I now feel myself amply compensated for all the perils I have undergone, and am happy to find myself in a situation to reward those generous tars, whose fate depends upon a hardy life.

> The wand'ring sailor ploughs the main,
> A competence in life to gain,
> Undaunted braves the stormy seas
> To find at last content and ease:
> In hopes, when toil and danger's o'er,
> To anchor on his native shore.
>   When winds blow hard and mountains roll,
> And thunder shakes from pole to pole,
> Tho' dreadful seas surrounding foam
> Still flatt'ring fancy wafts him home,
> In hopes when toil, &.
>   When round the bowl the jovial crew
> The early scenes of life renew,
> Tho' each his favourite fair will boast,
> This is the universal toast,
> May we when toil and danger's o'er
> Cast anchor on our native shore.

Exit.

SCENE 3. *A room in* CROP'S *house.*

ENDLESS *and* DOROTHY *discovered at a table laid for supper; at the back of the stage are several sacks, which appear full.*

DOROTHY. Indeed, mr. Endless, I wou'dn't do such a thing for the world.

ENDLESS *(aside).* I have carried on this action too precipitately. *(rises.)* But, my dear Dorothea, let us reason this affair together.

DOROTHY *(rises).* But what signifies our reasoning about a thing, which I know to be wrong.

ENDLESS. *I say,* what signifies our knowing a thing to be wrong, when nobody else knows any thing about the matter? A blot is *no blot,* 'till it's hit.

DOROTHY. Aye, but is there no such thing as conscience?

ENDLESS. But conscience can't be summoned into court; I never heard of a man's conscience being *subpoenaed* on a trial; if that was the case, there would be an end of our profession at once. Oh! it would be all Dicky with us.

Enter NELLY, *with a leg of boiled lamb, which she puts on the table, and exit.*

ENDLESS. But as Nelly seems to have been so busy for us, let us sit down, and finish the subject after supper. *(They sit down.)*

DOROTHY. I needn't ask you to make free, I hope, mr. Endless; as all you see on the table is your own.

ENDLESS. Don't mortify me, my sweet Dorothea, by calling it mine; you know it's all your's—at least, if your husband's money can make it so. *(aside.)*

DOROTHY. O dear! you are so obliging, I fear we shall never have it in our power to return your kindness, at least till George has gained his law-suit.

ENDLESS *(aside.)* I'll take care not to wait 'till then. —Don't mention any reward to me. I am sufficiently repaid in the happiness of *(rises and offers to kiss her; a loud knocking at the door.)* Who the devil's that? Do you expect any body here to-night? O Lord, the supper will be spoiled.

DOROTHY. Nelly, Nelly.

Enter NELLY.

DOROTHY. Run, Nelly; see who's at the door; if it's George, I am undone.

Exit NELLY, *she returns immediately.*

NELLY. O dear, it's my master, as I hope to be married.

ENDLESS. The devil it is!

DOROTHY. O dear! What shall we do with mr. Endless?

ENDLESS. Aye! there will be an end of mr. Endless.

CROP *(without).* Why wife! Dorothy! Dorothy!

ENDLESS. Zounds! put me any where; have you no closet, or snug corner I can creep into?

DOROTHY. No; but here I have it; creep into this sack.

ENDLESS. A sack!

DOROTHY. Yes, I'll get my husband to bed presently; and then I'll come and let you out.

ENDLESS. Creep into a sack! the thing's impossible; my new suit here will be totally spoil'd.

DOROTHY. No, no, it has only had flour in it, and that will easily brush off.

ENDLESS. Dam'me, but I wish I could brush off.

DOROTHY. Come, Nelly, help me to put it over him.

CROP (without). Why, Nelly, Dorothy, why don't you open the door? (DOROTHY and NELLY put a sack over ENDLESS, and place him among the other sacks. NELLY removes the lamb, and exit; returns directly, followed by CROP and MARGARETTA.)

CROP. Why, wife, one wou'd have thought by your keeping us at the door so long, you had been fast asleep; what were you dreaming of?

DOROTHY (aside). I am sure we never dreamt of you.

CROP. Poor Grist is dead, which made me come back to night, and on my way I met this young woman, who had lost her road; you must give her a night's lodging and a bit of supper.

MARGARETTA (aside). Where the deuce have they hid this roguish lawyer? I know he is here, by their confusion.

DOROTHY. Why, George, as I didn't expect you home to-night, I have got nothing for supper at all.

MARGARETTA (aside, after seeing the sack). Oh! you are there, are you, mr. Lawyer?

CROP. Hang it, I'm sorry there's nothing for supper, for I expect Robin here presently.

MARGARETTA (aside). What do I hear! Robin expected here!

CROP. He's only gone to the sea shore, to see if any thing was flung up by the tide.

ROBIN (without). Hallo! hallo!

CROP. 'Egad here he is; I'll go and bring out one of our cheeses; I dare say, he's hungry; he always had a good appetite.   Exit CROP.

MARGARETTA. I hope he has not forgot poor Margaretta.

Enter ROBIN, *with a small keg under his arm.*

ROBIN. Huzza! my boys, Robin's his own man again; with these fruits of honest industry, will I moor for life; and when I hear the winds rattle, I'll heave a sigh for all poor brother tars.

MARGARETTA (aside). Not a word of me yet.

Enter CROP *with a cheese.*

CROP. To think I should have nothing for supper but cheese! a plague of this ill-luck!

ROBIN. I'm so happy, I could dance a hornpipe on the head of a scupper nail.

CROP. What makes you so merry, Robin?

ROBIN. Why, George, I have now recovered my spirits.

CROP. What, in that keg, I suppose.

ROBIN. Aye! the finest in the world, drawn from all the parts of the globe; you shall taste them.

CROP. With all my heart; give us a glass, Nelly.

ROBIN. A glass, indeed! Lord love your lubberly head; give me a hammer. (CROP gives him a hammer; ROBIN unhoops the keg, and takes out a handful of gold.)

> Three years a sailor's life I led
>   And plough'd the roaring sea;
> For why her foes shou'd England dread,
>   Whilst all her sons are free?
> From France to Spain I earn'd my bread;
>   I thought it fair, d'ye see?
> And if a shot had ta'en my head,
>   Why there was an end of me.
> A medicine sure for grief and care,
>   I steer'd my course to find;
> Thenceforth an easy sail to bear,
>   And run before the wind.
> Their conj'ring skill let doctors boast,
>   And nostrums of their shop,
> Where'er we search, from coast to coast,
>   There's none like the golden drop.
> For gold we sail the world around,
>   And dare the tempest's rage,
> For when the sparklers once are found,
>   They ev'ry ill assuage.
> 'Twixt Jew and christian not a fig
>   Of difference here we find,
> The Jew no loathing has to pig,
>   If 'tis of the guinea kind.

Are not these the best cordials? these are the true golden drops, extracted from the Spanish mines, and I hope, from my soul, they will not be the last we shall draw from the same quarter.

MARGARETTA *(aside).* I am afraid now he's so rich, he'll marry a lady.

ROBIN. Here, Crop, you may want a few guineas, and as the keg is open, take a handful; and when you've recovered your law-suit, pay me, and now with the rest—

CROP. Aye, Robin, what will you do with the rest?

ROBIN. Carry it to Margaretta; and if she is still in the mind, marry her directly, and live happy all the rest of my life.

MARGARETTA *(aside).* My charming Robin!

ROBIN. If I cou'd but see her now.

MARGARETTA *(coming forward).* Aye! if you did, I fear you wou'd change your note.

ROBIN. Margaretta! *(runs and kisses her, and cries.)*

CROP. What's the matter, Robin?

ROBIN. My joy is so great, it has set my eye pumps a going.

MARGARETTA. I little thought of meeting you here, Robin.

ROBIN. And how came you here? I forgot to ask that.

MARGARETTA. Oh! that's too long a story to tell you now.

ROBIN. Well, then, let's hear it another time. O! dear Margaretta! I say—that—I say—you—that—O Lord! *(runs and kisses her very eagerly)* come let's now to supper and be merry. But where is the supper? What have you got in the house, brother Crop?

CROP. Why, I never knew any thing happen so unluckily; we have got nothing in the house; and I am as hungry as a lion myself.

DOROTHY. Why, what a fuss you make about supper! we are not all so rich as mr. Robin.

CROP. But what use are his riches now? we can't eat and drink gold.

ROBIN. 'Egad, if you can, you shall have it.

CROP. Faith, Robin, I can give you nothing but bread and cheese.

ROBIN. Well, bread and cheese, and kisses; hey! Margaretta, sit down, my girl.

MARGARETTA. Presently, Robin.— Now let me see if I can't furnish the table better. I smell the lamb yet. *(aside.)* *(*ROBIN *and* CROP *sit.)*

ROBIN. Come, Madge, give the landlord, and me one of the songs you used to sing, if you hav'n't forgot them. You don't know what a good pipe she has.

MARGARETTA. I'll sing you one that I heard this morning, which is quite new.

ROBIN. Aye! let's hear it.

MARGARETTA. The person who learnt it me, said it should never be sung before a poor meal; but you shall judge if he was right.

CROP. Well, begin, my girl.

MARGARETTA *(sings first verse).*

> Across the downs this morning,
> As by times I chanc'd to go,
> A shepherd lead his flock abroad,
> All white as driven snow,
>   But one was most the shepherd's care,
>   A lamb so sleek, so plump, so fair;
> It's wond'rous beauties, in a word,
> To let you fairly know,
> 'Twas such as Nelly from the fire,
> Took off not long ago.

CROP. Hold, hold, my girl, if I heard you right, I think you said such as Nelly took off the fire not long ago.

MARGARETTA. 'Tis part of my song, sir.

ROBIN. Aye! 'tis part of her song.

CROP. Well, but is it joke or earnest? Have you any lamb in the house, Nelly?

ROBIN. Come, Nell, let's overhaul your lockers.

CROP. Come, come, wife, I see how this is; you had a mind to surprise me agreeably.

DOROTHY. Why, that was the case, indeed, George; I knew you was very fond of lamb, so as it was only a small joint, I meant to give it you when you was alone.

CROP. I thought so; but bring it here, Nelly; I am one that don't like to see my guests fare worse than myself.

ROBIN. Come, bear a hand, Nell, stretch along the lamb halyards, and a knife or two. *(Exit NELLY, and returns with lamb, &c.)* 'Egad, Madge, it was lucky you happened to fall in with the sheep.

CROP. Sav'd it for *me*, did you? you and Nelly took care of a comfortable slice or two first.

ROBIN. Slice! dam'me, they've been at it yard-arm and yard-arm.

CROP. Come, let's hear the rest of the song.

MARGARETTA *(sings second verse).*

This lamb so blithe as midsummer,
His frolic gambols play'd,
And now of all the flock a-head,
The pretty wanton stray'd.
A wolf that watch'd with greedy eyes,
Rush'd forth, and seiz'd the tender prize.
The shepherd saw, and rais'd a stone,
So round, so large, I vow,
'Twas like the cake that Nelly laid
Upon the shelf just now,

CROP. Stop, my dear; didn't you say, like the cake Nelly laid on the shelf just now? Why, Nell, is there a cake in the house!

ROBIN. Aye! that there is.

CROP. Come, bring it out, Nell. *Exit NELLY; returns with cake.*

ROBIN. What! still the same madcap as ever, Margaretta?

CROP. 'Egad, this is a most excellent song.

MARGARETTA. Will you hear the rest of it, sir?

CROP. By all means; and if the latter part of it is as good as the former, it will be by much the best song I ever heard.

MARGARETTA. I'm afraid you'll be tir'd.

CROP. Not I; I love a song.

ROBIN. 'Egad, brother Crop, "No song no supper."

MARGARETTA *(sings third verse).*

This monstrous stone, the shepherd flung;
And well his aim he took;
Yet scarce the savage creature deign'd,
Around to cast a look;
But fled as swift, with footsteps light,
As he who brought the wine to night.
I tried to stop the thief! but he
Turn'd round in rage, good lack!
So mad the lawyer scarce can be,
That's hid in yonder sack.

CROP *(rises).* A lawyer hid in the sack! Zounds! what's all this?

ROBIN *(goes to the sacks).* O! impossible; these are full of corn. *(beats the sacks.)* Yes, faith, here's one seems to be heaving anchor. *(ENDLESS moves, and comes down to the front of the stage.)* 'Ecod, if they should all rise, you'll have a fine field of standing corn, brother Crop. *(Beats ENDLESS, who offers to go)* hold, hold, no exportation without inspection. *(Pulls off the sack, and discovers ENDLESS, who is covered with flour.)*

CROP. Endless! Oh! the devil!

ENDLESS. Assault me, if you dare; if you strike me, it's cognizable in court, as I wasn't found in any overt-act.

CROP. No, but you was found in a very *rascally one*, though.

ENDLESS. I don't care for that.

CROP. If these are your tricks, I know how to suit you.

ENDLESS. And you know how to *non* suit, I find.

CROP. To think I should entrust you to manage my affairs.

ROBIN. You might have had a young Crop before you look'd for it.

ENDLESS. I move for a habeas corpus out of this court: but take care how you insult a limb of the law, or you may chance to bring down the vengeance of the whole body. *Exit.*

ROBIN. If such limbs were lopped off, it would do the constitution good.

CROP *(to DOROTHY).* What have you to say for yourself, eh! you jade? so the lamb was for mr. Endless.

MARGARETTA. I should but half repay your kindness if I didn't tell you, that your wife has ever refused to listen to his addresses; this, I assure you, he said himself, when he little thought any one overheard him.

CROP. Say you so? then, wife, give me your hand; and let us for the future endeavour to live happy together, and the best way to do so, is to forget and forgive.

ROBIN. That's right, and now you'll bring her heart to an anchor for life.

Enter WILLIAM.

WILLIAM. O! Robin, all our fortunes are made; master Frederic is a rich 'squire, and is going to marry your niece; there will be oxen roasting, and wine and ale running about the streets; there are illuminations, and he has ordered the whole town to be set on fire.

Enter FREDERIC and LOUISA.

ROBIN. Master Frederic, I wish you joy; and d'ye see, Louisa, make him a good wife. This storm to night has blown back your lover, but remember, the *gentle gales of moderate weather*

must keep the husband within hail of you.

FINALE.

MARGARETTA, DOROTHY, *and* CROP:

Let shepherd lads and maids advance,
   And neatly trim be seen;
  To night we lead the merry dance,
    In circles o'er the green.

LOUISA *and* FREDERIC.

Beyond our hopes, by fortune crown'd,
   Here all our troubles cease
Each year that takes its jocund round,
   Shall bring content and peace.

MARGARETTA.

And whilst we sport and dance and play,
   The tabor blythe shall sound;
We'll laugh and chaunt our carols gay,
   While merry bells ring round.

DOROTHY.

Now mirth and glee, and pastimes light,
   The prolic hours shall share;
And sparkling eyes shall wake to-night;
   To-morrow's time for care.
And whilst we sport and dance and play,
   The tabor blythe shall sound,
We'll laugh and chaunt our carols gay,
   While merry bells ring round.

FINIS.